Delivering Culturally Competent
Nursing Care

Gloria Kersey-Matusiak, PhD, MSN, RN is Professor of Nursing at Holy Family University, Philadelphia. During more than 35 years of clinical practice in culturally diverse settings, Dr. Kersey-Matusiak developed a strong interest in multiculturalism and diversity. Since 2000, Dr. Kersey-Matusiak has served as the university's Coordinator for Diversity and Chair of the institution's Diversity Team. She holds a doctorate in Psycho-Educational Processes from Temple University and an Advanced Certificate in Culturally Competent Human Services from the former Multicultural Training and Research Institute at Temple University.

At Holy Family, Dr. Kersey-Matusiak has taught a variety of baccalaureate- and graduate-level courses including Medical-Surgical Nursing to undergraduates; Culture and Heath Care to RNs seeking BSNs; and Counseling Multicultural Populations to Counseling Psychology majors. Currently, Dr. Kersey-Matusiak teaches graduate courses in the MSN program and an interdisciplinary course in World Health in the university's Division of Extended Learning. Dr. Kersey-Matusiak's current research focuses on addressing the needs of ESL students. She coordinates an academic support program for nursing students for whom English is a second language.

Dr. Kersey-Matusiak has conducted numerous workshops and presentations for a variety of educational, health care, and business institutions and served as a diversity consultant for several institutions of higher learning. An article titled "Culturally Competent Care: Are We There Yet?" has recently been published in the journals, *Nursing* (February 2012) and *Nursing Management* (April 2012).

Delivering Culturally Competent Nursing Care

Gloria Kersey-Matusiak, PhD, MSN, RN

SPRINGER PUBLISHING COMPANY
NEW YORK

Springer Publishing Company, LLC
11 West 42nd Street
New York, NY 10036
www.springerpub.com

Acquisitions Editor: Margaret Zuccarini
Composition: Newgen Imaging

ISBN: 978-0-8261-9381-0
E-book ISBN: 978-0-8261-9382-7

12 13 14 15 / 5 4 3 2 1

The author and the publisher of this Work have made every effort to use sources believed to be reliable to provide information that is accurate and compatible with the standards generally accepted at the time of publication. Because medical science is continually advancing, our knowledge base continues to expand. Therefore, as new information becomes available, changes in procedures become necessary. We recommend that the reader always consult current research and specific institutional policies before performing any clinical procedure. The author and publisher shall not be liable for any special, consequential, or exemplary damages resulting, in whole or in part, from the readers' use of, or reliance on, the information contained in this book. The publisher has no responsibility for the persistence or accuracy of URLs for external or third-party Internet websites referred to in this publication and does not guarantee that any content on such websites is, or will remain, accurate or appropriate.

Library of Congress Cataloging-in-Publication Data
Kersey-Matusiak, Gloria.
  Delivering culturally competent nursing care / Gloria Kersey-Matusiak.
    p. ; cm.
  Includes bibliographical references and index.
  ISBN 978-0-8261-9381-0 – ISBN 978-0-8261-9382-7 (e-book)
  I. Title.
  [DNLM: 1. Cultural Competency. 2. Nursing Care. 3. Clinical Competence. 4. Cultural Diversity. WY 16.1]
  610.73—dc23   2012019908

Special discounts on bulk quantities of our books are available to corporations, professional associations, pharmaceutical companies, health care organizations, and other qualifying groups.

If you are interested in a custom book, including chapters from more than one of our titles, we can provide that service as well.

For details, please contact:
Special Sales Department, Springer Publishing Company, LLC
11 West 42nd Street, 15th Floor, New York, NY 10036-8002
Phone: 877-687-7476 or 212-431-4370; Fax: 212-941-7842
Email: sales@springerpub.com

Printed in the United States of America by Gasch Printing.

This book is dedicated to my parents,
Ernest and Doris Bonaparte

Contents

Contributors

Claire Dente, PhD, LCSW
Assistant Professor in Social Work
Westchester University
Westchester, Pennsylvania
(Chapter 9)

Barbara Jones, DNSc, MSN, RN
Professor
Master of Science in Nursing
Program Director
Gwynedd-Mercy College
Gwynedd Mercy, Pennsylvania
(Chapter 8)

Foreword

Globalization and advances in communication and transportation heightened our awareness of human diversity and the struggle to create unity amid differences. Health care is a microcosm of global society. Diversity is reflected in the differential access to health services and health outcomes across population groups. Improving the health of populations, however, necessitates measures beyond health care services. The Global Commission on Social Determinants of Health proposed that health achievement requires a commitment to the comprehensive reduction of social inequalities by improving the circumstances in which people live and work.

The impetus for cultural competence development of health professionals was prompted by the need to eliminate health disparities across population groups. Yet, health cannot be achieved by culturally competent health care services alone. Although access to quality care services can be facilitated by committed, culturally competent health care professionals, improving the environment where people live and work goes beyond health care provision. It requires advocacy for policies and programs that create better life conditions for the disadvantaged and vulnerable.

Cultural competence can be realized at the individual, organizational, and societal levels. Culturally competent individuals are the backbone of organizations and societies. Hence, cultural competence is only possible when more individuals develop the knowledge, abilities, and values of cultural competence. This book attempts to provide the base for cultural competence development for entry-level nurses. It behooves faculty using this book to provide the broader perspective of population health disparities and social inequities for students acquiring individual-level cultural competence.

Madeleine Leininger was a pioneer in advocating for culturally congruent care and declared Transcultural Nursing as a nursing specialty. Leininger, along with her colleagues and students, developed the body of knowledge for the discipline. Despite their efforts that began in the early 1950s, the mandate for culturally competent care did not gain momentum nationally across different disciplines until the Office of Minority Health of the Department of Health and Human Services developed the mandate for health care organizations to provide culturally and linguistically appropriate health care services. These standards were adopted by The Joint Commission and the Department of Health. The American Association of Colleges of Nursing created a national team of experts to facilitate integration of cultural competence in nursing education at the baccalaureate and master's level. Today, cultural diversity and cultural competence development are core concepts in education of all health care professionals in the United States.

This book addresses the challenge of cultural competence development in entry-level programs in nursing. A unique feature of this book is the Staircase Model toward cultural competence development with sample scenarios for application. The focus on critical self-reflection enhances the sensitivity of the individual toward differences between self and others. Self-reflection is a significant step in developing cultural sensitivity and respect for differences. Cultural competence is the opening of one's mind and spirit to differences in order to work effectively with diverse groups.

The book focuses on the process of cultural competence development applicable in different situations. It moves the emphasis from monolithic descriptions of different cultures that can endanger stereotypes about cultural groups. This process orientation creates a universal paradigm that allows self-reflection and evaluation of every encounter with diversity. Process-focused development promotes cultural fluency and adaptability to different situations. One of its strengths is the application of different models in cultural assessment. This eclectic approach exposes readers to different steps that can be used within the Staircase Model. The approach respects diversity in cultural competence development.

Dr. Kersey-Matusiak should be applauded for writing this practical and process-oriented book on culturally competent care delivery. This is an excellent introduction to cultural assessment and culturally competent decision making for entry-level nurses. Her book bridges content and evaluation of culturally competent care, thus providing a useful resource for entry-level nursing educators.

Dula F. Pacquiao, EdD, RN, CTN
Professor and Director
Center for Multicultural Education, Research, and Practice
University of Medicine and Dentistry of New Jersey
School of Nursing

Preface

More than 40 years ago, Madeleine Leininger identified the need for nurses to provide care that is responsive to the patient's own values, attitudes, and health beliefs. Since that time, despite encouragement by Leininger and her followers and the outcry of nurse leaders and professional nursing organizations, delivering culturally competent care remains a major challenge for many nurses. Although some nurses are making great strides in that direction, others remain perplexed about how they might accomplish this goal. Additionally, as the nation grows in its diversity, nursing, as a microcosm of society, is plagued by many of the same "isms" that challenge American society: ageism, sizeism, racism, homophobia, to name a few. These and other barriers to culturally congruent care create an imbalance in the equitable distribution of quality care for all.

The National Institutes of Health (NIH) continues to report health care disparities among African Americans, Hispanics, Native Americans, and Pacific Islanders. These groups experience "shorter life expectancy and higher rates of diabetes, cancer, heart disease, stroke, substance abuse, and infant mortality and low birth weight than did Whites." Research indicates that the causes of these disparities are multifactorial and include biological, environmental, and behavioral factors (NIH, 2010). Today, the shortage of racial minority health professionals; discrimination; and social determinants of health such as employment status, inequities in income, level of education, and access to health care are all believed to play a significant role in maintaining health care disparities (WHO, 2008). According to the American Association of Colleges of Nursing (AACN), building cultural competency skills among health care providers is one way to address health care disparities.

Nurses in particular who provide care that is culturally congruent with patients' health care values and beliefs are better able to promote health among culturally diverse populations, prevent complications from delayed treatment, and ensure quality care for all patients. By identifying populations at high risk for disease, and delivering effective and culturally appropriate care, nurses help reduce health care costs and health care disparities at the same time. However, despite the rapidly increasing body of knowledge on cultural competency, the goals of becoming culturally competent and reducing health care disparities are not easy to achieve. Many nurses continue to express concern and confusion about what it really means to be culturally competent. Some ask, "How can I fit one more nursing task into my already overwhelming workload?," "How can I learn all there is to know about the varieties of cultural groups and ethnicities I may encounter?," and, "Isn't just being a good nurse enough?" I believe that many good nurses have not yet accepted or bought into the idea that all interactions between the patient and the nurse are cultural (Campinha-Bacote, 2003).

Guided by AACN's Cultural Competencies for BSN graduates, this text is written to assist nursing students and practicing nurses in applying cultural competency skills to various patient care situations that nurses are likely to encounter in the 21st century. The author takes the position that the process always begins with the nurse's careful self-assessment. The Staircase Model, developed by the author and presented in Chapter 1, assists nurses in this process. By applying the Staircase Self-Assessment Model, nurses are guided toward a conscientious self-reflection that enables them to determine their personal level of cultural competency in the care of a particular patient population. Use of the model also helps nurses identify any personal limitations, determine strategies for overcoming them, and assist them in progressing to the next level. In this way, nurses practice delivering care that is meaningful to the patient, irrespective of the nurse's cultural beliefs and attitudes. Chapter 2 offers a description of current cultural assessment models to be used by the nurse to explore the patient's cultural background and health care needs. Chapter 3 focuses on nurses' interactions with one another as colleagues when there are language or cultural differences between them.

This text uses the concept of culture broadly to include the various groups or affiliations with which an individual identifies. Throughout the text, the concept of culture goes beyond racial, ethnic, or geographical traits, and encompasses the many human categories by which individuals are characterized. Members within each of these groups share certain circumstances and cultural values that influence health care access and type of health care. Therefore, in Chapters 4 through 11 the reader explores topics and case examples that focus on more challenging nurse–patient situations. These scenarios often cross race and ethnicity and include other salient aspects of differences between the patient and the nurse. The reader is asked to use each case scenario as a prototype of those the nurse might encounter in future clinical experiences. The reader is also encouraged to adopt the practice of self-assessment and patient cultural assessment when responding to the self-reflection questions posed in each chapter. Some topics include cultural considerations for patients who are migrant farm workers; morbidly obese, or have physical or psychological disabilities; who are gay, lesbian, bisexual, or transgendered; who are poor and without health care insurance; who come from a certain spiritual background; or who speak a language that differs from that of the nurse.

By addressing these more complex issues in culture care and by using the Staircase Self-Assessment Model, the reader develops skill in problem solving that can be used in any and all cross-cultural interactions.

NCLEX–type questions are provided at the end of each chapter to reinforce learning and to provide the reader with a sense of his or her developing cultural competency knowledge and skill. Answers for these questions can be found at the back of the book. The journey to cultural competency is one of ongoing, conscientious self-reflection, cultural assessment, and collaboration between the patient and the nurse. This book offers nurse readers a step-by-step approach to developing those skills.

Gloria Kersey-Matusiak

Acknowledgments

First and foremost, I am most grateful to the Divine and Holy Presence that guides my life and sustains my belief that everyone matters and that we have a collective and individual responsibility to one another. There are numerous individuals who have in some way shared my personal journey toward cultural competency during the writing of the manuscript, and without whom this book would not be possible.

To Claire Dente and Barbara Jones who never gave up on this project despite numerous iterations and misadventures. I am forever indebted to them for giving voice to two often-forgotten cultural groups—persons who are migrant farm workers and persons who are gay, lesbian, transsexual, or transgendered. Many thanks to Margaret Zuccarini whose guidance, positive energy, and encouragement helped me rekindle my resolve to complete this work. To Betsy who actively listened without judgment, thank you for enabling me to overcome a myriad of distractions to stay on course. To Cathy Jenner who offered endless words of encouragement from the very beginning; thank you for always being so caring. To Connie my friend and confidant since seventh grade, thank you for sharing the laughter and the tears on a day-to-day basis; what a treasure to have in my life! I am grateful also to Sister Betty Anne who provided spiritual guidance when the road ahead was unclear.

To my siblings, Ernestine, Barbara, Ernest, and Evon whose quiet support meant so much to me throughout this writing. A special thanks to Ernie, Barbara, and Harriet Green for their frequent but gentle reminders that kept me focused and on task. To my beloved husband, Bob, whose patience with my emotional absences waxed and waned, but his love and commitment was my anchor during difficult times, thank you for accepting me as I am. To my children, Robbie, Troy, and Brian, you are my heart, my soul, and inspiration. To Lil' Troy, Brennen, and Rakeem, my thoughts of you kept me smiling every day, you are the light of my life and great hope for the future.

Introduction

My own beliefs about cultural competency stem from the adage "to whom much is given, much is expected," and from my own ethnocentric views about what it really means to be a good nurse. Thus, I have come to appreciate that the road to cultural competency is not only personal, but spiritual and it requires a commitment to an ongoing journey of conscientious self-reflection. For this reason, the Staircase Model, a self-assessment model, developed by me years ago, is used as a component of cultural competency development throughout this text. Although the Staircase Model was primarily developed with nursing students and practicing nurses in mind, cultural competency is a responsibility of all caring health professionals, including physicians, psychologists, therapists, social workers, and counselors. However, among health care providers in the helping professions, nurses enjoy the privilege of a physical, emotional, and psychological intimacy with patients and clients that few others experience. Further, the literature attests to the high regard for nurses' integrity and ethical values society bestows upon the nurse (Donelan, Buerhaus, DesRoches, Dittus, & Dutwin, 2008). In response to the trust and respect society bestows, it is incumbent on nurses to hold themselves to the highest standard of practice and deepest level of self-reflection when caring for patients. This is especially true when planning care for a patient with whom the nurse fundamentally differs in values, attitudes, or health beliefs. So much depends on nurses being motivated to make the time in this fast-paced health care environment to communicate effectively even with patients with whom they may have little in common. Like detectives, nurses must seek ways to uncover barriers to care for culturally diverse groups through knowledge and skill development.

Yet, there are many nurses who still view cultural competency as an additional task, among others, to accomplish and rank it lowest among their priorities of care. But cultural competency needn't be thought of as an add-on task. When applying its major components, the nurse simply continues to apply the nursing process; assessing, analyzing, planning, implementing, and evaluating clinical data using additional cultural knowledge and skills that enhance or augment the skills the nurse already has. Good nurses, when demonstrating cultural competency skills, become even better nurses.

PURPOSE AND GOALS OF TEXT

With these thoughts in mind, this book is written to allay the nursing students' and practicing nurses' anxiety about becoming culturally competent, encourage them to conscientiously and regularly explore their own capacity to experience cross-cultural relationships with diverse patients, assist them in overcoming barriers to cross-cultural interaction, and provide useful information and strategies to aid them in the process of becoming culturally competent. In light of the current fast-paced, highly technical health care environment, I wish to help focus nurses' attention on the routine application of culturally competent skills to enhance the quality of care given to all patients. A second goal of writing this text is to assist nurses individually and collectively in reducing the health care disparities that currently exist in America. Nurses begin this process by exploring their own uniqueness to determine what it is that distinguishes them from the individuals, families, and communities they serve.

BARRIERS TO CULTURALLY COMPETENT CARE

This text also seeks to describe barriers that may interfere with the delivery of culturally competent care and identify the steps nurses need to take to overcome them. Personal and systemic barriers exist that interfere with nurses' ability to render quality care to members of some culturally diverse groups. Personal barriers include a nurse's lack of exposure to and/or knowledge about certain groups, misinformation, biases or prejudice, or an inability to communicate due to language differences. Systemic barriers impact patient's care by impeding health care access or the provision of adequate health care resources, through discriminatory health care policies or practices that target certain groups within a particular health care setting. Because such barriers exist, there is a need for nurses to adopt strategies to assist all patients and health care clients in overcoming them.

STRATEGIES FOR SKILL DEVELOPMENT

To foster cultural competency among nurses, this text uses the American Association of Colleges of Nursing (AACN) definition of cultural competency and offers a step-by-step approach to cultural competency development. Having a clear definition of cultural competency affords nurses a starting point from which to begin a thoughtful self-reflection about their readiness to apply cultural competency knowledge and skills to their clinical practice. Throughout the text, each chapter places emphasis on self-reflection, provides real-life case scenarios, utilizes multiple existing frameworks for cultural assessments of patients, and encourages culturally competent patient goal identification and evaluation.

Further, this text seeks to promote an understanding among nurses about the steps they need to take to acquire cultural knowledge and to determine exactly what that information should include. For example, when the knowledge gained during interactions with diverse groups includes information about the social factors that influence health, nurses are better able to discover effective ways to reduce the health care disparities that exist between groups in our society. Each aspect of the text is intended to ensure that student nurses and practicing nurse readers come away from each reading experience with new knowledge and an enhanced sense of their ability to deliver culturally competent care in clinical situations.

THE MEANING OF CULTURE

The concept of *culture* is used broadly in this text to include an individual's cultural background but also the various cultural groups to which individuals belong that may influence their health and well-being. The concepts *culture* and *cultural* may also be applied to individuals, groups, agencies, and institutions. Using this definition, one can appreciate various cultures that exist in society; the health care culture, the culture of poverty, culture of a hospital, or hospital unit, or the culture that exists within certain social groups or organizations. In that sense, all patients belong to various cultural groups. Each group membership potentially influences patients' health care decision making and the quality of care they receive. Moreover, there are many differences within each culturally diverse group. Individuals who share a particular cultural ethnicity or heritage may, through their particular life experiences, develop a very different worldview, use language differently, or hold values that are not shared by members of their reference group. As clients enter a particular health care setting with its own inherent and sometimes unfamiliar "culture" the nurse is often the individual who assists the patient in adapting to the new cultural environment. Organizational culture plays a significant role in patients' health care access and treatment; therefore, nurses must take this into consideration when planning care that is "culturally sensitive" to diverse patient needs.

ROLE OF THE CULTURALLY COMPETENT NURSE

All nurses have a responsibility to view each patient in the context of their various cultural memberships to gain insight into the totality of their health care needs. This is not new behavior, for nurses have always considered the various aspects of their patients from a physical, psychological, and spiritual perspective; holistic nursing has been stressed by the profession for a long time. Cultural competency expands on that holistic approach. Becoming culturally competent means that nurses view patients through their own cultural lens, rather than the narrow lens of the nurse or the Western health care culture. In developing an awareness and knowledge of one's own cultural memberships, nurses begin to see how multicultural all human beings actually are. Since everyone represents some form of diversity, nurses must not look solely to patients of color or persons from foreign lands for diversity, but must consider the broad range of differences that may exist between themselves and each patient they serve. Differences that exist between the nurse and the client come in many forms, but these differences must first be realized if they are to inform care planning.

THE RECIPIENTS OF CULTURALLY COMPETENT CARE

All patients require and deserve culturally competent care. However, for any group that has been placed outside the mainstream of American society receiving care that is culturally competent is critical if its members are to effectively negotiate the health care system and gain access to care. Such groups include, but are not limited to, the poor and uninsured; new immigrants; bariatric patients; persons who are gay, lesbian, or transgendered; persons who have disabilities; individuals for whom English is a second language; or those who are terminally ill. Members of these groups cross cultural, racial, and ethnic lines; thus the "difference" they share with one another is that of being considered outside of the mainstream of patients that most nurses commonly encounter. These patients, because of their unique circumstances, pose the challenge of requiring nurses to have additional knowledge, skill, expertise, and empathy to care for them.

It is also important for nurses and other health care providers to consider these differences, not from an ethnocentric position of authority and power, but from a sincere desire to gain cultural knowledge and insight to determine what is needed to render care that is sensitive and appropriate for each individual. With this perspective, nurses rediscover the common or universal needs that humans share and become better able to collaborate as partners with patients in health care decision making.

IDENTIFYING PATIENTS' NEEDS

Despite cultural differences that exist among patients there are many commonalities that nurses must consider when planning care for diverse groups. Maslow identified several basic human needs that he described as hierarchical; each is salient only when a lower need has been met. Maslow included physiological needs; security or safety needs; love, affection, and belonging needs; self-esteem; cognitive needs and aesthetic needs; and self-actualization or fulfillment needs. Culturally competent nurses consider this hierarchy in light of the historical, sociopolitical, geographical, and economic context in which the nurse discovers and interacts with the patient. Patients benefit when the nurse is able to discern which cultural needs are most salient from the patient's perspective and what level of the hierarchy is most in need of an intervention.

USING THIS TEXT

Each chapter is intended to provide practice opportunities for the nurse. The reader is introduced to a culturally relevant topic, then provided a brief, related case scenario. Self-reflection questions help readers determine their personal readiness for addressing the clinical situation using the Staircase Self-Assessment Model. The reader examines the patient's entire sociocultural context or situation, rather than focusing solely on the impact of culture, race, or ethnicity as it influences health. It is not the intent of this book to focus on assigned cultural attributes of a particular racial or ethnic group in each case example. However, specific cultural implications, where particularly salient, are incorporated in the narrative overview and discussions about the self-reflection questions. Cultural considerations are included in these narratives to emphasize the impact of the intersection of culture and context and their combined influence on health care. When addressing the pertinent issues identified in the case scenario, the reader is asked to select an appropriate model of cultural assessment to determine the specific needs of the patient. However, an appropriate cultural assessment model is also suggested by the author from among the various models that are discussed in Chapter 2.

It is the author's hope that this book serves as a clinical guide for undergraduate nursing students as a good resource during pre- and postconference or classroom discussion. The text can also be useful in nursing programs that offer a separate course on culture and health, or global health, to facilitate or augment class discussion. Learning objectives, case scenarios, glossary terms, NCLEX–type questions, and resources for further study of the topics presented in the case scenarios are provided. The author also highlights important points for the reader to take away from each chapter.

Nurses are lifelong learners and becoming culturally competent is a lifelong process. For student nurses this process begins in their school of nursing. For practicing nurses the process begins today at whatever point they find themselves along the cultural competency staircase. The 21st century is an important time in which to be a professional nurse. It is the author's hope that this text will support nurses in meeting the health needs of an increasingly diverse society, while reducing the health care disparities that have unfortunately resulted.

REFERENCES

Donelan, K., Buerhaus, P., DesRoches, C., Dittus, R., & Dutwin, D. (2008). Public perceptions of nursing careers: The influence of the media and nursing shortage. Special Report. *Nursing Economics, 26*(3), 143–165.

National Institute of Health. (2010). *NIH announces institute on minority health and health disparities.* Retrieved from www.nih.gov/news/health/sep2010/nimhd-27.htm

World Health Organization. (2008). *The Commission on Social Determinants of Health.* Final Report. Retrieved from www.who.int/social_determinants/the commission/finalreport/en/index.html

Defining Cultural Competency

GLORIA KERSEY-MATUSIAK

Faith is taking the first step, even when you don't see the whole staircase.
—MARTIN LUTHER KING JR.

LEARNING OBJECTIVES

1. Provide a rationale for a nurse to become culturally competent.
2. Define cultural competency as it relates to nursing practice.
3. Recall the American Association of Colleges of Nursing (AACN) cultural competencies for baccalaureate graduates.
4. Describe diversity in terms of health care populations and personnel in the 21st century.
5. Utilize the Staircase Self-Assessment Model as a means of determining one's level of cultural competency.
6. Determine strategies for strengthening culturally competent knowledge and skills.
7. Define related terms used in this chapter.
8. Identify relevant resources for further study of this topic.

KEY TERMS

Acculturate
Assimilate
CLAS standards
Cultural competence
Cultural humility

Cultural sensitivity
Culture
Diversity
Reflective listening

WHY CULTURAL COMPETENCY?

Throughout the history of the United States, diversity has always been a resilient and interwoven thread that strengthens the fabric of our society. No longer considered a melting pot, America has more recently been likened to a beautiful mosaic or quilt, reflecting the diverse colors and attributes of the many people who have come to this country from different shores. Most often, Americans have benefited from the rich contributions of its culturally diverse people.

At other times, differences in attitudes, beliefs, values, religion, language, and other characteristics threaten to undermine the ability of culturally diverse groups to coexist and to benefit equally from the nation's resources. **Culture**, for purposes of this text, is defined as, "the totality of socially transmitted behavioral patterns, arts, beliefs, customs, lifeways, and all other products of human work and thought characteristics of a population of people that guide their world-view and decision-making" (Purnell & Paulanka, 2008, p. 5). Culture is dynamic because individuals' values, beliefs, and attitudes change or evolve with their life experiences. For example, many new immigrants bring with them values, attitudes, beliefs, languages, and talents that they may or may not share with other immigrants from similar backgrounds. During an immigrant's stay in America that individual may hold fast to traditional beliefs and practices, but over time may adopt some of the cultural values and patterns of behavior of the dominant group. That culture is a determinant of one's health care decisions is well supported in the literature (Pennsylvania Department of Health, 2002; Spector, 2004; U.S. Department of Health and Human Services, 2000; 2004). Moreover, wide variations in access to health care and to specific treatment modalities have long been observed between members of culturally diverse groups. Linkages among culture, diversity, morbidity, response to treatment, and mortality are also well documented (Healthy People, 2010). In some cases, these linkages among diseases, life expectancy, and cultural group membership seem inexplicable, suggesting a need for further medical and nursing research (National Institutes of Health, 2006). The National Institutes of Health (NIH) and the Centers for Disease Control (CDC) report that such differences have led to health care disparities. These disparities include diseases and other illnesses that "disproportionately afflict individuals who are members of racial and ethnic minority groups" (NIH, 2006). High infant mortality rates, cancer mortality, death from coronary heart disease, and diabetes are some of the conditions that affect minority group members at higher rates than Whites in the United States. A vision held by the NIH is "A time when all Americans have an opportunity for long, healthy, and productive lives regardless of race, ethnicity, or socioeconomic status" (NIH, 2006). Many researchers emphasize the need for cultural competence in health care to address health disparities and to ensure equitable services for all (Drevdahl, Canales & Dorcy, 2008; Engebretson, Mahoney, & Carlson, 2008; Finley, 2008; Vaughn, 2009). In that article, the writer described models of cultural competence and methods of training and evaluation of cultural competency. Based on these observations, nurses have been called to action.

Nursing has taken a leadership role in accepting the diversity challenge. Since the 1950s, led by Madeleine Leininger, a nurse anthropologist, nurses have long considered the relationship between culture and diversity, and health care (Campinha-Bacote, 2010; Jeffreys, 2006; Leininger & McFarland, 2005). In 2002, the American Nurses Association, in cooperation with representatives from more than 40 national nursing organizations, identified diversity as an issue requiring immediate action. In its development of a strategic plan for the future of nursing, it recommended educational programs to develop nurses' skills in cultural competency in an effort to link cultural competency to patient safety and quality of care initiatives. In its 2010 report, Advancing Effective Communication, Cultural Competency, and Patient and Family Centered Care: A Roadmap for Hospitals, The Joint Commission made recommendations for hospitals. As one executive observed, hospitals may be able to determine gold standards for cultural competency based on this plan.

In support of these initiatives, others are advocating for a change in the way clinicians provide care to patients and in the way nurses are educated in light of the health disparities that exist (Alexander, 2008). Dergurahian (2008) discussed ways in which hospitals in Philadelphia are attempting to address the cultural needs of foreign-born patients who are seeking their services. Cultural competency frameworks and models are readily available to assist nurses in their journey toward cultural competency. Some of these frameworks are presented in Chapter 2. In other efforts, the American Association of Colleges and Universities (AACU, 2005) through its Making Excellence Inclusive programs, encourages curriculum developers in colleges and universities to consider the integration of diversity and inclusion into the curriculum and co-curricular activities as a means of promoting excellence. Cavillo, Clark, Ballantyne, Pacquiao, Purnell, and Villarruel (2009) described the work of the American Association of Colleges of Nursing's (AACN) Advisory Committee in identifying five competencies for cultural competency in Baccalaureate Nursing Education. AACN made suggestions for implementing curriculum, teaching cultural content, and evaluating nursing students' cultural competence outcomes. The AACN competencies are discussed later in this chapter. Milem, Chang, and Antonio (2005) discussed ways to transform the learning environment in ways that support the inclusion of culturally diverse learners while promoting excellence. Colleges and universities, through their mission statements, policies, and recruitment efforts, are attempting to strengthen their diversity. These institutions recognize the need to provide a more diverse and culturally rich college experience for their students to better prepare them for citizenship in a multicultural society.

For the purposes of this text, cultural competence is defined using the AACN's definition. This definition and the identified competencies are written as a framework for baccalaureate nursing graduates (AACN, 2012). **Cultural**

competence is defined as the attitudes, knowledge, and skills necessary for providing quality care to diverse populations. Although there are many other definitions found in the nursing literature (Kwong, 2009), most contain these three fundamental hallmarks of what it means for a nurse to be culturally competent. The *attitudes* one needs to be culturally competent include having an openness to an ongoing self-reflection about one's own values, beliefs, biases, and prejudices (Andrews, Boyle, & Carr, 2003), which everyone has, and having a willingness to consider another individual or group's perspective or worldview. This is not to say that culturally competent nurses adopt each patient's beliefs and attitudes; rather the nurse accepts that differences exist between themselves and the patient and is motivated to work toward transcending those differences for the sake of the nurse–patient relationship.

In addition to having attitudes that support positive interactions between nurses and culturally diverse patients, nurses must also be able to acquire cultural knowledge about themselves and the patient. The cultural assessment model that the nurse selects helps determine the kind of information needed to assess patients from diverse backgrounds. However, generally speaking, the nurse needs to know about the patient's history in the United States, geographical origin, the cultural or ethnic background, the context or situation, and the diversity within the group of reference. When nurses are able to obtain information about each of these areas, they are able to view the patient holistically and from the patient's cultural perspective.

The culturally competent nurse must also utilize various skills effectively to deliver care that is congruent with patients' cultural values. Primarily, these skills are communication skills that enhance the nurse–patient rapport and include reflective listening, speaking to patients using language they understand, interviewing the patient, using a cultural assessment tool, and critically thinking to problem solve cross-culturally. **Reflective listening** refers to a process of communication in which the nurse or other health care providers listen to the patient for understanding and intermittently seek clarification to be sure that they are accurately interpreting the patient's words. This style of communicating is especially important when the patient's verbal communication does not seem to reflect the nonverbal. Nurses must also keep in mind that medical jargon is a language all its own that is probably unfamiliar to most patients. Therefore, speaking to all patients in a language they understand means minimizing the use of medical jargon as much as possible and reserving it for use with colleagues and other health care providers. Communication is even more compromised when the patient and nurse speak different languages. When that happens, a medically trained interpreter is the ideal person to translate for the nurse. The process of interpreting is a skill in itself that requires training and knowledge that family members and other laypeople who speak the language may not have. To maintain the patient's privacy, confidentiality, and comfort, using children to translate should be avoided.

To obtain accurate cultural information about the patient, the nurse must *interview and assess* the patient and/or family using language and behaviors that are not offensive or inappropriate from the patient's perspective. Without some cultural knowledge of the patient's cultural norms and preferences, making offensive remarks or demonstrating behaviors that the patient considers inappropriate is nearly unavoidable. Therefore, nurses are encouraged to learn specific cultural knowledge about the populations they serve on a regular basis. It is impossible for nurses to know everything about all of the various culturally diverse groups they may encounter; however, there are many current texts that nurses can reference to gain specific knowledge about a particular group (Andrews & Boyle, 2008; Giger & Davidhizar, 2008; Purnell & Paulanka, 2008). The more nurses experience individuals from the same group, the more they are able to strengthen their cultural knowledge.

Critical thinking is a skill taught in nursing school; however, the culturally competent nurse is expected to apply those skills to problem solving cross-culturally. In other words, nurses who are able to think critically about the patient's cultural needs will also be able to identify potential cultural conflicts among individuals, families, and/or institutions. These nurses identify cultural differences, determine their impact on care, and develop strategies for overcoming them. Nurses who function at this level of cultural competency can serve as mentors for others. Each of the cultural competency skills described previously takes patience and time for the nurse to develop. Most importantly, skill development takes practice.

There are other terms found in the literature that refer to behaviors of the health care provider who aspires to becoming culturally competent. **Cultural humility** is another term often used to convey a similar idea. More specifically, Kosoko-Lasaki, Cook, and O'Brien (2009) described the concept of cultural humility as "the action and efforts by the nurse to understand and to eliminate biased, disrespectful, and prejudiced attitudes, beliefs, behaviors, polices, and practices." According to these authors, key to gaining this understanding is for health care professionals and institutions to first recognize that their own perspectives are influenced by the biomedical model and conceptual models; therefore, "their attitudes and beliefs are unconsciously biased, and their practices and policies often maintain dominance and superior power, typically aligned with whiteness and maleness" (p. 49). Purnell and Paulanka (2008) described **cultural sensitivity** in a similar way as having "more to do with attitudes and not saying things that might be offensive to someone from a cultural or ethnic background different from the healthcare provider's" (p. 6). Cultural sensitivity may also mean the use of "neutral language" and the intentional avoidance of other words, phrases, and categorizations in appreciation for the diversity of others (American Academy of Nursing Expert Panel on Cultural Competency, 2007). Thus, these terms—cultural competency, cultural humility, and cultural sensitivity—have similar meanings and are sometimes used interchangeably.

Duke, Connor, and McEldowney (2009) linked cultural competency to cultural safety for vulnerable people. These authors stressed the need for advancing generic skills to ensure cultural competency and provided a guide for its evaluation. The more knowledgeable nurses and other health care workers become about diversity as it impacts health care, the more likely they are to make a significant impact on health care disparities. The challenge, then, is for nurses and other health care providers to strive toward cultural competence and to begin implementing changes in care provision that respond to the needs of an increasingly diverse patient population.

DIVERSITY IN AMERICA

For the purposes of this text, **diversity** refers to all aspects of difference that may be found among health care populations. Increasingly, both the nature and scope of our nation's diversity has changed to include a wide range of differences between and among members of diverse groups. Diversity in health care today includes, but is not limited to, age, culture, race, gender, ethnicity, language differences, sexual orientation, socioeconomic status, immigration status, and any other group membership that may negatively influence one's access to culturally competent care. Moreover, intra-cultural or within-group differences may also have a significant influence on health care. Differences such as patterns or styles of communication, attitudes toward authority, ways of knowing, addressing conflict, and making decisions may all differ even within the same ethnic or racial group based on one's age, gender, or personality. Therefore, the author warns nurses against adopting a "recipe approach" to assessing patients' specific health care needs based on commonalities attributed to the cultural group of reference. Recognizing the intra-group differences within patient populations will ensure that care is based on an accurate assessment of patients' care needs. Immigrants also differ in their desire to **assimilate** or **acculturate** or not based on their reasons for immigration. To acculturate is to adapt or take on some parts of another culture. Assimilation refers to being absorbed into another culture and relinquishing one's own (*Webster's New World Dictionary*, 2002). Among new immigrants, some, but not all, are able to communicate fluently in English. Those who cannot are much less able to negotiate the health care system. New immigrants with limited English skills must rely on hospitals and health care personnel to identify and respond to their specific health needs despite difficulties in communicating with them. Today, a number of institutions have accepted this challenge.

The U.S. Department of Health and Human Services Office of Minority Health, in its publication of the National Standards for Culturally and Linguistically Appropriate Services (CLAS) in health care, affirmed the need for nurses to become culturally competent (DHHS, 2001, 2004). These standards serve as a guide for all health care providers. Some serve as mandates to hospitals to conform to those standards deemed necessary in providing culturally competent health care. These 14 guidelines and mandates are intended to ensure equitable care for all patients (Evans, 2007).

Since their inception, the response to the CLAS standards has been positive. Administrators of U.S. hospitals recognize the need for health care providers to understand the impact of language and culture on the quality of patient care. Patient safety is also impacted by the patient's and staff's ability to communicate effectively with one another. Therefore, qualified interpreters are needed to assist in improving health literacy and patient safety (Patient Education Management, 2007). Carlson (2008) examined patient care outcomes at a hospital in Anderson, South Carolina, and observed readmission rates among Spanish-speaking women decreased in the obstetrics department, after the hospital hired interpreters to help explain discharge plans.

In another example of compliance to CLAS standards, one writer discussed efforts at Children's National Medical Center to apply the CLAS standards through the hospital's integration of families and its community into standards of care. This hospital established family councils that taught the nurses about which staff behaviors were useful and those that interfered with patient care. When recruiting nurses, this hospital looks on its diversity as a strength, stating "we believe that we are more alike than different" (Evans, 2007). However, to address generational diversity between the nurses, the hospital provides flexible shifts to accommodate the different needs of baby boomers, Xers, and millennials among the staff. Generational diversity between and among staff members and patients is another aspect of difference that, although often overlooked, has the potential to impact the quality of care.

Having a diverse health care staff that is inclusive of age, culture, race, ethnicity, and religion is one way to better serve a diverse patient population. However, limited ethnic diversity within nursing's rank and file and society's general intolerance of difference, are factors that hinder nurses' progress in becoming culturally competent. Although there has been a gradual increase in diversity within nursing, gender and ethnic and racial diversity remains disproportionate to that of American society. For example, while gradually increasing their membership in the nursing profession, men account for only 7.1% of nurses in the United States. According to the U.S. population estimates for 2010, ethnic minorities represent nearly 30% of the U.S. population, with Asian Americans, 4.8%; Black Americans 12.6%; Hispanic or Latino Americans, 16.3%; and White Americans 72.4%. These estimates included Native Hawaiian and Other Pacific Islanders, 0.3%, and American Indian 0.3% and those indicating some other race 6.2%. Individuals representing two or more races are 2.9% (U.S. Census Bureau, 2010). In contrast, the 2008 Nurse Survey reported that nurses representing minority groups accounted for only 17.7% of the total nurse population with Black nurses 5.6%, Asian nurses 5.8%, and Hispanic/Latino nurses 3.9%. White nurses in 2008 accounted for 82.2% of the nurses surveyed. With the exception of Asian nurses, other minority groups remain significantly underrepresented in nursing (National Sample Survey, 2008). Thus, human resources that might enhance nurses' cross-cultural exposures and facilitate intercultural collaboration are limited.

Evans (2007) and Swinney and Dobal (2008) discussed the importance of having a diverse RN staff. The Embracing the Challenge (ETC) project is an example of recruitment efforts by one hospital in southwestern Massachusetts to increase the number of ethnic minority and disadvantaged nurses from Hispanic and African American communities in the nursing workforce. This project includes the goal of recruiting and retaining minority students in nursing by providing scholarships and stipends to economically disadvantaged students. Polacek (2009) also evaluated cultural competency at a U.S. hospital. In this study, the hospital conducted patient and doctor focus groups and employee surveys to assess cultural competency. Results of the study indicated that ethnicity and gender had an impact on language skills and awareness. The study also revealed that awareness and knowledge were influenced by an employee's position. Patients who were participants of the study expressed concerns about having access to care and respect from staff.

Another area of difference that exists among health care recipients is socioeconomic status. The impact of poverty on health, irrespective of one's race or ethnicity, is profound. Although minorities and some new immigrants represent a higher percentage of those who live below the poverty level, among all patients who are poor, many are medically uninsured and less able to access appropriate medical care.

Differences in sexual orientation are often overlooked in books that focus on cultural diversity and cultural competency; however, individuals who are gay, lesbian, bisexual, or transgendered bring unique issues and concerns to the health care arena. Recently, New York passed a law ensuring the right to marriage between gay couples, becoming one of six states to do so. Yet, there are still many people in America who view the family as consisting solely of a married man and woman and their children. In many states in the United States, gay and lesbian partners who are in long-term relationships may be denied health care benefits for their partners and consequently worry about accessing health care, particularly as they age.

Despite various differences among and between groups, as members of the human family, everyone is in need of acceptance and understanding. Nurses are challenged to acknowledge the uniqueness of all individuals, families, and groups while recognizing their patients' ties to the rest of society. Nurses who acknowledge cultural differences while establishing collaborative partnerships with patients from diverse populations maximize their potential to provide culturally competent care. These nurses gain new insights by acting with cultural humility and relinquishing their power over patients to determine what the patient actually needs and wants. Differences between the patient and the nurse are considered, but the patient is always treated with dignity and respect despite the differences. The reader is encouraged to view "diversity" from an inclusive perspective and consider all aspects of difference to have the potential to influence the quality of care a patient receives.

Nurses today practice in a time when the decision to develop cultural competency skills can no longer be viewed as optional. If nurses are ever to gain insight into the needs of their culturally diverse patients, they must view each individual's health care situation through the patient's own cultural perspective. To gain the respect and trust of the culturally diverse groups they serve, nurses must be willing to provide care that is relevant and congruent with patients' own health care values and beliefs.

Moreover, despite being the largest group of health care providers, nursing is but a microcosm of the society we represent. Consequently, the profession is plagued by the same societal ills, sexism, racism, homophobia, elitism, ageism, sizeism, and a host of other biases that exist in the larger society. Each of these characteristics can negatively influence the quality of care that some nurses provide and may prohibit them from being effective when working with individuals outside of their own reference groups. In becoming culturally competent, nurses learn to better address the specific needs of all patients and become much better prepared to work cooperatively as members of an increasingly diverse workforce. In settings where cultural competency is emphasized, nurses are encouraged to accept differences and to treat colleagues with cultural sensitivity and respect. Interactions between members of diverse groups offer opportunities for professional growth in cultural knowledge and skill development. In such settings nurses strive to provide one another the same degree of cultural awareness and sensitivity that they are expected to provide their patients. Despite the many challenges, becoming culturally competent can be a rewarding experience that enhances both nurse–patient and nurse-to-nurse interactions.

UTILIZING THE STAIRCASE SELF-ASSESSMENT MODEL

The Cultural Competency Staircase Model was developed in 1991 by the author as a self-assessment tool to assist student nurses and practicing nurses in assessing their personal level or degree of cultural competency. This model builds on ideas proposed by Terry L. Cross (1988) who described a continuum of cultural competency that included six stages: cultural destructiveness, cultural incapacity, cultural blindness, precompetency, basic cultural competency, and advanced cultural competency. As a nurse educator, the author over the past several years has observed both students and practicing nurses to be more easily grouped into the categories described by the Staircase Model. Another purpose of the Staircase Model is to provide nurses a method of progressive movement through the various steps. This approach fosters the ongoing development of a nurse's cultural awareness, knowledge, skills, and expertise in cultural competency. Therefore, culturally competent behaviors must be adaptable to the changing or evolving needs of individuals within culturally diverse groups.

The Staircase Model describes salient characteristics of the nurse at the various steps in becoming culturally competent; however, these characteristics may only be known to that individual. So it is important that nurses honestly evaluate themselves during this self-assessment. The model also offers a possible rationale for the characteristics observed, identifies typical patient care–related behaviors, and suggests strategies for moving toward the next step. Therefore, a staircase to illustrate upward mobility seemed most appropriate. However, while the model is linear, the staircase moves toward infinity, illustrating a primary assumption that cultural competency is a lifelong process and aspiration, not a final goal to be achieved. Another assumption of this model is that nurses who reach Level 5 or 6 in encounters with certain groups may easily find themselves at a much lower level when encountering new groups with whom they have little experience. Therefore, nurses can ascend or descend the staircase based on the experience or encounters a nurse has had with members of a particular cultural group. Through multiple encounters with the same group nurses gain more knowledge, skill, and facility in ascending the staircase. For example, a nurse may have much experience with Mexican patients through an emersion during which the nurse works with migrant farm workers. That nurse might well be able to demonstrate cultural competency in situations with Mexican patients at Step 5 or 6 of the staircase. At this level, the nurse is able to serve as mentor to other nurses who have not had such encounters. However, this same nurse may have little or no experience with Vietnamese clients and functions at Step 3 when caring for these patients. Nurses who perform a self-assessment on a regular basis when they encounter new groups will gain greater self-awareness, new insights about cultural care, and facility at ascending the staircase. These nurses also recognize the need to seek appropriate resources to assist them and begin to develop a network of support.

Staircase Model assumptions include the following. Culturally competent nurses:

- Increasingly develop self-awareness, cultural knowledge, and skills through encounters with culturally diverse patients.
- Strive to understand the patients or clients in their entire sociocultural context and with regard to all the dimensions of difference the patient represents; for example, a Black Muslim patient with multiple marriage partners; a new Vietnamese immigrant and single mother; a gay, Irish Catholic adolescent; a young married female newly diagnosed with multiple sclerosis (MS).
- Consider the patient's geographical origins, history in the United States, cultural background, and within group diversity.

- Make efforts to address health care disparities at the individual, institutional, or community levels through patient advocacy, mentoring, or educating other staff members, publications, or research.

FINDING YOUR PLACE ON THE STAIRCASE

Step 1. Nurses at Step 1 fail to recognize the significance of cultural influences when planning care. They may have completed nursing school before cultural content was introduced and/or have limited exposure to culturally diverse patients.

Step 2. Nurses at Step 2 have a growing awareness of the influence that culture has on health, but limited cultural self-awareness and limited knowledge about other cultural groups.

Step 3. These nurses have begun to develop cultural self-awareness, acquire cultural knowledge about one or two culturally diverse groups, and attempt to include cultural information in care planning.

Step 4. Nurses in this category have a strong cultural self-awareness and an expanded social network from which to derive cultural information about diverse groups. These nurses consistently incorporate that knowledge into their care planning.

Step 5. Nurses at Step 5 are highly aware and readily apply cultural knowledge to care planning. They also anticipate potential culturally related patient problems or staff issues. They may serve as mentors and role models.

Step 6. Nurses at this level have a high level of self-awareness; a wide knowledge of another or multiple cultures that differ from their own; and an ability to problem-solve across cultural groups and to teach other nurses through mentoring, publication, and or research. (Kersey-Matusiak, 2001. Reprinted with Permission from *Nursing Spectrum*.)

See Table 1.1 to find strategies for progression.

GENERAL STEP-CONSCIOUS QUESTIONS FOR NURSES TO ASK THEMSELVES TO DETERMINE THEIR LEVEL ON THE STAIRCASE

Step 1
- How much do I value becoming culturally competent?
- What actions have I taken recently or in the past when caring for members of culturally diverse patients that demonstrate my motivation?

Step 2
- How much do I know about my own cultural heritage or racial identity and its relationship to my own health care beliefs and practices?
- Have I discussed these issues with my parents, grandparents, or other relatives?

Step 3
- How much do I know about cultural groups that differ from my own?

Step 4
- How culturally diverse is my social network?
- How many encounters with cultural group members outside my own social network do I have; are these relationships superficial or do I have contact beyond the workplace?

Step 5
- Am I able to independently identify potential or actual problems that originate from cultural conflicts or am I surprised by them?
- Do I serve as a culturally competent role model/mentor for others?

Step 6
- Have I developed problem-solving strategies to manage cultural conflicts?
- Am I able to manage or resolve cultural problems or issues that arise?
- Do I have resources to call on to assist me when these conflicts occur?

AACN END-OF-PROGRAM CULTURAL COMPETENCIES FOR BACCALAUREATE NURSING EDUCATION

1. Apply knowledge of social and cultural factors that affect nursing and health care across multiple contexts.
2. Use relevant data sources and best evidence in providing culturally competent care.
3. Promote achievement of safe and quality outcomes of care for diverse populations.
4. Advocate for social justice, including commitment to the health of vulnerable populations and the elimination of health care disparities.
5. Participate in continuous cultural competence development.

TABLE 1.1 Cultural Competency Staircase Model

STEP	CHARACTERISTICS	RATIONALE	BEHAVIORS	STRATEGIES FOR PROGRESSION
Step 1	Health care (HC) provider fails to recognize the significance of cultural influences, lacks motivation	• Has not accepted influence of culture on own life or • Has had negative experiences with members of diverse groups or • Has had limited experiences with diversity or • Completed nursing school before cultural content was presented	• May treat all patients the same • May care for patients based on own values and beliefs • May make assumptions that may be unfounded • May stereotype or demonstrate bias, prejudice, or discrimination	• Explore own cultural origins through interviews of family members ethnographic study of one's cultural, ethnic heritage • Enhance internal motivation through encounters with members of culturally diverse groups; attend conferences and workshops • Seek culturally competent mentors, colleagues, and friends who are comfortable in cross-cultural situations
Step 2	HC provider is motivated, and has growing awareness of culture's influence on health, but limited self-awareness, or knowledge of other groups	• Is internally motivated to learn about own culture and culture of others • Is uncertain about how culture influences values	• May rely on texts for cultural information • Has limited experiences with diverse groups • May ignore intra-cultural differences • May make generalizations or stereotypes	• All of above. Utilize a cultural assessment tool to determine intra-cultural differences • Broaden one's personal contacts beyond comfort zone or usual social group in social and professional situations
Step 3	HC provider has developed a planned approach to developing cultural self-awareness and to acquire cultural knowledge about one or two culturally diverse groups	• Has developed a firm belief in the significance of culture and its impact on health and health care • Cultural competency is an identified value	• Attempts to include cultural information in care planning, but inconsistently • May overlook cultural competency behaviors when overwhelmed by other clinical roles and responsibilities	• All of above. Seek professional workshops and conferences that focus on cultural competency development • Consider immersions in a cultural group of interest or professional engagement • Identify culturally competent role models in the workplace

(continued)

13

TABLE 1.1 Cultural Competency Staircase Model *(continued)*

STEP	CHARACTERISTICS	RATIONALE	BEHAVIORS	STRATEGIES FOR PROGRESSION
Step 4	• Nurses have strong cultural self-awareness and an expanding social network. Consistently incorporates cultural knowledge into care planning	• Has observed cultural differences through interactions with family, close friends, and colleagues	• Consistently seeks to identify cultural information in plans of care	• All of above • Continue to seek additional cultural resources through community, state, and federal organizations
Step 5	• Nurses are highly self-aware, readily apply cultural knowledge in care planning, anticipate potential cultural conflicts in patient care or staff issues	• Has ongoing experience and training in cultural diversity and/or transcultural nursing	• Serves as role model and coach in demonstrating cultural competency behaviors in patient care settings	• All of above • Seek cultural/diversity support networks as resources
Step 6	• Nurses have attained a high level of self-awareness, a wide knowledge about a particular or multiple cultures, and have an ability to problem-solve cross-culturally	• Has had multiple and ongoing transcultural formal and informal learning experiences and training	• Serves in a leadership capacity in area of diversity or transcultural situations • Problem-solves cross-culturally • Considered an expert in some areas of diversity • Has areas of diversity needing development	• As above • Identify areas of diversity/transcultural nursing needing further development, e.g., language skills of interest (Spanish, Chinese) • Continue to attend workshops and conferences to strengthen knowledge • Utilize opportunities to immerse oneself in cultural learning experiences when possible

STRATEGIES FOR STRENGTHENING CULTURAL COMPETENCY

Nurses can use seven strategies when practicing culturally competent care. These strategies include:

- **Strategy 1**
  Review a patient care scenario

- **Strategy 2**
  Perform a self-assessment using the Staircase Model

- **Strategy 3**
  Select and apply a patient-centered cultural assessment to the scenario

- **Strategy 4**
  Identify potential or actual barriers to culturally competent care

- **Strategy 5**
  Establish patient care goals based on barriers and patient needs

- **Strategy 6**
  Develop a nursing action plan based on self-assessment, cultural assessment, barriers, and goals

- **Strategy 7**
  Evaluate the effectiveness of cultural competent care planning and revise as needed

This step also allows the nurse to reflect on whether the interventions were effective.

CASE SCENARIO

Mrs. G, a 48-year-old, married, Spanish-speaking, recent immigrant from Colombia, is brought to the ER via ambulance. She was brought to the ER after her 18-year-old son, Roberto, discovered her in a chair in the living room with a cigarette in her hand that had fallen into her lap. Mrs. G's son began beating Mrs. G's clothing to extinguish the fire that was starting to ignite Mrs. G's dress. During the episode, Mrs. G remained silent and appeared confused. Mrs. G has a history of hypertension and type 2 diabetes mellitus. She has smoked two packs of cigarettes a day for the past 40 years and has tried unsuccessfully to stop multiple times. Mrs. G is non–English speaking. Her son Roberto understands and speaks a little English, but has some difficulty communicating in English.

Roberto tells the nurse that his mother has been taking medication at home for DM and high blood pressure, but has not been to a doctor since coming to the United States 8 months ago.

The ER triage nurse becomes concerned when she realizes that the patient seems to be experiencing some neurologic changes. Communication with both the mother and son is difficult. Laboratory results reveal that the patient's blood sugar is 340mg/dl.

STEPPING UP TO CULTURALLY COMPETENT CARE

Apply seven strategies to ensure culturally competent care.

Strategy 1

Perform a self-assessment using the Staircase Model. The ER nurse in this situation has had many encounters with Spanish-speaking patients, but has not cared for patients from Colombia. The nurse is able to speak enough Spanish to obtain and explain basic information to the patient. When speaking with Mrs. G, she learns that Mrs. G is a widow. During a recent self-assessment, the ER nurse rated herself between Steps 4 and 5 using the Staircase Model. Today, she reflects on whether she needs the support of her colleague to assist her in this situation. The nurse knows a nurse practitioner who is fluent in Spanish and who she can call on to assist her in performing an assessment of the patient, if she needs her. Because of the complex nature of the patient's medical condition, which is likely to involve more than one diagnosis, the nurse decides to call on her friend, the nurse practitioner for assistance with the assessment, to expedite the assessment process.

Strategy 2

Review a patient care scenario. The ER nurse considers this patient's entire cultural context and considers:

1. This patient and her son are both new immigrants and may be unfamiliar with the U.S. health care system
2. The patient is unable to communicate in English. The son is not an appropriate translator or good historian, as he has limited English skills, too.
3. Patient has been taking unknown medications at home. She may be using herbal medicine or folk medicine to treat health problems; these may be incompatible with medicine ordered by physician in the hospital.
4. At age 48, is this patient employed, does she have health insurance? What is the socioeconomic, educational status of this patient? Have any of these issues impacted the patient's health in general, specifically blood pressure, or her understanding about her disease, or its treatment?

Strategy 3

Select and apply a patient-centered cultural assessment to the scenario. The nurse selects from among Purnell's Twelve Domains of Culture (2008), selecting those attributes relevant to a cultural assessment of this case example. The attributes selected include:

- Inhabited locality
- Communication
- Family roles and organization
- Workforce issues
- Biocultural ecology
- High-risk behaviors
- Nutrition
- Spirituality
- Health care practices
- Health care practitioners

Strategy 4

Identify potential or actual barriers to culturally competent care.
Example: Language barrier.

Strategy 5

Establish patient care goals based on barriers and patient's needs.
Example: The patient will understand health information and plan of care.

Strategy 6

Develop a nursing action plan based on above. A medically trained interpreter will assist with providing health information and plan of care in patient's own language.

Strategy 7

Evaluate the effectiveness of cultural competent care planning and revise as needed.

REFERENCES

Alexander, G. R. (2008). Cultural competence models in nursing. *Critical Care Nursing Clinics of North America, 20*(4), 415–421.

American Association of Colleges of Nursing (AACN). (2012). *Leading initiatives: Cultural competency in nursing education.* Retrieved from www.aacn.nche.edu/education-resources/cultural-competency

American Nurses Association. (2002, April). *A call to the nation: Nurses agenda for the future.* Retrieved January, 28, 2007, from www.nursingworld.org/naf/naf.pdf

Andrews, M., & Boyle, J. S. (2008). *Transcultural concepts in nursing care* (5th ed.). Philadelphia, PA: Wolters Kluwer/Lippincott Williams & Wilkins.

Andrews, M., Boyle, J., & Carr, T. J. (2003). *Transcultural concepts in nursing care* (4th ed.). Philadelphia, PA: Lippincott.

Association of American Colleges and Universities (AACU). (2005). *Making excellence inclusive: Diversity, inclusion, and institutional renewal.* Retrieved February 14, 2007, from www.aacu.org/inclusive_excellence/index.cfm

Calvillo, E., Clark, L., Ballantyne, J., Pacquiao, D., Purnell, L., & Villarruel, A. M. (2009). Cultural competency in baccalaureate nursing education. *Journal of Transcultural Nursing, 20*(2), 137–145.

Campinha-Bacote, J. (2010). *The process of cultural competence in the delivery of health care services.* (4th ed.). Cincinnati, OH: Transcultural C.A.R.E. Associates Press.

Carlson, J. (2008). Measuring Inclusiveness. *Modern Healthcare, 38*(44), 18–20.

Centers for Disease Control; National Prevention Information Network. (2011). *Cultural competence.* Retrieved from www.cdcnpin.org/scripts/population/culture.asp

Cross, T. (1988). *Cultural competence continuum.* Retrieved from www.casbrant.ca/files/upload/oacas/Reference Material/Agency Cultural Competence Continuum.doc

Dergurahian, J. (2008). Breaking Barriers. *Modern Healthcare, 38*(27), 28–30.

Drevdahl, D., Canales, M., & Dorcy, K. (2008). Of goldfish tanks and moonlight tricks: can cultural competency ameliorate health disparities?. *Advances in Nursing Science, 31*(1), 13–27. Retrieved from http://search.ebscohost.com/login.aspx?direct=true&db=rzh&AN=200986 1164

Duke, J., Connor, M., & McEldowney, R. (2009). Becoming a culturally competent health practitioner in the delivery of culturally safe care: A process oriented approach. *Journal of Cultural Diversity, 16*(2), 40–49. Retrieved from CINAHL Plus with Full Text database.

Engebretson, J., Mahoney, J., & Carlson, E. (2008). Cultural competence in the era of evidence-based practice. *Journal of Professional Nursing, 24*(3), 172–178. Retrieved from http://search.ebscohost.com/login.aspx?direct=true&db=rzh&AN=20099 45687

Evans, M. (2007). Culturally competent staff: Stories and learnings from Children's National Medical Center, Washington D.C. *Creative Nursing, 13*(1), 9–10.

Findley, T. E. (2008). *Cultural competence of nurses at the bedside.* Doctoral dissertation. Retrieved from http://web.ebscohost.com/ehost/delivery?vid=5&hid=106&sid-059b5377-al

Giger, J., & Davidhizar, R. (2008) *Transcultural nursing.* St. Louis, MO: Mosby Year Book.

Jeffreys, M. (2006). *Teaching cultural competence in nursing and health care.* New York, NY: Springer Publishing Company.

Kersey-Matusiak, G. (2001, April 2). An action plan for nurses: building cultural competence. *Nursing Spectrum, 10*, 7, 21–24

Kosoko-Lasaki, S., Cook, C. T., & O'Brien, R. L. (2009). *Cultural proficiency in addressing health disparities.* Boston, MA: Jones and Bartlettt.

Kwong, M. (2009). Applying cultural competency in clinical practice: findings from multicultural experts' experience. *Journal of Ethnic & Cultural Diversity in Social Work, 18*(1–2), 146–165. Retrieved from CINAHL Plus with Full Text database.

Leininger, M., & McFarland, M. R. (2005). *Culture care diversity and universality: A Worldwide nursing theory.* New York, NY: National League of Nursing Press, Publication No. 15–2402.

Milem, J. F., Chang, M. J., & Antonio, A. L. (2005). *Making diversity work on campus: A Research-based perspective.* Washington, DC: American Association of Colleges and Universities

National Institutes of Health. (2006). *Addressing health disparities: The NIH program of action.* Retrieved March 2007, from http://healthdisparities.nih.gov/whatare.html

Pennsylvania Department of Health. (2002). *State health improvement plan: Special report on the health status of minorities in Pennsylvania.* Pennsylvania, PA: Author.

Polacek, G. N. L., & Martinez, R. (2009). Assessing cultural competence at a local hospital system in the United States. *Health Care Manger, 28*(2), 98–110 Retrieved from http://web.ebscohost.com/ehost/delivery?vid

Purnell, L., & Paulanka, B. J. (2008). *Transcultural health care: A culturally competent approach.* Philadelphia, PA: F.A. Davis Company.

Qualified interpreters improve health literacy and patient safety. (2007) *Patient Education Management, 14*(7), 73–77.

Spector, R. (2004). *Cultural Diversity in Health and Illness* (6th ed.). Englewood Cliffs. NJ: Prentice Hall.

Swinney, J. E., & Dobal, M. T. (2008). Embracing the challenge: Increasing workforce diversity in nursing [Abstract]. *Hispanic Health Care International, 6*(4), 200–204.

U.S. Census Bureau. (2010). *People.* Retrieved from www.census.gov/people

U.S. Department of Health and Human Services. (2000). *Healthy people 2010: Understanding and improving health* (2nd ed.). Washington, DC: U.S. Government Printing Office.

U.S. Department of Health and Human Services. (2001) *National standards for culturally linguistically appropriate services in health care.* Washington, DC: Author.

U. S. Department of Health and Human Services; Office of Minority Health. (2004). *Setting the agenda.* Washington, DC: Author.

Vaughn, L. (2009). families and cultural competency: where are we? *Family & Community Health, 32*(3), 247–256.

Webster's New World Dictionary and Thesaurus (2nd ed.). (2002). New York, NY: Hungry Minds Inc.

Patient-Focused Cultural Assessment Models

GLORIA KERSEY-MATUSIAK

The only place where true change can occur and where the past can be dissolved is the Now.

—ECKHART TOLLE (2001)

LEARNING OBJECTIVES

1. Describe the rationale for utilizing a patient-centered cultural assessment model.
2. Describe selected cultural assessment models developed specifically for nurses.
3. Discuss the components of a selected group of cultural assessment models used for other health professionals.
4. Utilize an appropriate cultural assessment model to enhance communication when delivering care to culturally diverse patients.
5. Integrate cultural assessment findings in care planning for culturally diverse clients.

KEY TERMS

Biocultural ecology
Cultural assessment
Cultural encounter
Culturally congruent
Culture care
Culture Care Diversity and Universality
Generic or folk systems
Sunrise Model

SELECTING A CULTURAL ASSESSMENT TOOL

Opportunities to conduct **cultural assessments** occur each time there is contact between the patient and the nurse or other health care provider. These *encounters* may occur face-to-face, but can also occur during phone conversations, teleconferences, or other means through which there is interaction between the client and the nurse (Campinha-Bacote, 2003). Each encounter is an opportunity for the nurse to establish or affirm a trusting, supportive relationship with the patient (Keller, 2008). It is also an opportunity for nurses to gain insights about their patients' culture, health attitudes and beliefs, and to explore the entire situation or context in which the patient's cultural health beliefs exist. Armed with this knowledge, the nurse is able to partner with the patient to establish mutually agreed on and **culturally congruent** goals for care. It is important to note here that no one is expected to learn all there is to know about any particular culture during a single, brief clinical encounter. However, the nurse must place emphasis on learning about what is deemed most significant from a cultural perspective from the patient's point of view. The nurse must also recognize that there may be differences about what is culturally important between members of the same group. Using a cultural assessment model, the nurse can explore how the patient feels about a variety of factors that impact health. These include, but are not limited to, the patient's beliefs about the illness, hospitalization, Western medicine, health care decision making, nutrition, medications, and values and beliefs about life, death, and spirituality. It may not be possible to have extended periods during which to gather important cultural information, so the nurse is encouraged to use each opportunity during which there is interaction with the patient to seek this information.

There is a wide variety of cultural competency assessment models that are found in the nursing literature (Alexander, 2008; Campinha-Bacote, 2003, 2008; Giger and Davidhizar, 2008; Jeffries, 2006, Purnell & Paulanka (2009). Each model offers its own constructs and/or parameters to use as a basis for either determining one's own level of cultural competency, or performing a cultural assessment. The author of this text encourages nurses to use a model that is most suitable for their communication style, care setting, and patient situation. By learning about many of the models and frameworks currently available, the nurse builds an arsenal of strategies to use at the appropriate time to meet the situation at hand. The purpose of this text is to assist nurses in practicing cultural competency skills routinely, so when giving nursing care, a description of various models is presented here. Case scenarios are presented at the end of the chapters to provide the reader with practice opportunities using the models. An assessment model is suggested for application to each of the cases throughout the text.

Many of the models found in the literature are specifically intended to assist nurses in integrating cultural information into their clinical nursing assessments and care planning. Stein (2010) also identified assessment models such as ETHNIC, LEARN, BATHE, and GREET models that, although not initially developed for nurses, are applicable in patient care situations, and therefore useful to nurses.

Before beginning any cultural assessment the nurse must first be motivated to engage in the assessment process. Campinha-Bacote (2008) refers to this motivation as the "desire" that actually fuels the process of becoming culturally competent. Nurses at Step 1 of the Staircase Self-Assessment Model (discussed in Chapter 1) may believe that having knowledge of the patient's physiologic needs, which the nurse discovers during a health and/or physical assessment, is all that is needed. However, obtaining a cultural assessment is an essential cultural competency that skill nurses must practice to gain cultural information and to become proficient at doing so.

Fortunately, the more nurses interact with patients from culturally diverse groups, the more likely they are to gain an understanding of differences and similarities that exist between themselves and their patients. Nurses who are able to overcome cultural differences can provide care that is holistic and patient-centered.

Some institutions have already begun incorporating cultural assessment questions within the nursing history questionnaires used during patient admission surveys. When assessing the patient's cultural values, attitudes, and beliefs, "the most important phenomenon for the healthcare provider to understand is the client's worldview" (Pedersen, Draguns, Lonner, & Trimble, 2008, p. 40). One may think of worldview as "the objective, subjective and symbolic meanings we ascribe to people, places, and things" (p. 40). One's thoughts on morality, esthetics, and social behavior would be a reflection of one's worldview. Worldview is influenced by regional and national values, which is why it is important for the nurse to consider the patient's geographical region of origin. One's gender, familial values, and degree of religiosity or spirituality also influence a person's worldview (Richmond & Guindon, 2008, p. 290).

Although many persons from the same cultural or ethnic group generally share a worldview, there are differences within the same ethnic group based on life experiences. Each person is unique, so when conducting a cultural assessment and planning care, nurses must identify the specific beliefs, attitudes, and needs of that individual. As observed previously, all patients present with visible and invisible aspects of culture. Much like an iceberg, at the visible tip one can observe some characteristics easily. Skin color, dress, language usage, gender, age, communication style, and body size may be apparent while other traits, such as one's values, political views, spiritual needs, health beliefs, and sexual orientation are often hidden below the surface. For this reason, nurses act as detectives uncovering that which is unknown to ensure that health care decision making is congruent with the patient's values, health beliefs, and wishes. Cultural assessment models assist the nurse in accomplishing this task. An overview of selected cultural assessment models follows.

NON-NURSING MODELS

One of the earliest frameworks for a cultural assessment was Kleinman (1992) who posed eight questions for physicians to guide the process of appraisal in counseling; it was one of the first models to include the client in the problem-solving approach (Wiley, Online Library, 2009). Using this explanatory model, the nurse or other health care provider explores the personal and social meaning the illness has for the patient, as well as the expectations about the appropriate treatment, goals for care, and the expected outcomes. The model also enables the clinician to determine if there are areas of conflict to be addressed through collaboration and negotiation with the patient (Wiley Online Library, 2009). The model is useful in a variety of health care situations. Kleinman's explanatory model includes several open-ended questions and is useful in situations:

1. What do you call your problem?
2. What do you think has caused your problem?
3. Why do you think it started when it did?
4. What do you think your sickness does to you? How does it work?
5. How severe is it? Will it have a short or long course?
6. What do you fear the most about your sickness?
7. What are the chief problems your sickness has caused for you?
8. What kind of treatment do you think you should receive?
9. What are the most important results you hope to receive from this treatment?

Taking this approach affords the nurse or other health provider a baseline from which to begin a collaboration with the patient. The nurse is able to share health information based on the patient's understanding and health care beliefs.

The ETHNIC Model

The ETHNIC Model of culturally competent care was developed in 1997 by Steven J. Levin, Robert C. Like, and Jan E. Gottleib. ETHNIC stands for *explanation, treatment, healers, negotiation, intervention*, and *collaboration*. This model allows the nurse to determine what the client expects to happen during the illness, based on that person's cultural beliefs. The model also affords a collaboration between the nurse and the client in planning culturally appropriate care. An example of a question the nurse might ask when using this approach is: Do you receive advice about your care from persons outside of the medical profession, such as traditional healers?

The LEARN Model

The LEARN Model enables the nurse to overcome barriers in communication between the patient and the nurse. This model was developed in 1983 by Elois Ann Berlin and William C. Fowlkes Jr. The acronym LEARN represents *listen, explain, acknowledge, recommend*, and *negotiate*. Nurses using this model will acknowledge and discuss similarities and differences between the patient's explanation and the clinical or medical explanation of that patient's illness. The authors of this model suggest that the provider *listens* with a sympathetic ear and then *explains* their perceptions of what the patient is saying. This process is also referred to as *reflective* or *active listening*, which originated in the field of counseling psychology. Reflective listening is associated with Carl Rogers's "client-centered" approach to therapy, which involves restating or clarifying, and responding with acceptance and empathy to what the speaker is saying (Fisher, 2011). (See the following website for more information about active listening: www.analytictech.com/mb119/reflecti.htm.) At that point, the provider attempts to identify differences and similarities in perceptions between the patient and provider, and *recommends* treatment. The idea of recommending treatment suggests that the nurse or other health care providers finally *negotiates* the treatment plan with the patient and offers clinical options based on the patient's values and goals for care, rather than have them imposed by the provider.

The BATHE Model

The BATHE model was developed by Marian Stuart and Joseph Lieberman in 2002 for use by psychotherapists. The acronym refers to *background, affect, trouble, handling,* and *empathy*. This model seeks to enhance communication between the client and care provider by focusing on the psychosocial context of the client. When exploring the *background*, the nurse attempts to gain knowledge of the circumstances surrounding the patient and influencing the patient's perceptions of the illness. *Affect* refers to the feelings the patient has related to the illness or condition. Asking the patient what is *troubling* about the illness is an attempt to explore how the illness is impacting the patient's life. It also helps the provider determine an area to focus attention in planning care. The patient is then asked about how he or she is *handling* the illness. *Empathy* refers to statements that the provider uses to affirm or legitimize what the patient has said in an effort to provide psychological support (Stuart & Lieberman, 1993). Although the model was intended originally for mental health physicians, one can see the potential benefits for using the models in nursing.

The GREET Model

The GREET Model is specifically intended for non-native patients (Stein, 2010). GREET signifies *generation, reason, extended family, ethnic behavior,* and *time* living in the United States. Learning when and why the patient has come to the United States and what supports the individual has are all important pieces of information to ensure effective cross-cultural information.

Each of these models illustrates strategies for ensuring enhanced cross-cultural communication. The provider must first understand patients' situations or circumstances, perceptions of their illness, and be willing to collaborate and negotiate with them to determine goals and interventions that are culturally congruent.

NURSING MODELS

Any discussion of nursing models begins with Madeleine Leininger's **Sunrise Model** and Theory of **Culture Care Diversity and Universality**. As a cultural anthropologist and nurse, as early as the 1950s, Leininger, founder of Transcultural Nursing, conceptualized **culture care**. These concepts mean providing care that is congruent with the cultural values of the patient. Leininger described several dimensions of culture and social structure that influence caring practices, well-being, and the experiences of health and illness among individuals, families, and groups. These dimensions or factors include cultural values and life ways, political factors, economic factors, educational factors, technological factors, religious and philosophical factors, kinship, and social factors. Patients engage in diverse health systems including **generic** or **folk systems** and professional systems. The Sunrise Model illustrates three ways in which nursing may provide culturally competent care through culture care preservation and/or maintenance, culture-care accommodation and or negotiation, and/or culture care repatterning and/or restructuring.

Among those who have been recognized with Leininger as leaders in the field of Transcultural Nursing are Rachel Spector (2009), Giger and Davidhizar (2008), Andrews and Boyle (2007), Larry Purnell (2008), and Campinha-Bacote (2003, 2008). Each has made a distinct contribution to the transcultural nursing body of knowledge and references to their work will be made throughout the text where appropriate. When conducting physical assessments, nurses must also apply their cultural knowledge about physical, physiological, and biological variations that may influence the interpretation of results (Campinha-Bacote, 2003; Giger & Davidhizar, 2008).

One model that is particularly useful to include in the physical assessment of clients is Giger and Davidhizar's Transcultural Assessment Model. In this model, there are six essential cultural phenomena that address *communication, space, social orientation, time, environmental control*, and *biological variations*. The phenomenon of biologic variations is used by the nurse when conducting a full physical assessment (Giger & Davidhizar, 2008). The authors have identified several questions to determine culture-specific biologic information. For example, when examining lab work and reviewing the hemoglobin results, the nurse considers the possibility of sickle cell phenomenon in the Black or Mediterranean client (Geiger & Davidhizar, p. 10). During examination of the skin the nurse must pay attention to variations based on ethnic or racial norms, rather than compare all skin types to color changes that occur in the dominant group, or white skin. Pallor, petechiae, erythema, ecchymosis cyanosis, and jaundice must all be evaluated based on the patient's normal skin tones (Campinha-Bacote, 2003). Please see Giger and Davidhizar (2008) for a more in-depth discussion on a physical and cultural assessment.

Rachel Spector (2009) focuses on the relationship between one's *cultural heritage* and health care choices. She describes the traditional health beliefs and practices of selected North American groups and emphasizes the influence of sociopolitical changes and demographics on current perceptions of health and illness. Spector emphasizes the interconnectedness of heritage, culture, ethnicity, religion, socialization, and identity, diversity, and demographic change, population, immigration, and poverty. The author relates these to the concepts of health, illness, and healing. In Spector's latest text, the author suggests five steps to climb toward cultural competency. A tool for conducting a heritage assessment is also provided.

In another text, Andrews and Boyle (2008) apply principles of transcultural nursing across the life span and in various health care settings. These authors focus on seven components to include in a cultural assessment, *family and kinship systems, social life, political systems, language and traditions, worldview, value orientations,* and *cultural norms, religion, health beliefs, and practices.* They also discuss the transcultural aspects of pain among other nursing considerations and offer culturally appropriate interventions.

Purnell (2008) offers a cultural competency assessment model utilizing 12 domains that are applicable to all cultures when performing a cultural assessment. The Purnell Model for Cultural Competence and its organizing framework is applicable to all health care providers and disciplines. Purnell's domains include *localities and topography, communication, family roles and organization, workforce issues,* **biocultural ecology,** *high-risk health behaviors, nutrition, pregnancy, and child-bearing practices,* and *death rituals.* These constructs may be used to assess both the health care client as well as the provider.

A text by Marianne Jeffreys (2006) provides a resource for faculty and graduate nurse educators in teaching cultural competency skills in schools of nursing. A model of learning outcome assessment is also provided in her text and may be used with the author's permission.

Campinha-Bacote (2011) provides a model, the Process of Cultural Competence in the Delivery of Healthcare Services, that defines cultural competence as "the process in which the healthcare professional continually strives to achieve the ability and availability to effectively work within the cultural context of a client (family, individual, or community)." Campinha-Bacote describes it as a lifelong process of becoming, rather than being culturally competent. The model identifies five constructs that define cultural competency, cultural awareness, cultural knowledge, cultural skill, cultural encounters, and cultural desire. One's journey toward cultural competency begins with the cultural encounter, which serves as "the pivotal construct" that energizes the nurse and provides a foundation for future cultural interactions. Using the ASKED mnemonic, which represents the self-examination questions regarding one's awareness, skill, knowledge, encounters, and desire, health professionals are able to informally assess their level of cultural competence. (Please visit Dr. Campinha-Bacote's website for more in-depth information about this model at www.transculturalcare.net/Cultural Competence Model.htm.)

During all encounters with patients one of the most important things for the nurse to keep in mind comes from a remark by a student nurse who came to the realization through a cultural immersion experience. "You (the nurse) are the most important thing in patient care" (Bosworth, 2006). The statement is interpreted by this author to mean that nurses can view themselves as the most important tool in the process of delivering culturally competent care. In light of the nation's increasing cultural diversity and the persistence of health care disparities, health care providers need to be able to deliver care using an efficient and effective approach to communicating with patients that meets the needs of a diverse society (AHRQ, 2007; Tucker et al., 2007). The literature offers many models and conceptual frameworks from which nurses might choose one that is best suited for their clinical situation. Some of those models have been presented here for application in practice or real-life situations.

The author hopes to encourage nurses to approach cultural encounters in a new and creative way with the help of a guiding framework to facilitate communication between the nurses and their clients. As nurses develop skills in using a self-assessment and patient-focused cultural assessment model, they become better able to demonstrate competence, cultural sensitivity, and cultural humility. As nurses' confidence in their ability to deliver culturally competent care increases, so, too, does their desire to experience newer and more challenging multicultural patient care encounters. Nurses who reach this level of confidence as culturally competent nurses will help reduce the disparities that exist between groups and serve as role models and mentors for other nurses.

IMPORTANT POINTS

- In addition to a self-assessment, culturally competent nurses must assess their patients/clients based on cultural criteria.
- The nursing literature provides a variety of nursing and non-nursing cultural assessment models.
- The nurse should select a model that is appropriate for the nurse's communication style, the patient's situation, and the clinical setting.
- Data gathered through the cultural assessment is used to inform patient care planning.

CASE SCENARIO

A male nurse admits a 40-year-old woman, Mrs. V of Asian Indian descent, to the medical-surgical unit. The patient had sustained a head injury and was confused and somewhat disoriented. Her husband, who spoke some English but had a heavy Indian accent, accompanied her. While the patient was very quiet, the husband, who answered all questions addressed to his wife, seemed very anxious and annoyed. The nurse attempted to reassure Mr. V that everything was going to be okay. Nevertheless, he insisted on seeing a doctor right away and stated, "I don't want to keep speaking to a nurse, I need to speak with the doctor." The admitting nurse explained to the patient that the doctor would be in as soon as possible, but in the meantime decided to conduct a cultural assessment. During the assessment the nurse learned that the husband was a recent immigrant to the United States from India and was not used to, and therefore uncomfortable with, the idea of his wife having a male nurse. The nurse later explained to the patient and her husband that he would remain the nurse primarily in charge of the patient's care, but that he would have a female assistant nurse provide her personal care. Mr. V was satisfied with this arrangement, but with the staff's permission, remained at the bedside throughout her hospitalization.

Selected Cultural Considerations Using the Giger and Davidhizar Transcultural Assessment Model

Relevant aspects of this model are selected for this case. The nurse selects this cultural assessment model by Giger and Davidhizar and focuses on the following seven parameters when interviewing the patient and her spouse:

Communication: The patient is unable or unwilling to communicate verbally; husband answers for patient, has good English command, but heavy accent. Both husband and wife speak Indian dialect in the home. Patient tends to defer to husband when questioned. Nurse may need to investigate need for a medical interpreter.

Space: Both the patient and the nurse seem comfortable with close personal space, but do not like touching or close contact unless necessary for clinical procedures. Cross-gender touching is culturally unacceptable to the patient and her spouse.

Social orientation: There is an obvious gender role difference in expectations between what the nurse expects and what the patient's spouse expects in terms of spousal roles. This husband is very attentive and protective of Mrs. V and chooses to stay with wife at all times. The nurses will need to be creative in planning to incorporate Mr. V in the care of this patient.

Time: Since Asian Indians are believed to be present, past, and future oriented, the nurse will need to assess the specific orientation of the patient and family during the patient–nurse encounter.

Environmental control: During the cultural assessment, when asked what Mr. G believes is a cause of this illness, he responds, "This is what God wants and we must always obey His will."

Biological variations: Because Mrs. V has sustained a head injury, the nurse will need to include among the various components of a neurological assessment monitoring Mrs. V for skin color changes for indications of inadequate breathing patterns, ineffective airway clearance, and impaired gas exchange. Mrs. V is Indian and is dark skinned. The nurse will need to observe the patient's normal skin tone to establish a baseline and compare later skin assessments to her own norm.

Plan: Using this model the nurse will establish the following culturally competent goals for the patient. This is not an exhaustive list.

Goal 1: The patient will be able to communicate clearly with staff and staff will provide needed materials in a language the patient clearly understands. A medical interpreter can help with clarifying information that the patient or family attempts to convey. The interpreter can also make sure that the patient and her spouse understand the staff.

Goal 2: The patient's spouse will be included in patient's care and be encouraged to stay with her as much as is possible.

Goal 3: The patient will be treated with respect regarding cultural preferences regarding issues of personal privacy, touching, and so on. A female nurse will administer personal care.

Goal 4: The patient will have spiritual care based on her expressed wishes.

Goal 5: The patient will have adequate gas exchange. Among the assessment parameters monitored, the nurses will provide appropriate skin assessments based on the patient's norm.

NCLEX-TYPE QUESTIONS

1. A nurse selects a cultural assessment model when performing a nursing history of a newly admitted recent immigrant from Cambodia. The primary reason for selecting the model is to:
   A. Determine the nurse's ability to provide culturally competent care.
   B. Assess the patient's ability to communicate in English.
   C. Gain cultural knowledge about factors that may influence the patient's health care decision making.
   D. Determine the patient's readiness to utilize Western medicine.

2. When using Purnell's 12 domains to perform a cultural assessment, the culturally competent nurse understands that the term *biocultural ecology* refers to:
   A. Physical, biological, and physiological variations such as skin color
   B. Differences in geographic location
   C. Attitudes toward preserving the environment
   D. One's country of origin

3. When performing a cultural assessment, the nurse utilizes Giger and Davidhizar's Transcultural Assessment Model. When assessing the construct of space, the nurse considers the patient's:
   A. Visual depth perception
   B. The patient's comfort level regarding social distance

   C. The adequacy of the patient's prior reception

   D. The patient's sense of physiologic balance

4. In Leininger's Sunrise Model, "generic or folk systems" refers to:
   A. Western medicine
   B. Systems of medicine that are antiquated and no longer useful
   C. Health practices of the elderly
   D. Traditional health care practices and belief systems used as alternatives to Western medicine

5. The culturally competent nurse recognizes that the most appropriate time for performing a cultural assessment is:
   A. When obtaining a health history
   B. After the nurse has met with the patient and the family
   C. During each patient–nurse encounter
   D. During the physical examination

6. During a cultural assessment, the nurse utilizes the ASKED mnemonic. The E in this model refers to:
   A. Education needed to be culturally competent
   B. Evidence-based practice
   C. Eagerness of the nurse to become culturally competent
   D. Encounter each time the nurse and patient interact

7. The nurse discovers that a newly admitted patient is unable to speak or understand English. In taking a patient-centered approach to care, what is an appropriate goal of care? *Please select all that apply.*
   A. The patient will understand the diagnosis and treatment plan in his own language.
   B. The patient will learn some English to communicate with the staff.
   C. The patient's family will be included in the care planning as the patient desires.
   D. The patient's children will be utilized to translate to minimize the need for a medical translator.

8. The culturally competent nurse uses Kleinman's Explanatory Model during a cultural assessment. This model was selected because the nurse wants the patient to focus on:
   A. The patient's perceptions about his illness
   B. The patient's allegiance to his family
   C. The patient's concerns about his spiritual beliefs
   D. The patient's concerns about the hospital staff

9. When using any of the cultural assessment tools, the culturally competent nurse employs a particular type of listening technique that requires the nurse to:
   A. Question the patient's comments
   B. Restate and clarify
   C. Discuss the situation from the nurse's point of view
   D. Offer advice based on the nurse's medical knowledge

10. The ETHNIC Model affords the nurse an opportunity to learn about the patient's:
    A. Genetic predispositions to diseases
    B. Socioeconomic problems
    C. Health beliefs, practices, preferences, and expectations
    D. Racial background

AACN COMPETENCIES ADDRESSED IN THIS CHAPTER

1. Apply knowledge of social and cultural factors that affect nursing and health care across multiple contexts.
2. Use relevant data sources and best evidence in providing culturally competent care.
5. Participate in continuous cultural competence development.

REFERENCES

Agency for Healthcare Research and Quality. (2007). *National healthcare disparities report at a glance.* Retrieved from www.ahrg.gov/gual/nhdr07/nhdr07.pdf

Alexander, G. (2008). Cultural competence models in nursing. *Critical Care Nursing Clinics of North America, 20*(4), 415–421. Retrieved from http://search.ebscohost.com/login.aspx?direct=true&db=rzh&AN=20101415

Andrews, M. M., & Boyle, J. S. (2008). *Transcultural Concepts in Nursing Care* (5th ed.). Philadelphia, PA: Lippincott Williams &Wilkins.

Bosworth, T. L.; Haloburdo, E. P.; Hetrick, C.; Patchett, K. Thompson, M. A., & Welch, M. (2006). International partnerships to promote quality care: faculty groundwork, student projects and outcomes. *The Journal of Continuing Education in Nursing,37*(1), 32–38.

Campinha-Bacote, J. (2003). *The process of cultural competence in the delivery of health care services.* Cincinnati, OH: Transcultural Care Associates.

Campinha-Bacote, J. (2008). Cultural desire: Caught or taught. *Contemporary Nurse,28,*(1–2), 141–148.

Centers for Disease Control. Office of Minority Health. (2009). National partnerships for action ongoing discussions. Retrieved from www.minorityhealth.hhs.gov/assets/pdf/checking11/camarajones

Dayer-Berenson, L. (2011). *Cultural competencies for nurses: Impact on health and illness.* Boston, MA: Jones and Bartlett.

Fisher, D. (2006). Reflective listening. In *Communication in Organizations.* Fenton Books. Retrieved from http://www.analytictech.com/mb119/reflecti.htm

Giger, J., & Davidhizar, R. E. (2008). *Transcultural nursing: Assessment and intervention* (5th ed.). St. Louis, MO: Mosby Elsevier.

Jeffreys, M. R. (2006). *Teaching cultural competence in nursing and health care.* New York, NY: Springer Publishing.

Keller, T. (2008). Mexican American parent's perceptions of culturally congruent interpersonal processes of care during childhood immunization episodes—A pilot study. *Online Journal of Rural Nursing and Health Care, 8*(2), 33–39. Retrieved from http:findarticles.com1particles/mi_mo555/is

Leininger, M. (1978). *Transcultural nursing: Theories, concepts and practices*. New York, NY: John Wiley & Sons.

Pedersen, P. B., Draguns, J. G., Lonner, W. J., & Trimble, J. E. (2008) *Counseling across cultures*. Los Angeles,CA: Sage.

Purnell, L. D., & Paulanka, B. J. (2009). *Guide to Culturally Competent Health Care* (2nd ed.). Philadelphia, PA: F.A. Davis Company.

Purnell, L. D., & Paulanka, B. J. (2008). *Transcultural Health Care: A culturally competent approach* (3rd ed.). Philadelphia, PA: F. A. Davis Company.

Richmond, L. J., & Guindon, M. H. (2008). European Americans. In G. (Ed.), *Culturally alert counseling: A comprehensive introduction* (pp. 255–291). Los Angeles, CA: Sage

Spector, R. (2009). *Cultural diversity in health and illness* (7th ed.). Upper Saddle, NJ: Pearson, Prentice Hall.

Stein, K. (2010). Topics of professional interest. Moving cultural competency from abstract to act. *Journal of the American Dietetic Association, 110*(2), 180. Retrieved from http://webscohost.com/ehost/delivery?vid

Tucker, C. M., Ferdinand, L. A. Mirsu-Paun, A., Herman, K. C., Delgado-Romero, E., van den Berg, J. J., & Jones, J. D. (2007). The roles of counseling psychologists in reducing health disparities. *The Counseling Psychologist, 35*, 650–673. doi:10. 1177/0011000007301687

Wiley Online Library. (2009). *Achieving cultural competency: A care based approach to training health professionals*, pp. 217–220. Retreived from http://onlinelibrary. wiley.com/doi/10.1002/9781444311686.app2/pdf

IMPORTANT WEBSITES

For information about diseases, conditions, health risks, fact sheets, and what to do.

Centers for Disease Control
http://cdc.gov
National Institute of Health
www.http://nih.gov
Office of Minority Health
www.minorityhealthhhs.gov
Provider's Guide to Quality and Culture. Techniques for Taking a History. Kleinman's Explanatory Model
http://erc.msh.org/aapi/tt11.html
Toolkit for Cultural Competency
http://sklad.cumc.columbia.edu/nursing/programs/pdf/toolkitCult CompetNursingEd.pdf

Why Can't They Speak Our Language?

Working With Culturally Diverse Colleagues

GLORIA KERSEY-MATUSIAK

Everything that irritates us about others can lead us to an understanding of ourselves

—CARL JUNG

LEARNING OBJECTIVES

1. Identify personal barriers to effective communication between culturally diverse coworkers.
2. Develop strategies for enhancing positive interactions between culturally diverse coworkers.
3. Recognize institutional barriers to positive interactions between culturally diverse colleagues.
4. Develop strategies for addressing institutional barriers to enhance interaction between culturally diverse coworkers.

KEY TERMS

Acculturated
Bicultural
Culturally immersed
Traditional interaction style

OVERVIEW

Issues of diversity in health care go beyond relationships between the patient and the nurse. Today, as the diversity of the nation's population increases, many are touting the benefits of a multicultural and diverse workforce

(Batchelor, 2004; Bristow, 2004; Christian & Porter, 2006; Edwards, 2009; Evans, 2004, 2007; Harper 2007; Michell & Lassiter, 2006; Truneh, 2006). As stated in the previous chapters, diversity in this text is defined broadly and refers to attributes that include such characteristics as age, ability, culture and ethnicity, gender, race, religion, and sexual orientation (Gwell, 2010; Roberts, 2009; Stevens & Ogunji, 2010). For the benefit of the institution, organizational leaders are encouraged to maximize the advantages of the unique talents and experiences that a diverse workforce has to offer (Stevens & Orgunji, 2010). As Friedman and Amoo (2002) observed, organizations are strengthened by the collective varied experiences of diverse groups.

DIVERSITY ISSUES AND CONCERNS

However, nurses from diverse groups bring their cultural characteristics, attitudes, and health beliefs to the workplace and these sometimes conflict with those of their American peers (Mattson, 2009). As a result, cultural conflicts and communication problems may impact interactions between nurse colleagues and other members of the health team. These conflicts become more problematic when differences between the dominant and minority group members are not recognized or acknowledged (Beecham, 1995; Gwell, 2010; Hunt, 2007; Mannix & Neale 2005; Smith Trudeau, 2002). For example, Smith (2002) identified differences in values, point of view, language, and personal preferences among those that RNs, LPNs, and nursing assistants in a work group might experience. These variations may be based in part on differences in perceptions about the nature of caring based on the nurse's level of nursing education. One researcher found that nurses with higher education levels were more likely to value differences and build trusting relationships with others (Beheri, 2009) than those who were less educated.

In another example of difference, nurses who are foreign-born and educated bring with them their own cultural values about the meaning of work, beliefs about being a health care provider, as well as a collectivist perspective about being a team member (Mattson, 2009). One might also consider the generational diversity that exists among nurses. The average age of practicing registered nurses is 46.8 years, yet currently four generations of nurses coexist in the workplace, which include veterans, boomers, Xers, and millennials. Each group has its own values and beliefs regarding issues of employment. One author noted the importance of building a coalition between generational groups, maximizing their strengths through careful study of their similarities, and changing their differences to strengths (Ward, 2009). Moreover, having a collective sense of inclusion among members of a diverse workforce team is positively associated with enhanced performance and productivity (Avigdor, Braun, Konkin, Duzmycz, & Ferdman, 2007). Thus, among nurses, diversity may exist on many levels and its impact on the team's performance and outcomes is dependent on the work group's members' ability to transcend those differences and work effectively as a team.

Barriers to Cross-Cultural Interaction

Since 1986 the American Nurses Association (ANA) has made a commitment through its mission and position statements and strategic planning to enhance diversity in nursing, yet progress remains slow (Lowe, 2009). This lack of progress is due to a number of obstacles or barriers to positive group interaction, which include a limited number of culturally diverse nurses, lack of gender diversity, cultural differences, racial discrimination, differences in interaction styles, and a lack of cultural self-awareness and sensitivity by many nurses from all cultural groups.

According to the 2008 RN Sample Survey, although racial and ethnic diversity is increasing in the RN population, only about 16.8% of the employed RN population comes from non-Caucasian backgrounds. Additionally, men in nursing still comprise only 10% of RNs employed in nursing (HRSA, 2010). Nevertheless, increasingly, nursing departments are made up of individuals who represent racial, ethnic, and gender diversity. These individuals have been born and educated both within and outside of the United States. Therefore, despite nurses' shared membership in the nursing profession, all nurses bring with them their own unique set of values and behaviors that are products of their racial, cultural, ethnic, and gender identities. Livers and Caver (2003) remind us, "Because race and gender are unchangeable aspects of one's identity, their impact on work experiences depends to a great degree on the perceptions and reactions of others" (p. 87). Each of the differences discussed, and the tendency of many individuals to avoid acknowledging them, may act as barriers to cross-cultural communication. Thus, although there are many benefits derived from having a diverse workforce, there are also limitations (Manix & Heale, 2005).

Additionally, each health care institution and nursing unit has its own unique culture to which new members must acclimate. Overcoming individual and organizational cultural differences becomes a dual responsibility for new graduate nurses, or new employees who must learn to adapt their preferred style of interacting to that of the institution and the members of the work team. In light of the current nurse shortage, one author notes, "creative solutions to the nursing shortage necessitate not only building teamwork but also tapping the unique perspectives of the teams' diverse members" (Loney, 2003, p. 15). Yet many times when new nurses express values and beliefs, or demonstrate behaviors that differ from those of the staff, they are viewed unsuitable or as "not fitting in" to the work environment. This label is particularly damaging for recent graduates who are attempting to adjust to a new role as a professional nurse and as a member of the work team.

Unfortunately some minority nurses also experience this labeling when they come from backgrounds that are different from the dominant group members of the staff. For example, within the U.S. workforce, the discrimination and prejudice experienced by African Americans in society is sometimes carried over into the workplace (Beecham 1995; Livers & Cavers, 2003; Purnell, 2008). For example, African Americans adhere to a strong work ethic, but often experience ethnic or racial tension in the workplace (Purnell, 2005, 2008).

Mannix and Neale (2005) described similarity-attraction theory and principles of homophilia, which indicate that individuals are attracted to and seek other individuals who they perceive as being like themselves and will experience more social integration in homogeneous groups (p. 31). This theory explains why during the recruitment and hiring process, the tendency is for search teams to seek nurses who are most likely to "fit in" with the dominant members of the work team. In some settings, this desire, coupled with the tendency for individuals to seek others who look and speak like themselves, make it difficult for some qualified nurses of color to be hired or to advance to a higher level or position. To make matters worse, other health team members often bypass African American nurses who hold these positions when they are attempting to identify the "nurse in charge." Another problem for some ethnic nurses of color occurs when some patients request not to be assigned "that foreign nurse." Usually this request is made because of a perceived language barrier, despite the nurses having met the employment requirements. Culturally competent nurses can reassure the patient of the foreign nurses' professional competence and explain the institutional policy on discrimination.

Avery, Richeson, Hebl, and Ambady (2009) focused primarily on Black and White relationships in describing interracial interaction in the workplace. These researchers found White employees were less likely than their non-White counterparts to have significant prior experience engaging in interracial interactions. Having this kind of prior experience was found to promote greater comfort in subsequent interracial encounters.

Avery et al. (2009) found "heightened anxiety associated with Black-White interracial workplace interactions." Uncertainty about what to say or do during these interactions; a resultant discomfort; a desire to "avoid being perceived a racist, or perceptions of workplace discrimination" were underlying causes of this anxiety. These researchers suggest that high anxiety may lead to some White individuals' avoidance behavior in promoting interracial interaction. This avoidance may negatively impact individuals' or work group performance.

On the other hand, White nurses who find themselves in the minority in work settings have also expressed the feeling that their opinions and suggestions were less valued than members of the dominant group. Identifying and openly acknowledging differences between nurse colleagues and the conflicts that differences sometimes create is a way of alleviating conflicting underlying perceptions and mistrust and to build understanding and respect between members of diverse groups (Livers & Cavers, 2003).

STRATEGIES FOR POSITIVE INTERACTIONS

The commitment for promoting an inclusive work environment must begin at the top with a well-communicated statement of the institution's vision and mission in this regard. That vision is then shared with managers and staff. Administrators and line managers provide resources that support the staff in meeting the institution's diversity goals. Examples of activities to strengthen diversity include opportunities for mentoring of new culturally diverse staff members as well as diversity staff development opportunities for all nurses is aimed at enhancing cross-cultural understanding between groups. Evaluations and promotion prerequisites should include documentation of demonstrated commitment and achievement of the established diversity goals of the institution and the unit.

When working with culturally diverse colleagues, nurses must begin by becoming aware of their own attitudes, beliefs, and behaviors. Be careful not to take on an ethnocentric perspective, that is to say, believing one's own values and beliefs are superior, because this is another important step in the process. Most of us view others through our own cultural lens; however, when individuals are ethnocentric in their views, they are more likely to judge others' values and beliefs as inferior. Both majority and minority nurses must be careful in avoiding this dilemma and both must aim toward bridging cultural gaps between diverse groups.

Strategies to help minority group members establish better relationships with members of the dominant group include building trust by gradually establishing open and honest dialogue with others, going slowly and respecting areas considered private, being willing to give others the benefit of the doubt, demanding equitable treatment for yourself and others, and attempting to understand how your behaviors are perceived (Livers & Capers, 2003). If all members of the staff are provided opportunities for sharing formally and informally about themselves an appreciation and respect for diversity can be fostered. In an atmosphere such as this, new members can be familiarized in a nonthreatening way with the unit culture, which includes the norms and expectations of the work group. In order to accomplish this goal, members of the nursing staff will need to actively listen to one another. In other words, when communicating with one another, nurse colleagues will need to seek clarification when uncertain about each other's intended meaning. This process is accomplished by restating the message to the speaker and stating, "I believe that you are saying…this." Finding a trusted individual among the group members to assist a colleague in analyzing personal attitudes and behaviors is another useful strategy in developing effective cross-cultural communication skills. An atmosphere in which open dialogue about personal values and beliefs regularly occurs also provides an opportunity for nurses to validate and support one another.

To ensure better interracial interactions among work team members, Avery et al. (2009) recommended staff development activities aimed at reducing the uncertainty about what to say or do in initial interracial encounters. One way this is achieved is by employers providing opportunities for employees that offer "behavioral strategies for improving interracial interaction." The literature suggests both groups, Blacks and Whites, "desire to engage in greater inter-group contact, but are apprehensive about doing so," so diversity training should build on that desire (p. 1389). Some examples offered by the researchers include "meet-and-greet" ice breakers during employee orientations, introductions during meetings, self-disclosure, and sharing of personal information. In this way, individuals introduce themselves and their roles to the group prior to beginning a working relationship. Such interactions can set the tone for future encounters between members of diverse groups.

A clear benefit of a multicultural work team is that it affords opportunities for sharing cultural knowledge that may be applied to care planning for culturally diverse patients. With this important benefit in mind, nurse leaders set the tone on the unit by utilizing their management skills to facilitate the interaction between culturally diverse team members.

When working with a culturally diverse nursing team, an effective nurse manager establishes a trusting relationship with her staff and strives to understand each member's cultural values, personality, attitudes, and interaction style. While assessing staff members' communication patterns, the nurse manager should consider both verbal and nonverbal styles of communication and become aware of how an individual's preferred style may impact cross-cultural interactions and relationships.

It is also helpful to know which of the four interacting styles, identified by Bell and Evans (as cited in Campinha-Bacote, 2003; Purnell, 2003), is dominant. These interacting styles include the acculturated interpersonal style, the culturally immersed style, the traditional impersonal style, and the bicultural interacting style. Persons who are **acculturated** are willing to abandon their own cultural values, practices, and beliefs. Individuals who preferred this style would be able to fully embrace the unit culture, and to behave in a way much like their nursing colleagues. If, however, the nurse belongs to the **culturally immersed** group he or she will find it difficult to relinquish personal values, attitudes, and practices and may often be in conflict with staff members and patients from the dominant group. Consequently, his or her relationships within the organizational culture and the unit culture may be compromised.

Persons who adopt a **traditional interaction style** are those who fail to recognize or acknowledge their own cultural identity and its impact on their behavior. Individuals who are unaware of their own fundamental beliefs and values are also unable to appreciate the differences that exist between themselves and others. As a result, cross-cultural interactions may result in conflicts between members of culturally diverse groups that remain outside of the person's awareness. People who demonstrate a **bicultural** interacting style are able to take pride in their own cultural traditions while maintaining a certain level of comfort when interacting with members of the dominate society.

While an individual nurse is responsible for acculturating to an assigned unit, "the complexity of nursing requires a substantial and consistent support system to ensure the success, satisfaction, and retention of nurses" (Greene & Puetzer, 2002, p. 69). As novices to clinical practice, all nurses need the support of a culturally sensitive and caring mentor. One author describes a mentor as an experienced and competent staff member who can commit to a 1-year relationship with an assigned new staff member. The mentor functions as a role model, a socializer, and educator (Greene & Puetzer, 2002; Tracey & Nicholl, 2005). "The mentor demonstrates how a competent nurse performs and integrates the mentee into the social culture of the unit, making the mentee feel welcome in the peer group, while providing feedback" (Greene & Puetzer, 2002, p. 70). In most cases, the nurse manager would assume the responsibility of determining and assigning an appropriate mentor for a new staff nurse. When there is no formal structure in place, any culturally sensitive member of the nursing team may assume this role.

IMPORTANT POINTS

- Since 1986, the nursing profession, through the ANA, has made a commitment to diversity, yet progress has been slow.
- Every member of the work team, as well as institutional administrators, is responsible for maintaining a welcoming and supportive institutional culture and work environment.
- Variations in worldviews, values, and beliefs exist between work group members from culturally diverse groups.
- New members of the workforce must strive to acclimate to the new cultural environment through open and honest dialogue.
- Differences in values, attitudes, and beliefs between the dominant and minority group members should be addressed through planned opportunities for cultural sharing.
- When working with culturally diverse coworkers, active listening is an important strategy for effective communication.

CASE SCENARIO

Kim is a shy 23-year-old RN who was born in Vietnam. Several years ago, at age 12, she immigrated with her parents as a refugee to the United States from Cambodia. While in Cambodia, Kim learned to speak English moderately well, but still has a strong accent and sometimes forgets the appropriate word to use when she is anxious. After coming to the United States Kim attended high school with a small group of other Cambodian refugee students whose families had also recently come to America. This small group became Kim's social network while in high school. Kim continued to strengthen her language skills through an English-as-a-second-language (ESL) program. After graduating from high school, Kim attended a BSN program from which she recently has graduated.

Throughout her education, Kim, although very bright, has been uncomfortable with her English when she is around a group of native English speakers and finds it difficult to contribute to group discussions.

The nurses on a busy surgical unit have been complaining for some time about the staffing shortage, high patient acuity, and the rapid patient turnover rates. They are concerned that the quality of care is being compromised. In response, the administration has recently added an additional full-time position to the unit's budget. Kim, the Vietnamese nurse, was recently hired to fill the position. Since Kim's arrival, members of the staff have complained among themselves about her inability to "fit in" as a member of the group. The major problem, as they see it, is Kim's poor language skills. Kim says little in communicating with other staff members. One of Kim's patients has even requested to have "another nurse, someone who speaks better English." On the other hand, many of Kim's other patients say that she is a caring and conscientious nurse. Some staff members complain, "Why can't these people learn the language if they want to work here?" One colleague laments, "I don't think she knows what she's doing" and "having Kim is like having no help at all." The staff decides to discuss the matter with the head nurse.

Kim is unaware of the staff's attitudes toward her, but senses that she has not yet been fully accepted as a member of the group and does not believe her input about patient care is valued. Still, Kim tries hard to befriend members of the staff through one-on-one interactions with them. She loves her job as a staff nurse, enjoys caring for patients, and is eager to learn as much as she can about her new role. She frequently offers to work overtime and to assist others as needed during her scheduled shifts. Kim wants so much to be accepted by the group and to make her mother and father proud of her success as a member of this nursing staff.

WHAT NURSES NEED TO KNOW ABOUT THEMSELVES ▬▬▬▬

APPLICATION OF THE STAIRCASE MODEL: SELF-REFLECTION QUESTIONS

1. Where am I on the Cultural Competency Staircase? How can I progress to the next level? (see Chapter 1 progression)
2. How many encounters with people from Kim's background have I had, to prepare me for interactions with Kim?
3. What do I know about members of this specific Asian group; Vietnamese or Cambodian?
4. What assumptions, stereotypes, or generalizations underlie my beliefs about Kim or about other members of Kim's cultural group? Am I prejudiced toward her?
5. What do I really know about Kim's attitudes, values, health beliefs, and work ethic and how do these differ from my own?

6. How much have I tried to communicate with Kim personally?
7. How willing am I to extend myself to establish a positive and collegial rapport with this new member of the nursing staff?
8. What are some potential interpersonal problems or potential cultural conflicts based on this case scenario?
9. How can I overcome them?
10. Are there any legitimate patient-care issues that may be addressed through staff development, such as mentoring?

Please note: The selection of a nurse of Vietnamese heritage is a proto-type; these questions may also be applied to encounters with other cultural groups.

Responses to Self-Reflection Questions 3, 4, 5, 6, 7, and 10

Response to What do I know about members of this specific Asian group, Vietnamese or Cambodian?

Many of the sources discussed in Chapter 1 offer culture-specific information about various cultural groups. A brief overview, such as the one that follows regarding Vietnamese culture, might assist nurses in having a better understanding of Kim and other nurses who are immigrants to the United States.

Vietnamese Culture
More than 1 million Vietnamese have emigrated to the United States, many seeking asylum from war, persecution, or fear of death (Yoder-Stouffer, 2004). Like other immigrants, the Vietnamese are not a monolithic group. Among the earliest South Vietnamese immigrants who came to America between 1975 and 1977 were business people, military officers, or professionals who came from urban areas, with knowledge of American culture and the ability to speak English. Later immigrants (1980–1986) came from less fortunate circumstances, were unable to speak English, and had little understanding of Western culture. These "boat people," as they were often called, came to escape communism (Nowak, 2003). However, of those who survived the refugee camps or the perilous trip to America, many remained unemployed or in menial jobs. These groups had much more difficulty acculturating to the United States. Some of the Vietnamese are Christian, while the majority practices Buddhism, Confucianism, and Taoism. Vietnamese religious practices and traditions are based on these ancient philosophies.

A dominant force for most Vietnamese is that they wish to bring honor and prosperity to the family, which is the central reference point for the individual throughout his life (Giger & Davidhizar, 2004; Nowak, 2003; Purnell & Paulanka, 2005). The family may be nuclear or extended with many generations living together. Among Vietnamese, an individual's responsibility to family transcends all others. Traditionally, men serve as the decision maker while women care for the children and the household. Children are expected to honor and obey their parents and respect the older adults.

Although emphasis is placed on the family and its needs, most Vietnamese values enable them to be successful in the workplace. They have a high regard for authority and are willing to work hard and to sacrifice comforts to maintain a steady income. They also value a harmonious work environment in which they readily adapt to work cooperatively with their peers. Purnell (2003) notes that "They may be less concerned about such factors as punctuality, adherence to deadlines, and competition" (p. 332). It is important to keep in mind that this statement may be true for some Vietnamese, but not necessarily all of them.

Communication
Vietnamese Americans usually speak one or more of four languages. The first, Vietnamese, is similar to Chinese, and has many dialects reflecting the geographical origin of the speaker. Vietnamese immigrants may also speak Chinese, French, or English. However, despite having knowledge of the English language, most Vietnamese do not feel competent when speaking English. Language variations may make it difficult for individuals from one part of Southeast Asia (e.g., Vietnam) to understand the language of people who come from another (e.g., Cambodia) (Nowak, 2003; Yoder-Stouffer, 2004).

Vietnamese Americans differ from mainstream Americans in their style and patterns of verbal and nonverbal communication. As compared to the dominant group, Vietnamese people are often considered passive. Generally speaking, they are nonconfrontational and they communicate in a soft-spoken tone of voice. Overt expressions of emotions, such as raising one's voice or verbally expressing disagreement, are typically avoided. The Vietnamese consider these behaviors to be disrespectful and inappropriate. Vietnamese do not usually discuss their personal feelings, but are more likely to open up in a one-on-one basis. Women typically avoid discussions about sexuality, childbirth, and sensitive topics of this nature in the presence of males (Purnell & Paulanka, 2005; Yoder-Stouffer, 2004).

In observing nonverbal communication with Vietnamese American colleagues, it is important to recognize that avoiding eye contact while interacting with others is a demonstration of respect for those of "higher status." Vietnamese consider age, education, gender, nurses, and doctors, and other professionals with high regard. A quiet smile may reflect a variety of emotions, including joy, acknowledgment, or an absence of feelings entirely. Nodding one's head may not necessarily indicate an affirmation; rather it may represent an acknowledgment of what has been heard (Yoder-Stouffer, 2004).

Vietnamese Americans prefer a more extended social distance or space when communicating than do Euro-Americans (Nowak, 2003).

Demonstrations of affection are limited to inside the home and it is considered an insult for a man to touch a woman in the presence of others. Holding hands with members of the same gender is considered appropriate among Vietnamese. For Vietnamese the head of the body is considered sacred and should not be touched. The feet as the lowest part of the body should not be placed on a desk or table, as this would be considered a sign of rudeness and disrespect. Pointing one's fingers at someone or motioning with the finger to summon an individual are also considered signs of disrespect (Nowak, 2003).

Using this general overview of Vietnamese culture, nurses can begin to build cultural knowledge and gain some insight into Kim's dilemma in attempting to acculturate to this nursing unit. This knowledge is useful to those seeking to identify appropriate ways of assisting her in orienting to the unit and in assuming her new role as a staff nurse.

Response to What assumptions, stereotypes, or generalizations underlie my beliefs about Kim or about other members of Kim's cultural group? Am I prejudiced toward her?

The nurses have communicated to one another their frustration regarding Kim's inability to communicate effectively with them in the statement, "Why can't these people learn the language if they want to work here?" They have also indicated a general mistrust in Kim's ability to function as a staff nurse. This is evident in their statements, "I don't think she knows what she's doing" and, "Having Kim is like having no help at all." These feelings expressed by the nurses may be based on legitimate observations of Kim's performance in clinical situations.

However, it is possible that these feelings are based on the staff's inability to get to know Kim and to gain a sense of trust and confidence in her. Anxiety about Kim may also come from the fear of what is unknown about Kim as an individual who comes from a foreign background. Some nurses may have an unconscious bias toward Asian or other nurses from foreign countries, or non-Caucasian backgrounds as being inferior to nurses from the dominant group.

Kim and her colleagues must be willing to acknowledge the cultural differences that exist between them and between Kim and some of her patients. As members of the health care team, nurses are encouraged to respect all people. This requires that they develop an open mind, seek cross-cultural relationships, recognize the stereotypes that they may have accepted as true or partially true about certain groups, and make an effort to free themselves of these influences (Livers & Cavers, 2003).

Although the nurses can do little to change the attitudes of their patients toward Kim, they can demonstrate their acceptance and collegial respect for Kim as a professional nurse and by setting an example of acceptance, foster in patients a greater degree of confidence in Kim's ability to care for them.

Response to What do I really know about Kim's attitudes, values, health beliefs, and work ethic and how do these differ from my own?

It is important for nurses to realize that the answer to this question can only be found through frequent encounters with her. Despite having a general knowledge about Asian or Vietnamese culture, one cannot assume that Kim adopts all of these cultural values and beliefs. There is much intracultural diversity between members of the same group. Much will partly depend on when Kim actually immigrated to America and whether she has acculturated to American norms. Perhaps during lunch, the nurses might encourage Kim to talk about her background, her nursing preparation, and her general experiences as an immigrant to the United States. Members of the larger group might also share their own backgrounds and experiences in diversity with her. Later, as Kim becomes more comfortable with the staff, she might be asked to share her learning experiences in an open forum with other nurses throughout the hospital. By sharing cultural knowledge, both she and the staff can begin to identify cultural conflicts or patient-centered problem areas and strategies for addressing them.

Response to How much have I tried to communicate with Kim personally?

Kim, the nurse manager, and the nursing staff, as well as the staff development department, share the responsibility of facilitating Kim's transition to her new role as staff member. As the newest member of the nursing team, Kim also has a responsibility to develop strategies for assessing the new culture (the nursing unit) she has entered. In cooperation with her nurse manager, she will need to determine effective ways of acculturating to it.

Response to How willing am I to extend myself to establish a positive and collegial rapport with this nurse?

Without the sincere motivation to work cooperatively with members of culturally diverse groups, it is impossible to overcome the many barriers to cross-cultural communication that cultural differences in values, beliefs, attitudes, and behaviors can create. Accomplishing this goal requires a joint effort by Kim and the staff. Bridging the cultural gap serves the best interest of both the individual who is attempting to assimilate as a new member of the group and the nursing team that benefits from the addition of a more culturally competent and better-prepared team member. Most importantly, through the achievement of these goals, patient care is ultimately enhanced.

Response to *Are there any legitimate patient-care issues that may be addressed through staff development, mentoring, and so on?*

In this case, a culturally competent nurse manager might assign a nurse mentor to determine effective methods of bridging the existing cultural gaps between Kim and the staff. The individual assigned to act as a mentor for Kim would be able to give her honest feedback about her ability to communicate with patients and to address their patient care needs.

This approach would assist in promoting Kim's growth and productivity as a professional nurse. The resultant close one-on-one relationship with a mentor who is also a native speaker of English would assist Kim in strengthening her language skills as well.

WHAT NURSES NEED TO KNOW WHEN WORKING WITH CULTURALLY DIVERSE COLLEAGUES

SELECTING A CULTURAL ASSESSMENT MODEL

Apply a cultural assessment model to help identify cultural information about Kim that could be used to establish more effective communication with her. One cultural assessment model that might be appropriate in this situation is Andrews and Boyle's Assessment Guide for Individuals and Families. This model includes multiple components that are to be evaluated within "context" (see Chapter 4). In Kim's case, the context to be taken into consideration is the professional work environment.

ASSESMENT QUESTIONS FOR GAINING RELEVANT CULTURAL INFORMATION

1. What is Kim's country of origin?
2. Immigration status, new versus old immigrant?
3. Family network and other social supports in the United States; who does Kim live with, marital status?
4. What language does Kim speak in the home; what English language problems does Kim have? Are the staff members able to communicate with her effectively? If not, what resources are available to assist Kim in overcoming the language barrier? What strategies can I use to enhance my communication with Kim?
5. Does Kim have a collectivist or individualistic perspective? How does Kim view her role as a member of this health care team?
6. Does Kim hold values and beliefs or health care practices that differ from my own?
7. What cultural information can I learn from Kim to utilize in future cross-cultural interactions?
8. How can I assist Kim in acclimating to this unit, this hospital, this community?

Use the information gained about Kim from these assessment questions to complete the following case exercise. Discuss your responses with a friend, a classmate, or a colleague.

CASE EXERCISE ON WORKING WITH CULTURALLY DIVERSE COLLEAGUES

A. Pretend that you are one of the nurses working with Kim. Identify three ways that you can assist Kim in acclimating to the unit.
1.
2.
3.
B. Identify three ways that you can assist the patients in becoming more accepting of Kim.
1.
2.
3.
C. Imagine yourself as a new member of a staff. You are the only representative member of your racial/ethnic, gender, or cultural group on the staff. What can you do to be a more effective team member?

NCLEX-TYPE QUESTIONS

1. In a culturally competent work setting, the responsibility for Kim's success as a new nurse on the unit lies with:
   A. Human resources
   B. Kim
   C. The staff
   D. Kim, human resources, and the nursing staff

2. The primary cross-cultural barrier in this case scenario is a problem due to:
   A. Kim's lack of experience in the United States
   B. Kim's educational preparation in nursing
   C. Challenges in communication
   D. Differences in worldview

3. Having knowledge about Kim's cultural background is useful because (select all that apply):
   A. It enables the nurses to get to know Kim's cultural values and beliefs.
   B. It provides cultural information as a resource for the nurses' future encounters with patients who share Kim's ethnicity.
   C. It assists in overcoming the language barrier.
   D. It helps prevent problems in miscommunication.

4. A culturally competent nurse recognizes that cultural group members who have a collectivist perspective value:
   A. The needs of the group or team over that of the individual
   B. The needs of the individual
   C. Needs based on the circumstances
   D. The demands of the team leader

5. According to some researchers, minority group members can establish better relationships with members of the dominant group by (select all that apply):
   A. Building trust through honest dialogue.
   B. Being vigilant in watching for any signs of prejudice or bias toward them.
   C. Being willing to give others the benefit of the doubt.
   D. Demanding equitable treatment for themselves and others.
   E. Striving to understand how their behaviors are perceived.

6. When culturally competent nurses are working with diverse colleagues, the first step in the process is to:
   A. Determine the new colleague's level of communication.
   B. Explore one's own attitudes, beliefs, and behavior.
   C. Share cultural knowledge about your own cultural background.
   D. Explore cultural differences that exist between themselves and the new staff member.

7. To ensure the cultural acclimation of newly hired nurses from culturally diverse backgrounds, nurse administrators and human resource personnel can assist by (select all that apply):
   A. Providing staff development opportunities that promote cultural sharing.
   B. Orienting culturally diverse nurses to the culture of the unit and the institution.
   C. Setting a deadline by which new staff must complete their orientation.
   D. Assigning a mentor to work specifically with a new nurse.

8. The culturally competent nurse is working with a colleague who adopts a traditional interpersonal style. The nurse recognizes that persons practicing this style are more likely to:
   A. Be willing to abandon their cultural values.
   B. Find it difficult to relinquish their beliefs and attitudes.
   C. Fail to recognize or acknowledge their cultural identity.
   D. Take pride in their own culture while being comfortable interacting with members of another.

9. Active listening is a strategy used by culturally competent nurses. This means that during communication, the culturally competent nurse:
   A. Allows the speaker to speak without ever interrupting.
   B. Seeks clarification to ensure accuracy.
   C. Uses nonverbal communication for emphasis.
   D. Actively engages the speaker by sharing stories.

10. When a patient asks to have someone other than a culturally diverse coworker to care for them, culturally competent nurses can respond by:
    A. Speaking supportively about the professional competence of the nurse.
    B. Agreeing to take the assignment on behalf of the nurse.
    C. Insisting that the patient will have to accept the hospital's policy on nondiscrimination.
    D. Refusing to care for the patient.

SUMMARY

Acknowledging biases that may be based on ignorance or assumptions about persons of Asian or Vietnamese heritage or any other ethnic group is a first step in curtailing their influence on cross-cultural interactions. Utilizing multiple formal and informal opportunities to share cultural knowledge will strengthen the relationship between Kim and the staff. In the mutual sharing of cultural information Kim will also be able to grow in her understanding of U.S. culture and its implications in the workplace. Staff members will gain knowledge that will assist them in caring for Vietnamese patients.

Besides having knowledge and understanding, skills in communication, which promote active listening and open and honest dialogue between culturally diverse groups, are needed to avoid major cultural conflicts that threaten positive cross-cultural communication. Having a clear understanding of Kim's values, attitudes, health beliefs, work ethic, and interacting style will enable the nurses on the unit to identify commonalities as well as differences between them.

Establishing a trusting relationship with at least one member of the team that can serve as a provider of feedback as well as a sounding board for Kim's frustrations would be equally useful in facilitating Kim's psychological transition and professional development in her nursing role. When Kim and the nursing staff are able to bridge the cultural gap that exists between them, everyone wins.

REFERENCES

Avery, D. R., Richeson, J. A., Hebl, M. R.,Ambady, N. (2009). It does not have to be uncomfortable. *Journal of Applied Psychology, 94*(6), 1382–1393. doi: 10.1037/a0016208

Batchelor, J. (2004). First among equals. *Nursing Management, 11*(6), 8–9.

Beecham, L. (1995). Black and Asian nurses in the national health service report harassment. *British Medical Journal, 311*(7015), 1247.

Beheri, W. (2009). Diversity within nursing: Effects on nurse-nurse interaction, job satisfaction, and turnover. *Nursing Administration Quarterly, 33*(3), 216–226. doi: 10.1097/NAQ.0b013e3181accacc

Bristow, L. R. (2004,). IOM advances the call for greater workforce diversity. *AHA. News, 40*(11), 5.

Campinha-Bacote, J. (2003). *The process of cultural competency in the delivery of health care services* (4th ed.). Cincinnati, OH: Transcultural C.A.R.E. Associates Press.

Christian, J., Porter, L, & Moffitt, G. (2006). Workplace diversity and group relations: An Overview. *Group Process & Intergroup Relations, 9*(4), 459–466.

Edwards, K. (2009). Promoting quality care by increasing the diversity of the professional nursing workforce. *Journal of Cultural Diversity, 16*(2), 39.

Evans, M. (2004). Healthcare's minority report: Sullivan Commission, IOM try to make patient, hospital staff makeup more reflective of the nation's ever-changing population. *Modern Healthcare, 34*(39), 6–7.

Evans, M. (2007). The cure is in the melting pot. *Modern Healthcare, 37*(23), 32–36.

Friedman, H., & Amoo, T. (2002). Workplace diversity: The key to survival and growth. *Workforce Diversity.* Retrieved April 11, 2007, from www.westga. edu/~bquest/2002/diversity.htm

Greene, M. T., & Puetzer, M. (2002). The value of mentoring: A strategic approach to retention and recruitment. *Journal of Nursing Care Quality, 17*(1), 67–75.

Gwele, N. (2009). Diversity management in the workplace: Beyond compliance. *Curationis, 32*(2), 4–10.

Harper, D. (2007). A diverse environmental public health workforce to meet the diverse environmental health challenges of the 21st century. *Journal of Environmental Health, 69*(6), 52–53.

HRSA. (2010). HRSA study finds nursing workforce is growing more diverse. Retrieved from www.hrsa.gov/about/news/pressreleases/2010/100317_hrsa_ study_100317_finds_nursing_workforce_is_growing_and_more_diverse.html

Hunt, B. (2007). Managing equality and cultural diversity in the health workforce. *Journal of Clinical Nursing, 16*(12), 2252–2259.

Husting, P. M. (1995). Managing a culturally diverse workforce. *Nursing Management, 26*(8), 26–32.

Livers, A., & Cavers, K. A. (2003). Can't we all just get along? *Black Enterprise, 33*(12), 87–89.

Lofton, K. (2007). Diversity needed in the C. suite. *Modern Healthcare, 37*(23), 26.

Loney, M. (2003). It takes a team to make a difference. *ONS News, 18*(4), 15.

Lowe, J., & Archibald, C. (2009). Cultural diversity: the intention of nursing. *Nursing Forum, 44*(1), 11–18. doi: 10.1111/j.1744–6198.2009.00122.x

Mannix, E., & Neale, M. A. (2005). What differences make a difference? The promise and reality of diverse teams in organizations. *Psychological Science in the Public Interest, 6*, 31–55.

Mattson, S. (2009). A culturally diverse staff population: Challenges and opportunities for nurses. *Journal of Perinatal & Neonatal Nursing, 23*(3), 258–262. doi:10.1097/ JPN.0b013e3181aedf19

Mitchell, D. A., & Lassiter, S. L. (2006). Addressing health care disparities and increasing workforce diversity: The next step for the dental, medical, and public health professions. *American Journal of Public Health, 96*(12), 2093–2097.

Noone, J. (2008). The diversity imperative: strategies to address a diverse nursing workforce. *Nursing Forum, 43*(3), 133–143. doi:10.1111/j.1744-6198.2008.00105.x

Nowak, T. T. (2003). People of Vietnamese heritage. In L. D. Purnell & B. J. Paulanka (Eds.), *Transcultural health care: A culturally competent approach* (2nd ed., pp.327–343). Philadelphia, PA: F.A. Davis Company.

Purnell, L. D., & Paulanka, B. J. (Eds.). (2003). *Transcultural health care: A culturally competent approach* (2nd ed.). Philadelphia, PA: F. A. Davis, p. 41.

Purnell, L. D., & Paulanka, B. J. (2005). *Guide to culturally competent health care.* Philadelphia, PA: F. A. Davis, pp. 426–447.

Roberts, W. (2009). Diversity in the environmental health workforce. *Journal of Environmental Health, 72*(3), 4.

Smith-Trudeau, P. (2002). Diversity consciousness: From conflict to collaboration. *Vermont Nurse Connection, 5*(1),11.

Stevens, R. H. & Ogunji, E. (2010). Managing diverse organizational environments for strategic advantage: Exploring the value of developing business diversity curriculum in higher education. *Journal of Management Policy, 11*(4). Retrieved from www.na-businesspress.com/JMPP/StevensWeb.pdf

Tracey, C., & Nicholl, H. (2005). Mentoring and *networking*. *Nursing management,* 12(10), 28–32.

Truneh, H. (2006). The power of diversity: Three cultures, three perspectives, one vision. *Stanford Nurse, 26*(1),14–15.

Umphress, E., Smith-Crowe, K., Brief, A. P., Dietz, J., & Watkins, M. B. (2007). When birds of a feather flock together and when they do not: Status composition, social dominance, and organizational attractiveness. *Journal of Applied Psychology, 92*(2), 396–409.

Ward, K., & Parsons, L. (2009). A look at generational diversity: managing the differences. A reprint of a feature originally published in SCI Nursing 23.4. *SCI Nursing, 26*(3), 18–23.

Yoder Stouffer, R. U. (2004). Vietnamese Americans. In J. N. Giger & R. E. Davidhizer. *Transcultural nursing* (4th ed., pp. 455–488). St. Louis: MO: Mosby Inc.

IMPORTANT WEBSITES

For more comprehensive information about Vietnamese people and their cultural heritage.

Impact of the Vietnamese war on immigration
http://pages.prodigy.net/meng25/mchs/immig.htm
Vietnamese culture
www.vietnam-culture.com/zones-6–1/Vietnamese-Culture-Values.aspx
Vietnamese Embassy of the United States
www.vietnamembassy-usa.org
Vietnamese Culture and Science Association
www.vhkhun.org/vhkh
Vietnamese Touch
www.viettouch.com
http://web.ebscohost.com/ehost/pdfviewer/pdfviewer?sid=05133855–3a67–45e8-b257–114ad578dc72%40sessionmgr114&vid=4&hid=123

Cultural Considerations When the Patient's Religious or Spiritual Needs Differ From One's Own

GLORIA KERSEY-MATUSIAK

Everything in your life is there as a vehicle for transformation. Use it!

—RAM DASS

LEARNING OBJECTIVES

1. State a personal definition of spirituality.
2. Explain the difference between spirituality and religion as they relate to the delivery of culturally competent care.
3. Describe the significance of spirituality from both the nurse's and patient's perspective.
4. Recognize clinical indicators of spiritual distress.
5. Identify selected religious groups that are currently practicing in the United States.
6. Identify important religious considerations when delivering culturally competent care.
7. Select appropriate interventions to promote patients' spiritual well-being.

KEY TERMS

Agnosticism
Atheism
Humanist
Monist
Religion
Secularist
Spirituality
Theist

DEFINING SPIRITUALITY

Spirituality and/or **religion** are aspects of everyone's culture. Therefore, both the patient and the nurse bring to each nurse–patient encounter their own spiritual values and religious beliefs. When the patient and the nurse come from different backgrounds, the nurse may have little knowledge of the patient's spiritual needs or religious views. For example, in some situations, it may be difficult for the nurse to appreciate the impact that faith and prayer have on healing from the patient's perspective. It may be even more challenging for the nurse to appreciate a patient's spirituality needs when the individual seems to lack religious conviction, is atheistic (**atheism**), or agnostic (**agnosticism**). In any case, irrespective of the nurse's or the patient's religious affiliation, culturally appropriate, evidence-based, and holistic nursing care must include interventions that address the patient's spiritual needs (de Souza, Maftum, & Bais, 2008; Gibson & Hendricks, 2006; Kreitzer, Gross, Waleekhachonloet, & Pesut, 2009; Reilly-Spong, & Byrd, 2009; Tyler & Raynor 2006; Wright, 2008). But, what then is spirituality?

According to the nursing literature, spirituality may be defined differently based on one's philosophical perspective. However, for purposes of this text, we will use the definition as written by Spector (2009): "Spirituality connotes the way we orient ourselves to the Divine, the way we make meaning out of our lives, the recognition of the spirit (breath) within us, a cultivation of a lifestyle consistent with this presence, and a perspective to foster purpose, meaning, and direction to life" (p. 86). In another definition, McAuliffe (2008) defined spirituality as a means by which people maintain inner relationships with themselves, others, and the universe.

Pesut (2008) explored the various ways spirituality might be integrated into one's life from a monistic, theistic (**theist**), or humanistic (**humanist**) viewpoint. **Monists** believe in the interconnectedness of all of creation and the need to collectively strive toward a higher level of consciousness. Absent from this thinking is the concept of an external being or God. Theists, on the other hand, believe in God as an independent creator that sustains all of creation. At the same time, theists believe that man is empowered to make choices as unique individuals, while living cooperatively with others during this physical existence in preparation for the next life. Humanists view spirituality as an intangible, innate, and mysterious attribute of all humans that "provides meaning and a reason for existence" (Pesut, 2008, p.101). Humanists share a belief in a connectedness, but the object of the connection may vary with individuals and may or may not be attached to a belief in God. Nurses who have an understanding of the various ways in which spirituality may play out based on these ideologies will have an advantage when trying to identify their patients' spiritual care needs.

THE SIGNIFICANCE OF SPIRITUALITY

The current nursing literature is replete with stories about the significance of spirituality in the provision of nursing care (Agrimson & Taft, 2009; Cuevas, 2010; Dunn, 2008; Lackey, 2009; Wright, 2008). These articles not only emphasize the impact that spirituality has on patients' views about their illness, but on nurses' views of themselves as care providers. Spirituality, then, is a significant dimension of both the persons giving and receiving care, which ultimately influences patients' health outcomes, as well as nurses' attitudes about the quality of care they provide.

McAuliffe (2008) examined the relationship of spirituality and breast cancer survivors. In this study the participants' spirituality and belief in God as healer was a source of hope and coping with illness. Nurses can be instrumental in enhancing patients' ability to cope with illness by fostering a positive spiritual connection between themselves and their patients.

Just as nurses are encouraged to assess their own cultural values and beliefs when caring for culturally diverse patients, evaluating one's spiritual well-being is a vital component of a cultural assessment. Nurses who are able to maintain their own spiritual well-being are better able to provide spiritual care for their patients. At the same time, nurses must be careful not to impose their own religious or spiritual views on their patients.

Many factors influence the nature of one's spiritual well-being, including one's developmental stage of life, family relationships, cultural beliefs, religion, and various life events (Taylor, 2005). Obviously, some life events make more of an impact than others. For example, when individuals are experiencing life-threatening illnesses, they are often compelled to think about the meaning of life in a way most individuals tend to avoid. Loss of loved ones also puts people more in touch with the idea of their own mortality and the value of life as they currently know it. Nurses can maximize opportunities to enhance these spiritual moments when caring for patients if they themselves are in a place of spiritual well-being that enables them to do so. Preston (2008) writes, "I leave the room revitalized—the patient comforted, moments of shared humanity. It is a gift" (p. 18). Ravari, Vanaki, Houmann, and Kazmnejad (2009) found that many nurses derive spiritual gratification through their work with patients. In this study, Iranian nurses discussed the "spiritual rewards" of caregiving as a significant factor influencing their job satisfaction. Nurses in this study believed, despite the heavy job demands, inadequate pay, and sometimes unkind treatment by supervisors, patients remained a source of contentment and moral fulfillment that energized them, enhanced their personal lives, and "provided an opportunity for serving God" (p. 27). These nurses also equated sacrificing one's time and energy, irrespective of monetary rewards for services, with "conscientious care, spiritual commitment, devotion in care, improvement in their patients' health, and pleasant feelings." According to these authors, other positive personal outcomes for the nurse when giving care include "increased joy, peace, serenity, and improved productivity" (p. 28). Tyler and Raynor (2006) described "serenity," as a "spiritual experience of inner peace" (p. 8). In a randomized trial of organ transplant recipients, participants in this study were given an abbreviated form of the Serenity Scale to examine the impact of mindfulness-based stress reduction. According to these authors, patients who achieve serenity are able to accept situations, decrease perceived stress, and improve health.

DIFFERENTIATING SPIRITUALITY FROM RELIGION

The nursing literature distinguishes between spirituality and religion, and reminds us that one can certainly be spiritual without being religious. Among the distinguishing characteristics of spirituality cited in the literature is its tendency to be internalized and used by the individual as a resource for inner strength and direction for one's life. A central aspect of spirituality is hope (Stanley, 2005). As such, it serves as a "means for coping with major stressors" (Gibson & Hendricks, 2006). McAuliffe (2008) differentiated religion from spirituality by identifying three major differences between them. According to this author, religion relies upon doctrines and rules, and is primarily external and exclusive, while spirituality has no doctrines and is internal and inclusive. Religion is also considered "a specific system of values and beliefs and a framework for ethical behavior that its members must follow" (Stanley, 2005 p. 269).

In a doctoral study of individuals with chronic illnesses, but without religious affiliations, Noto (2006) concluded, "the participants who believed they were treated as unique individuals by the nurse also experienced spiritual nursing care." The nature of caring was defined as "an extension of self by the nurse to their (the patient's) inner core." Conversely, many participants experienced alienation when they did not experience such a connection between their inner core and the nurse. The author encouraged nurses to develop "increased consciousness" of the spiritual needs of ill individuals, especially when the patient is without religious affiliation.

Swinton (2006) reminds us of the difficulty some nurses have who hold spirituality as a value, yet lack the time to make it a priority when they are providing care. These authors further note that as nurses themselves experience a work environment that is increasingly overwhelming, their own personal sense of spirituality is often neglected, making it far less likely for them to be able to address this dimension in others. In light of the growing demands of the health care environment, nurses will need to explore ways to tap into their own personal spiritual reserves to sustain their ability and motivation to nurture spirituality in others.

As Dunn (2008) suggests, because of nurses' close and frequent contact with patients, it is likely that the nurse's spirituality will influence the care the patient receives. Dunn offers nurses a conceptual model to assist them in gaining insight into their own spirituality and encourages them to become aware of their spiritual perspectives. Dunn also reminds us that religion is a way to express spirituality and cited studies that indicate that "nurses with a religious affiliation are more likely to provide spiritual care in practice" (p. 4).

RELIGION

In the United States there is a wide variety of religious affiliations. The large majority of Americans are Christians (76.5%), which includes Protestants (39%) and Catholics (24%); however, there are significant differences in religious perspectives between Christians who identify with conservative or traditional groups and those who are more liberal in their beliefs. A significant number of individuals (15%) report being **secularists**, humanists, agnostics, and nonbelievers (McAuliffe et al., p. 513). Individuals who practice Judaism represent about 1.3% of the U.S. population, Islam, 0.5 %, Buddhism 0.5%, and Hinduism 0.4%. Table 4.1 illustrates the various religious groups found in the United States. Affiliations to a particular religion vary across the United States (Pew, 2008).

In a recent landmark study of religious affiliations in the United States, the researchers interviewed 35,000 participants across the nation (Pew, 2008). Data analysis provided detailed information about the demographic aspects of various religious groups including regional distribution, age, gender, racial and ethnic composition, and educational and income distribution. The study results revealed wide intra-group variations in belief in God, significance of religion in one's life, frequency of attendance at religious services, frequency of prayer, attitudes toward religious doctrine, and sociopolitical views among members of the same religion.

Further, the data demonstrated a tendency by many individuals, who self-identify with a particular religious group or denomination, to disagree with one or more of its major tenets. This study is useful in demonstrating the need for nurses to remain open-minded and nonjudgmental about a patient's religious or spiritual views despite their stated affiliation. Studies like this also assist nurses in acquiring evidence-based knowledge about religions that may otherwise be unfamiliar to them.

Knowledge of intra-group differences among members of the same religion provides a rationale for nurses to attempt to determine the impact religion has on an individual patient, rather than the religious group, during the care-planning phase. This determination can best be made by the nurse who conducts a spiritual assessment.

COMPONENTS OF A SPIRITUAL ASSESSMENT

In today's fast-paced work environment, a spiritual assessment can be integrated into the nursing history-and-care plan, rather than be thought of as an add-on to the many tasks that nurses already perform. Tanyi (2002) offered several suggestions that nurses might include in an assessment of patients' spirituality. The nurse initiates a conversation with the patient about spirituality during the admission assessment, demonstrates respect of the patient's spiritual and cultural practices, listens attentively for spiritual cues, remains nonjudgmental and open-minded, and consults with other health care professionals as needed to administer appropriate spiritual care. Geiger and Davidhizar (2008) included pertinent questions to assess an individual's spiritual needs within their transcultural nursing model (p. 11). Determining whether the patient believes in God, has any spiritual practices that may need to be moderated during the illness or hospitalization, has certain attitudes about death and dying, or other relevant spiritual information will enable the nurse to plan care more effectively. The nurse might also question how the patients' beliefs are linked to their daily activities, particularly while they are hospitalized. Is there a specific need for a religious leader to be present at a particular time? By asking these questions, nurses acknowledge patients' right to spiritual care and provide a means by which individual patients can share information about their spiritual concerns. *Potential for Enhanced Spiritual Well-Being and Spiritual Distress* is a nursing diagnoses that captures the essence of spirituality (Taylor, 2005). As part of the spiritual assessment, nurses can, on a regular basis, observe patients for signs of spiritual well-being or of spiritual distress. Spiritual assessment questions should focus on positive indicators of spiritual well-being including patients' acceptance of their own physical limitations, illness, or impending death. Evidence that the patient maintains loving and caring relationships with family and friends and has the ability to reconcile past sources of anxiety or frustration is also a good indicator of spiritual well-being. On the other hand, spiritual distress may be evidenced by such behaviors as crying, apathy, anger, changes in sleep patterns, and/or depression. The spiritual care of patients involves such interventions as contacting a spiritual advisor that the patient chooses, or an on-call chaplain, praying for patients, and praying with patients at their request or with their permission.

In summary, the literature suggests that an individual's spiritual nature serves as an internal resource for experiencing oneself and others, while managing life's stressors with some degree of hope. Membership in any of the various religious groups often provides a social support network and sense of belonging for its members. Based on these descriptions of spirituality and religion, nurses can assume that patients they encounter will be influenced by one or both of these dimensions in their daily lives. Therefore, besides having their own sense of what religion and spirituality means to them personally, it is important for nurses to have an understanding of the meaning religion and spirituality hold for the patients for whom they are caring. Lackey (2009) suggests careful listening to assist patients in answering their own spiritual questions. To ensure that each patient receives holistic, culturally competent, and evidence-based care, the nurse must take the spiritual and/or religious nature of the individual into consideration as care is being provided.

All of these measures enable the nurse to help patients avoid physical and emotional consequences of spiritual crisis. As one author noted, often with serious illness and/or personal losses comes a sense of grieving or loss that may be accompanied by a profound questioning of life's meaning (Agrimson, 2009). At such times, the nurse provides support that ameliorates the situation so that patients can better cope with their situation. Wright (2008) invites nurses to "enter into the encounter of suffering with individuals and families, allow them to share their stories...and to listen with our hearts" (p. 407).

IMPORTANT POINTS

- There are important differences between spirituality and religion.
- It is important for nurses to be mindful of their own spiritual well-being if they are to be effective in delivering spiritual care to their patients.
- Not all patients are religious, but everyone is in need of spiritual care, even those who are agnostic or nonbelievers.
- Patients who share the same religion may not all have the same religious perspectives or values.
- When delivering spiritual care, nurses must be careful not to impose their own spiritual and/or religious views on their patients.
- Signs of spiritual distress include crying, apathy, anger, changes in sleep patterns, and/or depression.
- Providing spiritual care involves listening to patients for spiritual clues and assessing for spiritual despair.
- Spiritual care includes seeking a spiritual advisor of the patient's choosing, praying for and with patients, and providing space and time for private prayer.

In the following two case examples, a Jewish patient and a patient who is a Jehovah's Witness are being presented as prototypes to illustrate situations in which two nurses are caring for someone whose religion or spirituality needs differ from their own. It is not the intent of the author to examine a variety of religious or spiritual belief systems here, but to examine ways in which nurses might acquire, through this reading, methods of incorporating

TABLE 4.1   Selected Religious Groups in the United States

RELIGIOUS AFFILIATION	
RELIGION	**% IN U.S.**
Christian	78
Protestant	51
Evangelical Protestant	26.3
Mainline Protestant	18.1
Hist. Black Protestant	6.9
Catholic	23.9
Mormon	1.7
Jehovah's Witness	0.7
Orthodox	0.6
Other Christian	0.3
Other Religions	5
Jewish	1.7
Buddhist	0.7
Islam	1
Hindu	0.4
Other World Religions	0.3
Other Faiths	1.2
Unaffiliated	16.1
Don't Know/Refused	0.8
RELIGION	**SIZE WITHIN U.S. POPULATION (%)**
Catholic	23.9
Buddhist	0.7
Evangelical Protestant	26.3
Hindu	0.4
Historically Black Baptist	6.9
Jehovah's Witness	0.7
Jewish	1.7
Reform	0.7
Conservative	0.5
Orthodox	0.3
Other	0.3
Mainline Protestant	18.1
Mormon	1.7
Muslim	0.6
Sunni	0.3
Shia	< 0.3
Orthodox	0.6
Unaffiliated	16.1

Source: Pew Forum on Religious Life, U.S. Religious Landscape Survey (2007 data)

spiritual care into their daily nursing practice. Before beginning to address the religious or spiritual needs of patients, nurses must define both terms for themselves, have a general understanding of their own attitudes and beliefs about spirituality and religion, and be open-minded and nonjudgmental about the spiritual beliefs and practices of the patient.

CASE SCENARIO

A JEWISH PATIENT

Yetta is a 71-year-old Jewish patient. She has been a resident of an upscale Lutheran long-term care facility for the past 2 years. Yetta has been married for 50 years and is quite concerned about her husband who has recently fallen ill and now rarely visits her. The couple has three children. Two of them, a daughter and a son who is a physician, are married with children. The third child, another son, has a mental disability.

Over the past 15 years, Yetta has suffered from a variety of chronic health problems including multiple sclerosis and related quadriplegia, diabetes mellitus, hypertension, obesity, decubitus ulcers, and depression. As a result of her multiple clinical problems, she is now totally dependent on the staff for assistance with activities of daily living. Since her admission, Yetta has become progressively more demanding and difficult in her interactions with others. Some of the nurses have commented that this behavior is "typical of Jewish patients." Others have suggested that, perhaps, Yetta is now experiencing a form of dementia.

During a state inspection of the facility, Yetta complained to an official that the staff frequently ignored her. Consequently, the institution established a policy that required all nurses caring for Yetta to visit her at least once each hour. A few of the staff members do so grudgingly and avoid going into her room beyond the designated times. In addition, Yetta's family members visit her infrequently and limit the time of their visits to less than an hour.

Yetta spends much of her time checking her watch and calling for the nurses shortly before her scheduled treatments, meals, medications, and procedures. Karen, one of Yetta's nurses, is frustrated by her patient's behavior. Like many of the other nurses, she dreads going into Yetta's room and caring for her, because the patient constantly criticizes everything she does for her and never seems satisfied. One day Karen noticed that the only time that Yetta seemed reasonably comfortable was when she was talking to her about her former lifestyle, during which she was much more active in her synagogue. There was a certain twinkle in her eye as she spoke of the many social events that she and her husband participated in through her synagogue. Yetta stated that in the past they had a close relationship with the rabbi. She also described fond memories of her children's Bar and Bat Mitzvahs.

Karen also noticed that although Yetta's conversation with her family is often tense, she seems grateful for the Kosher food her family brings during their brief visits. Karen, a Catholic, knew little about the Jewish religion, or Jewish customs and practices. This was her first experience caring for anyone who was of Jewish heritage. She wondered whether Yetta's behavior might be partially a reflection of her separation from her family, cultural traditions, and religious practices. She also wondered if providing Yetta with opportunities to talk more about herself might be helpful in assisting Yetta to better cope with her health care problems and relationships with health care providers during her stay at this long-term care facility. Karen decided to further investigate Judaism and to learn about ways to incorporate Yetta's faith and cultural traditions into her care planning.

WHAT NURSES NEED TO KNOW ABOUT THEMSELVES

APPLICATION OF THE STAIRCASE MODEL: SELF-REFLECTION QUESTIONS

When considering Yetta's case, ask yourself the following questions. If you are the nurse caring for Yetta:

1. What feelings would you have in caring for this patient? On what are these attitudes and feelings based?
2. Where are you on the Cultural Competency Staircase regarding the care of this patient?
3. How will you progress to the next level? (see Chapter 1)
4. What are your feelings, attitudes, and beliefs about the role spirituality and religion play in coping with illness?
5. Does your religious affiliation differ from the patient's in this case? How might this impact your ability to assist her with spiritual/religious care?
6. How much do you know about the values, traditions, religious, and health beliefs of Jewish patients? What are some ways the nurse might learn?
7. Based on your own religious beliefs and values, what spiritual resources would you seek for yourself if you were hospitalized? Are those kinds of resources applicable in this case?
8. Do you have any underlying assumptions or biases that may interfere with positive intercultural communication (barriers) with a patient who behaves like Yetta?
9. How easily would you be able to communicate with the patient and her family to assess the patient's cultural/spiritual needs?
10. What cultural assessment tool would you use to collect data about this patient's spiritual needs?

WHAT THE NURSE NEEDS TO KNOW ABOUT THE PATIENT

Selecting a Cultural Assessment Model

Andrews and Boyle's (2003) *Transcultural Nursing Assessment Guide for Individuals and Families* is a good model to follow here (Table 4.2). When assessing this patient, the nurse can use this assessment model or select another one of his or her choosing, addressing the areas that are relevant to this patient's situation.

TABLE 4.2   Transcultural Nursing Assessment Guide for Individuals and Family

DOMAINS OF CULTURAL KNOWLEDGE	ASSESSMENT DATA FOR YETTA
• Biocultural variations	• Dependent on origins of immigration; Tay-Sachs disease and Gaucher's disease are prevalent among some individuals of Jewish descent
• Communication	• In this case, poor communications between patient and nursing staff
• Cultural affiliations	• Jewish ethnicity
• Cultural sanctions and restrictions	• Is Yetta restricted in any way by cultural values?
• Developmental considerations	• Patient is age 71 (late adulthood). Developmental task (integrity vs. despair)
• Educational background	
• Health beliefs	• Does Yetta hold traditional health beliefs or share those of Western medicine?
• Kinship and social networks	• Family is very significant in Jewish culture. Yetta has a strained relationship with her family
• Nutrition	• Does patient prefer Kosher food?
• Religious affiliations	• Jewish religion: Need to determine what role religion plays in Yetta's life. Is she Orthodox or Reform?
• Values orientation	• As above, family is important to Yetta

A Rationale for Care

There is evidence in the information provided that a number of factors are having a direct impact on the patient's quality of life while living in this extended care facility. It may be helpful to identify physiologic reasons that might explain the patient's anxiety and related behavior (patient's blood sugar, blood pressure, level of clinical depression, and specific medications) as these add to our understanding of both her physiologic and psychological needs. Despite the fact that the medical care that Yetta requires is probably being provided, it is obvious that the patient is unhappy with her care and that many other psychosocial needs are going unmet. This aspect of Yetta's care is the primary focus of this discussion.

According to the standards of professional nursing practice, it is the responsibility of the nurses "to carry out nursing actions which promote patients' psychological as well as physiological well being, involve the family in the planning of care, and evaluate the quality of the care provided on an ongoing basis" (ANA, 2003). Further, based on CLAS standards developed by the Department of Health and Human Services, and those established by The Joint Commission, nurses also have a responsibility to "ensure that patients receive from all staff members effective, understandable, and respectful care that is compatible with their cultural health beliefs and practices."

Implications of the Patient's Religion and Culture

The fact that Yetta happens to be of Jewish heritage and has, for reasons unknown, been placed in a religious facility that is different from the religion she practices may be complicating an already challenging situation. Some staff members have implied having some assumptions about Jewish patients and find it difficult to relate to her. Yetta's estrangement from her husband due to his illness, her limited contact and somewhat strained relationship with her family, and multiple chronic health problems provide many sources of stress and frustration for her.

Like all patients hospitalized, or in tertiary care facilities for chronic illnesses, there are several physiologic and psychological care needs to be addressed. More specifically, in this case it is important that nurses caring for Yetta have an understanding of her health care beliefs, spirituality needs, family relationships and support systems, patterns of communication, and dietary preferences in order to provide her with culturally competent nursing care (Scott, 2008).

Planning Culturally Competent Care: Staircase Self-Assessment

If Yetta is to receive culturally competent care, the nurses must begin with a self-assessment. During this assessment, nurses acknowledge their own personal feelings and attitudes when caring for this patient and recognize the impact these have on the quality of care they are able to provide. Culturally sensitive nurses will also reflect on their personal attitudes and beliefs about the role spirituality plays in the promotion, maintenance, and restoration of health and how these attitudes may differ from those of the patient. Recognizing anxieties, biases, and frustrations is the first step in preventing barriers to communication between the patient and the nurse. Those nurses who express feelings that Yetta's behavior reflects a cultural or ethnic norm must consider this a personal bias that is probably based on limited information about patients who are Jewish. Caring for even 25 Jewish patients does not afford nurses enough exposure to make generalizations about all of them.

Considering Jewish Traditions

There is evidence in this case scenario that suggests there are reasons other than cultural heritage that may explain Yetta's behavior. The roles spirituality and religion may be playing cannot be overlooked. If dementia does exist, this is a medical diagnosis that must become a factor when planning the patient's care. There are ethical considerations when caring for all patients with dementia, but there are specific implications for care of a patient with dementia who happens to be Jewish (Jotkowitz, 2005).

A wide variation exists between members of the Jewish religion and cultural group based on their denomination and adherence to Jewish law and traditions. Additionally, all persons have unique characteristics based on their personality. Since one of the nurses has already established that "Yetta seems happier" when discussing her religion, further conversation should be encouraged to determine how much Yetta's religion means to her. Would she benefit by having a rabbi or members of her own or a neighboring synagogue called in to see her?

The Jewish Culture: A Brief Overview as a Reference for This Case Scenario

Besides the information needed to plan care to address Yetta's physiologic needs, it is important that nurses caring for her attempt to understand what being Jewish means to Yetta. Equally important is for nurses to have some basic knowledge about important aspects of Judaism. This knowledge should incorporate information about Yetta's cultural values and health care beliefs. What does Yetta believe about her illness and its consequences and her ability to lead a normal life? What are her expectations of the staff nurses and physicians? Nurses can assess Yetta's knowledge level, feelings, and attitudes using a variety of assessment measures and begin to develop a plan that is more congruent with the patient's goals.

As is the case in every cultural group, there is no monolithic group of Jewish patients. Individual members of the same cultural group differ in ways that are specific to their own personality traits and circumstances. Therefore, there is no standard culturally sensitive way to manage the care of patients who happen to be Jewish, especially when they are experiencing complex medical problems like Yetta's. Nurses can benefit from knowing some important aspects of Jewish culture that may be applicable in providing care to patients of Jewish heritage. However, it is equally important to keep in mind the aspects of Yetta's or other Jewish patients' situations that make them unique. Jewish patients may belong to one of three main branches of the Jewish religion, *Orthodox* (highly traditional), *Conservative* (less strict), or *Reform* denomination (considered liberal or progressive). While *Ultra-Orthodox* Jews, like Hasidics, adhere strictly to all religious laws and practices of Judaism, Conservative Judaism places emphasis on obeying most of the Jewish laws with some degree of compromise with modern times (Zavato, 2003). Reform Jews modify traditional practices to incorporate contemporary social and cultural norms, which include being flexible regarding the use of Hebrew for religious services and dietary practices. There are many converts to Judaism and many of these become more conservative in their adherence to Jewish law than some of those who are born Jewish. Given this range of participation in the Jewish faith, it is helpful for the nurse to know to which group the patient belongs.

For all practicing Jews, religion is based on the Torah, which is the first five books of the Hebrew Bible or Old Testament of the Christian Bible. The Talmud is the body of scholarly teaching about early Jewish civil and religious law. Prominent Jewish scholars provide a third source of Jewish legal authority in the Responsa Literature, which provides an interpretation of the Bible and Talmud, while keeping it relevant to contemporary times (Geiger & Davidhizar, 2008; Goldstand, Rosenberg, & Gordon, 2001). In Judaism the spiritual leader is the *rabbi*, who is often consulted regarding questions having to do with Jewish religious law. Jews are permitted to question or challenge tenets of the religion as a means of enhancing their understanding. Jews celebrate the Sabbath on Saturday, beginning at sundown Friday evening and ending sundown on Saturday evening. This time is considered a holy day of rest for observant Jews.

The language spoken for religious services is *Hebrew*. Major faith beliefs lie in the sanctity and preservation of life and living up to one's potential. According to Jewish tradition all life is God-given and the value of one's life is determined by the good deeds, "mitzvah," done during one's lifetime (Andrews & Hanson, 2003). Members of the Jewish religion are required to perform good deeds and are also mandated to pray for relief from suffering and to visit the sick as part of their responsibility to the community. Judaism stresses one's responsibility to others. Depending on which tradition of Judaism is practiced, the patient may or may not adhere strictly to Jewish laws regarding life and death rituals and dietary practices.

Family Roles and Relationships

According to Jewish tradition, the family is the primary and central unit of Jewish society. Jewish devotion to family life, loyalty to kin, and a strong spirit of ethnocentrism are aspects of Jewish tradition (Goldstand, Rosenberg, & Gordon, 2001). Historically, these characteristics offered a support to Jewish people through years of trauma and environmental obstacles that threatened their existence. Thus, although American Jewish men and women are acculturated to American society, there is a strong, highly valued communal relationship between them as members of the Jewish religion and culture.

Like other ethnic families in America, contemporary Jewish families assume traditional male and female designated responsibilities. Men are considered the provider or head of household, while women maintain more responsibility for the care of the home and the children. Today, these roles are often shared as both partners may be working outside the home. Jewish children are highly valued and are educated in the Jewish religion and cultural traditions.

They may attend a secular and/or Hebrew school. Increasingly there is an increased rate of intermarriage between Jewish and non-Jewish Americans. However, Jewish cultural and religious identity greatly influences parenting styles, children's self-perceptions, and all aspects of family life. Among less conservative Jews, Jewish children are encouraged to respectfully question parental authority and are permitted some freedom in embracing the religious laws and cultural practices. Maturity is reached at age 13 for a male child and age 12 for a female.

Communication Patterns

Yiddish, a Judeo-German dialect is spoken among older adult, first-generation Jewish people, but English is the primary language of Jewish American people. While speaking English, Jews often incorporate Yiddish idioms throughout their conversation. Non–Jewish Americans have also adopted many of these terms into the English language. As patients, Jews are demonstrative in their expressions of pain and discomfort. Therefore, it is culturally acceptable to indicate one's distress. Ultra-Conservative Jews, for example, Hasidics, are formal in their interactions with others and may not look directly in their eyes. Hasidic men are not permitted to touch women other than their wives. However, among other Jewish people, short spatial distances are preferred and touching is permissible.

Dietary Concerns

The need to strictly follow Jewish dietary laws and to maintain Kosher standards is variable among Jewish people. This depends on where they are on the continuum between highly conservative and liberal or reform Jewish traditions. A Kosher diet is based on Jewish religious law and includes concerns about the "slaughter, preparation, and consumption of food." Therefore, Kosher foods are those that have met certain standards for the slaughter of animals and the preparation and handling of food that ensures that it remains clean or "fit to eat." For example, according to Jewish tradition milk and meat should not be mixed. Consequently, religious Jews would utilize separate utensils and plates to prevent this occurrence. It is important to establish early on if the patient requires Kosher food for religious purposes. For the less conservative Jews this accommodation may not be necessary.

Health Care Values, Practices, and Beliefs

Health care decisions are made within the context of the family, the religion, and the community. The rabbi is often sought to assist in decision making. Because Jews highly value the sanctity of human life, every effort is made to sustain life and to promote the highest quality of life.

There is much that nurses can do in this situation to enhance Yetta's quality of life. Channels of communication among the patient, the patient's family, and the nursing staff must be opened for culturally sensitive nursing care to be achieved. Although Yetta's cultural and religious beliefs and values are not the only factors influencing Yetta's emotional outlook, they offer a starting point for addressing Yetta's psychosocial needs and for making her long-term experience at the institution a more fulfilling one.

Key Strategies for Providing Culturally Competent Care

The Jewish patient represents a prototype. You may apply the following points to any religious difference between the patient and nurse.

- To which of the three denominations of the Jewish religions does Yetta belong?
- Determine what roles Yetta formerly played in her synagogue, community, and so on. Is there some aspect she might resume?
- Arrange for visits with her rabbi, or other members of her synagogue on a regular basis, or volunteers from a nearby synagogue.
- Meet with Yetta's family members to discuss their feelings and to plan interventions for her.
- Discuss with Yetta's family the possibility of arranging some way for Yetta to communicate regularly with her husband.
- Provide opportunities for Yetta to participate in useful activities that utilize her knowledge and skills.
- For a more in-depth understanding of Judaism, please refer to any of the following websites:
  - Judaism 101 www.jewfaq.org/index.htm
  - Movements of Judaism www.caic.org.au/world/judaism.htm
  - Hebrew for Christians www.hebrew4christians.com/index.html

CASE SCENARIO 2

A JEHOVAH'S WITNESS PATIENT

Tyrone Jackmon, a 46-year-old African American male patient, was admitted to a surgical trauma unit with multiple bilateral fractures of upper and lower extremities, multiple contusions, and a pelvic fracture. Mr. Jackmon was a victim of a multiple-car collision near his place of employment. Remarkably he was awake, alert, and oriented during his admission to the unit. Mr. Jackmon arrived at the unit accompanied by his wife of 20 years. Shortly after his transfer to the floor, the nurses received his laboratory reports by phone and learned that Mr. Jackmon's hemoglobin was 6g/dL on admission to the emergency room. Following the report from the ER nurse, the primary nurse, Susan, immediately contacted the physician to determine if blood products were to be administered. The physician had ordered two units of packed red blood cells to be given over the next 6 hours. When Susan met with the patient to obtain the nursing history, Mr. Jackmon informed her that he was a Jehovah's Witness and would not accept blood as it was "against his religion." Susan explained to the patient that without the transfusion, Mr. Jackmon's hemoglobin was likely to drop even more. Still, Mr. Jackmon refused. Susan felt strongly that the patient should change his mind about accepting the transfusion, since his hemoglobin was so low. Susan decided to discuss the matter with Rachel, another staff nurse on the unit. Rachel explained to Susan that there were alternatives to being transfused with packed cells when the patient objected to having a blood transfusion. Rachel added that she believed it was important to respect the patient's religious values. Susan called the physician so that he might meet with the patient to discuss the dilemma and determine the next course of action. Both nurses were anxious to stabilize Mr. Jackmon medically and recognized that the patient was becoming anxious about his medical situation. Despite his anxiety, Mr. Jackmon remained alert and oriented, and steadfast in his religious commitment. Later, that afternoon, a second laboratory report revealed a hemoglobin of 3g/dL. Susan feared that time might be running out for Mr. Jackmon and something needed to be done soon. Perhaps it was the morphine he was receiving for pain that was clouding his judgment, one of the nurses remarked. "I don't understand some of these patients, how can you help them when they won't try to help themselves?"

WHAT NURSES NEED TO KNOW ABOUT THEMSELVES ▓▓▓▓▓▓

APPLICATION OF THE STAIRCASE MODEL: SELF-REFLECTION QUESTIONS

In attempting to address Mr. Jackmon's case, ask yourself the following questions if you are the nurse caring for Mr. Jackmon:

1. Where am I on the staircase in relation to this patient? How can I move to the next level?
2. How familiar am I and the nursing and medical staff with the religious beliefs, values, and attitudes of people who are Jehovah's Witnesses?
3. What major differences exist in health beliefs of followers of this religion and other Christian traditions? How different is this religion from my own?
4. What feelings and attitudes do I have about Mr. Jackmon's beliefs about receiving blood?
5. How helpful are these attitudes toward the development of cooperative interaction between myself and the patient?
6. Are there alternative ways of treating this patient's hemoglobinemia?
7. On what religious beliefs does Mr. Jackmon base his refusal of blood, despite his need for it?
8. From whom could the nursing staff gain more insight about the patient's health care beliefs?
9. What strategies might be useful in meeting the physiological and psychological needs of this patient?
10. What resources might the nursing staff utilize to assist them in meeting the needs of this patient?

WHAT NURSES NEED TO KNOW ABOUT THE PATIENT ▓▓▓▓▓▓

Selecting a Patient-Focused Cultural Assessment Model

An assessment model that may be useful in this case example was developed by Berlin and Fowkes (1982) and can be found at www.ncbi.nlm.nih.gov/pmc/articles/PMC1011028/?page=5. In this model, the authors use the mneumonic LEARN and identify five steps in the cultural assessment process. The framework was first developed by the authors to enhance physician-patient communication and promote better compliance of treatment plans. The model has since been used by all health care providers as a tool in improving cross-cultural communication. During the first step the nurse *listens* to the client to determine his understanding of his illness and related problems. At Step 2, the nurse *explains* his or her perception of the problem. At Step 3, the nurse *acknowledges* similarities and differences in perception between the patient and the nurse. Campinha-Bacote urges nurses to "recognize differences, but build on similarities." At the next step, the nurse makes *recommendations* in collaboration with the patient and in the final step *negotiates* a mutually agreed on plan of treatment.

Some hospitals are already beginning to utilize cultural assessment tools in obtaining patient admission histories. Collecting this kind of data early on enhances the nurse's understanding of the patient's needs and provides a foundation from which nurses can build an arsenal of knowledge about future patients who share the same cultural backgrounds or faith traditions. It is important for nurses to recognize that while many commonalities exist between members of the same ethnic, cultural, or religious groups, there are often individual differences in attitudes and beliefs. For example, "not all patients who identify themselves as Jehovah's Witness agree with the blood policy" (McInroy, 2005, p. 271).

Listen

The nurse caring for this patient must focus attention on the patient's health-related beliefs, religious orientation and values, and treatment efficacy. Obviously, this is a critical time in this patient's hospitalization. Mr. Jackmon's immediate clinical problem is not only anxiety producing, but also life threatening. Nevertheless, the patient's perspective on his illness and preferred treatment approach must be heard.

Explain

It is equally important that the patient fully understand the consequences of his health care decisions, but that he also be given adequate information about alternative methods of treating his hemoglobinemia. Today there are many strategies for replacing blood loss in patients who do not wish to be transfused. These methods include treatment with recombinant human erythropoietin, albumin, and recombinant activated factor VII. Autologous autotransfusion and isovolemic hemodilution may also be used (Hughes, Ullery, & Barrie, 2008). Many Jehovah's Witnesses, but not all, will submit to autologous blood transfusions. Acceptance of this approach will depend on the method in which the blood is retrieved

(Giger & Davidhizar, 2008). It is important for nurses to recall that for Jehovah's Witnesses, "the determination to abstain from blood is based on references to scripture" (Andrews & Boyle, 2003). Since many Jehovah's Witnesses are strong believers in the Bible, it may be useful to provide time and privacy for scripture reading as a means of offering emotional and spiritual support (Andrews & Hanson, 2003).

Acknowledge

As McInroy (2005) states, "it is imperative that the nurse acts as a voice for the patient and respects his/her autonomy" (p. 270). Nurses can also act as advocate for this patient by making his values and beliefs known to other members of the health care staff.

During the initial assessment, the nurses caring for Mr. Jackmon must fully determine the patient's level of understanding about the nature of his illness, its cause, possible consequences, and methods of treatment. It is equally important for the nurse to be knowledgeable about the value that this patient places on his religious and spiritual beliefs. Several authors provide information about caring for clients who are Jehovah's Witnesses that will aid nurses in providing care for members of this religious group (Andrews & Boyle, 2003; Geiger & Davidhizar, 2008; Spector, 2004). With this knowledge, nurses will be able to conduct a thoughtful and comprehensive evaluation of the patient's cultural background and health care attitudes and beliefs to plan an effective treatment approach.

Spirituality and Jehovah's Witnesses

According to the Watch Tower Society (2009) there are millions of Jehovah's Witnesses in more than 230 lands. The world headquarters for the Jehovah's Witnesses is located in Brooklyn, New York. There are also more than 100 branch offices around the world. The King James version of the Christian Bible serves as the basis of Jehovah's Witnesses' religious beliefs.

Members believe in the value of a strict interpretation of the scriptures as the Word of God and a guide for life. Jehovah, the Hebrew name for God, is believed to be the source of all human life and that all life is sacred and precious to Him. Among other values shared by members of this religion are: loving their fellow man, teaching others about God's Kingdom, and avoiding political and social controversies. Many Jehovah's Witnesses are conscientious objectors as they do not support any acts of war or aggression against their fellow man. Additionally, other taboos of the religion include a disdain for gambling, lying, stealing, taking revenge, fornication, premarital relations, incest, and homosexuality.

Members hold meetings for bible study in Kingdom Hall, the Witnesses' place of worship. Jehovah's Witnesses recognize Jesus as the son of God, but do not celebrate traditional Christian holidays such as Christmas and Easter. They do observe the night of the Last Supper as a memorial of Christ's death on a day that corresponds to Nisa 14 of the Jewish calendar, which occurs sometime in March or April (Andrews & Boyle, 2003). Members of the Jehovah's Witnesses congregation do not believe in magical spells or practice faith or spiritual healing, nor do they celebrate birthdays, as they believe that this practice is derived from ancient false religions. Within the congregations volunteer "elders" or "overseers" serve as leaders and provide spiritual comfort and guidance, without pay or special status, to the congregants. All members and elders willingly visit the sick and pray with them, so this is an excellent resource for nurses seeking psychological support for patients who are members of this religion. Naturally, a better place to start, in this particular case, is with the patient's own family.

Family Roles and Traditions

Based on biblical beliefs, Jehovah's Witnesses consider the husband the head of the household and he is expected to honor and respect his wife, serve as spiritual leader for the family, and provide food, clothing, and shelter for the family. The wife is expected to assist her husband in caring for the children and teaching them the tenets of the religion. Children are required to obey their parents and to study the Bible with them. Within the marriage partners are encouraged to be forgiving through marital difficulties and to use the Bible in confronting these issues. Divorce is frowned on and adultery is the only acceptable grounds for divorce for a Jehovah's Witness.

In light of this background information about Jehovah's Witnesses, one realizes that there are many facets of this patient's situation that represent either a real or perceived threat to his personal integrity. As breadwinner and head of household, he may worry about his family's ability to sustain themselves through what is potentially a long-term illness with loss of employment days. Once the patient's health situation is stabilized, culturally sensitive nurses in cooperation with social workers and the patient's family can work together to find methods of support.

Health Care Beliefs and Values

All life is deeply valued and respected by Jehovah's Witnesses; therefore, abortion, suicide, euthanasia, and violence against others are all unacceptable practices. Unhealthful practices that do not support a healthy life, such as smoking, taking drugs, and excessive drinking are also forbidden by practicing members of this group (Andrews & Boyle, 2003).

Blood is also considered sacred and Jehovah's Witnesses consider it wrong to eat the meat of an animal that has not been appropriately bled (Watch Tower Bible and Tract, 2011). Some members of this religious group also consider it wrong to accept a blood transfusion even when the patient's own blood is the source. They believe that this is a serious sin against God. At times, children have been made wards of the court when physicians, seeking authorization for transfusions, have believed that a medical condition necessitated a blood transfusion (Andrews & Boyle, 2003).

Nonblood volume expanders, surgical procedures without accompanying blood transfusions, surgical procedures, and biopsies are accepted by Jehovah's Witnesses, but adherence to God's laws is valued over sustaining one's life.

Applying Principles of Cultural Competency

Nurses caring for Mr. Jackmon will need to recognize that the ability to provide culturally sensitive and congruent health care is jeopardized when the desire to impose one's own values (in this case, regarding adherence to Western medical practices) conflicts with the desire to do what is in the best interest of the patient (from the patient's own perspective). The inability to respect Mr. Jackmon's right to decide about what medical interventions are acceptable based on his religious convictions is a critical factor interfering with positive cross-cultural communication between some of the nurses and this patient. Nurses who are able to accept the patient's perspective, even as it conflicts with their own personal views, are in a much better position to establish a trusting relationship based on mutual respect, and to act most effectively in this patient's behalf.

Culturally sensitive nurses and other health care providers will utilize cultural assessment measures that explore the patient's level of understanding about his health risks, clinical status, and alternative methods of treatment for the patient's hemoglobinemia. Measures will be taken to utilize the family and community supports to provide spiritual and emotional support during this time of crisis.

Role of Spirituality

In caring for this patient, the nurse will need to determine what role religion and spirituality play in Mr. Jackmon's and his family's life and incorporate this in his plan of care. A meeting with his wife to further assess Mr. Jackmon's level of anxiety about his hospitalization and other stresses is necessary. As patient advocate, the culturally competent nurse can collaborate with the physician and other health professionals to determine appropriate treatment options for him.

IMPORTANT POINTS

- Jehovah's Witnesses don't celebrate birthdays or Christian holidays like Christmas and Easter.
- Jehovah's Witnesses place much emphasis on physical, mental, moral, and spiritual cleanliness, and will not eat meat that has not been bled properly, or accept blood transfusions.
- Jehovah's Witnesses will accept blood substitutes, or plasma expanders.
- Witnesses believe that we live in an unclean world and that Witnesses must strive on a daily basis to overcome threats to their moral integrity and indirectly their relationship with God. Truth-telling, keeping a clean house, and avoiding people who do not adhere to God's laws is a way of life for Jehovah's Witnesses.
- Members are also encouraged to teach God's word at least 10 hours each month.

NCLEX-TYPE QUESTIONS

1. What statement below is accurate about the difference between spirituality and religion? (select all that apply)
   A. Religion is internal and spirituality is external and exclusive.
   B. Spirituality relies on doctrines and rules.
   C. Religion is focused on specific values, beliefs, and a framework for ethical behavior.
   D. Spirituality is internal and inclusive.

2. The culturally competent nurse recognizes that within each major religious group in the United States:
   A. There are significant differences in religious perspectives.
   B. Most groups are strongly traditional in their religious thinking.
   C. Most Protestants are conservative.
   D. Most Catholics are liberal.

3. During a cultural assessment, when asked about his religion, the patient tells the nurse that he is an agnostic. The nurse acknowledges that this term means:
   A. The patient believes in the oneness of the human family.
   B. The patient does not believe in God.
   C. The patient is uncertain about the existence of God.
   D. The patient believes that there are many deities.

4. The culturally competent nurse questions patients to learn about the value they place on God and religion in their lives because:
   A. Attitudes about God and religion vary among individuals.
   B. Some patients will not require spiritual care.
   C. Most patients are religious.
   D. This is a sign of a patient's coping capacity.

5. It is important for the nurse to assist patients in maintaining their spiritual well-being because spirituality is believed to:
   A. Give patients a sense of purpose
   B. Provide a means for coping with stress
   C. Positively influence the nurse–patient relationship
   D. Strengthen patients' religious beliefs

6. According to research, the large majority of Americans are:
   A. Catholic
   B. Protestants
   C. Muslims
   D. Christians

7. The percentage of Americans who consider themselves secularists, humanists, agnostics, and nonbelievers is:
   A. 2%
   B. 5%
   C. 15%
   D. 30%

8. When defining spirituality, one common theme seems to be that spirituality is an expression of one's views about:
   A. Religion
   B. Meaning, purpose, and direction of life
   C. Cultural attitudes
   D. God

9. When the culturally competent nurses administer spiritual care to diverse patients, they recognize that it is important to focus their attention on the spiritual well-being of:
   A. The patient only
   B. The patient and his family
   C. The patient and the nurse
   D. The nurse only

10. Some important aspects of spiritual care are (select all that apply):
    A. Listening for spiritual clues
    B. Remaining nonjudgmental
    C. Consulting with other health care professionals as needed
    D. Incorporating one's own religious and moral views in patient care decision making

11. The culturally competent nurse observes patients for indications of spiritual distress which include (select all that apply):
    A. Depression
    B. Crying
    C. Apathy
    D. Insomnia
    E. Moodiness

12. Ideally, the nurse selects a spiritual advisor for the patient based on:
    A. The nurse's knowledge of the patient's religion
    B. The patient's expressed desire
    C. The availability of a spiritual advisor within the health care system
    D. The family's wishes

AACN COMPETENCIES ADDRESSED IN THIS CHAPTER

1. Apply knowledge of social and cultural factors that affect nursing and health care across multiple contexts.
3. Promote achievement of safe and quality outcomes of care for diverse populations.
5. Participates in continuous cultural competence development.

REFERENCES

Agrimson, L. B., & Taft L. B. (2009). Spiritual crisis: A concept analysis. *Journal of Advanced Nursing, 65*(2). 454–461.

American Nurses Association. (2003). *Nursing: Scope and standards of practice.* Silver Spring, MD: Nursebooks.org.

Andrews, M., & J. S. Boyle. (Eds.). (2003). *Transcultural concepts in nursing care.* Philadelphia, PA: Lippincott.

Andrews, M., & Hanson P. (2003). Jehovah's Witnesses. In M. M. Andrews & J. S. Boyle. (Eds.), *Transcultural concepts in nursing care* (4th ed., pp. 480–481). Philadelphia, PA: Lippincott.

Andrews, M., & Hanson P. (2003). Religion, culture, and nursing. In M. M. Andrews & J. S. Boyle (Eds.), *Transcultural concepts in nursing care* (4th ed., pp. 518–519). Philadelphia, PA: Lippincott.

Campinha-Bacote, J. (2002). The process of cultural competence in the delivery of healthcare services: A model of care. *Journal of Transcultural Nursing, 13*(3), 181–184. doi:10.1177/10459602013003003

Cuevas, J., Vance, D., Viamonte, S., Lee, S., & South, J. (2010). A comparison of spirituality and religiousness in older and younger adults with and without HIV. *Journal of Spirituality In Mental Health, 12*(4), 273–287. doi:10.1080/19349637.2010.518828

de Souza, J. R., Maftum M. A., & Bais, D. D. H. (2008). Nursing care facing the recognition of patient's belief or religión: Undergraduates' perceptions. *Online Brazilian Journal of Nursing, 7*(2). Retrieved from www.objnursing.uff.br/index.php/nursing/article/view2.27

Dunn, L. (2008). Spirituality and nursing: Personal responsibility. *Online Journal of rural nursing and health care, 8*(1). Retrieved from web.ebscohost.com.holyfamily.idm.oclc.org/ehost//pdfviewer/pdfvie

Gibson, M., & Hindricks, C. S. (2006). Integrative review of spirituality in African American breast cancer survivors. *ABNF Journal, 17*(2), 67–72.

Giger, J. N., & Davidhizar, R. E. (2008). *Transcultural nursing. Assessment and intervention* (5th ed.). St. Louis, MO: Mosby.

Goldsand, G., Rosenberg, Z., & Gordon, M. (2001). Bioethics for clinicians: Jewish bioethics. *Canadian Medical Association Journal, 164*(2), 219–222.

Hughes, D. B., Ullery, B. W., Barrie, P. S. (2008). The contemporary approach to the care of Jehovah's witnesses. *Journal of Trauma,65*(1), 237–247.

Kreitzer, M. J., Gross, C. R., Waleekhachonloet, O., Reilly-Spong, M., & Byrd, M. (2009). *Journal of Holistic Nursing, 27*(7), 7–16.

Lackey, S. A. (2009). Opening the door to spiritually sensitive nursing care. *Nursing, 39*(4),46–48.

Mok, E., Wong, F., & Wong, D. (2010). The meaning of spirituality and spiritual care among the Hong Kong Chinese terminally ill. *Journal of Advanced Nursing, 66*(2), 360–370. doi:10.1111/j.1365-2648.2009.05193.x

Noto, E. C. (2008). The meaning of spirituality and spiritual nursing care for the individual with no religious affiliation. *Southern Online Journal of Nursing Research, 8*(2). Retrieved from web.ebscohost.com.holyfamily./dm.oclc.orglehost/detail?vid=25&h

Pesut, B. (2008). A conversation on diverse perspectives of spirituality in nursing literature. *Nursing Philosophy, 9,* 98–109.

Pesut, B. (2009). Incorporating patients' spirituality into care using Gadow's ethical framework. *Nursing Ethics, 16*(4), 418–428. doi: 10.1177/0969733009104606

Pew Research Center. (2008). *The Pew Forum on Religious Life: U.S. Religious Landscape Survey (2007)*. Retrieved from http://religions.pewforum.org/affiliations

Purnell, L., & Selekman, J. (2008). People of Jewish Heritage. In L. Purnell & B. J. Paulanka (Eds.), *Transcultural health care: A culturally competent approach* (3rd ed.). Philadelphia, PA: F.A. Davis Company.

Ravari, A., Vanaki, Z., Houmann, H., & Kazemnejad, A. (2009). Spiritual job satisfaction in an Iranian nursing context. *Nursing Ethics, 16*(1), 19–30.

Scott, B. J. (2008). Celebrating Jewish culture. *Long Term Living: For the Continuing Care Professional, 57*(3), 18, 20.

Simpson, S., Preston A., Ghafior S., Page, L., Keith, P., & Havers, C. (2008). Search for meaning. *Nursing standard, 22*(21). 18–20.

Swinton, J. (2006). Editorial: Critical reflections on the current state of spirituality-in-nursing. *Journal of Clinical Nursing, 15*(7), 801–802.

Tanyi R.A. (2002). Toward clarification of the meaning of spirituality. *Journal of Advanced Nursing, 39*(5), 500–509.

Tyler, I., & Raynor, J. (2006). Spirituality in the natural sciences and nursing: An interdisciplinary perspective. *ABNF Journal, 17*(2), 63–66.

Watch Tower Bible and Tract Society of Pennsylvania. (2011). What does God require of us: Showing respect for life and blood. Retrieved September 29, 2011, from www.watchtower.org

Watch Tower Society. (2009). What does the bible really teach? Retrieved June 27, 2009, from www.watchtower.org

Wright, L. (2008). Softening suffering through spiritual care practices: One possibility for healing families. *Journal of Family Nursing, 14,* 394–411.

Zavatto, A. (2003) *The pocket idiot's guide to Judaism*. Indianapolis, IN: Pearson Education.

ADDITIONAL RESOURCES

Institute for Jewish Medical Ethics: Accessed June 8, 2009 at www.ijme.org

Jewish Community Online's Internet Resources (Family/Health and Bioethics). Retrieved June 9, 2009, from www.jewish.com/search/Family

Jewish Outreach Institute. Retrieved June 11, 2009, from http://joi.org/blog/?cat=4

Judaism 101. Retrieved June 8, 2009, from www.jewfaq.org/toc.htm

The Watchtower Bible and Tract Society of Pennsylvania. (2009). Transfusion alternative strategies: Simple, safe, effective. Retrieved June 27, 2009, from www.watchtower.org/e/vcnb/article_01.htm

Cultural Considerations When Caring for Patients With Physical, Psychological, or Intellectual Disabilities

GLORIA KERSEY-MATUSIAK

Just because a man lacks the use of his eyes, doesn't mean he lacks vision.
—STEVIE WONDER

LEARNING OBJECTIVES

1. Describe the various types of disabilities found in American society.
2. Discuss the impact of discrimination or bias on persons with disabilities.
3. Examine the demographics found among persons with disabilities.
4. Identify groups and organizations that may be used as resources when caring for persons with disabilities.
5. Explore common attitudes of health care providers toward persons with disabilities.
6. Recognize the implications for nurses when caring for persons with disabilities.
7. Determine strategies and intervention to enhance the quality of care for persons with disabilities.

KEY TERMS

American with Disabilities Act (ADA)
Arc
Disability
Disability disparities
Learning Disability Association of America (LDA)

DEFINING DISABILITIES

The **Americans with Disabilities Act (ADA)** defines **disability** in terms of the person's physical, mental, or emotional functioning problems that coexist with his or her levels of participation in the activities required to be integrated into the social world. According to the American Disability Association (2009), 10% of the world's population—more than 650 million people—are persons with disabilities; 80% of these individuals live in developing countries. The CDC (2011) reported that, "during 2001–2005, almost 30% of the non-institutionalized adult U.S. population (approximately 62 million people) has some basic movement, sensory, cognitive, or emotional difficulties. More than one-fifth of this population has conditions that limit their basic physical activities, such as walking, bending, climbing stairs, reaching, lifting, or carrying. About 13% of people with disabilities report problems with vision or hearing, while 6% of the population struggle with emotional or cognitive difficulties" (National Center for Health Statistics, 2008). According to the World Health Organization (WHO), "the number of people with disabilities is increasing due to population growth, ageing, emergence of chronic diseases, injuries such as those due to road crashes, conflicts, falls, HIV/AIDS, and other communicable diseases" (WHO, 2009). Despite these facts, many Americans have never seen or interacted with a person with a disability. Therefore, many are unaware of, and insensitive to, the various problems members of this group experience. Unfortunately, unfair stereotyping and bias by able-bodied members of society are sometimes unintentionally directed toward people who have physical or mental disabilities when the able-bodied encounter them.

DISABILITIES AND DISCRIMINATION

Global attitudes toward persons who are disabled vary depending on one's cultural attitudes and beliefs and the nature of the disability (Purnell, 2008). As earlier researchers recognized, "societal attitudes toward persons with disabilities are often based on a lack of understanding, fear of the unknown, and stereotypes learned from others" (Thompson, Emrich, & Moore, 2003). The Rehabilitation Act of 1973 and the Americans with Disabilities Act (ADA) of 1990 are both aimed at prohibiting discrimination and protecting the civil and constitutional rights of persons with disabilities. More specifically, these acts prohibit discrimination by employers, state and local governments, and private enterprises. In addition to government agencies, other associations and organizations work with, and on behalf of, the various groups of persons with disabilities.

LEARNING DISABILITIES

The **Arc** is one of several organizations of and for people with intellectual and developmental disabilities. This organization provides services for the 7 million people and their families who struggle with intellectual disabilities.

Members of this and other organizations that support persons with disabilities seek their inclusion in society and the workplace. The Arc philosophy includes the idea of people first and the belief "that all people with intellectual and developmental disabilities have strengths, abilities and inherent value; are equal before the law; and must be treated with dignity and respect" (Arc, 2009). The Arc represents, supports, and acts on behalf of individuals and their families regardless of level of disability or membership in the organization. The organization empowers people with disabilities by providing needed resources to assist them in making informed decisions and choices. This philosophy is shared in the United Kingdom and expressed through an initiative sponsored by the Department of Health, Valuing People Now, a strategy by the government of the United Kingdom to respond to a 2008 report that provided compelling evidence that people with learning disabilities have greater needs than others, yet have less access to that care and poorer outcomes. This initiative identifies five priorities with the primary one being improved access and health outcomes for people with learning disabilities. In the United States, the **Learning Disabilities Association of America (LDA)** reports that, "the prevalence of learning disabilities has 'spiraled ever higher'" among students in American schools over recent years. The LDA attributes this trend to better diagnostics, environmental hazards, and poor instructional methods that may cause some populations to be misdiagnosed (LDA, 2009).

NEW TRENDS IN CARING FOR PERSONS WITH LEARNING DISABILITIES

Today the care of persons with learning disabilities has moved away from long-term care facilities toward more frequent use of general health services. Therefore, it is more likely that nurses may see persons with learning disabilities during their professional careers. Persons with learning disabilities may enter hospitals and other health care settings for reasons related to their learning disability or for physical or mental health issues experienced by the rest of society (Slevin, Mcconkey, Truesdale-Kennedy, & Tagart, 2008). In any case, nurses are encouraged to use a partnership approach when caring for learning-disabled clients that promotes the client's involvement in decision making whenever possible (Leyson & Clark, 2005). Caring for patients or clients with learning disabilities also necessitates using a multidisciplinary approach that is holistic and focused on addressing the needs of patients based on the patient's perspective. In a paper describing actual experiences of a patient with a learning disability, the authors discuss feelings of powerlessness that professionals experience when caring for individuals with learning disorders. They suggest that these feelings arise because there is no cure for the disability and health providers become vulnerable in the process of recognizing this problem. As the authors noted, "The challenge is for professionals to acknowledge and reflect on the dynamics of power and powerlessness within the therapeutic relationship" (p. 214). The reader is encouraged to read the article cited in the reference list by Manners (2006) on working with patients with learning disabilities.

CULTURAL DIVERSITY, DISABILITIES, AND DISPARITIES

Lewis (2009) emphasized the urgency in addressing cultural competency to meet the "multiple accountability demands" on rehabilitation and disability providers. In a web broadcast Lewis discussed a proposed model for rendering care to patients with disabilities with cultural humility, cultural efficacy, and cultural competency. In the web broadcast, the terms were used interchangeably. The model Lewis proposes expands on Section 21 of the Rehabilitation Act amendment, which first addressed the concept of "**disability disparities**." Like health care disparities, disability disparities refer to differences in service delivery, disability experiences, or clinical outcomes based on one's membership in a particular group, such as one's age, race, culture, ethnicity, or socioeconomic status. For example, Ho, Kroll, and Kehn (2007) discussed the problems encountered by low-income, working-age adults with physical disabilities, which included transportation accessibility, and privacy barriers. Of the 28 people who participated in the study, 13 lived in a homeless shelter, 7 in a nursing home, and 8 in a private home. In this study, half of the participants had spinal cord injury and paralysis and relied on Medicaid or a local public program for health insurance. Respondents perceived public and private transportation either unreliable or inaccessible and lacked access to a regular physician, and dental care, which is not covered under their Medicaid plan. Participants who lived in a nursing home or shelter also expressed concerns about having a lack of privacy and security. In this situation, while ethnicity or race is not a factor, the lack of health care insurance or the level of poverty is the common factor that influences the care these individuals receive. Chevarley (2006) reported that the proportion of Black non-Hispanic women who had three or more functional limitations was higher than for Hispanic women and White non-Hispanic women. Moreover, women with functional limitations were more likely to rate their health as fair or poor than women with no functional limitations. Those with more functional limitations were also more likely to smoke, have hypertension, be overweight, and experience mental health problems. Women with greater functional limitations were also less likely to have had mammograms and Pap smear exams within the previous year. Bowen and Gonzolez (2008) observed that although disability rates among older adults have decreased, Blacks and Latinos continue to be overrepresented among persons with disabilities. These researchers also report that Blacks and Latinos were less able to carry out activities of daily living (ADL) than Whites and had more mobility limitations. The researchers concluded that equal economic access alone, although important, may not guarantee equal access to care for Blacks and Latinos. Pollard and Barnett (2009) studied health literacy among people who are deaf and found that nearly a third of the participants, despite having college degrees, scored below the ninth-grade level. The authors noted that individuals who are unable to understand health-related words are at risk for health care disparities. The researchers encourage health care professionals to develop better health education materials to prevent worse health outcomes for individuals who are deaf. These examples are but a few of the disparities that are noted in the literature. Developing cultural competency skills is one way for nurses and other providers to address them.

Lewis's proposed disability disparity model includes five domains; each domain on the five-point continuum represents the total disability experience. At the beginning of the continuum the client/patient's disability begins. The end point on the continuum represents the point at which outcomes are achieved at the end of the rehabilitation services. In the model, Lewis hypothesizes what accounts for differential experiences and offers a set of reasons to explain the differences based on a cultural orientation at each of the five points. Lewis explains these differences from a macro—big-picture or conceptual level, as well as a micro—practitioner, or clinician level. At the micro level, the model offers service providers opportunities to explore various things that may be happening from a cultural perspective to influence the disability experience. For example, in Domain 1, at the macro level certain factors account for a higher incidence of disabilities among a selected culturally diverse group. These factors may reflect cultural characteristics like biological or genetic traits that are linked to membership in a particular ethnically diverse group. At the micro level practitioners can consider factors in the environment, coping strategies, level of stress, and so on, that may be impacting clients' behaviors, and consequently their access to care or their disability outcomes. The model also includes a consideration of systemic health care biases that currently permeate the health care system and act as barriers to access for members of culturally diverse groups. An example of a systemic bias may be Western practitioners' over-reliance on Western medicine as a treatment modality. In Chinese culture, some Eastern treatment modalities like acupuncture or herbal medicine may be preferred. For a more detailed description of the model, please see the Project Empowerment: Disability Disparities website listed at the end of this chapter. Lewis is not alone in advocating for a change in practice strategies for providers to provide more culturally relevant care for persons with disabilities (Au, 2006; Laino, 2007; Matziou, 2009; ten Klooster, 2009; Thompson, 2003).

IMPLICATIONS FOR NURSES

Nurses in particular have special opportunities to interact with people who have disabilities. However, the context in which nursing occurs plays a role in determining the type of nursing care, the quality of resources, and services that are made available to the patient with disabilities. For example, in rehabilitation nursing, nurses in close collaboration with other rehabilitation team members are prepared to provide care that more specifically addresses the needs of patients with disabilities. In these settings a multidisciplinary planned approach that focuses on potential and actual problems that may be related to the client's cultural background is already in place. When persons with physical disabilities find themselves in acute or chronic health care settings for reasons having little to do with their disability, it is still often the nurse who determines the quality of care the patient receives (Jenkins, 2009). By acting as patient advocate the nurse sets the tone for other members of the health team. In recognizing the specific needs of individuals with disabilities nurses can make a tremendous positive difference in ensuring that care is appropriate and culturally sensitive. Because nurses' attitudes mirror those of society some nurses demonstrate negative attitudes and consequently negative behaviors that reflect our society's views (Matziou et al., 2009; Seccombe, 2007; Thompson, Emrich, & Moore, 2003). However, the nursing literature reveals differing attitudes by nurses toward persons with disabilities. Melville (2005) found that nurses played a key role in addressing the unmet needs of people with disabilities and had positive attitudes toward them. On the other hand, Lehman (2009) in a study of advanced practice nurses' attitudes toward disabilities in a primary care setting reported that nurses do not lack knowledge, but because of the unsupportive work environment, nurses may not be able to provide optimum care for women with disabilities. Baker (2009) highlighted some of the issues nurses face in providing care to patients with long-term neurological conditions such as Huntington's disease, vegetative states, locked-in syndrome, Parkinson's and MS, and the high demands on the nurse in the care of these patients. This researcher observes that care of the long-term patient depends on attitudes of the nurse. Lanio (2007) examined nurses' knowledge of mental disabilities, attitudes, interaction skills, and competence in meeting mentally disabled patients' needs. Respondents felt that their knowledge was "quite poor, outdated, limited, and insufficient."

Thompson (2003), Au (2006), and ten Klooster (2009) studied student nurses' attitudes toward persons with disabilities. Au compared occupational therapy, physical therapy, and social work, and nursing students in Hong Kong to professionals in the respective fields and reported that nurses had the least favorable attitudes toward people with disabilities and even less positive than student nurses. The researcher recommended modifying the training and curriculum to enhance the quality of service to persons with disabilities and develop more positive attitudes. Ten Klooster (2009) examined attitudes of Dutch nursing students' attitudes toward physically or intellectually disabled people as compared to non-nursing peers' attitudes. This research revealed that nursing students were more positive toward persons with disabilities than their peers. An important determinant of attitudes in this study was having a relative or friend with a disability. Recommendations from this study include educational interventions that focus on forms of contact with persons with disabilities beyond formal care relationships. This recommendation supports the idea that by increasing encounters with the selected group, the nurse or health provider builds a greater understanding and desire to provide culturally sensitive care. Thompson (2003) in a descriptive study to determine if a change in the curriculum had an effect on nursing students' attitudes found more positive attitudes after students completed the senior year. This researcher also suggested education about and experiences with people with disabilities to promote positive attitudes of nursing students toward persons with disabilities.

Matziou (2009) investigated professional pediatric nurses' first-year nursing students', and post-diploma nurses' attitudes toward disabled children. He found that first-year students and females in the study had more positive attitudes toward children with disabilities than nurses. This researcher concluded that carefully designed curricula should be integrated into special courses in nursing education to change negative attitudes. As Seccombe (2007) stated, "effective nursing care can be severely compromised through negative attitudes." At times, these behaviors simply illustrate a nurses' lack of understanding about the psychosocial needs of persons with disabilities. It is helpful for those nurses to realize that the needs of individuals with disabilities are not unlike those of the general public, which include the desire to be treated with dignity, respect, and understanding.

DEMOGRAPHICS AMONG THE DISABLED

Like everyone else, persons with disabilities from culturally diverse groups share some commonalities; they experience joy, sadness, anger, fear, and loneliness. Yet, among culturally diverse persons with disabilities, differences do exist between cultural and ethnic groups and also within them. Researchers have identified sociodemographic characteristics of persons with disabilities and report that women are overrepresented among persons with disabilities. Sixty percent of adults with either complex activity limitations or basic action difficulties are women. Women are also overrepresented among individuals with emotional disabilities. "Adults under the age of 65 made up the majority (64%) of persons with complex activity limitations and approximately one-half of adults with emotional disorders were under 45 years of age" (National Center for Health Statistics, 2008). The racial and ethnic distribution of the population with disabilities differs from the racial and ethnic distribution of the population without disabilities. For example, "The population with complex activity limitation included far fewer people of Hispanic or Asian adults versus Blacks whose numbers more closely mirrored their proportion in society" (National Center for Health Statistics, 2008). Other demographic differences between people with and without disabilities include differences in education, employment, and family income. In a 2001 to 2005 study, people without disabilities were more than twice as likely to have a college degree as people with complex activity limitation and 70% more likely than people with basic action difficulties. Although the majority of people with disabilities acquire them after they have completed their education, some disabilities may limit opportunities for higher education and account for this difference.

Employment among persons with disabilities is impacted by the nature of the disability, as are the tendencies toward cigarette smoking, lack of regular physical exercise, and obesity. Forty percent of persons with complex activity limitations or basic action difficulties reported smoking as compared to 22% of persons without disabilities. Only 15% of persons with complex activity limitations or 21% with basic actions difficulties exercised as compared to 35% of nondisabled individuals. Almost 30% of persons with basic action difficulties and 33% of persons with complex activity limitations reported being obese as compared to 19% of persons without these limitations. During the 2001 to 2005 study, the researchers also discovered that adults 18 to 44 years of age were more likely to lack a usual source of medical care, regardless of disability status. This is especially significant for adults with emotional disabilities, because these tend to occur at a younger age. An awareness of these statistics is helpful in identifying potential risk factors and problems when caring for persons with disabilities. In addition, from the patient's perspective, much depends on how recently the disability was acquired, the severity of the disability, whether the disability is permanent, and the extent to which there are adequate family or other support systems. Certainly patients who have recently become disabled due to trauma, stroke, or other unanticipated events, will experience psychological effects that will need to be considered when planning care. Other patients with long-standing disabilities may have adapted to the inconveniences of the disability itself and may not consider it a "problem" at all.

ATTITUDES OF HEALTH CARE PROVIDERS TOWARD PERSONS WITH DISABILITIES

During the course of more than 16 years of rehabilitation nursing and numerous interactions with persons with physical disabilities, the author has had many conversations with patients about their perceptions of health care providers' attitudes toward persons with disabilities. Throughout these conversations several common themes have emerged that have also been found in the literature: (1) some able-bodied persons use terms or descriptors that are demeaning and offensive when discussing people with disabilities; (2) some able-bodied nurses and other health care workers discount the individuality of people with disabilities; (3) some health providers talk to and treat persons with disabilities as though they were children; (4) and some able-bodied health providers look on the disability as a handicap, where as many patients view their disability as but one aspect of their life (ODEP, 2002).

A myth that exists about people with disabilities is that there is nothing one person can do to help eliminate the barriers and myths encountered by people with disabilities. Despite that belief, the ADA suggests that "everyone can contribute to the inclusion and empowerment of people with disabilities in our society." The International Council of Nurses (ICN) advises that national nurses associations should play a visible role in influencing and advocating public policy on the care of people with disabilities. The ICN Position Statement on the Prevention of Disabilities and the Care of Persons with Disabilities identifies strategies to maximize nursing effectiveness in caring for individuals with disabilities. For example, nurse educators are encouraged to address "competencies for the prevention of disabilities and the care and rehabilitation of people with disabilities; promote fuller understanding of the particular problems faced by people with disabilities and their families…and support people with disabilities and their families to access education, information and support services that allow them to lead fulfilling lives" (ICN, 2002). To that end, nurses can begin by setting an example among health care providers in using a person's first language, which places that person before the disability. As Snow argues, "sadly disability diagnoses are often used to define a person's value and potential…the real problem is never a person's disability, but the attitudes of others" (p. 2). Nurses must seek to understand persons with disabilities by accepting them as individuals with cultural characteristics that transcend the nature of their disability. This behavior must be demonstrated during each encounter with persons with disabilities. Conducting a cultural assessment will enable nurses to identify the pertinent health needs that are relevant to the individual and to plan care that is culturally congruent with the patient's attitudes, beliefs, and health care needs. An injury or disease that causes a person to require a wheelchair does not change that person's personality or cultural values. Nor does it change that person's abilities. Emphasis should be placed on what a person with a disability values and what that person is able to do, rather than what he or she cannot do (Snow, 2008).

CASE SCENARIO 1

Jimmy Watson is a 28-year-old White male patient with paraplegia caused by falling two stories from a ladder while doing construction work. This event occurred 4 months ago and Jimmy has had extensive previous hospitalizations for multiple trauma injuries during the acute and subacute phase of his injury. Jimmy was transported from the very rural area in which he lives to a rehabilitation hospital in an urban area several hundred miles from his hometown. This occurred because there was no facility of this kind in the area in which he lived. Jimmy's father and younger brother live several hundred miles away and are unable to visit.

During the first weeks of his admission to the unit, Jimmy was pleasant and cooperative in his interactions with the hospital staff. All of the nurses enjoyed working with him. Jimmy worked very hard to cooperate with the rehabilitation team in following his treatment regimen. After several weeks of hospitalization and several setbacks, including wound infections, high fevers, and several discharge postponements, Jimmy became despondent.

At times, he became hostile when interacting with the staff. He frequently apologized for his discourteous behavior, but became increasingly unhappy with his care. The nurses were perplexed. Bob, one of the nurses, comments, "I know he doesn't like the food here and wants to go home, but I don't understand why he seems to have given up. We are doing the best we can for him."

CASE SCENARIO 2

Milton Thomas, a 26-year-old Black male patient with quadraplegia, is admitted to a medical surgical unit. Four years ago he was a victim of a gunshot wound to his spine. He has since been living at home with his wife. He is admitted to a medical surgical unit with a urinary tract infection, large sacral decubitus ulcer, and a fever of 103. He arrived on the unit on a stretcher accompanied by his wife. Milton and his wife were escorted to a room that was occupied by an older adult male patient with dementia. Kate, a young White female nurse, came into the room to perform the nursing history and initial assessment and discovers an angry and hostile Milton who is requesting a room change. The nurse explains that presently there are no other beds available, but they will consider moving him when possible. In assessing Milton, the nurse determines that because of his quadriplegia, need for extensive wound care, and problem with urinary retention, he will need much assistance with his personal care. Over the next several days, Milton's condition slowly improves but his attitude toward the hospital personnel becomes increasingly strained. He has several altercations with different members of the staff. One nurse comments, "I actually felt sorry for him at first, but I am fed up with his abusive behavior." Nurses assigned to work with Milton complain that he is uncooperative and at times rude toward them. Others are intimidated by his behavior and avoid going into his room at all. Another nurse refuses to answer Milton's call bell at night, because, she says, he deliberately puts on the light as soon as the nurse leaves the room. A psychologist and social worker have been consulted. It is determined that Milton is having some marital difficulties and he anticipates possibly being placed in a nursing home following his discharge. His wife feels that she is no longer able to care for him because she has to work and Milton is unable to care for himself at home.

CASE SCENARIO 3

Carlotta, a 38-year-old Spanish-speaking married mother of three, is admitted to a medical unit after several weeks of neurological changes that involved progressive weakness of her lower extremities. Prior to this, Carlotta and her family had recently moved to Philadelphia from Puerto Rico, where she had a full-time job as a secretary. She has been active in her church and community. She and her husband also enjoyed swimming, but she has not felt up to doing any of these activities for the past several weeks. She was brought to the unit in a wheelchair. When Steve, Carlotta's nurse, attempts to assist Carlotta to the bed, the patient waves him away. "I'm okay," she says. "I can do it." The admitting nurse learns that Carlotta is being evaluated to determine if she has MS or some other neurological disease.

During the interview, the nurse learns that Carlotta speaks only a little English. She is able to determine that Carlotta has three teenage children. The patient denies any complaints beyond the general muscle weakness that she is currently experiencing in her lower extremities. The nurse tries to explain that over the next 2 days testing has been planned to determine the nature of Carlotta's illness. That afternoon, Carlotta interacts pleasantly with the nursing staff and enjoys a visit with her husband and several other members of her family. While giving a report the nurse states, "She is a nice lady, but a real puzzle. I don't understand why, despite her growing weakness, she does not really let you do anything for her. She wants to do it all by herself." Later that evening, on making her rounds, the evening nurse discovers Carlotta sobbing in her room.

WHAT NURSES NEED TO KNOW ABOUT THEMSELVES

APPLICATION OF THE STAIRCASE MODEL: SELF-REFLECTION QUESTIONS

The patients in these cases presented earlier are experiencing various stages in their encounter with disabilities and each has unique circumstances that influence the patient's ability to cope with their disability and to participate in their care. In attempting to address the cases above, ask yourself the following questions. If you were the nurse caring for these patients how would you respond?

1. Where are you on the staircase in working with patients with disabilities? How will you prepare to progress to the next level?
2. Which case would be the most challenging for you and why?
3. What attitudes and feelings would you have toward the patients in each of these scenarios? How might these attitudes influence care?
4. What skills or resources would be useful to you and the other nurses when caring for these patients?
5. What information would you need to provide these patients with culturally sensitive and competent care?
6. During each patient–nurse encounter, what strategies would strengthen the nurse–patient relationship?

Responses to Self-Reflection Questions 3, 4, 5, and 6

***Response to What attitudes and feelings would you have toward
the patients in each of these scenarios? How might
these attitudes influence care?***

In all of the cases, the nurses' attitudes toward the patient seem directly related to the attitude and/or behavior of the patient. In Case 1, Bob, Jimmy's nurse, indicates his frustration with Jimmy's depression and is somewhat defensive in stating, "We're doing all we can for him." In Case 2, the nurses express a range of emotions that include anger, feeling intimidated, and "feeling sorry for the patient." Again, each of these emotions is a direct reflection of the patient's behavior toward the nurses. In Case 3, the nurses again expressed "feeling sorry for the patient" in the wheelchair and confusion about the patient's insistence on remaining independent.

As a human being, it is difficult to believe that you are doing the best that you can on someone's behalf and feel that it is unappreciated by that person. However, none of these attitudes or feelings expressed by the nurses, including "feeling sorry for the patient," really helps meet the patient's needs. However, acknowledging rather than denying frustration, anger, intimidation, or even sympathy toward the patient during peer group discussions may help alleviate some of the related stress that is associated with these feelings. This acknowledgment enables nurses to focus their energy on identifying and responding to the specific needs of the patient rather than focusing on their own personal feelings. By so doing, nurses become better able to confront patient care issues more objectively, while providing support for one another.

***Response to What skills or resources would be useful to you
and the other nurses when caring for these patients?***

Regardless of the nature and type of the disability, it will be helpful for the nurse to gain specific knowledge about the patient's health-related beliefs and practices and cultural values; disease incidence and prevalence; and treatment efficacy. This includes learning from patients how they view the world, what they value or really care about, and what they believe about their illness, disease, or clinical situation. It also involves gaining information about any predispositions to disease or health risks that may be attributed to ethnicity or race and determining the effectiveness of the treatment plan being utilized. Another consideration is the preferred style of interaction or communication that the patient utilizes. This style is usually dependent on whether the patient is "culturally immersed" in his own culture, or acculturated to another. Many American patients will use a "traditional style" that neither rejects nor accepts their cultural identity. In this case, patients will frequently say, "I'm just an American." Members of culturally diverse groups may be more likely to be acculturated, bicultural, or culturally immersed, rejecting all values except those held by their own cultural group.

In any case, nurses must recognize that there are also intra-cultural differences. For example, Americans from rural, suburban, and urban areas may choose different styles of interacting when placed in an environment that is new to them. Besides learning that is acquired through textbooks and conferences, health care professionals must gain cultural knowledge directly through interactions with the patient as well. Cultural knowledge comes through asking questions, seeking clarification, and sharing cultural information about differences and commonalities between the patient and the nurse.

Response to What information would you need to provide these patients with culturally sensitive and competent care?

In these three cases it would be helpful for the nurses to first select and utilize a cultural assessment model that will enable them to develop a profile of the patient, identify pertinent health care needs, and plan care that is culturally congruent with the patients' values and beliefs. Because patients who are disabled are a heterogeneous population, they will have a wide variation in background factors that will contribute to both their responses to illness and their specific needs for care. McKenna (2003) identified such factors as ethnicity, cultural traditions, social and economic situations, living arrangements, employment status, and migration history. In addition, the developmental stage and age of the patient will also have an impact on the type of care they will require. In culturally assessing the patient, the nurse can gain information about the patient's family support systems, values, religion and spirituality needs, food preferences, and health beliefs, and attitudes.

One approach the nurse can utilize is the assessment model first proposed by Purnell and Paulanka (1998). This model focuses on 12 interconnected domains that may be applied in assessing individuals' families and groups within various cultures. These attributes include overview, inhabited localities, and topography, communication, family roles and organizations, workforce issues, biocultural ecology, high-risk health behaviors, nutrition, pregnancy, childbearing practices, death rituals, spirituality, health care practices, and health care practitioners. Obviously, the nurse will need to decide which of the domains is relevant in the care of a particular patient or selected population. When applying any assessment model nurses will also need to utilize good communication skills. Particularly, it is critical that the nurse has the ability to actively and objectively listen to their patients without making judgments about their statements or attributing negative connotations to issues about which the patient and the nurse disagree. Human resources to assist the nurse in planning culturally sensitive care include the family, clergy, social service personnel, interpreters, and other members of the health team when needed.

Response to During each patient–nurse encounter, what strategies would strengthen the nurse–patient relationship?

Each patient care encounter affords the nurse opportunities to learn more about the patient and to apply that information to patient care planning. For example, in Case 1 during interactions with Jimmy, nurses can attempt to learn more about the differences between the rural lifestyle and hospital experiences that the patient is accustomed to and his experience in this urban hospital outside of his local region. In what ways can nurses assist the patient in coping with those differences? It is especially helpful to determine how significant the absence of family members is to this patient. Are there extended family members nearby? Could the nurse facilitate periodic phone conversations between the patient and the family? If interaction between the patient and his family is not possible, what kinds of social supports or activities can be arranged for this patient? What are some food preferences or substitutes that may be acquired through consultation with dietary services? In resolving some of these issues, the nurse may be better able to assist the patient in coping with his medical situation.

Clearly the nurse–patient encounter in Case 2 encounters have not been positive ones. The nurses are angered and frustrated by the interactions they are having with this "hostile patient." However, the psychological consultations have revealed some underlying reasons for the patient's angry behavior. Are there also race and gender issues influencing the nurse–patient interaction in this situation? Can these issues be explored by assigning a male nurse or nursing assistants from the patient's ethnic background to assist the other nurses with his care? If this is not possible, perhaps the nurses can collaborate with the psychologist, clinical nurse specialist in psychology, or other members of the health care team to identify effective strategies for interacting with the patient.

In encounters with patients like the patient in Case 3, who speaks little English, the nurse can use a model proposed by Like that uses the mnemonic TRANSLATE to determine how to utilize a medical interpreter when working with a patient who speaks English as a second language: The model addresses the issues of *trust, roles advocacy, nonjudgmental attitude, setting, language, accuracy,* and *ethical issues* (Like, 2000).

The model assists the nurse in determining:

- How trust will be established between the patient and the interpreter
- What role the interpreter will play
- How advocacy and support for the patient and family will occur
- How a nonjudgmental attitude will be maintained

- The appropriate setting for the encounter between the patient and the interpreter
- How linguistic competence will be evaluated
- How the patient will be provided with thorough and accurate information
- How time will be managed
- How confidentiality and other ethical issues will be handled during patient encounters

Despite the nurse's best intentions and best efforts, it is sometimes difficult for both the nurse and the patient to like one another. Nevertheless, the culturally competent nurse must be willing to respect differences while remaining flexible in adapting care so that it is culturally congruent with the patient's values and needs. Additionally, regardless of the patient's behavior, the nurse remains accepting of the patient as partner in the development of an appropriate plan of care. Without sincere cultural humility and motivation to provide culturally sensitive care to patients it is impossible to do so.

In caring for patients with physical disabilities, besides the considerations mentioned previously, there are some general guidelines that may be helpful to include when planning care. All of these are based on the fact that physically disabled people do not want to be viewed as handicapped,

IMPORTANT POINTS

Strategies for Delivering Culturally Competent Care

Adapted from "People First: Communicating With and About People with Disability," New York State Department of Health, 2009.

1. **Treat adults as adults.** Address people with disabilities by their first name only after they have given permission. Never patronize them by patting them on the head or shoulders, regardless of their age.
2. **Be aware of and sensitive to factors influencing the patient's experience of illness** such as the nature of the disability, the realistic problems it creates, the person's attitude, material resources, attitude of the patient's family and or social group (Vacc & Clifford, 1995).
3. **Avoid looking down on patients** who utilize wheelchairs either figuratively or literally. Be seated for face-to-face encounters that allow you to make direct eye contact with them.
4. **Listen attentively when you are talking to people who have difficulty speaking.** Be patient! Do not interrupt them, correct them, or speak for them. Do not pretend to understand. Repeat what you understand and allow them to elaborate.

(continued)

IMPORTANT POINTS

(continued)

5. **Avoid leaning or hanging onto a person's wheelchair.** The chair is part of their personal space.
6. **Avoid negative language,** for example, use of words like *afflicted, handicapped, stricken, deaf and dumb, retarded, victim, confined to wheelchair, unfortunate,* and so on. Refer to a person with a disability as a person first who has a particular disability.
7. **Remember that issues of sexuality are important.** Although these issues are frequently ignored by the nurse and other health professionals, they are often of great concern for young and older persons experiencing new onset or permanent disabilities (Vacc & Clifford, 1995).
8. **Seek appropriate resources** to assist in addressing the patient's concerns.
9. **Consider issues of mobility from the patient's perspective** to ensure that patients are permitted to move freely and to have the most autonomy that the clinical situation permits. This may require collaboration with the physical or occupational therapy staff.
10. **Be flexible** in allowing adequate time for the patient to perform ADLs at a pace that is appropriate, given the nature of the disability.
11. **Provide privacy and assistance** with physical or body requirements such as catheterizations, toileting, or wound care according to the patient's specific needs.
12. **Teach the patient with disabilities new skills** to assist them in adapting to their environment.
13. **Utilize available resources** (see References) to address home care needs of patients with disabilities when planning for the patients' discharge. For example, the Individuals with Disabilities Education Act (IDEA) provides transitional services for children 16 years or younger, such as transportation, rehabilitation counseling, social work assistance, and other services.

but as individuals with a disability who, like everyone else, can benefit by understanding and receiving tactful help in meeting problems.

A more complete list of do's and don'ts when communicating with people with disabilities can be found at People First Language www.disabilityis-natural.com.

Vacc and Clifford (1995) identified direct services and advocacy measures that helping professionals can provide to individuals with disabilities. Those direct services relevant to nurses in acute care or rehabilitation settings include: providing career, personal, and social counseling; assisting individuals in participating in social activities; assisting individuals in making transitions from one setting to another; identifying needs of family members; and evaluating the efficacy of treatment programs for persons with disabilities; sensitizing other staff members to practices and materials that may be prejudicial to individuals with disabilities; informing family members of mandates and regulations concerning the rights and opportunities of individuals with disabilities; assisting individuals in seeking resources; cooperating with significant others to develop and review or revise nursing plans of care; and conducting or attending in-service programs and workshops that address issues of caring for patients with disabilities are other ways to ensure culturally competent care to persons with disabilities.

In short, nurses caring for patients with disabilities, must have an awareness of their own attitudes, values, and beliefs, have cultural knowledge about patients for whom they care, be skilled at optimizing each nurse patient encounter, and most importantly, be highly motivated to provide care that is congruent with what the patient needs and desires.

NCLEX-TYPE QUESTIONS

1. When planning care for persons with disabilities, the nurse recognizes that according to the Americans with Disabilities Act, a disability is defined as:
   A. A person's physical, mental, or emotional functioning problems that alter an individual's ability to participate and be integrated into the social world.
   B. A physical limitation or bodily impairment that disallows freedom of mobility.
   C. An emotional or psychological illness that interferes with learning.
   D. A psychological impairment that hinders a person's normal development.

2. According to the Department of Health and Human Services, what percent of the U.S. population has some basic movement, sensory, cognitive, or emotional difficulties?
   A. 10%
   B. 15%
   C. 30%
   D. 40%

3. When caring for a patient who is newly diagnosed with a disability, the nurse's best response is to:
   A. Minimize the patient's involvement in care to avoid embarrassing situations.
   B. Encourage the patient's participation as much as they are able.
   C. Encourage the family to assist the nurse in providing care.
   D. Seek an additional staff person to provide one-on-one supervision in the nurse's absence when possible.

4. The nurse is caring for a person who is confined to a wheelchair who questions why able-bodied people are sometimes so insensitive to the needs of persons with disabilities. The nurse explains that according to some researchers:
   A. Most able-bodied persons have had little prior exposure to persons with disabilities and are unaware of the problems they face in society.

B. Persons who are insensitive are those who usually lack social skills or compassion.
C. Most able-bodied persons try hard to demonstrate compassion when meeting persons with disabilities.
D. Persons who have disabilities are often given considerations that able-bodied persons are denied.

5. For nurses caring for persons who have disabilities, it is important to remember that issues of sexuality:
    A. Have little or no significance after diagnosis of a physical disability.
    B. Are of great concern to persons with disabilities, but are often ignored by the nurse.
    C. Are meaningless when learning or cognitive disabilities exist.
    D. Only affect persons who are able-bodied.

6. The nurse considers the care needs of a person who is confined to a wheelchair. When planning care, the nurse recognizes that the best approach is to (select all that apply):
    A. Plan activities that will maintain the patient's immobility and limit the patient's safety risks.
    B. Encourage the patient to move freely and to have the most autonomy that their clinical situation allows.
    C. Encourage activities that force the patient to develop stronger motor skills.
    D. Sit facing the patient to maintain eye-to-eye contact.

7. The nurse is teaching a community class about the incidence of disabilities in the United States. According to the World Health Organization, what factors account for the increasing number of persons with disabilities in the United States?
    A. Ageing
    B. The emergence of chronic diseases
    C. Injuries caused by road crashes
    D. HIV/AIDS
    E. All of these

8. Two organizations that primarily provide support for persons with intellectual and developmental disabilities are:
    A. ADA and ICN
    B. WHO and ADA
    C. The Arc and LDA
    D. NIH and WHO

9. The nurse caring for persons with disabilities recognizes that the concept of people first refers to the belief that:
    A. All persons with disabilities have strengths, abilities, and inherent value and are equal in the law.
    B. Persons with disabilities should be given first priority in clinical settings.
    C. Persons with disabilities must first overcome them before actively participating in society.
    D. Persons with disabilities should be first to receive health care benefits.

10. What situation describes the problem of disability disparities among persons with disabilities?
    A. Low-income, working-age adults with physical disabilities experience problems with transportation accessibility and privacy barriers.
    B. A person is born with a learning disability.
    C. Children who have cerebral palsy experience problems with mobility.
    D. There is a high percentage of physically disabled among the young.

11. The nurse is interviewing a patient with a disability who has a problem speaking clearly. The patient is struggling to explain a situation. The best initial action by the nurse is to:
    A. Correct the patient's mispronunciations and unclear statements.
    B. Listen patiently without interrupting, then question to clarify.
    C. Speak directly to a family member instead who is able to interpret the patient's meaning.
    D. Pretend to follow the conversation to minimize the patient's embarrassment.

12. The culturally competent nurse recognizes that the use of certain language can be demoralizing to persons with disabilities. Which of these statements suggest that the nurse is using culturally appropriate language when caring for clients with disabilities?
    A. The nurse giving a report at change of shift mentions that the patient is afflicted with mobility problems and has recently been stricken with multiple sclerosis (MS).
    B. The ER triage nurse explains that, "since you are handicapped, I'll place you in a larger cubicle for your assessment."
    C. The nurse explains to the doctor, "I believe this young lady may have a hearing impairment."
    D. A nurse exclaims, "I was just assigned to a mentally retarded patient."

13. The nurse is caring for a patient who is paralyzed from the waist down due to a gunshot wound of the spine. In an effort to encourage the patient's participation in his care the nurse offers the patient a basin with hot soapy water. On the nurse's return a half hour later, the patient is still washing himself. The best initial response by the nurse is to:
    A. Take over for the patient and complete the bath.
    B. Ask if he needs any assistance or wants the nurse to return later.
    C. Take the wash basin away as this is taking too long.
    D. Ask a nursing assistant to work with the patient to complete his bath.

14. When admitting a 73-year-old patient with dementia to his unit, what approach by the nurse is most appropriate?
    A. Calling the patient by her first name to establish an informal and relaxed rapport with her.
    B. Asking the patient by which name she wishes to be called.
    C. Stating her own name, but referring to the patient as "sweetie."
    D. Avoiding the use of names in relating to the patient.

AACN COMPETENCIES ADDRESSED IN THIS CHAPTER

1. Apply knowledge of social and cultural factors that affect nursing and health care across multiple contexts.
3. Promote achievement of safe and quality outcomes of care for diverse populations.
5. Participate in continuous cultural competence development.

REFERENCES

Altman, B., & Bernstein, A. (2008). *Disability and health in the United States, 2001–2005.* Hyattsville, MD: United States Department of Health and Human Services.

American Disability Association. (2009). Statistics. Retrieved from www.adanet.org

Au, K. W., & Man, D. W. K. (2006). Attitudes toward people with disabilities: A comparison between health care professionals and students. *International Journal of Rehabilitation Research, 29*(2), 155–160. Retrieved from www.cinahl.com/cgi-bin/refsvc?

Baker, M. (2009). Providing care for adults with complex neurological disabilities. *British Journal of Nursing, 18*(7), 1050–1054.

Bowen, M. E., & Gonzalez, H. M. (2008). Care quality and treatment differences may Underlie greater functional disability among older blacks and Latinos: The health and retirement study. *Gerontologist 48*(5), 659–667. Retrieved from www.ahrq.gov/research/feb09/0209RA2.htm

CDC (2011). *Disability and Health Data and Statistics.* Retrieved from www.cdc.gov/ncbddd/disabilityandhealth/data.html

Chevarley, F.M., Thierry, J. M., Gill, C. J. (2006). Women with disabilities report poorer health and more problems accessing health care than other women. *Women's Health Issues 16,* 297–312. Retrieved from http://www.ahrq.gov/research/may07/0507RA16.htm

Ho, P. S., Kroll, T., & Kehn, M. (2007). Health and housing among low-income adults with physical disabilities. *Journal of Health Care for the Poor and Underserved, 18*(4), 902–915. Retrieved from www.ahrq.gov/research/aug08/0808RA26htm

International Council of Nurses. (2000). Position statement prevention of disability and care of people with disabilities. Retrieved from http://www.icn.ch/psdisability00.htm

Jenkins, R. (2009). Nurses's views about services for older people with learning disabilities. *Nursing Older People, 21*(3), 23–27. Retrieved from http://webscohost.com/ehost/delivery?vid=36&hid=107&sid

Laino, E. (2007). Does a mentally disabled person bewilder a nurse? *Sairaanhoita, 80*(2). Retrieved from www.cinahl.com/cgi-bin/refsvc?

Lehman, C. A. (2009). APN knowledge, self efficacy, and practices in providing women's services with women with disabilities. *Rehabilitation Nursing: The Official Journal of the Association of Rehabilitation Nurses, 34*(5), 186–194.

Like, R. (2000). TRANSLATE: For Working With Medical Interpreters. *Patient Care, 34*(9), 188–190.

Like, R. C., Steiner, R. P., Rubel, J. (2009). Recommended core curriculum guidelines on culturally sensitive and competent health care. Retrieved from www.stfm.org/group/minority/guidelines.cfm

Lewis, A. (2009). Disability disparities a beginning model. *Disability and Rehabilitation, 31*(14), 1136–1143. Retrieved from www.cinahl.com/cgi-bin/refsvc?jid=609&accno=2010337148

Lewis, A., Wilson, K., Imparato, A., & Rumril, P. (2009). *Project empowerment: Improving minority disability research capacity: Disability disparities* [Webcast]. Richmond, VA: Virginia Commonwealth University. Retrieved from www.vcu-projectempowerment.org/training/viewWebcast.cfm/151

Leyson, S., & Clark, L. L. (2005). Legal and ethical issues in seeking consent of adults with learning disability. *British Journal of Neuroscience Nursing 1*(3), 126–131. Retrieved from www.cinahl.com/cgi-bin/refsvcjid=2989&accno=2009073470

Manners, P. J.(2006). Working reflexively in learning disabilities: What Emma taught us. *Journal Compilation, 34*, 211–214. doi:10.1111/j.1468-3156.2006.00391.x

Matziou, V., Galanis, P., Tsoumakas, C., Gymnopoulou, E., Perdikaris, P., Brokalaki, H. (2009). Attitudes of nursing professionals and nursing students toward children with disabilities: Do nurses really overcome children's physical and mental handicaps? *International Nursing Review, 56*(4), 456–460.

Melville, C. A., Finlayson, J., Cooper, S., Allan, L., Robinson, N., Burns, E., Martin. G., & Morrison, J. (2005). Enhancing primary health care services for adults with intellectual disabilities. *Journal of Intellectual Disability Research, 49*(3), 190–198. doi:10.1111/j.1365-2788.2005.00640.x

National Center for Health Statistics. (2008). *Disability and Health in the United States 2001–2005: Sociodemographic characteristics of the population with disabilities.* Retrieved from www.cdc.gov/nchs/data/misc/disability2001-2005.pdf

New York State Department of Health. (2009). *People first language: Communicating with and about people with disabilities.* Retrieved from http://www.nyhealth.gov/puplications/0951

Pollard, R. Q., & Barnett, S. (2009). Health related vocabulary knowledge among deaf adults. *Rehabilitation Psychology, 54*(2), 182–185. Retrieved from http://www.ahrq.gov/research/dec09/1209RA11.htm

Purnell, L., & Paulanka, B. J. (2005). *Transcultural health care: A culturally competent approach.* Philadelphia, PA: F.A. Davis.

Seccombe, J. A. (2007). Attitudes towards disability in an undergraduate nursing curriculum: A literature review. *Nurse Education Today, 27*(5), 459–465.

Slevin, E., MCConkey, R., Truesdale-Kennedy, M., & Taggart, L. (2008). People with learning disabilities admitted to an assessment and treatment unit: impact on challenging behaviours and mental health problems. *Journal of Psychiatric and Mental Health Nursing, 15*, 537–546.

Snow, K. (2008). *People first language.* Retrieved from www.disabilityisnatural.com

Thompson, T. L. C., Emrich, K., & Moore, G. (2003). The effect of curriculum on the attitudes of nursing students toward disability. *Rehabilitation Nursing, 28*(1), 27–30.

ten Klooster, P. M., Dannenberg, J., Taal, E., Burger, G., & Rasker, J. J. (2009). Attitudes towards people with physical or intellectual disabilities: Nursing students and non-nursing peers. *Journal of Advanced Nursing, 65*(12), 2562–2573.

United States Department of Labor. Office of Disability Employment Policy (ODEP). (2002).*Communicating with and about people with disabilities.* Retrieved from www.dol.gov/odep/pubs/fact/comucate.htm

Vacc, N., & Clifford, K. (1995). Individuals with physical disability. In N. Vacc, S. B. Devaney, & J. Wittmer (Eds.), *Experiencing and counseling multicultural population* (pp. 251–271). Bristol, PA: Accelerated Development.
World Health Organization. (2009) *New HIV recommendations to improve health, reduce infection, and save lives.* Retrieved from www.who.int/mediacentre/news/releases/2009/world_aids_20091130/en/index.html

IMPORTANT WEBSITES

American Disability Association
http://www.ada.gov/publicat.htm
American Association of People with Disabilities
http://www.aapd.com/Membership/benefits.html
The Arc
http://www.thearc.org/NetCommunity/Page.aspx?pid=1910
Disabilities and Health in the United States 2001–2005
http://www.cdc.gov/nchs/data/misc/disability2001–2005.pdf
http://www.cdc.gov/nchs/data/misc/disability2001–2005.pdf
Project Empowerment: Improving Minority Disability
http://www.vcu-projectempowerment.org/training/viewWebcast.cfm/151
Valuing People Now (UK)
http://www.dh.gov.uk/en/SocialCare/Deliveringadultsocialcare/Learningdisabilities/index.htm
http://www.dh.gov.uk/dr_consum_dh/groups/dh_digitalassets/documents/digitalasset/dh_093375.pdf

Cultural Considerations When the Patient Speaks a Different Language

GLORIA KERSEY-MATUSIAK

The language of the lips is easily taught, but who can teach the language of the heart.

—MAHATMA GHANDI

LEARNING OBJECTIVES

1. Describe the impact of language barriers on patients' access to quality health care.
2. Recognize the various types of language diversity and their impact on nurse–patient interactions.
3. Explain some myths related to language diversity.
4. Discuss the influence of linguistic style and nonverbal communication on nurse–patient communication.
5. Develop strategies for overcoming language barriers when working with culturally diverse groups.

KEY TERMS

CLAS standards
Language barrier
Linguistic style
Literacy
Nonverbal communication

UNDERSTANDING THE NEED FOR CULTURALLY LINGUISTIC CARE

America continues to be viewed as a haven for people around the globe seeking to improve their living and socioeconomic conditions. According to the Federation for American Immigration Reform (FAIR), a Washington, DC–based advocacy group, about 20% of immigrants come from Mexico, and 5% to 7% come from India, China, and the Philippines. Lesser numbers come from Vietnam, El Salvador, Cuba, Haiti, Bosnia, Canada, the Dominican Republic, Ukraine, Korea, Russia, and Nicaragua (FAIR, 2009). As a result, the 2010 United States Census reported that 20.6% of the population speaks a language other than English in the home. As the diversity of the United States increases, so does the variety of languages that nurses and other health care providers encounter in their day-to-day communications with patients. According to the 2010 Census, more than 36 million American speakers of a foreign language speak Spanish. The second largest group of speakers of a foreign language in the United States speaks Chinese. Additionally, a variety of other Asian languages are also listed among the top 10 languages spoken in homes across the country. These include Tagalog, the language of the Philippines, Vietnamese, and Korean. Additionally, the number of people who speak Chinese, Vietnamese, Russian, Arabic, or French Creole is rapidly increasing.

In a self-report of people speaking a language other than English in the home, of more than 48 million speakers of a second language, more than 21 million reported having some degree of difficulty speaking English. Of these, many are children or teenagers (U.S. Census, 2010). Given these facts, as nurses increasingly interact with culturally diverse patients, they can be certain to encounter **language barriers** at some point during their careers. Communicating effectively with patients requires nurses to be able to listen, observe, and understand the beliefs and needs of their patients and to use culturally relevant concepts when communicating with them (Flaskerud, 2007).

The National Standards for Culturally and Linguistically Appropriate Services in Health Care (**CLAS standards**) have challenged nurses and health care institutions to provide services that address the linguistic needs of patients (U.S. DHHS, 2007). More specifically, in Standard 4 of this document health care agencies are mandated to "provide to patients/consumers in their preferred language both verbal offers and written notices informing them of their right to receive language services. Language enables us to establish a rapport with our patients, communicate our ideas, and negotiate our plan of care. It is the primary way nurses communicate caring"(Stinson, 2009).

Obviously, when the patient and the nurse speak different languages, or have only minimal understanding of one another's primary language, this greatly inhibits the establishment of a culturally sensitive and ethically appropriate nurse–patient relationship (Bartlett, Blais, Tamblyn, Clermont, & MacGibbon, 2008; Meddings & Haith-Cooper, 2008). The literature tells us that "linguistic barriers between nurses and patients can threaten quality nursing care by perpetuating stereotypes and fostering the delivery of care based on misinformation and assumptions" (Carnevale, Vissandjee, Nyland, & Vinet-Bonin, 2009; Collins, Gullette, & Schnepf, 2005; Squires, 2008; Thon, 2008; Wu, 2009).

Moreover, in a research study that examined ethical norms for cross-linguistic nursing, five principal ethical norms were identified, including: (1) "respect for the patient as a unique person; (2) respect for the patient's right to self determination; respect for patient privacy and confidentiality; respect for one's own competence, judgment and action; and responsibility to promote action better to meet the needs of patients, families, and groups" (Carnevale, Vissandjee, Nyland, &Vinet-Bonin, 2009, p. 813). These authors found the problems of linguistic barriers to be more problematic for nurses than physicians. However, the process of strengthening communication between members of culturally diverse groups entails far more than the nurse and the patient having an understanding of one another's spoken language.

LANGUAGE DIVERSITY

Sometimes problems in communication are encountered when patients have some knowledge of English, but lack the confidence in their ability to speak it with native speakers. Because lacking English speaking skills is often stigmatized in America, foreign speakers of English sometimes fear ridicule or negative judgments about their intelligence. Besides being able to manage the English as a second language issue, nurses must also learn to bridge the communication gap that is created by differences in patients' **linguistic style**, dialect, **literacy**, and **nonverbal communication** patterns. For each of these aspects, communication can significantly influence cross-cultural interactions between the patient and the nurse.

Another important nursing consideration during cross-linguistic communication is the cultural context in which the language is spoken. When speaking in their language, some cultural groups rely on the use of many words to convey a particular message. Such groups are considered "low context." The English, German, and French fall under this category. High-context languages use fewer words and meaning is found between the lines as more attention is paid to the nonverbal or cultural cues transmitted through body language. High-context languages include Native American languages and Chinese (Giger, 2008; Purnell & Paulanka, 2009).

Linguistic style refers to the way in which words are used to send messages. This includes tone of voice, rate of speed, and degree of loudness. It also reflects the speaker's vocabulary pace, pitch, and intonation choices. It also relates to an individual's tendency to be direct or indirect when communicating (PBS, 2005). Linguistic style is influenced by a variety of cultural factors such as ethnic background, geographical origin, and gender. It is useful for nurses to recognize that linguistic style and dialect variations are reflections of a cultural group's shared patterns of communicating, usually due to geographical norms. Consider a speaker who comes from Rhode Island and another from the rural south. One way of speaking is not superior to another, nor is linguistic style an indication of one's intelligence or ability. However, language-related conflicts occur due to feelings and attitudes of fear and mistrust of "otherness" as reflected by a difference in one's style of communicating. These attitudes emerge from long-held assumptions about differences that may be inaccurate.

There are also variations in patients' levels of literacy, or their ability to read and write the spoken word whether it be in English or in the patient's native language. The term *health literacy* refers to the ability of patients to understand their health information (Patient Education Management, 2007). Therefore, the nurse cannot assume that patients understand medical forms or documents even when distributed in the patient's language. Just as in America, some persons who speak their own language at a conversational level of fluency are unable to read it, so nurses must assess reading capacity of patients from both English-speaking and linguistically diverse backgrounds. To members of some cultural groups, nonverbal communication is even more important than the spoken word. Often by our gestures, facial expressions, eye contact, stance, or hand movements, we communicate to others messages we do not intend. When communicating cross-culturally it is especially important for nurses to pay attention to differences in patterns of nonverbal communication between themselves and the patient. When differences in linguistic style and nonverbal behavior coexist with the inability to share a common language, either the patient and/or the nurse may become frustrated and abandon efforts to communicate at all. This is evidenced by the tendency by some nurses to avoid the patient's room who may have a different way of communicating that is offensive or intimidating to the nurse. An attitude of unwillingness to seek new ways to overcome language barriers is the greatest barrier of all. Failure of the nurse to communicate effectively with patients can lead to serious consequences for the patient (Aboul-Enin & Ahmed, 2006; Bartlett, Blais, Tamblyn, Clermont, & MacGibbon, 2008). Specifically, barriers to communication can adversely affect patients' access to health care, ability to give informed consent, medical and nursing diagnosis, health education, and health care outcomes (Garcia & Duckett, 2009). To overcome the barriers created by differences in language and communication style between the patient and the nurse, nurses must first be aware of their own patterns and styles of communication. By acknowledging differences that exist between themselves and their patients and the potential problems these differences create, they are able to identify appropriate strategies to overcome them.

Myths About Language Diversity

Two myths about language diversity may influence nurses' judgment about linguistically diverse patients. First, some believe that emphasizing the importance of Americans gaining knowledge of a second language other than English may minimize the importance of English as the primary language of the United States. The fact is, America is a multilingual nation with 20% of its population speaking at least one other language besides English (Census, 2010). Yet, English remains the dominant language. Second, there are those who believe that minority members, especially recent immigrants, are not eager to learn English. However, experience in local communities tells us that there are many programs throughout the country that provide English-learning programs. These programs are highly sought out and attended by recent and older immigrants who seek to prepare themselves for living and working in the United States (Vårheim, 2011).

STRATEGIES TO ADDRESS LINGUISTIC BARRIERS

When the nurse identifies language barriers it is best to determine the patient's primary language and his or her ability to read and write it. It is also helpful to know the extent to which English is spoken and/or understood. When the nurse communicates with patients who speak English as a second language there are three important strategies the nurse can use. First, the nurse must listen *actively* while paying particular attention to the patient's use of silence throughout the conversation. Listening actively means asking for clarification when the patient uses unfamiliar terms or the nurse is unclear about the patient's use of English terms. The nurse should also seek to clarify nonverbal communication to avoid misinterpretation. Third, regardless of the type of language barrier, the nurse should remember to strive to convey patience and caring through nonverbal measures. These actions by the nurse include moving about in a nonhurried manner, facing the patient when communicating, touching when culturally acceptable, and smiling. In this way the nurse acknowledges an appreciation of how stressful cross-cultural interactions may be for the patient. This approach also signals to patients the nurse's desire to minimize their anxiety and ultimately bridge the cultural gap that exists in these situations.

Additionally, Stinson (2009) discussed the pros and cons of a variety of methods that health care facilities can utilize to provide language access to patients. These strategies include "having a bilingual clinical staff, telephone interpreting services, translators and translation software for written materials, language classes for staff, video medical interpreting services, and on-site medical interpreters" (p. 21). These authors encourage hospitals to choose the services most suitable for their institution.

Using an Interpreter

Many texts outline the best approach when utilizing an interpreter (Andrews & Boyle, 2008; Purnell & Paulanka, 2009). When a nurse recognizes that the patient is unable to speak English, the nurse should attempt to recruit someone who can address the patient in his or her native language. In an effort to maintain patients' privacy and confidentiality, family members should be avoided as interpreters or translators when possible. Ideally, a person selected to assist the nurse in interpreting and providing patient care education should be a trained medical interpreter who is not only fluent in the language but able to understand the nuances of the culture. This individual should be knowledgeable of medical terminology and procedures as well as patients' rights in a clinical setting. Preferably age and gender are considered when sensitive or personal issues related to sexuality are being discussed. Understandably, in urgent situations where a trained interpreter is not available, nurses must rely on other individuals such as age-appropriate family members.

Purnell and Paulanka (2009) advise nurses to utilize an interpreter to interpret the meaning of the patient's words rather than a translator to just translate them. These authors also warn that differences in social class between the patient and the interpreter may result in interpreters withholding information from the nurse that they deem insignificant. The nurse should plan adequate time for an unhurried session that includes both translation and interpretation. During the exchange, the communication should focus on the patient. The nurse should maintain eye contact, direct questions to the patient, avoid using medical jargon or idiomatic expressions, and observe the patient for nonverbal cues. Using phrase books or picture cards will enhance the patient's understanding. At the end of the session the nurse reviews and summarizes ideas and the patient's responses (Purnell & Paulanka, 2009).

A general guide for working with and without an interpreter is included in the important points at the end of this section. Other resources include telephone interpreting services, phrase books and the use of flash cards that illustrate the meaning of selected basic words to enhance clinical communication, translated written materials, and communication boards. Another useful tool discussed by Robertson (2006) was a form developed to promote understanding of non–English-speaking patients' needs related to pain control and basic needs. A 15-item questionnaire with both the foreign and English translation allowed patients to circle yes and no responses indicating their needs.

IMPORTANT POINTS

- Twenty percent of the U.S. population speaks a language other than English as a primary language.
- CLAS standards are national guidelines and mandates that compel hospitals and health care providers to provide culturally linguistic care.
- Language diversity includes ESL issues as well as linguistic style, dialect, literacy, and nonverbal communication patterns.
- Literacy refers to the ability to read and write.
- Linguistic style refers to the way in which words are exchanged. This includes tone of voice, rate of speed, and degree of loudness.
- Linguistic style does not reflect an individual's intelligence or ability.
- Language barriers can adversely affect patients' access to health care, ability to give informed consent, medical and nursing diagnosis, health education, and health care outcomes.

(continued)

IMPORTANT POINTS

(continued)

- Some myths about language diversity influence nurses' attitudes about caring for linguistically diverse patients.
- The person selected to assist the nurse by translating and interpreting for the patient should ideally be a trained medical interpreter.
- Using family members, especially children may violate patients' confidentiality and privacy rights.
- Strategies for caring for linguistically diverse patients includes actively listening, seeking clarification, using an appropriate interpreter and paying attention to nonverbal communication.
- It is important to document the session and its outcome with the interpreter (Smith, 2007).
- Working with an interpreter (adapted from Andrews & Boyle, 2008, *Transcultural Concepts in Nursing*):
  - Meet with the interpreter beforehand to describe the nature of the translation meeting with the patient.
  - Plan to utilize more time for the session with the patient and interpreter.
  - The conversation should always be focused on the patient.
  - Speak only a sentence or two before allowing the interpreter to translate.
  - Use simple language; avoid medical jargon.
  - Be attentive to nonverbal clues by the patient.
  - Be polite and formal.
  - Greet the patient using their last name; offer a handshake or nod. Smile.
  - Speak in a low moderate voice.
  - Attempt to use any words you know in the patient's language.
  - Use simple words.
  - Pantomime words and simple actions while verbalizing them.
  - Validate the patient's understanding.
  - Obtain phrase books from a library or bookstore.

CASE SCENARIO

Anna Garcia is a 67-year-old woman who is visiting her daughter from Puerto Rico. She suddenly experiences an episode of severe chest pain. Her daughter Rita, who recently delivered a healthy 8-pound newborn, calls for an ambulance, but is unable to accompany her mother to the hospital. Although Rita speaks English fluently, Anna Garcia speaks only Spanish and can understand only a little English. Anna is rushed to the nearest hospital where the staff struggles to communicate with her as best they can. In the emergency room Anna holds her hand over her chest and grimaces as the pain seems to grow more severe.

One of the ER nurses grabs Mr. Rodriquez, a member of environmental services, and asks him to assist by translating for the nurses and doctors caring for Mrs. Garcia, because it is 8 a.m. and the only Spanish-speaking medical interpreter, Mr. Sanchez, is not due in this morning until 10 a.m. Based on the EKG findings and first lab results, the staff believes that Mrs. Garcia is experiencing an MI. They ask that Mr. Rodriquez explain to her that they are awaiting the results of other laboratory studies to confirm the medical diagnosis, but believe that she probably had a heart attack and will need further testing to confirm the medical staff's suspicion. Mrs. Garcia becomes extremely anxious and begins to cry. The staff is baffled about what to do next.

WHAT NURSES NEED TO KNOW ABOUT THEMSELVES

APPLICATION OF THE STAIRCASE MODEL: SELF-REFLECTION QUESTIONS

1. Where are you on the Cultural Competency Staircase regarding this patient's language and culture? How will you progress to the next level? (review Chapter 1 and the Staircase Model)
2. What knowledge do you need to have about this patient, including cultural/language needs, to provide this patient with culturally sensitive care?
3. What would you personally do to address the needs of this patient?
4. What resources do you need and how would you obtain them?
5. What cultural assessment model would you plan to use to assess this patient?

Responses to Self-Reflection Questions

Response to Where are you on the Cultural Competency Staircase

Finding your place on the Cultural Competency Staircase enables you to determine your readiness for caring for this patient. Wherever you find yourself, it is important to think of ways to progress up the staircase. Is it knowledge of the culture you lack, or the ability to communicate in the language? In this chapter, we examined strategies for communicating with individuals who speak languages other than English. Which of these strategies can you apply here? Do you need an interpreter?

Response to What knowledge do I need to provide culturally sensitive care?

A good question to ask yourself in this situation is, what do I know about the specific Hispanic culture represented in this case scenario? Although many texts offer information generally about Latinos/Hispanics, you really want to identify relevant information about Puerto Ricans. Texts by Andrews and Boyle, Purnell, and Paulanka (2009), and Spector (2009) provide specific information about this cultural group. For example, Spector reminds us that there is diversity among members of this group. For example, many Puerto Ricans are Catholic, but there are also many Protestants among the group. Puerto Ricans vary in their level of education and socioeconomic status. Some are highly educated, while some others may be illiterate both in English and in Spanish. Through the patient, her family, and an interpreter you can gain insight into the patient's cultural attitudes and beliefs, dietary preferences, spirituality needs, and health beliefs.

Response to What would you personally do to address the needs of this patient?

Because of the emergent medical problem, it is important for the nurse to have some general medical information about this patient immediately. Calling the family and attempting to speak with someone who can give information about the onset of Mrs. Garcia's symptoms and precipitating factors is important. We know that Mrs. Garcia's daughter is an adult and is able to speak English. Whether you are able to speak Spanish or not, there are some verbal and nonverbal ways to communicate with this patient. Emphasis should be placed on reducing this patient's anxiety through the nurse's verbal and nonverbal communication of support. Using phrase cards or other visual devices that enables the nurse to communicate caring to the patient is important.

Response to What resources do you need and how would you obtain them?

If the daughter is available, she may be an age-appropriate alternative when the interpreter is not available. Because the patient is experiencing a medical crisis, it is critical to contact either the daughter or the interpreter at home to provide this service for the patient. The environmental services person is of least effectiveness in this situation, because of the medical knowledge limitations and potential for breaching the patient's confidentiality and privacy rights.

WHAT NURSES NEED TO KNOW ABOUT THE PATIENT

Selecting a Cultural Assessment Model

It is important to select a model that can be quickly applied in this situation. The LEARN Model is one of several that seems appropriate here. Remember, the acronym stands for *listen, explain, acknowledge, recommend, negotiate.*

The nurses then *listen* with sympathetic ears to the patient and the interpreter and then *explain* their perceptions of what the patient is saying, in this case through an interpreter, while always facing and addressing the patient. This process is also referred to as reflective or active listening. During interviews with Mrs. Garcia, the nurse restates and/or clarifies information always responding with acceptance and empathy to what Mrs. Garcia says. See Chapter 2 for the discussion on the LEARN Model and more information about active listening at www.analytictech.com/mb119/reflecti.htm. The nurses in this case should attempt to identify differences and similarities in perceptions between the patient and her family and the medical staff, as they *recommend* appropriate treatment. After the nurse and the other health care providers finally *negotiate* the treatment plan with the patient, they should offer her clinical options based on the patient's values and goals for care.

NCLEX-TYPE QUESTIONS

1. The culturally competent nurse recognizes that the consequences of misunderstandings between the nurse and linguistically diverse patients are most likely to result in (select all that apply):
   A. Misdiagnosis
   B. Suboptimal pain management
   C. Reduction in the cost of care
   D. Poor patient satisfaction
   E. Enhanced treatment of chronic care

2. When delivering cross-linguistic nursing (CLN), to ensure evidence-based practice, the nurse reviews the literature on cultural competency and finds which statement below is accurate about language differences between nurses and their patients? Language differences between patients and nurses often:
   A. Perpetuate discrimination and compromise care
   B. Impact doctors and nurses equally
   C. Impact doctors more than nurses
   D. Enhance nurse–patient interactions

3. When the nurse uses informal or ad hoc translators such as family members or untrained hospital staff, it potentially (select all that apply):
   A. Breaches patient's confidentiality
   B. Ensures compliance with the Office of Minority Health
   C. Meets ethical standards
   D. Is intrusive of patients' privacy rights

4. The nurse admits Mr. Smith, a member of the Cherokee Tribe to the unit. When preparing to conduct the initial nursing interview and assessment, the nurse considers that Mr. Smith's cultural heritage suggests that his language is most likely to be:
   A. Low-context
   B. High-context
   C. Nonverbal
   D. Mid-context

5. The nurse complains to his charge nurse that one of his patients is threatening and intimidating because of his loud and forceful tone of voice. The culturally competent charge nurse recognizes that this behavior most likely reflects this patient's:
   A. Cultural beliefs
   B. Linguistic style
   C. Language context
   D. Cultural language

6. When the nurse plans cross-linguistic care for her newly admitted patient, she is most concerned by patient behaviors that suggest differences in:
   A. Linguistic style
   B. Language context
   C. Literacy
   D. Cultural attitudes

7. When language diversity is first suspected, the initial response by the nurse should be to:
   A. Provide an interpreter.
   B. Notify the physician of this concern.
   C. Determine the patient's primary language and his or her ability to speak and read it.
   D. Conduct a full cultural assessment.

8. A female patient who is unable to speak English is discovered by the nurse crying alone in her room. What *initial* action by the nurse is most appropriate?
   A. The nurse goes to contact the family before entering the room.
   B. The nurse approaches the patient smiling and offers the patient tissues.
   C. The nurse contacts an interpreter.
   D. The nurse speaks in English and tells the patient that everything will be all right.

9. The nurses on a medical-surgical unit are offered an opportunity to take a night course in Spanish for health care personnel. One nurse refuses to take the course because she believes that this action by the nurses would discourage Spanish-speaking patients to appreciate the importance of learning and speaking English. This way of thinking is based on:
   A. Myths about language diversity
   B. Evidence-based practice
   C. Cultural sensitivity
   D. Linguistic diversity

10. The interpreter arrives on the unit to see Mr. Nam, a Vietnamese patient. The nurse's initial action before beginning the interpreting session is to:
    A. Discuss the clinical situation and goals of the interview with the interpreter.
    B. Introduce the patient and interpreter.
    C. Provide a list of questions to ask the patient.
    D. Allow the interpreter an opportunity to determine how the interview should be conducted.

AACN COMPETENCIES ADDRESSED IN THIS CHAPTER

1. Apply knowledge of social and cultural factors that affect nursing and health care across multiple contexts.
2. Use relevant data sources and best evidence in providing culturally competent care.
3. Promote achievement of safe and quality outcomes of care for diverse populations.
4. Advocate for social justice, including commitment to the health of vulnerable populations and the elimination of health care disparities. (Based on application of nursing ethics as it relates to culturally linguistic nursing care.)
5. Participate in continuous cultural competence development.

REFERENCES

Aboul-Enein, F. H., & Ahmed, F. (2006). How Language Barriers Impact Patient Care: A Commentary. *Journal of Cultural Diversity, 13*(3), 168–169.

Andrews, M. M., & Boyle, J. S. (2008). *Transcultural Concepts in Nursing Care* (5th ed.). Philadelphia, PA: Lippincott Williams &Wilkins.

Bartlett, G., Blais, R., Tamblyn, R., Clermont, R. J., & MacGibbon, B. (2008). Impact of patient communication problems on the risk of preventable adverse events in acute care settings. *CMAJ: Canadian Medical Association Journal, 178*(12), 1555–1562. doi:10.1503/cmaj.070690

Bartlett, R., Williams, A., & Lucas, R. (2011). A common language is so basic! *Issues in Mental Health Nursing, 32*(9), 608–609. doi:10.3109/01612840.2011.597539

Carnevale, F. A., Vissandjée, B., Nyland, A., & Vinet-Bonin, A. (2009). Ethical Considerations in Cross-Linguistic Nursing. *Nursing Ethics, 16*(6), 813–826.

Collins, A., Gullette, D., & Schnepf, M. (2004). Break through language barriers. *Nursing Management, 35*(8), 34–38.

Federation for American Immigration Reform. (2009). Immigration facts. Retrieved from www.fairus.org/site/PageNavigator/facts/national_data.html

Flaskerud, J. H. (2007). Cultural competence column: What else is necessary? *Issues in Mental Health Care, 28,* 219–222. doi: 10.108/01612840601096487

Garcia, C. M., & Duckett, L. J. (2009). No te entiendo y tú no me entiendes: Language barriers among immigrant latino adolescents seeking health care. *Journal of Cultural Diversity, 16*(3), 120–126.

Giger, J. & Davidhizar, R. E. (2008). *Transcultural Nursing: Assessment and Intervention* (5th ed.). St. Louis, MO: Mosby Elsevier.

Meddings, F., & Haith-Cooper, M. (2008). Culture and Communication in ethically appropriate care. *Nursing Ethics, 15*(1), 52–61.

Patient Education Management. (2007). Qualified interpreters improve health literacy and patient safety. *Patient Education Management, 14*(7), 73–77.

PBS (2005). *Communicative choices and linguistic style.* Retrieved from www.pbs.org/speak/education/curriculum/high/style/#ncte

Purnell, L. D., & Paulanka, B. J. (2009). *Guide to culturally competent health care* (2nd ed.). Philadelphia, PA: F.A. Davis Company.

Robertson, S. (2006). The use of a tool to assess symptoms in non-English speaking patients. *Oncology Nursing Forum, 33*(2), 415.

Singleton, K., & Krause, E. S. (2009). Understanding cultural and linguistic barriers to health literacy. *Online Journal of Issues In Nursing, 14*(3), 2.

Smith, L. S. (2007). Documenting use of an interpreter. *Nursing, 37*(7), 25.

Spector, R. (2009) *Cultural diversity in health and illness* (7th ed.). Upper Saddle, NJ: Pearson, Prentice Hall

Squires, A. A. (2008). Language barriers and qualitative nursing research: Methodological considerations. *International Nursing Review, 55*(3), 265–273. doi:10.1111/j.1466-7657.2008.00652.x

Stinson, S. (2009) Open to interpretation. *Minority Nurse, Winter,* 20–23.

Thom, N. (2008, October 23). Why do nurses refuse to use interpreter services? *British Journal of Nursing, 17*(19), 1206.

U.S. Census Bureau. (2010). *Census Report 2010.* Retrieved from http://factfinder.census.gov/servlet/STTable?_bm=y&-geo_id=01000US&-qr_

U.S. Department of Health and Human Services. The Office of Minority Health. (2007). Standards on culturally and linguistically appropriate services (CLAS) Retrieved from http://minorityhealth.hhs.gov/templates/browse.aspx?lvl=2&lvlID=15

Vårheim, A. (2011). Gracious space: Library programming strategies towards immigrants as tools in the creation of social capital. *Library & Information Science Research (07408188), 33*(1), 12–18. doi:10.1016/j.lisr.2010.04.005

Wu, M., Kviz, F. J., & Miller, A. (2009). Identifying individual and contextual barriers to seeking mental health services among Korean American immigrant women. *Issues in Mental Health Nursing, 30*(2), 78–85. doi:10.1080/01612840802595204

IMPORTANT WEBSITES

Do You Speak American?
http://www.pbs.org/speak/education/curriculum/college/style/
Guidance and Standards on Language Access Services
www.oig.hhs.gov/oei/reports/oei-05-1000050.pdf
Language Policy and Practice in Health Care: Hablamos Juntos: We Speak together
http://www.hablamosjuntos.org/mtw/default.toolkit.asp:
Practicing Medical Spanish
http://www.practicingspanish.com/
The Exchange—Talking About Language and Health
http://www.health-exchange.net/language.html

7

Cultural Considerations When Caring for the Patient Who Is Terminally Ill

GLORIA KERSEY-MATUSIAK

Let us touch the dying, the poor, the lonely and the unwanted according to the graces we have received and let us not be ashamed or slow to do the humble work.

—MOTHER TERESA

LEARNING OBJECTIVES

1. Examine beliefs about death and dying and its influence on care provision to members of culturally diverse groups.
2. Discuss variations in attitudes regarding advanced directives, life support, disclosure of diagnosis, and the designation of decision makers during terminal illness.
3. Identify variations in beliefs, practices, and traditions during death and dying experiences between culturally diverse groups.
4. Assess the psychological, cultural, spiritual, and/or religious factors influencing the death and dying experience of members of culturally diverse groups.
5. Examine selected cultural practices related to the care of the body and burial after death.
6. Describe the impact of attitudinal barriers impacting the death and dying experience of patients with HIV/AIDS.
7. Analyze the role of the nurse in assisting culturally diverse patients during death, dying, and grieving experiences.

KEY TERMS

Acculturation
Advance directive
Culture
Espirituista
Hospice
Life support
Palliative care
Stigma
Terminal illness

In the United States approximately 13% of the population is older than 65 years of age and the current life expectancy for both genders is 78.2 years (CDC, 2011). The five most common causes of death are heart disease, malignant neoplasms, chronic lower respiratory diseases, strokes, and accidents. About 10% of individuals die from sudden, unexpected events such as an MI or an accident. However, more than 90% of persons who are ill die from an extended life-threatening illness that includes a "relatively short terminal phase" (Vitas, 2002). Of those individuals 75% die in health care facilities; 57% in hospitals, and 17% in long-term care facilities. Yet, when asked where patients prefer to die, "9 out of 10 cite their home as the preferred site of care" (Institute of Medicine [IOM], Committee on Care at the End of Life). At the end of life nurses are the largest and most likely group of professionals to play a critical role in ensuring that the wishes and goal of patients are met.

THE ROLE OF THE NURSE

One of the most challenging roles of the nurse is that of caring for patients who are terminally ill. As the cultural diversity of the U.S. patient population increases, nurses caring for terminally ill patients face the added challenge of providing terminal care that meets their patients' specific cultural needs. As a result, nurses will need to become knowledgeable about the important cultural aspects of care to address during these experiences. Moreover, members of culturally diverse groups will vary in their preferences for aspects of nursing care and place a different emphasis on religion and/or spirituality during the process of death and dying.

In America a tension often exists between the battle to sustain life through technology and the legal right of the patient to refuse treatment or let nature take its course. Shalev (2010) suggests a "patient-centered approach" that goes beyond having advance directives, which direct the patient's treatment during the end of life. Instead, this author recommends more in-depth communication between the health care providers and patients, especially patients and families. During such encounters, doctors relinquish domination over the encounter and focus on the patient's psychosocial needs to promote a deeper understanding of what the patient wishes. Ideally, family members should be included in this exchange; however, confronting the impending death of a loved one may be emotionally challenging for all concerned. To ensure that patients who are dying receive care that enhances, rather than detracts, from their quality of life, both the health care provider's and the patient's views about the care that should be provided must be congruent. What the patient values and how those values are prioritized during this phase of life can be determined through an appropriate cultural assessment by the nurse. That assessment should then be utilized in establishing mutually agreed upon goals among the patient, the nurse, and all members of the health care team to provide care that optimally meets the needs of patients and their families during this significant period in their lives. Nurses can facilitate such encounters by "creating an open, safe, and supportive space in which the conversation can take place" (Shalev, 2010, p. 143). Attentive listening to enable the patient's voice to be heard is a critical element of this process.

The American Nurses Association's (ANA) Position Statement on the registered nurse's role at the end of a patient's life (2010) reminds nurses that, "interaction between the RN and the patient occurs within the context of the values and beliefs of the patient and the nurse" (ANA, 2010). The nurse's own cultural values, attitudes, and beliefs about death and dying often set the tone for assisting patients during this significant period in their lives (Braun, Gordon, & Uziely, 2010). However, the ANA encourages nurses to be "mindful of the patient's cultural and spiritual beliefs and to advocate for them without personal bias." To ensure the delivery of culturally sensitive care to individuals and families, nurses need to have an awareness of their own attitudes and beliefs about **terminal illness** and the process of death and dying. Having this knowledge enables nurses to consider potential differences between their own and their patient's view of appropriate care at the end of life. By focusing on what the patient and their families value, nurses avoid imposing their own cultural attitudes and beliefs during death and dying experiences.

Nurses can begin the process of planning end-of-life care for culturally diverse groups by first expanding their perspective about what **culture** means. In a study that examined dying in hospitals, the researchers warned nurses against limiting the concept of culture to refer only to ethnicity (Chan, Macdonald, & Cohen, 2009). Rather, they urge nurses to consider culture in its broadest sense, to view the patient and the family holistically and in "their total context." This means including gender, age, race, immigration status, social position, sexual orientation, and so on. Additionally, the researchers encouraged nurses to include an examination of the culture of the health care setting as well as that of biomedicine when trying to explore the patient's health care context. Having this expanded view affords nurses an opportunity to consider factors within the health care setting that may influence end-of-life decision making. From this perspective, nurses and doctors examine the entire context in which patients make end-of-life health care choices and gain a better understanding of why these choices are made.

When exploring a particular health care institution's capacity for delivering culturally appropriate end-of-life care, nurses and other health care providers can ask themselves several important questions. For example: Does the institution have available resources and personnel to effectively respond to the needs of culturally diverse terminally ill patients? Are there language or attitudinal barriers that might need to be addressed before the hospital or a particular group of staff members can perform a cultural assessment or provide information to patients in their own language? Are the patients who utilize the hospital services coming from communities of affluence or poverty that may impact their access to care? Regarding biomedicine, are the doctors who are prescribing medicine mindful of some patients' use of herbal medicine or other folk practices that potentially interact with prescribed medications? Are the doctors also aware of variations among some ethnic groups in their responses to Western medicine? Acknowledging barriers to communication between patients and providers is the first step in finding ways to resolve them.

Variations also exist between and among culturally diverse groups in their attitudes about aspects of death and dying including disclosure of the diagnosis and its prognosis; advance directives; life support; beliefs, practices, and traditions around grief; care of the body after death; and burial procedures (ANA, 2010). For this reason, it is critical that nurses not make assumptions or predictions about the care needs of individuals based on their knowledge of a particular cultural group. Despite having some knowledge of cultural tendencies among members of a particular group, the nurse confers with patients and their families to determine their specific preferences. When caring for patients at the end of life, nurses have both the privilege and responsibility of ensuring that the final goals and wishes of the patient are met. To ensure culturally competent care, nurses are expected to listen attentively, initiate honest, open, and compassionate discussions with families, and assess patients' psychosocial as well as physical symptoms to determine anxiety, depression, sense of loss, grief, feelings of isolation, and/or spiritual distress (ANA, 2010).

Nursing generally has its own set of goals for patients who are terminally ill. Such goals are based on American culture and traditions as well as the ethical standards that guide nursing practice. One example is the primary goal of **palliative care**, which is to "prevent and relieve suffering and to support the best quality of life for patients and their families regardless of their stage of disease or need for other therapy" (National Consensus Project, 2007). However, there are times when nursing goals may differ from those of the patient. For example, nurses in the United States strive to maintain patients' autonomy in health care decision making. Yet, some cultural groups do not wish the patient to know of the seriousness of a diagnosis and/or its prognosis. At such times, nurses are encouraged to first determine whether the patient has the capacity and desire to speak for himself or has designated a surrogate to speak on his behalf. If so, the nurse supports the decision of the patient and/or his designee and acts accordingly.

The challenges of caring for the terminally ill are universally experienced by nurses and other health care providers around the world; therefore, this section focuses on examining selected studies from a global and historical rather than from a solely national perspective. Earlier researchers (Hurtig & Stewin, 1990) focused on nurses caring for patients who were terminally ill and concluded that, "until nurses learn to cope with the specter of death, they will be inclined to put a distance between themselves and the dying" (p. 30). The researchers advocated a brief education on dying for nurses and discussed the need for having "a reconciliation" with death. In a later study of nurses in Denmark, Veijlgaurd, and Addington-Hall (2005) explored nurses' attitudes toward palliative care and care of terminally ill patients. In this study, researchers found that nurses held more positive attitudes than doctors and found the care of dying patients more rewarding, 90% versus 63%. Respondents also believed that caring for dying patients makes one aware of their own feelings regarding death. This study supported a need for education to change attitudes about care of the terminally ill. Hung-La Wu and Volker (2009) described the experiences of Taiwanese **hospice** nurses in their care of dying patients in hospices. These researchers identified three subthemes in their analysis: holistic and meaningful care through close relationships, confronting and managing negative beliefs about hospice, and managing the dying process. Nursing care for Taiwanese patients is done in the context of patients' cultural attitudes and beliefs. When providing holistic and meaningful care, nurses in this study facilitated communication among patients, their families, and health care professionals, became good listeners, and treated patients as though they were part of their own families. The nurses also tried to help patients make sense of their suffering, and find meaning in their lives and the dying experience (Hung-La Wu & Volker, 2009). Managing the dying experience included helping patients transition from life to death. In order to live with the challenges and demands of caring for patients who are terminally ill, nurses in this study needed to develop effective strategies to prevent burnout. Therefore, the participants in this study included dependence on their colleagues, families, and friends for support, their own religious beliefs, and lifestyle strategies to replenish them and manage stress. Lifestyle strategies included "eating healthy foods, sleeping well, exercising regularly, and engaging in relaxing activities" (p. 582). As a result of their efforts, nurses received positive feedback from patients and their families, felt happy and energetic, and gained a greater sense of self-worth.

By considering the results of these studies nurses can begin to care for the terminally ill from an evidence-based perspective. Nurses begin this process by reflecting on their own attitudes and beliefs, then educating themselves through in-service or continuing education workshops and conferences that enable them to determine what actions are needed to assist patients and families in managing the dying process. Most importantly, in this effort nurses should strive to assist patients in finding personal meaning in the dying and death experiences. To enable nurses to sustain their ability to carry on the day-to-day tasks required of them during this challenging time in patients' lives, strategies like those mentioned earlier must be incorporated in their daily lives. In addition, maintaining one's own spiritual well-being is also an important aspect of this process if the nurse is to be effective in delivering culturally relevant care.

In hospice and palliative care settings, the nurse appreciates the need for psychological and spiritual care and looks on the process of dying as a normal aspect of life. Nurses in other health care settings may also find themselves having to deliver care for patients who are dying. At such times, nurses should seek the guidance and expertise of these hospice nurse colleagues. Nurses who have a clear understanding of their patients' beliefs and attitudes about the death experience are better able to make each nurse–patient encounter meaningful from the patient's cultural perspective. The nurse has several opportunities to listen actively to determine what the patient wishes during the dying experience. This nursing behavior is particularly useful when significant others are not available to act as resources for the staff.

CULTURAL FACTORS AND SPIRITUALITY

The ability of patients who are dying to negotiate this often lonely and frightening final stage of their life is influenced by the cultural and spiritual values they hold. Research supports the idea that cultural factors play a major role in determining patients' decisions about end-of life care (Johnson, Kuchibhatla, & Tulsky, 2008; Kwak & Haley, 2005; NGO-Metzger, August, Srinivasan, Liao, & Meyskens, 2008). The American Academy of Family Physicians (AAFP) established cultural proficiency guidelines and developed an ethical policy statement, which attempts to guide the care at the end of life. It states, "Care at the end of life should recognize, assess, and address the psychological, social, spiritual/religious issues and cultural taboos realizing that different cultures may require significantly different approaches" (AAFP, 2008; Gibson, 2006).

Within the realm of cultural considerations, the nurse examines the patient's spiritual needs. The Oncology Nursing Society (ONS) takes the position that, "Sensitive and appropriate spiritual care issues are assessed and integrated into the nursing care plan to promote adequate coping for patients, families, and significant others. Yet, while patients with life-threatening illnesses believe that psycho-spiritual support during a terminal illness is critical, it is often overlooked by many healthcare providers" (Searight & Gafford, 2005). As the patient experiences the dying process, the nurse may need to utilize the expertise of the patient's identified spiritual counselor or religious leaders. Priests, ministers, rabbis, lay ministers, *espirituista*, and others are among the many religious leaders with whom a patient may wish to confer. These individuals can assist the nurse in providing support for the patients and their families during grieving or other times of spiritual need. For patients who are religious, spiritual leaders can also assist patients during sacred times based on their religion. Spector (2009) reminds us that it is important for the nurse to know when these sacred times occur, including days of rest, religious holidays, or other considerations that afford the patient an opportunity to continue religious practices as desired.

Even patients who are religious will vary in their desire to incorporate prayer into their daily routine. Nurses can ask patients about their need for solitude, companionship, or for special religious items to assist them in prayer rituals. When a dying patient's anxiety is high or when grief is overwhelming, some patients welcome the opportunity for the nurse to sit quietly with them during prayer. In today's hectic health care environment, the nurse needs to be proactive and identify patients' care needs early and plan to incorporate strategies to address them into their daily schedule. Most hospitals have a generic place of worship to direct patients' families who wish to have private moments for meditation or prayer. Health care facilities usually have at least a lay minister to call on to meet the spiritual needs of patients. The Nursing Oncology Society's Position Statement encourages nurses to provide interpreter services and culturally sensitive materials in the patient's own language (ONS, 2007). These services enable patients to make optimum use of spiritual services that are available.

CULTURAL VARIATIONS AND BARRIERS

Siriwardena and Clark (2010) discussed end-of-life care for ethnic minorities and included cultural or religious differences, access to services, and diverse health beliefs among some of the barriers to care and support. In Kwak and Haley's (2005) review on end-of-life decision making among culturally diverse groups, variations in preferences among members of ethnically diverse groups were found. These variations were found in preferences toward **advance directives; life support**; disclosure and communication of diagnosis and prognosis; and designation of primary decision makers. Within-group variations were based on patients' cultural and demographic characteristics, level of **acculturation**, and knowledge of end-of-life treatment options. Additionally, as Spector (2009) observed, "Countless ethnocultural and religious differences can be found in the ways we observe dying, death, and mourning" (p. 130). These differences range from attitudes about caring for a dying patient and his family, care of the body after the patient has died, and the postmortem procedures and services in commemoration of the person's death (Spector, 2009). In multicultural societies ideas about death reflect one's personal worldview, while in Western society, the concept of death has been dominated by a culture of scientific medicine and a strong effort to fight against it (Shalev, 2010).

Johnson, Kuchibhatala, and Tulsky (2008) also studied differences on end-of-life decision making among racially and ethnically diverse groups. Results indicate that non-White racial groups lacked knowledge about advance directives, preferred the use of life supports, and were less likely than Whites to support advance directives. Asians and Hispanics were more likely to prefer family-centered decision making. They found that African

Americans were less likely to hold favorable beliefs about hospice care, were more likely to express discomfort about discussions around death and dying, and were more likely to want aggressive treatment. African Americans were also more likely to have spiritual beliefs that were in conflict with principles of palliative care and distrusted the health care system.

Some studies focused on determining a "good versus bad" death from both the nurses' and patients' perspectives (Borbasi, Gordon, & Uziely, 2005; Good et al., 2004; Komoromy, 2005). Komoromy found that these definitions "vary according to different historical and cultural contexts" (p. 40). In this article, the author identifies a number of choices people make about what they would like to happen when they are dying. For example, some sought solitude, while others wanted their family present. Some sought a religious presence, while another stated, "I don't want any [thing] religious around, nor do I want any religious ideas expressed" (p. 40). Many individuals consider death that involves pain a "bad death"; however, some cultural groups, based on their religious beliefs, may consider the pain they experience a form of cleansing or atonement in preparation for the next life. These variations in what patients want make it impossible for the nurse or other health care providers to know unless the patient is questioned about his or her preferences.

"Denial of death is common in western cultures," state Braun, Gordon, and Uziely (2010). Therefore, the concept of death is difficult to articulate and many euphemisms are used to express the process of death and dying (Purnell, 2008). The exception may occur when patients are cared for by nursing and physician specialists in the area of palliative and hospice care. Consequently, both patients and health care providers often interact during this period, without making any references to the realities of the dying process even while the patient is experiencing them. In some cases, this behavior may be acceptable to both the patient and the nurse. As Kellehear (2009) observed, "Some dying people show calm, autonomy and agency in their dying conduct" (p. 389). In such cases, patients may or may not need to discuss their situation. At other times, when the nurse and/or physician is unable or unwilling to address the realities of the patient's terminal status, without strong family supports the patient is forced to walk this final journey alone. Consequently, for some, "collapse, anxiety, and active distress" have been associated with the dying experience (Kellehear, 2009). As Shalev (2010) observed, for the patient approaching death, "there is a need for facilitation of an intimate encounter where patients can speak about their concerns with their loved ones" (p. 134). Some patients who have an awareness of a terminal diagnosis derive mechanisms for coping from religious or spiritual traditions. These traditions enable many patients to approach death in a positive and peaceful manner. Others may lack a religious affiliation or sense of their own spirituality and find it more difficult to cope with the psychological and emotional stress of dying.

Oxlad, Wade, Hallsworth, and Koczwaru (2008) studied concerns and needs of women who had completed primary treatment for breast cancer.

In this study, the researchers found that many had "a sense of apprehension about the future" among many other concerns. Anderson (2008) examined advanced cancer patients' verbal expressions of negative emotions. These feelings included feeling "scared, concerned, worried, depressed, and nervous." Anxiety, fear, depression, and anger were among the emotions expressed by the participants. The researchers found that respondents included among the topics of interest, their symptoms, functional concerns, medical diagnosis and treatment, and social issues, but only a few mentioned having concerns about dying (2%). Grant et al. (2004) studied cancer patients in the last year of life. In this study, the participants were asked to describe their spiritual needs and how they might be addressed. Results of the study indicate that patients' spiritual needs focused on loss of roles, self-identity, and fear of dying. There was also a need to make sense of the "sacred world." Anxiety, insomnia, and despair increased the need for support from health professionals. The authors concluded that when patients felt affirmed and valued by health professionals they experienced an improved quality of life and reduced need for health resources.

In another study Kim and Lee (2003) surveyed 185 acute-care hospital nurses in Korea to determine their attitudes about elements that would describe a "good death." They found comfort in not being a burden to the family, a good relationship with family members, a readiness to die, and a belief in perpetuity elements characteristic of a "good death." Conversely, elements of a "bad death" included a persistent vegetative state, sudden death, pain and agony, dying alone, and being a burden to the family. The majority (90%) of the respondents did not wish to receive life-perpetuating treatments. Sixty-seven percent of the respondents stated that they would be willing to discuss their own death and dying; this was dependent on the nature of the illness. Economic status and the disease states were variables influencing the elements of a "bad death."

Because there are such wide variations in preferences around death and dying experiences, nurses must utilize a careful cultural assessment of their terminally ill patients and include their significant others in the process. Gathering information that is specific and relevant to the patient is the best way to ensure that the patient's desired outcomes are achieved.

ATTITUDINAL BARRIERS AND DEATH AND DYING

For some patients, the experience of dying is compounded by the psychological trauma that results from attitudinal barriers that are imposed by society because of the nature of the patient's illness. One example of this situation is the patient who is dying from AIDS. For this patient, the emotional pain, grief, and fear associated with dying occurs from the time of the suspected diagnosis, but is made more difficult because of the **stigma** that is still associated with this particular disease (Zukoski & Thorburn, 2009). According to the Centers for Disease Control (CDC, 2009), "HIV disease remains a lead-ing cause of death among persons 25–44 years old, particularly among those who are black/African American, or Hispanic. There are increasing num-bers of women, persons older than 45 years old, and residents of the South, among those who now die of HIV related deaths each year" (AIDS Alert, 2007; CDC, 2009). In the United States, by the end of 2007, 14,561 adults and adolescents died from AIDS-related deaths. The total number of deaths since its inception through 2007 was 583,298. Of this number, 4,891 were children under 13 years old. In 2007, the estimated number of AIDS cases among racial and ethnic groups included 228 American Indians, 455 Asians, 21,549 Blacks/African Americans, 46 Native Hawaiian and Pacific Islanders, and 12,556 Whites (CDC, 2009).

Since its initial outbreak during the 1980s, for many of its victims a diag-nosis of HIV/AIDS has meant living with the sheer terror of knowing that one has a debilitating and fatal disease. The perpetual anxiety and fear that accompanies the diagnosis is a very human reaction to a disease that causes a devastating impact on the quality of one's life and offers an unpredicta-ble clinical course and outcome. As a terminal illness, it forces its victims to immediately confront their own mortality whether they are psychologi-cally ready or not. In addition, AIDS victims are stigmatized by a society that still blames the victims by pointing a finger at them for having acquired the disease in the first place.

Since the beginning of the AIDS pandemic, several studies have described nurses' and other health care workers' changing attitudes about caring for persons living with AIDS. Earlier studies indicated that negative attitudes toward persons with AIDS reflected the fear and anxiety nurses and other health care workers held about contracting the disease (Cole & Slocum 1992; Forrester & Murphy, 1992; Gebbie, 1999; McCann 1997; Place, 1995). More-over, in the early days, AIDS was considered a homosexual disease. Atkin-son (1995) discussed the earlier intolerance that society expressed toward homosexuals and the view it held that homosexuality was both a sin and a crime. These attitudes were also reflected in early study results indicat-ing that nurses were largely unwilling to care for the AIDS patients because many of them attached moral, religious, or ethical implications to contracting the disease, or were convinced of the notion that patients living with AIDS brought this disease on themselves.

As McCann (1997) reported, one study of nurses and doctors found that "most, though not all, nurses and doctors are prepared to work with these individuals" (p. 1033). However, in a study of the impact of HIV/AIDS on maternity care in Kenya, researchers found that fears of becoming HIV infected and the resulting stigma and discrimination were among the negative effects of caring for HIV/AIDS patients (Turan, Bukusi, Cohen, Sande, & Miller, 2008). Generally, recent studies indicate that nurses have become more willing to care for certain AIDS patients, but today remain less willing to care for some others. For example, two studies revealed that nurses and doctors were no longer judgmental about homosexuals who were diagnosed with HIV/AIDS, but were less willing to care for patients with HIV/AIDS who they believed contracted the disease through IV drug abuse (Cole & Slocum, 1992; Forrester & Murphy, 1992). Despite the fact that most health professionals view drug abuse a serious medical problem in itself, the nurses in this study were much less tolerant of patients whose risk-taking behavior—that is, IV drug abuse—led to a diagnosis of AIDS. This biased attitude toward certain AIDS patients, and not others, because of the way in which the disease was acquired, forms the basis for yet another "ism" in our society. Consequently, at times the death and dying experience of persons diagnosed with HIV is further complicated by the need for the patient to find ways to cope with feelings and attitudes of society and health care providers who blame the patient himself (Fair & Ginsburg, 2010). Some individuals may be compelled to use coping mechanisms that are detrimental and that detract from the quality of their remaining life. For example, Kelly, Bimbi, Izinicki, and Parsons (2009), in a study of HIV-positive men who were gay and bisexual, found that many of the respondents reported using substance abuse and sex as a strategy for coping with the stigma and physical consequences of the disease.

Today, society recognizes that this dreaded disease attacks its victims across age, race, class, gender, sexual orientation, and socioeconomic lines. With advances in technology and a greater understanding of the disease process, and as more individuals who are heterosexual become victims of AIDS, society views the disease and its victims differently.

Although society's attitude has changed somewhat over the last two decades, as Kabash, El-Gueneidy, Sharaf, Hassan, and Al-Nawawy (2008) observed, "the impact of HIV is devastating in all measured dimensions of health and its related quality of life." Further, these researchers noted, "AIDS is still considered a shameful disease and people look down on those who have it" (p. 1317). There remains a residual of attitudinal barriers that prohibit some AIDS patients from obtaining the same quality of health care that patients with other diseases are able to receive. Consequently, many patients living with HIV or AIDS who are most in need of compassionate and supportive health care are those who are the least likely to receive it.

In a study in the United States of 66 homosexual men who were HIV-positive, participants reported greater stigma, gay-related stress, self-blame, and having sex under the influence of drugs as a means of coping with the diagnosis (Kelly, Bimbi, Izienicki, & Parsons, 2009). The researchers encourage health care providers to assist patients who use poor coping strategies to identify more effective methods of managing issues of stress and coping.

Paparini, Doyal, and Anderson (2008) studied African men living with AIDS in London. The participants, who identified themselves as gay or bisexual, experienced a "double stigma" because of their sexuality and HIV status; "within African communities both HIV and homosexuality carry a substantial stigma" (p. 602). This might also be said of the African American communities in the United States. Consequently, the participants in the study were fearful of disclosing information about their sexuality, or health status, particularly to members of their own ethnic group. As a result, recruitment for this study was difficult and yielded only eight participants. Ages of participants ranged from 27 to 43. In this study, interviews with the men revealed that participants were not only fearful of returning to their native lands because treatment was not available, but also because they would experience "blackmailing, harassment, violence, and arrest" (p. 602). They also thought that others would blame them for contracting the disease. Living in London, the men felt unable to share the diagnosis with family members or associates, but did disclose to their current partners. Although five of the men were employed, some believed that the physical and psychological health problems, HIV-related stigma, and immigration status inhibited their chances for employment. For most of the participants the diagnosis of HIV came as a shock and they believed they were going to die immediately. The men also expressed concerns about "racist attitudes in gay networks as well as cultural differences that might lead to misunderstandings" (p. 603).

Courtenay-Quirk, Wolitsky, Parsons, and Gomez examined HIV/AIDS stigma within the gay community. Stigma was found to be associated with "increased levels of anxiety, loneliness, depressive symptoms, engaging in avoidant coping strategies, and history of suicidal ideation" (p. 56).

In a study of 153 Egyptians infected with HIV, Kabbash, El-Gueneidy, Sharaf, Hassan, and Al-Nawawy (2008) tried to determine the psychological and health needs of persons living with HIV/AIDS. In this study, fear of stigmatization, feelings of anxiety, hopelessness, and depression were frequently reported. The researchers concluded that decreasing stigma and providing psychosocial support would enable patients to develop coping strategies to better manage the consequences of this disease. Anderson et al. (2008) studied 25 Caribbean people, the majority were Jamaican, who were HIV-positive living in the United Kingdom. In this study, interviews revealed participants' awareness of the stigma surrounding their diagnosis, which they attributed to "fear of contamination, homophobia, and ignorance, reinforced by religious beliefs" (p.117). The participants identified violence and employment discrimination as possible outcomes among the HIV/AIDS stigma discrimination they experienced.

Makoae et al. (2008) identified strategies for coping with HIV-related stigma among 251 patients living with HIV and their families in five southern African countries. The researchers identified prejudice, discrimination, and hostility related to the stigmatization of AIDS. This research yielded strategies for patients and nurses in coping with the illness and the stigma. The 17 self-care strategies are presented in Exhibit 7.1. The authors conclude that coping with the illness is only modestly helpful in coping with stigma.

EXHIBIT 7.1 ■ COPING STRATEGIES FOR NURSES AND PERSONS LIVING WITH HIV/AIDS

• Restructuring	• Disclosing one's HIV status
• Seeing oneself as okay	• Speaking to others with the same problem
• Letting go	• Getting counseling
• Turning to God	• Helping others to cope with the illness
• Hoping	• Educating others
• Changing behavior	• Learning from others
• Keeping oneself active	• Acquiring knowledge and understanding
• Using humor	about the disease
• Joining a social or support group	• Getting help from others

Source: Makoae et al. (2008). *Journal of the Association of Nurses in AIDS Care Strategies.*

In the United States, although a diagnosis of HIV is no longer an immediate death sentence for its victims, AIDS remains a chronic and terminal illness. Because of the intimate nature of the nurse–patient relationship, nurses are critically positioned to work toward limiting the impact of stigmatization on the patient's health care experiences. Acknowledging the powerful and sometimes devastating impact that stigmatization can have on the psychological and emotional well-being of patients with HIV/AIDS is a first step toward helping the patient overcome it.

During encounters with patients who are dying with HIV/AIDS, nurses can determine ways to demonstrate their respect and appreciation of the patient's value as a human being. By so doing, the nurse establishes a trusting relationship that encourages patients to share their needs and desires about end-of-life care more readily. Culturally sensitive nursing care then focuses on utilizing strategies to assist the patient in coping with stigmatization and addressing the patient's specific needs and goals for care. This approach by the nurse assists patients in freeing their psychic energy so that they are better able to cope with the other psychological and physiologic aspects of their illness. Moreover, this kind of care enables patients who are dying with HIV/AIDS to die with the dignity all patients deserve.

In the same way that nurses understand the culpability of the chronic cigarette smoker with chronic obstnctive pulmonary disease (COPD), the alcohol abuse of some patients with cirrhosis, the sedentary lifestyle and dietary habits that lead to hyperlipidemia in some cardiac patients, they also appreciate the serious impact of risk-taking behavior (e.g., IV drug abuse) in the case of some patients who have contracted HIV/AIDS. In each of these clinical situations the victim has been noncompliant in practicing known preventative measures toward health promotion. Yet often victims of AIDS are looked on differently. In all of these situations, the need for health promotion is apparent. However, although such strategies as educating patients is clearly indicated, there remains the need for health care providers to remain sensitive, supportive, and nonjudgmental in their approach. This is especially true when the etiology of the disease is uncertain and the patient is forced to add stigmatization and fear of death to the list of other stressors associated with the disease. Most importantly, as culturally competent nurses, we recognize that all patients, regardless of their race, class, gender, diagnosis, lifestyle, sexual orientation, disease etiology, or other personal attribute, deserves to be treated with dignity, respect, and culturally competent care.

The impact of the stigmatization of HIV/AIDS on the patient only compounds the physiological and psychological trauma the disease causes its victims (Dallas, 2011). Negative attitudes toward patients with HIV/AIDS critically impact the victim at a time when the patient is the most vulnerable. Patients in this situation require health care that focuses on identifying their cultural and spiritual needs and appropriate strategies for addressing them. Providing culturally sensitive care for patients with HIV/AIDS begins during the diagnostic phase of this disease when stigmatization threatens to overwhelm the patient's psychological and emotional reserves even before the diagnosis has been made and treatment options have been considered. All health care providers, including doctors, nurses, and technicians, have an opportunity during this time to assist the patient in approaching the possibility of this devastating illness with less recrimination, hopelessness, and fear of the unknown.

IMPORTANT POINTS

- Caring for patients who are terminally ill requires nurses to first confront their own beliefs and attitudes concerning death and dying.
- Traditional and ethical goals of nursing may differ from those of the terminally ill patient.
- Anxiety, fear, and depression often accompany the death and dying experience.
- Differences exist between culturally diverse groups in their attitudes toward advance directives, life support, disclosure of diagnosis, and the designation of the decision maker.
- A variety of health practices and rituals related to death and dying are found among culturally diverse groups.
- The nurse will need to assess the patient's psychological, cultural, spiritual, and religious views when caring for terminally ill patients.
- The nurse should utilize a variety of resources to assist in providing culturally competent care to patients who have terminal illnesses.
- Negative attitudes held by society toward persons with HIV/AIDs further complicate a terminal illness causing additional psychological stress.
- When caring for patients with HIV/AIDS it is important for the nurse to remain sensitive, supportive, and nonjudgmental.

CASE SCENARIO 1

Ms. Vera Talsford, a 65-year-old widow, mother of two daughters, and grandmother of two young boys, arrived in the ER of a busy metropolitan trauma center complaining of a severe headache with increasing pain, dizziness, and nausea with movement. After the physical examination, the physician ordered a CAT scan, which revealed a left occipital mass. Ms. Talsford was admitted with a brain tumor. During the next few days, MRI studies, a PET scan, and other tests revealed that Ms. Talford had lung cancer with metastases to her brain. A friend of the family was with the patient when the doctor spoke with her. He asked Ms. T, as everyone called her, if it was okay with the patient to speak about her situation while the visitor was present. Ms. T said that was okay with her. The doctor spoke encouragingly and told Ms. T that everything would be done to remove the tumor from her brain. Over several days, Ms. T made a slow neurological recovery from the surgery, but became more despondent, after being told about the severity of her illness. She was starting to eat less each day and lost 20 pounds in a short period. Ms. T was well liked and had a room full of visitors each day. The nurses on the unit were confused about how to best care for Ms. T. They weren't sure if she appreciated the significance of her diagnosis. One day Karen, one of the staff nurses, asked Ms. T if she'd like to see a minister or other clergymen during her hospitalization. Ms. T stated, "Well I'm not really the religious type." Karen was stunned by Ms. T's comments and stated, "Okay, I'll be back in a little while." She left the room perplexed about what to do next to assist Ms. T.

WHAT NURSES NEED TO KNOW ABOUT THEMSELVES

APPLICATION OF THE STAIRCASE MODEL: SELF-REFLECTION QUESTIONS

1. Have you considered the significance of your own death?
2. Do you believe in life after death?
3. Where are you on the Cultural Competency Staircase when caring for patients who are terminally ill? How will you progress to the next level?
4. How comfortable are you caring for Ms. Talsford and discussing issues related to the death and dying process with her and/or her family?
5. What cultural information about the patient will you need to obtain to provide culturally sensitive care during the end of life?
6. What kinds of psychological, emotional, and spiritual support would you need if given a similar diagnosis?

Responses to Self-Reflection Questions

Response to Have you considered your own death? Life after death? Where are you on the Cultural Competency Staircase?

There are many exercises to help nurses explore their feelings and attitudes about death and dying that can be found on the web. Getting in touch with one's true feelings can open the mind toward understanding other's attitudes and beliefs. The authors recommend these exercises as a first step in assisting patients who are terminally ill during grieving stages of illness.

Response to How comfortable are you working with this patient and discussing issues related to death and dying?

As stated earlier, nurses begin by exploring their own attitudes about death and dying. One opportunity can be found at www.durbinhypnosis.com/deathdying.htm, Paul Durbin's (2004) tribute to Dr. Kübler Ross (*Death & Dying, Death & Grief: A Tribute to Dr. Kübler Ross*). Other nursing actions include reviewing content provided by nursing and medicine on principles guiding cross-cultural end-of-life care.

Several websites are recommended that provide relevant content on this subject, and can be found at the end of this chapter.

WHAT NURSES NEED TO KNOW ABOUT THE PATIENT

Selecting a Cultural Assessment Model

Response to What cultural information will you need to know when caring for patients at end of life?

Nurses caring for patients at end of life will need to be aware of the patient's knowledge and understanding that the illness is terminal. This may or not be culturally appropriate based on the patient and family's cultural perspectives about sharing this information. Nurses should also explore what resources and coping mechanisms are available to the patient. It is particularly useful to determine the patient's religious attitudes and beliefs regarding what constitutes a happy or peaceful death; the patient's attitudes about life after death might also be discussed if the patient wishes.

Response to What kinds of psychological, emotional, spiritual care would you need if given this diagnosis?

This is very individual and will depend on the results of your cultural assessment. The degree to which people need supportive care depends on family support, and their psychological, emotional, and spiritual preparation and personal readiness for death. When speaking with the patient and the family, the nurse can determine if the patient wishes to see a clergyperson or other spiritual leader or counselor. If desired, the nurse should afford the patient private time for prayer as needed on a routine basis.

CASE SCENARIO 2

Bill Hamilton is a 48-year-old African American faculty member at a local college. Bill is gay and has been living in a monogamous relationship with Henry, his male partner for the past 22 years. Since revealing that he was homosexual at age 16, he has been estranged from his parents and three siblings, a sister and two brothers.

Bill is uncomfortable sharing any of this information with anyone other than his primary physician, Carol Safer. During a visit to Dr. Safer, Bill complained of having a fever, frequent productive cough, and tightness in his chest. He was also experiencing high anxiety, and a sensation of impending doom. After reviewing his preliminary laboratory results, the doctor suggested that Bill also be tested for HIV. Bill quietly accepted his physician's suggestions, but was terrified about the possibility of having AIDS.

Dr. Safer reassured Bill that this was only a possibility at this point, and that she needed to rule out HIV before exploring other possibilities. She explained further that the test results would take several days, but that in the meantime, due to his worsening clinical status, she would admit him to the community acute care center for evaluation and to rule out pneumocystis carinii pneumonia and AIDS. Bill was nearly paralyzed with fear and anxiety about his illness. He was also concerned about the potential impact a diagnosis of HIV or AIDS might have on his relationship with Henry and his employment. He decided not to call Henry at work until he was settled into his room at the hospital. Bill's first encounter at the hospital was with a male technician who had been asked to draw Bill's blood. The technician approached him without comment, and began placing the tourniquet on his arm and palpating for a vein. His only verbal communication with Bill was to tell him, "If you are discharged, you will need to pick up these results yourself, since we can't give this kind of information over the phone." Bill was too embarrassed to speak. Finally, several hours after being admitted, Bill was taken to a floor where Sandy, a 23-year-old woman, was assigned as his nurse. It was the end of the day shift, so Sandy and a nursing assistant quickly glanced at his chart and assisted the patient to his assigned room. Bill was placed in a double-occupancy room that was then unoccupied. The nurses helped him to bed, administered pain medication at the patient's request, and performed a brief nursing history. During the interview, Sandy noticed that the patient was alone. She asked Mr. Hamilton if he was married or accompanied by anyone when he arrived. Bill stated that he was single and did not mention his relationship with Henry. He simply stated that a longtime friend would be in later that evening after he left work. He also told her that he did not wish to alarm any members of his family at this time. After completing Mr. Hamilton's admission to the unit, Sandy began the change of shift report.

While sharing the limited information she had gathered about the patient's medical diagnosis and clinical status with two older nurses, Jane, the evening nurse asked, "So, is this patient gay?" "I don't know," Sandy responded. "I didn't ask. I guess I was uncomfortable asking, I figured if he was and wanted to tell me, he would have." "Yes, I understand," Jane responded. "But it's an important question." "Did anyone come in with him; does he have family in the area?" Jane asked. "He said he doesn't want to alarm them, but he told me a friend would be in tonight." Mary, the other evening nurse remarked, "Is there any IV drug abuse history?" "I don't recall seeing anything on the chart," Sandy replied. "Well, just because it's not there, doesn't mean it's not the case," Mary remarked. "I've seen it over and over, they come in with HIV/AIDS and you find out later why, and it's either IV drug abuse, promiscuity, or both." "That's not true," Jane responded. "Exposure to HIV occurs because of exposure to the virus. Many women, children, as well as some men have been victims through heterosexual contact with the virus; therefore, it's not really fair to judge anyone about the cause. Besides, isn't AIDS being ruled out as a possibility?" Sandy became really uncomfortable with this conversation. She thought about a recent cultural competency class during which she had learned about exploring the patient's cultural and social history. By glancing too quickly at this patient's chart, and not really spending too much time questioning him, she was uncertain about whether she had enough information to effectively plan his care. She had been distracted by her need to complete other nursing tasks required of her before the end of her shift and had hurried through the admission history taking.

Sandy was also uncomfortable asking the patient too many personal questions. She had assumed that the patient might be gay, but had not given much thought about the possible etiologies of the patient's disease. She didn't care why her patient might have contracted AIDS. Based on her coworker's remarks and the limited information that she was able to provide about Mr. Hamilton, she wondered if the patient would receive the supportive care he needed that evening from his assigned nurse. He really seemed like a nice guy who was clearly alone and afraid. She wondered what she could do to help, but was intimidated by Mary who had far more years of experience. Before she left the unit, she spoke privately with Jane and asked her if she would mind taking care of Mr. Hamilton that night, and Jane agreed.

WHAT NURSES NEED TO KNOW ABOUT THEMSELVES

APPLICATION OF THE STAIRCASE MODEL: SELF-REFLECTION QUESTIONS

1. Where are you on the staircase regarding delivering care to patients who are terminally ill?

2. What encounters have you had in caring for patients with HIV/AIDS?
3. How do the nurses in this case example feel about caring for Mr. Hamilton? How would you feel? Why?
4. What cultural knowledge and skills are needed in caring for a patient diagnosed with HIV/AIDS?
5. What factors influence your motivation to provide culturally sensitive care to patients with HIV/AIDS?
6. What other patient information is important for nurses to know or to understand in order to provide this patient with culturally competent care?

Responses to Self-Reflection Questions

Response to Where are you on the staircase when caring for patients who are terminally ill?

Think of ways to move beyond where you are to progress to the next level while caring for this patient. Begin by doing exercises that allow you to tap into your feelings about death and dying (see tribute to Kübler Ross, earlier).

Response to What encounters have you had with patients diagnosed with HIV/AIDS?

During each nurse–patient interaction, nurses have the opportunity to assess the patient, to determine a nursing diagnosis, and to plan or implement culturally competent care. In this case, at the time of the admission, the nurse might have easily determined this patient's need for psychosocial support simply based on the primary admitting medical diagnosis. An effort could have been made, despite time constraints, to determine if the patient needed or wanted someone from among the resource personnel mentioned earlier with whom to speak. When the nurse returned with the medication, she might have said, "I noticed that you came to the hospital alone. Is there someone you'd like me to contact?" The fact that the patient is alone is also indicative of the need for more frequent visits to his room by members of the staff who are comfortable caring for HIV/AIDS patients.

During the next shift, a careful cultural assessment by the evening nurse may have elicited more information about the patient's attitudes about his clinical situation and his need for care. The nurse who is able to project complete acceptance of the patient, including his sexuality, can establish a trusting relationship through which his care needs can be identified and mutually agreed on goals and interventions can be established.

Response to How do the nurses in this case example feel about caring for Mr. Hamilton? How would you feel and why?

The technician seems callous and insensitive in not making any attempt to introduce himself or to converse with the patient, if only to allay the patient's anxiety. Sandy, the receiving nurse, seems to be aware of her feelings about caring for Mr. Hamilton, but is preoccupied with trying to complete her assignment and prepare for the change of shift report. Mary, one of the evening nurses, has indicated a certain bias toward the patient that reflects a combination of biases toward AIDS patients, homosexuals, and IV drug abusers. These attitudes underlie the stigma that is associated with a diagnosis of HIV/AIDS. Mary seems to lack awareness of her biases. Fortunately, Jane confronts Mary about her remarks. Both Jane and Sandy seem to be aware of the impact negative attitudes can have on the quality of care. That awareness may enable them to explore ways to provide culturally sensitive care during subsequent encounters with the patient.

Response to What skills are needed in caring for a patient diagnosed with HIV/AIDS?

Research on HIV/AIDS shows high levels of stigma and discrimination associated with HIV status continue to exist and provoke feelings of social rejection, isolation, and feelings of being treated differently. For this reason, among the many skills needed by nurses caring for AIDS patients, is the ability to perform careful cultural assessments and utilize skillful and active listening to obtain relevant psychosocial information about the patient. There are a variety of assessment tools from which nurses might choose. The author suggests the use of the *Framework for Cultural Assessment and Intervention Techniques* by Giger and Davidhizar (2008). This model utilizes six dimensions for assessment, including communication, space, social organization, time, environmental control, and biologic variations. Nurses must also be able to demonstrate that they appreciate the inherent value of this individual as a fellow human being. In this case, we are not yet sure if the patient actually has AIDS. Yet, he already has to confront behaviors by health care providers that reflect stereotyping and prejudice. Without some real evaluation of who this patient really is and how that individual is affected by his illness, it is impossible to develop a relevant and culturally congruent plan of care.

By respecting and valuing the patient the nurse is able to provide hope and encouragement in even the patient who is terminally ill. Also, nurses need to be able to create a partnership between themselves and their patients through which health care decision making is negotiated. In the case example earlier, a careful cultural assessment would reveal this patient's fear and anxiety among other nursing diagnoses. The nurse could then collaborate with the patient to determine the appropriate resources, for example, counselors, psychologist, and minister to support him in his care.

Response to What factors influence the nurse's motivation to provide culturally sensitive care to patients with HIV/AIDS?

Professional nurses' accountability that is due to the professional standards of practice, not conditional on any other consideration, is one of many factors influencing nurses' willingness to care for and treat HIV/AIDS patients. Another important factor is the belief that providing care and treatment for such patients is a rewarding experience (McCann 1997). According to this author, "care and treatment must also be voluntary, and not coerced by senior colleagues" (p. 1033). Some nurses view the opportunity to work with AIDS patients an opportunity to gain new and challenging information from a biomedical and psychosocial perspective. Others considered care of AIDS patients an opportunity to develop longer-term professional relationships because of the chronicity of this disease. Previous experience with stigmatized groups and the ability of the nurse to be nonjudgmental and to be tolerant of diverse sexual orientations are other factors influencing the nurse's willingness to care for these patients. Although actual encounters with patients with AIDS might dispel some negative attitudes or myths about caring for these patients, in other cases these negative attitudes may be reinforced. For example, situations in which the family and colleagues are fully involved and nurses can converse with them about the patient's care tend to have a more positive influence on the nurses' desire to provide culturally sensitive care. On the other hand, when the patient's family is absent or colleagues are unsympathetic toward the patient, nurses are less motivated to care for them. It is ironic that when the patient is most in need of support he is less likely to receive it.

Response to What do the nurses need to know about this patient in order to provide this patient with culturally competent care?

In the case earlier, the nurses' knowledge about this patient is limited. Being culturally competent requires knowledge of the patient's health-related beliefs, practices, and values. Knowledge of the history, incidence, and prevalence of disease in the population from which the patient comes is also important. In this case, the patient is African American. Many health care disparities exist between African Americans and White Americans. The incidence and prevalence of HIV/AIDS is higher among African Americans than it is for any other ethnic grou; therefore, there is a great need for health promotion and education in this community regarding HIV. Another important area in which nurses must gain information about the patient is in understanding the patient's preferred style of interacting. In gaining this knowledge, the nurse is able to minimize offensive language and behavior, and to elicit pertinent information through an ongoing cultural assessment. Nurses caring for ethnically diverse groups must also be aware of the efficacy of treatment, including medications that may vary in their effectiveness when administered to members of culturally diverse groups.

SUMMARY

When caring for persons with HIV/AIDS, in order for nurses to establish a trusting and meaningful nurse–patient relationship, they must demonstrate awareness, knowledge, skill, and a strong desire based on a sense of duty to care. In providing culturally competent care to persons either diagnosed with AIDS or who are suspected of having AIDS, nurses must have a strong sense of their own attitudes toward patients who have been infected with HIV, and any other marginalized groups the patient may represent. Nurses must also be willing to confront their own attitudes about human sexuality and appreciate the diverse ways in which sexuality may be expressed.

Culturally competent nurses are also skilled in conveying warmth, acceptance, and understanding through active listening and comprehensive cultural assessments. During these assessments, the nurse observes for intra-cultural differences that may be revealed.

The nurse communicates effectively with the patient in a language the patient understands, avoiding medical jargon or slang that the patient may not understand. When necessary, the nurse is also skillful in engaging the support of other health care providers that include social workers, ministers, psychologists, interpreters, and others to support the provision of care.

Caring for the patient with HIV/AIDS and other sexually transmitted diseases also requires that nurses be knowledgeable of the patient's cultural, ethnic, and racial background, including culture-bound illnesses, health care disparities, or pharmacological considerations that may place the patient at greater risk of disease or complications. To serve as an effective resource for the patient, nurses must also be knowledgeable about the disease process and its impact on the patient's physical and psychological health. Every nurse–patient encounter should be viewed as an opportunity to employ the nursing process and to build a partnership with patients that allows him or her to actively participate in his or her care. Through meaningful partnerships in which both the patient and the nurse identify mutually determined goals and interventions, patients gain more satisfaction with their care. The more encounters there are and the more nurses experience success in providing care to persons with AIDS, the more they are likely to be motivated to care for them.

NCLEX-TYPE QUESTIONS

1. The nurse begins planning care for a patient newly diagnosed with pancreatic cancer. The patient has not yet been told of the diagnosis. The initial action by the nurse is to:
   A. Conduct a cultural assessment to determine the needs of the patient.
   B. Reflect on personal beliefs and attitudes regarding terminal illness.
   C. Offer the patient spiritual reading material.
   D. Disregard the diagnosis and treat the patient like any other patient.

2. The primary role of the nurse in caring for patients who have terminal illnesses is to ensure that:
   A. The patient has a happy death.
   B. Pain is minimized and controlled.
   C. The patient is protected from unnecessary stress.
   D. The patient's goals and wishes related to death and dying are addressed.

3. A terminally ill patient states that she believes the pain associated with her illnesses is God's way of purifying her of her sins before death; consequently, she is refusing pain medication. What statement by the nurse caring for a patient who is terminally ill suggests a need for further staff development?
   A. "That statement makes no sense, I believe we should add pain meds to her food."
   B. "The patient has a right to decide the care they receive as long as they are cognitively sound."
   C. "Let's continue to offer the medication just in case she changes her mind."
   D. "Perhaps we can offer some magazines or music therapy to divert her attention from her pain."

4. The staff development nurse conducts a workshop on caring for terminally ill patients. What statement by the nurse is accurate about culturally diverse groups and terminal illness?
   A. Members of the same cultural, racial, or ethnic groups generally share the same attitudes about death and dying.
   B. The nurse can assume there are variations among culturally diverse groups regarding death and dying beliefs and practices.
   C. Members of the same religious group share beliefs about postmortem procedures.
   D. To avoid confusion, it is best to care for all patients in the same way.

5. The hospice nurse comes to visit a terminally ill patient who has just been placed in her care. The nurse asks the patient whether he wishes to enter a hospice care facility or receive care at home. The nurse recalls that current research reveals most terminally ill patients prefer:
   A. Staying in the hospital where they feel safe.
   B. Being discharged from nursing care, because they cannot expect a cure for their illness.
   C. Going to a long-term care or rehabilitation facility.
   D. Going home to die in the presence of their loved ones.

6. The literature suggests that nurses caring for terminally ill patients will need to find ways to avoid burnout. One strategy is to (select all that apply):
   A. Eat a healthy diet.
   B. Get adequate sleep.
   C. Limit conversations about death and dying with the patient.
   D. Exercise regularly.

7. In the United States, ideas about death and dying are most often a result of America's focus on the medical model of care and:
   A. One's personal view of death.
   B. A desire to engage in the afterlife.
   C. An effort to fight against death.
   D. A concern for a peaceful death.

8. According to the CDC, HIV remains a leading cause of death among which of the following age groups?
   A. 25–44
   B. 30–45

C. 45–55

D. 50–60

9. During a cultural assessment, the nurse learns that a patient is a member of the Cherokee Nation. What *initial* action by the nurse is *most* appropriate.
   A. The nurse plans care for the patient based on personal knowledge about Cherokee Indians.
   B. The nurse performs a cultural assessment to learn about the individual care needs of the patient.
   C. The nurse plans to get an interpreter to speak with the patient.
   D. The nurse will review a cultural competency textbook to learn more about the Cherokee Nation.

10. A Muslim patient who is terminally ill refuses to eat during Ramadan. What statement by the nurse demonstrates a good understanding of culturally competent care to patients who are terminally ill?
   A. "You don't have to honor Ramadan at your stage of illness."
   B. "Fasting will only make you sicker. You must really try to eat something."
   C. "Your health is the most important consideration at this time."
   D. "I will bring you a tray after sundown."

REFERENCES

AIDS Alert. (2007). Increasing numbers of older Americans are coping with HIV infection and stigma: Their number has more than tripled in recent decades. *AIDS Alert, 22*(2), 13–16. Retrieved from http://web.ebscohost.com/ehost/pdfviewer/pdfviewer?sid=1bdfa30f- 34f4–4e35-a329–47827fbde43c%40session mgr104&vid=5&hid=127

American Nurses Association. (2010). Revised position statement: Registered nurses' role and responsibilities in the provision of expert care and counseling at the end of life. Retrieved from www.nursingworld.org/MainMenuCategories/EthicsStandards/Ethics-Position-Statements/etpain14426.pdf

Anderson, M., Elam, G., Gerver, S., Solarin, I., Fenton, K., & Easterbrook, P. (2008). HIV/AIDS-related stigma and discrimination: Accounts of HIV-positive Caribbean people in the United Kingdom. *Social Science and Medicine, 67*(5), 790–798.

Anderson, W. G., Alexander, S. C., Rodriquez, K. L., Jeffreys, A. S., Olsen, M. K., Pollak, K. I.,…Arnold, R. M. (2008). "What concerns me is…" Expression of emotion by advanced cancer patients during outpatient visits. *Supportive Care in Cancer: Official Journal Of the Multinational Association of Supportive Care in Cancer, 16*(7), 803–811. Retrieved from http://web.ebscohost.com/ehost/delivery?vid=70&hid=5&sid=d1936c5d-48cb

Atkinson, D. R., & Hackett, G. (1995). Treatment of gay men and lesbian women: Society's treatment of gay people. In D. R. Atkinson & G. Hackett (Eds.), *Counseling diverse populations* (pp. 56–69). California: William C. Brown.

Borbasi, S., Wotton, K., Redden, M., & Chapman, Y. (2005). Letting go: A qualitative study of acute care and community nurses' perceptions of a good versus a bad death. *Australian Critical Care, 18*(3), 107–113.

Braun, M., Gordon, D., & Uziely, B. (2010). Associations between oncology nurses' attitudes toward death and caring for dying patients. *Oncology Nursing Forum, 37*(1), E43-E48. doi: 10.1188/10.ONF.E43-E49

Centers for Disease Control. (2009). Centers for Disease Control summary of annual HIV/AIDS surveillance report. Retrieved from www.cdc.gov/hiv/surveilance/resources/reports/2009report/pdf/20

Chan, L. S. Macdonald, M. E., & Cohen, S. R. (2009). Moving culture beyond ethnicity. Examining dying in hospitals through a cultural lens. *Journal of Palliative Care* 25(2), 117–124.

Cole, F., & Slocumb, E. (1992). Nurses' attitudes toward patients with AIDS. *Journal of Advanced Nursing, 18*(7), 1112–1127.

Courtenay-Quirk, C., Wolitski, R. J., Parsons, J. T., & Gomez, C. A. (2006). Is HIV/AIDS stigma dividing the gay community? Perceptions of HIV-positive men who have sex with men. *AIDS Education and Prevention, 18*(1), 56–67.

Dallas, E. (2011). *Everyday stigma may take toll on lesbians and gays.* Medline Plus. Retrieved from www.nlm.nih.gov/medlineplus/news/fullstory_117371.html

Fair, C., & Ginsburg, B. (2010). HIV-related stigma, discrimination, and knowledge of legal rights among infected adults. *Journal Of HIV/AIDS & Social Services, 9*(1), 77–89. doi: 10.1080/15381500903583470

Forrester, D.,& Murphy, P. (1992). Nurses' attitudes toward patients with AIDS and AIDS-related risk factors. *Journal of Advanced Nursing, 17*, 1260–1266.

Gebbie, K. (1999). Which came first: Social prejudice or fear of the disease? *AIDS READ, 9*(3), 160–166.

Gibson, C. A., Lichtenthal, W., Berg, A., & Breitbart, W. (2006). Psychologic issues in palliative care. *Anesthesiology Clinics, 24*(1), 61–80.

Good, M. D., Gadmer, N. M., Ruopp, P., Lakoma, M., Sullivan, A. M., Redinbaugh, E., ...Block, S. D. (2004). Narrative nuances on good and bad deaths: Internists' tales from high technology work places. *Social Science and Medicine, 58*(5), 939–953. Retrieved from http://web.ebscohost.com/ehost/detail?

Grant, E., Murray, S. A., Kendall, M., Boyd, K., Tilley, S., & Ryan, D. (2004). Spiritual issues and needs: Perspectives from patients with advanced cancer and nonmalignant disease. A qualitative study. *Palliative and Supportive Care, 2*(4), 371–378.

Hurtig, W. A., & Stewin, L. (1990). The effect of death education and experience on nursing students' attitude toward death. *Journal of Advanced Nursing, 15*, 29–34.

Johnson, K. S., Kuchibhatla, M., & Tulsky, J. A. (2008). What explains racial differences in the use of advance directives and attitudes toward hospice care? *Journal of the American Geriatric Society, 56*(10). 1953–1958. Retrieved from www.ncbi.nlm.nih.gov/pubmed/18771455

Kabbash, I. A., El-Gueneidy, M., Sharaf, A. Y. , Hassan, N. M., & Al-Nawawy, A. N. (2008). Needs assessment and coping strategies of persons infected with HIV in Egypt. *La Revue de Sante de la Mediterranee orientale, 14*(6), 1308–1319.

Kellehear, A. (2009) On dying and human suffering. *Palliative Medicine 23*, 388–397. doi 10.1177/0269216309104858

Kelly, B. C., Bimbi, D. S., Izienicki, H., & Parsons, J. T. (2009). Stress and coping among HIV-positive barebackers. *AIDS and Behaviour, 13*(4), 792–797. Retrieved from http://web.ebscohost.com/ehost/delivery.com/ehost/delivery?vid

Kim, S., & Lee, Y. (2003). Korean nurses' attitudes to good and bad death, life sustaining treatment, and advance directives. *Nursing Ethics, 10*(6), 625–635.

Komaromy, C. (2005). Improving quality of dying: What makes a good death? *Nursing and Residential Care, 7*(1), 40–42.

Kwak, J., & Haley, W. E. (2005). Current research findings on end-of-life decision making among racially or ethnically diverse groups. *Gerontologist, 45*(5). 634–641. Retrieved from www.ncbi.nlm.nih.gov/pubmed/16199398

Makoae, L. N., Greeff, M., Phetlhu, R. D., Uys, L.R., Naidoo, J.R., Kohi, T. W., ... Holzemer, W. L. (2008). Coping with HIV-related stigma in five African countries. *The Journal of the Association of Nurses in AIDS Care Strategies, 19*(2), 137–146.

McCann, T. V. (1997). Willingness to provide care and treatment for patients with HIV/AIDS. *Journal of Advanced Nursing, 25*, 1033–1039.

Miller, D. K., Chibnall, J., Videen, S. D., & Duckro, P. (2005). Supportive-affective group experience for persons with life-threatening illness: Reducing spiritual, psychological, and death related distress in dying patients. *Journal of Palliative Medicine, 8*(2), 333–342.

National Consensus Project for Quality Palliative Care (2007). *Framework for hospice and palliative care.* Retrieved from www.nationalconsensusproject.org

NGO-Metzger, Q., August, K. J., Srinivasan, M., Liao, S., & Meyskens, F. L. (2008). End-of-life care: Guidelines for patient-centered communication. *American Family Physician, 77*(2), 167–174.

Oncology Nursing Society (ONS). (2007). Oncology Nursing Society and Association of Oncology Social Work Joint Position on palliative and end-of-life care. *Oncology Nursing Forum, 34*(6), 1097–1098.

Oxlad, M., Wade T. D., Hallsworth, L., & Koczwaru, B. (2007). I'm living with a chronic illness, not...illness, not dying with cancer: A qualitative study of Australian women's self-identified concerns and needs following primary treatment for breast cancer. *European Journal of Cancer Care, 17,* 157–166. doi: 10.1111/j.1365-2354.2007.00828.x

Paparini, S., Doyal, L., & Anderson, J. (2008). I count myself as being in a different world: African gay and bisexual men living with HIV in London. An exploratory study. *AIDS Care, 20*(5), 601–605. doi: 10.1080/09540120701867040

Place, A. (1995). Hospital staff want more infection control education. *Australian Nursing Journal, 3*(1), 8–10.

Purnell, L. (2008). The Purnell model for cultural competence. *In* L. Purnell &, & B. J. Paulanka (Eds.), *Transcultural health care: A culturally competent approach.* (3rd ed., pp. 19–55). Philadelphia, PA: F.A. Davis.

Searight, H. R., & Gafford, J. (2005). Cultural diversity at the end of life: Issues and guidelines for family physicians. *American Family Physician, 71*(3), 515–522. Retrieved from www.aafp.org/afp

Shalev, C. (2010). Reclaiming the patient's voice and spirit in dying: An insight from Israel. *Bioethics, 24*(3), 134–144. doi: 10.1111.j.J467–8519.2009.01790x

Shih, F., Lin, H., Gau, M.., Chen, C., Hsiao, S., Shih, S.,...Sheu, S. (2009). Spiritual needs of Taiwan's older patients with terminal cancer. *Oncology Nursing Forum, 36*(1). doi: 10.1188/09.ONF.E31-E38

Sirwardena, A. N., & Clark, D.A. (n d). End of life care for ethnic minority groups. *Diversity in Medicine, 6*(1), 43–47.

Spector, R. (2009). *Cultural diversity in health and illness* (7th ed.). Upper Saddle, NJ: Prentice Hall.

Turan, J. M., Bukusi, E. A., Cohen, C. R., Sande, J., & Miller, S. (2008). Effects of HIV/AIDS on Maternity Care Providers in Kenya. *JOGNN, 37*(5), 588–595. Retrieved from http://jognn.awhonn.org. doi: 10.1111/j.1552–6909.2008.00281.x

United States Department of Health and Human Services. Center for Disease Control and Prevention (CDC). (2011). *National vital statistics report.* Retrieved from www.cdc.gov/nchs/data/nvsr/nvsr59/nvsr59_04.pdf

Vejlgaard, T. (2005). Attitudes of Danish doctors and nurses to palliative and terminal care. *Palliative Medicine, 19,*119–127.

Wu, H. L., & Volker, D. L. (2009). Living with the death and dying: The experience of Taiwanese hospice nurse. *Oncology Nursing Forum, 36*(5), 578–584.

Zukoski, A., & Thorburn, S. (2009). Experiences of stigma and discrimination among adults living with HIV in a low HIV-prevalence context: A qualitative analysis. *AIDS Patient Care & Standards, 23*(4), 267–276. doi: 10.1089/apc.2008.0168

IMPORTANT WEBSITES

AACN: Peaceful Death: Recommended Competencies and Curricular Guidelines for End of Life Care

www.aacn.nche.edu/elnec/peaceful-death

American Academy of Family Physicians: Cross-Cultural End of Life Care

www.aafp.org/online/en/home/clinical/publichealth/culturalprof/quality-care-diverse-populations/watch-videos/qdcp-eolcare.html

Chaplain Paul G. Durbin, PhD. *Death & Dying, Death, & Grief: A Tribute To Dr. Kübler Ross*

http://www.durbinhypnosis.com/deathdying.htm

Cultural Considerations When Caring for the Geographically Displaced Client

BARBARA JONES

We draw our strength from the very despair in which we have been forced to live. We shall endure.

—CESAR CHAVEZ (1927–1993)

LEARNING OBJECTIVES

1. Describe the breadth of cultural diversity within the three dominant migrant streams.
2. Specify factors that limit or impede access of farm workers and their dependents to health services.
3. Discuss major health risk factors associated with the migratory lifestyle.
4. Acknowledge the critical importance of the nurse's advocacy role in modifying the social, economic, political, and environmental factors that result in migrant farm work; considered one of the most dangerous occupations engaged in within the United States.

KEY TERMS

Botanicas
Hazard vulnerability
Migrant worker
Promotores de salud
Santa Ana Test
Vulnerable populations

OVERVIEW

When we shop in the produce section of the grocery store, do we make a connection between the availability of this bounty and the crucial, indispensable role of the **migrant** agricultural worker in bringing ripe fruits and vegetables to market? For most of us, the answer is probably no. Despite the essential nature of their work, migrants are neither recognized nor rewarded by society. It is estimated that 3 million migrant farm workers and their dependents traverse the United States each year for the purpose of harvesting a variety of crops, 85% of which must be cultivated and picked by hand. Examples include citrus and broccoli in Florida, peaches in South Carolina, cucumbers and sweet potatoes in North Carolina, apples in Washington and New York, and potatoes and blueberries in Maine. Migrant agricultural workers are the backbone of the United States' multibillion-dollar agricultural industry.

There are three major streams of migrant agricultural workers that travel the United States annually picking and processing fruits and vegetables. The western stream begins in Southern California and travels up the west coast. The Texas stream fans out throughout the central United States and generally ends its season in Michigan. The eastern stream is based in Northern Florida in the region around Lake Okochobee. Its migrants travel up the coast until they reach upstate New York. All groups are on the move a minimum of 9 months each year and may relocate 11 to 13 times during this period. They follow the ripening crops then circle back to their home base and soon begin their cycle again.

Migrants generally are recruited and organized by a crew leader who contracts with growers to harvest crops. Generally, migrants return to the same farms each season. Housing is provided by the grower. Typically, accommodations involve groups of cinder-block houses called camps, which include common space for meals and recreation. Small bedrooms are designed to sleep four or more workers. Cots and bedding are provided along with shelves for personal belongings. Families are generally housed in different buildings than are workers traveling by themselves.

Farm workers generally lack their own transportation. Consequently, they are unable to travel to nearby towns to shop for essentials. Customarily camps are located several miles from population centers, which tend to be small, rural, ethnically and racially homogeneous communities. As a group, farm workers experience significant social isolation. They are often not welcome in the community and are expected to stay close to their camp. As a result, crew leaders purchase items in bulk and resell them to workers at a profit thereby eroding workers' already substandard incomes. Crew leaders also make cigarettes, wine, beer and, on occasion, illegal drugs available to workers at inflated charges. More than 30% of America's migrant workers earn below the poverty line.

There are significant health risks associated with agricultural work, which is ranked among the top three most dangerous occupations in the United States. During the harvesting season, the typical workday is 10 to 12 hours with few breaks permitted. Camp cooks deliver water and meals to workers in the field. Workers are continuously exposed to environmental hazards including prolonged exposure to sunlight and pesticides. They are at high risk for falls from ladders, lacerations, and snakebites. Repetitive-motion injuries, such as carpal tunnel syndrome and erosion of cartilage in the knees, are also of high incidence.

The social isolation associated with the migratory lifestyle, limited access to recreational resources, crowded congregate living conditions, cultural mores associated with limited use of contraception, and access to drugs and alcohol have contributed to a high incidence of sexually transmitted diseases and HIV/AIDS linked to drug use and prostitution. Farm workers as a group exhibit rates of seropositivity that are 8 times the national seropositivity rate. Five percent of farm workers are infected with HIV/AIDS, nearly 10 times the national average of 0.6%. Education regarding safe sex is complicated by information gleaned from research data regarding condom use by Hispanic/Latino males. In a research study conducted in rural Georgia (Villaruel & Rodriguez, 2003), nearly 80% of Hispanic farm worker respondents indicated that they never used condoms. Their decision not to use condoms was influenced by their religious and cultural practices. Most respondents reported that they were raised in the Roman Catholic faith. Catholic teaching prohibits the use of condoms because they are viewed as a contraceptive. Female partners of men who did use condoms indicated feelings of shame and embarrassment.

Migrant farm workers are at increased risk for tuberculosis related in part to living in crowded, substandard conditions. More than 40% of adult agricultural workers have positive tuberculosis (TB) skin tests and must undergo additional diagnostic testing to determine the presence of active disease. Early detection efforts can be complicated by state requirements for processing sputum specimens. In some instances, migrants have moved on prior to the local health department's receipt of test results. Lack of transportation and short stays in areas complicate implementation of directly observed therapy for TB. Efforts are made to determine the worker's next stop and to provide referral for follow-up care; however, many clients are lost to follow-up. It is also difficult to notify the client's contacts so that they may be screened and treated as necessary.

Pesticide exposure is a major risk factor for the development of acute and chronic health problems in the migrant population (Snipes et al., 2009). Half of all farm workers experience pesticide-related illness during their working life. More than 20,000 incidences of acute pesticide poisoning are reported annually. Workers report that they are instructed to cover their face with a bandana in order to limit exposure; this is an ineffective strategy. In California, 60% of grape workers stated that they were required to taste the fruit by eating unwashed grapes to determine whether they were sweet and ready for harvesting (Farmworker Justice, 2011). Long-term effects of pesticide exposure include cancer, infertility, birth defects, and neurological problems.

According to the Farm Worker's Health Study, conducted by the National Institute of Health's Institute for Environmental Health Services, having done farm work was associated with poor performance on four neurological tests—digit span, finger tapping, **Santa Ana Test**, and postural sway (Kamel, Rowland, Stallone, Ramirez-Garcia, & Sandler, 2003). Longer duration of farm work was associated with worse performance on neurological tests.

The Environmental Protection Agency (EPA) requires that every 5 years growers must explain concepts of basic pesticide safety to their workers. Interpretation of this responsibility has been problematic. The grower hires the crew leader who in turn hires the migrant workers, so the grower can legally be said to have only one employee, the crew leader. A grower may comply with EPA regulations by discussing pesticide issues with the crew leader; however, this crucial information may never reach the individual workers. Federally funded projects, such as Project Be Smart, Be Safe, are now focusing on peer health education related to pesticide safety. In Project Be Smart, Be Safe, 3,000 peer health educators, often called *promotores de salud*, were trained and received pocket-size books in English and Spanish for distribution to farm workers. The booklet describes each pesticide used during the growing cycle, lists signs and symptoms of potential pesticide-related health problems, and indicates when to seek help. Similar lay peer educator programs have been developed to focus on environmental risks linked to lead poisoning and asthma. An additional example of the use of lay peers in community-based education is the Wise Women program, which prepares volunteers to convey information about breast health including how to perform breast self-examination, warning signs of breast cancer, availability of free mammograms, and the importance of early detection for long-term survival (*Trained Peers...*, 2011).

Migrant health care is generally provided by local county health departments or by nonprofit groups that have organized to serve this population. Services include primary care of adults and children, screening for infectious disease, prenatal care, and referrals for more complex health care needs. Payment for health services tends to be on a sliding scale or free of charge. Migrant health centers report that less than 12% of their revenues are derived from Medicaid. Follow-up appointments are often missed as the camp empties and its workers move on. Outreach is a critical component of any health care program serving migrant farm workers and their dependents.

Compliance with therapeutic regimens, including medications, is a significant issue for migrant farm workers. Their long work hours, limited wages, and lack of transportation make it difficult for them to obtain needed supplies or medication refills, or to comply with special diets. Migrant children often fail to complete their immunization series. When farm workers seek care at their next stop, they may have lost their health records and be unable to remember the name of the facility or program where they received care. A survey of migrant workers in the Texas stream revealed that 98% of participants used herbal and other "natural" remedies because of tradition, perceived effectiveness, and lower costs (Poss, Pierce, & Prieto, 2005). Use persists even among highly culturally assimilated workers (Anthony, 2011).

Prenatal care is often sporadic and of late onset. This increases the pregnant worker's risk of complications of pregnancy and premature birth. Pesticide exposure also affects pregnancy outcomes.

Dental services are extremely rare. Migrant farm workers exhibit extraordinarily high rates of gingivitis with as many as 82% of the population affected. Forty-seven percent of children and adolescents have untreated decay. Migrant workers are among the majority of the U.S. population lacking dental insurance. In addition, most migrant farm workers do not have access to fluoridated water because they work and live in rural areas.

As noted above, farm workers are a culturally diverse group. They include individuals and families representing all racial and ethnic groups. Farm workers in the western stream are primarily Hispanics of Mexican heritage; however, there are also workers who are of Asian heritage and have arrived from Vietnam, Cambodia, and the Philippines. The Texas and east coast streams include African Americans, White non-Hispanics, Filipinos, and Haitians as well as Hispanic/Latino workers of Mexican, Puerto Rican, and Dominican ethnicity. Twenty percent of migrant farm workers are women.

CASE SCENARIO

Milagros Amaro is a 23-year-old Mexican American migrant agricultural worker who is traveling the migrant stream with her husband Reynaldo, her mother Rosa, and their three children—Carmencita, age 6, Angel, 4, and Rosamel, 17 months. Milagros and Reynaldo are currently harvesting peaches in a region of South Carolina known as the Midlands. They work long hours. When the weather is dry, they are in the orchards 7 days a week from 6 a.m. until dusk during peak season. On rainy days, they work in the many packing sheds preparing fruit for shipping. There is plenty of work available; however, the season is short. While they are in the orchards, Rosa cares for the children in the migrant camp provided by the grower.

The Amaro family generally works in South Carolina each year from the end of May until the end of July. They then move on to North Carolina to harvest vegetables and tobacco, then on to Delaware for tomatoes and peppers, then continue moving northward to New Jersey, Pennsylvania, and finally to New York where they harvest onions, apples, and winter vegetables. When the season ends, they return to their home base in Frostproof, Florida, where they reside with Reynaldo's extended family. They harvest citrus fruit throughout the winter months then prepare for their annual trek upstream.

Milagros tells the nurse practitioner at the migrant health clinic that she is experiencing pain on urination, right-sided flank pain, and a low-grade fever. She suspects that she has a urinary infection. She would also like to discuss family planning issues. She is currently taking oral contraceptives and has questions about their long-term safety. She also would like the children to have physicals and to catch up on their vaccinations. Her command of English is excellent. She is a U.S. citizen and was raised in Florida. Carmencita is fully bilingual, and Angel knows many words in both languages. Milagros tells the nurse that her husband knows some English but is more comfortable communicating in Spanish. She states that Reynaldo has a hernia but is reluctant to come to the clinic for two reasons. First, he is a Mexican citizen who has an agricultural worker visa, which has now expired. Second, his hernia is in the groin area, and he feels self-conscious about having an examination.

As the nurse completes the health history on the Amaro children, she learns that Milagros does not have their vaccination records available. She shares information about when and where their vaccinations were administered. She has a variety of cards with her that identify a number of clinics where they sought services while traveling the stream. The nurse notices that Milagros's surname is different on some of the cards and asks the clinic's social worker to telephone the clinics and request that health records be faxed after Milagros signs a consent form.

Physical examination of the children reveals that all are above their recommended weight for height. Otherwise, they are healthy youngsters who have achieved their developmental milestones. The two older children are curious about the nurse's activities, and they each want to listen to their heartbeat. Their mother disciplines them verbally, and they quiet immediately.

While the nursing assistant talks with Carmencita and Angel about healthy snacks, the nurse obtains a urine sample for culture and sensitivity from Milagros. She encourages her to increase her intake of water and juices and to take an over-the-counter analgesic as needed. Milagros explains that she does not have a kitchen or refrigerator in her room at the camp; all meals are taken in the camp's cookhouse. She, therefore, has minimal control over her family's diet but feels she can request extra fluids. The nurse asks Milagros to call for her lab results in 48 hours to learn if she will need to begin antibiotic therapy. She then asks about Milagros's current contraceptive practices and provides her with information about other options.

The social worker returns and states that she cannot reach any of the clinics other than the one in Florida because they operate only during the harvesting season. The records from the Frostproof clinic do provide a list of immunizations received there and dates of administration. The social worker also accessed the Migrant Clinicians Network, but the only information in its database came from the Frostproof clinic. After the nursing staff expresses frustration, the nurse practitioner decides to begin immunizing the children using the CDC Catch-Up Schedule based on the official records from Florida. She also orders that a TB skin test be administered to the children and to Milagros. The nurse tells Milagros that if her urine culture does not indicate infection and she therefore does not need to return to the clinic, she will drive out to the camp to read the skin tests. She then faxes the information about today's immunizations back to the clinic in Frostproof. She also gives a copy of the vaccination records to Milagros. She asks if Milagros's mother has any health-related needs. She replies that Rosa takes medication for hypertension but her supply has run out; she requires a new prescription. The nurse suggests that when Reynaldo visits the clinic it would be beneficial for him to bring Rosa with him for a blood pressure check and a prescription if indicated.

WHAT NURSES NEED TO KNOW ABOUT THEMSELVES

APPLICATION OF THE STAIRCASE MODEL: SELF-REFLECTION QUESTIONS

1. What are your feelings, attitudes, and beliefs about people who live a transient lifestyle?
2. Does your concept of the Hispanic or Latino client and family reflect common stereotypes or reflect the broad diversity of this population?
3. What does the nursing staff at the clinic need to know about Milagros's Mexican American heritage, her values, traditions, and health beliefs in order to deliver quality care to her and to her family?
4. What is the response of the staff to Milagros's incomplete health records on her children? What assumptions underlie this response?
5. What occupation-related issues are important when caring for migrant agricultural workers?
6. What attributes do nurses working with migrant agricultural workers need in order to function as effective advocates for their clients?

WHAT NURSES NEED TO KNOW ABOUT THEIR PATIENTS

Application of the Staircase Model

Nurses choose to practice in settings serving agricultural migrants because they are committed to working with **vulnerable populations** and desire to increase their cultural awareness, knowledge, and skill through encounters requiring immersion into the farm worker culture (Staircase Model, Step 2). Despite their desire to serve these clients, they will often discover that they possess stereotypes about this population that they previously did not recognize within themselves (Step 1). To deliver culturally competent care to Reynaldo and Milagros Amaro and their three children, it is important for the nurse to acquire awareness and knowledge related to two distinct cultures—their migrant agricultural culture characterized by transience and marginality, and their identity as Mexicans and Mexican Americans (Step 3). Aspects of the migratory lifestyle will be considered first because it is the migratory lifestyle, rather than attributes and behaviors of specific cultural groups, that contributes to discontinuity of health care, erratic management of health problems, and noncompliance with therapeutic regimens. Nurses and other health care workers delivering services to farm workers may hold stereotypical views of the migrant population. A classic stereotype is that individuals and families become involved in a migratory lifestyle because they have no options. They may perceive farm workers as lacking a work ethic or as being homeless (Step 1). Nurses who possess this stereotypic belief have difficulty understanding that love and reverence for the land, experiencing agricultural bounty during different seasons and in different regions, and a family legacy of an agricultural lifestyle can motivate individuals and families to migrate. Many migrant workers are members of families who have traveled the agricultural circuit for generations. They frequently travel with their extended families including children of all ages. Children attend school in their family's home-base area and are then placed in local schools for short periods as their family travels the migrant stream.

Other workers are single men and women of diverse backgrounds who are recruited by crew leaders. Some are unskilled individuals who have been unable to find other work. Others do have poor or sporadic work histories, have legal problems such as active warrants for their arrest, have violated parole, are homeless, mentally ill, or have addiction problems. In some instances, crew leaders deliberately target addicted individuals. To fill their quota of workers, crew leaders promise ready access to alcohol or drugs. Workers recruited in this manner are often in poor physical health and are at increased risk for both accidents and other-related violence in the camps.

Frustrated health care personnel may find themselves blaming farm worker clients for their poorly controlled diabetes or interruption of drug treatment for tuberculosis (Step 1). Health care workers may fail to understand the complexity of accessing medical resources, arranging for payment, acquiring prescriptions and equipment, and working therapeutic regimens into a daily work routine that has the client outdoors for extended periods.

Migrant farm workers comprise a vulnerable client population for multiple reasons. Approximately 61% live in poverty; half earn an annual income of less than $7,500 per year. Only 7% have employer-provided health insurance, and 32% of male farm workers in California report that they have never been treated by a physician while on the road. They rarely have access to workmen's compensation coverage, health insurance, disability compensation, or occupational rehabilitation. Some are Medicaid eligible in their home base state; however, Medicaid coverage ceases when they travel to other states as benefits do not transfer. Migrant workers are ineligible for unemployment benefits despite the reality that their jobs are seasonal and intermittent. Most do not receive any public benefits such as food stamps or welfare.

As a group, they lack fluency in English. It is estimated that only 12% of migrant workers are fluent (Anthony, 2011). The median educational level is low with a mean of 6 years of formal education with 20% having 3 years or less. These three factors—poverty, language abilities, and low educational levels—contribute to vulnerability to illness and limit health care access. An additional factor is fear of repercussion should they speak out against their employers. As migrant workers, they are often politically disenfranchised as they are on the road at the time when elections are being held in their home districts.

Although migrant workers are a racially and culturally diverse group, 83% are Hispanic (National Center for Farm Worker Health, 2011). Hispanics/Latinos are the fastest growing minority group in the United States and comprise nearly 13% of the total U.S. population. It is crucial that the nurse recognize that not all Hispanic/Latino clients are alike and appreciate the diversity of this population (Step 4). A first generation immigrant from Central America is likely to have little in common with a third-generation Cuban American. Factors to be considered when assessing Hispanic/Latino clients include: country of origin of the client, his parents, and extended family; language use and preference, amount of time in the United States, participation in schooling in the United States, type and frequency of contact with family of origin, and gender-based roles. Most anthropologists agree that there are core attributes that appear to transcend the diversity of the Hispanic/Latino culture. These include:

- Respect for others. Clients expect to receive care in a supportive atmosphere. There is particular reverence for older members of the extended family. Empathy and privacy are essential. Communication processes often conflict with approaches used by health providers from the dominant American culture who tend to be blunt, frank, and hurried. Hispanic/Latino clients expect to be approached respectfully, to engage in polite small talk, and to then move on to the main topic. Abrupt communication is felt to convey disrespect.
- Health perspective. Health is perceived as a balance of body, mind, and spirit. Holistic treatment is expected. Spiritual care and religious rituals are often essential components of health care and stress management. Some clients will incorporate certain herbs or spiritual practices into their health care activities. *Botanicas* and pharmacies in communities where there is a significant population of Hispanics/Latinos commonly offer a variety of herbs, teas, and elixirs as well as religious articles including candles and symbols. It is always critical that the health provider ask what the client believes will aid in improving his or her health (Step 4).
- Strong kinship system. Most Hispanics/Latinos participate in an extended system of kinship involving mutual obligations for emotional support, personal and economic assistance, and encouragement. Historically, families have not relied on extensive support from outside the family; their cultural pattern is to obtain support from within their family group. This has implications for nurses caring for Hispanic/Latino farm workers traveling without their families (Weyr, 1989).

Mexicans comprise the largest Hispanic/Latino migrant subgroup. The words *Hispanic* and *Latino*, though used synonymously, have meanings that differ slightly in denotation. The term Hispanic indicates that an individual traces his ancestry back to Spain. The term Latino, in contrast, focuses on ethnic roots that trace back to one of the Latin American nations, including the countries comprising Central America and islands such as Puerto Rico and the Dominican Republic. The histories of most of the nations mentioned above include invasion by Spanish conquistadors followed by subjugation and at times extermination of indigenous peoples, so the term Latino minimizes the connection to Spain and is preferred by many of Spanish heritage.

Many Hispanic/Latino clients utilize their mother's name as their surname. For example, Milagros's daughter Carmencita may be identified as Carmen Amaro Torres because Torres is Milagros's maiden name. When Milagros enrolls Carmencita in school, she may decide to Americanize Carmencita's name as Carmen Torres Amaro. Her husband, Reynaldo Amaro, may at times utilize the name Reynaldo Amaro Rodriguez because Rodriquez was his mother's last name. Traditionally, lineage descends through the mother's family. These practices create the potential for discrepancies in health, school, insurance, and legal records.

Certain stereotypes related to the Hispanic/Latino culture may affect delivery of health care. Many health providers appear to have internalized the belief that Latinos are passive and fatalistic in their worldviews (Steps 1 and 2). Although some individuals do possess these traits, many others embrace the values of the dominant U.S. culture, perceive that they have control over many aspects of their health, and follow current health promotion recommendations.

Success of outreach efforts to migrant health workers is contingent on the nurse's ability to develop cordial relationships with growers and crew leaders because their permission is required to visit camps. Typically, the nurse and other migrant health clinic staff visit each camp early in the season to provide information about the location of the clinic, hours of service, types of services available, and payment options. They also attempt to develop a positive relationship with the cook who will notify the clinic in times of crisis or accidents as well as facilitate access for health screening and education. Social service workers assist clients who need to exit the migrant stream due to acute health deviations by arranging transportation to tertiary care facilities or facilitating return to their home base.

Communication skills are an essential part of delivering culturally competent care. Some nurses working with populations who are primary speakers of Spanish attempt to develop proficiency in the language themselves. Others respond by ensuring that translators are available during all hours in which the clinic is open for services. In the past, it was common to ask family members who were more proficient in English to translate for the client. This practice is declining. Health providers now recognize that all clients have the right to privacy. They may not wish their relative or friend to know about their diagnosis or treatment. Also, when informal translators are used, it is hard for the nurse to validate what is really being communicated to the client. There is the potential for the translator to misconstrue what is being discussed. To provide culturally competent care to clients, health care facilities should employ translators who agree to assist clients with limited English proficiency while maintaining privacy and confidentiality. When working with clients who do speak English, it is important for the nurse to recognize that the ability to speak English well does not mean that the individual is skilled in reading or writing the English language. The nurse should always ask the client whether he or she would prefer to receive health education materials in English or Spanish (Step 6).

In addition to excellent communication, assessment, and interpersonal skills, nurses who work with migrant agricultural populations require skills related to advocacy and political action. Many farm workers have extreme difficulty accessing resources to which they are entitled. The migratory lifestyle makes it difficult to follow through with required appointments and paperwork. As they travel the migrant stream, workers needing ongoing pharmacologic management of chronic illness, such as Rosa who was featured in the case study, have difficulty obtaining and paying for needed supplies and refills. Because they lack access to transportation and sometimes demonstrate low levels of English proficiency, workers often do not seek care when symptoms arrive. As a result, they may overuse emergency rooms as sources of primary care. Payment for services is also an issue. Nurses can provide key information about economic programs that assist such clients. Nurses can also advocate for clients by informing growers about unsafe conditions in the camp. The nurse conveys that, from an economic perspective, illnesses associated with such conditions have the potential to negatively impact worker productivity. This may prove to be a stronger impetus to improve conditions than would appeals to provide a living environment that supports human dignity.

Nurses working with migrant workers must be committed to social change. America's treatment of migrant farm workers has long been considered a national disgrace. The Migrant and Seasonal Agricultural Worker Protection Act of 1983 was designed to protect farm workers on matters of pay and work-related conditions (U.S. Department of Agriculture, Agricultural Labor Affairs). The act required crew leaders to register with the U.S. Department of Labor and to disclose to workers information about wages, hours, working conditions, and housing, which must meet minimum safety standards. Nevertheless, serious infractions persist and violations of the act are underreported due to intimidation of workers by crew leaders. As a result, the plight of the migrant as depicted in John Steinbeck's classic book *The Grapes of Wrath* (1939) and in the 1960s documentary *Harvest of Shame* continues to exist today.

Application Exercise

The following is an exercise in applying knowledge acquired through reading this chapter to the case study presented earlier.

A. What strategies would be most beneficial in encouraging Reynaldo to visit the migrant health clinic for assessment of his inguinal hernia?

1.
2.
3.

B. How could the nurse increase the likelihood that Milagros will have her children's immunization records available when she reaches their next stop along the migrant stream?

1.
2.
3.

C. What concerns do you have about Rosa, a hypertensive older adult, who remains in the camp caring for the children while Milagros and Reynaldo work in the fields? What other health problems is she at increased risk for?

1.
2.
3.

NCLEX-TYPE QUESTIONS

1. The migrant worker is at increased risk for negative health outcomes as a result of:
   A. Overcrowded living conditions.
   B. Delay in seeking care.
   C. Lack of social support.
   D. Mistrust of health care providers.

2. The incidence of adverse drug reactions is higher in workers with H-2A guest worker visas because:
   A. They are likely to be taking medications available without prescription that were obtained outside the United States.
   B. They are less likely to be able to access health resources.
   C. Farm workers demonstrate immunity to most infectious agents due to cumulative exposure.
   D. They have access to a network of informal health providers recommending herbal remedies.

3. When completing physical assessments on Hispanic/Latino clients, it is important for the nurse to recognize that the client will be:
   A. Unable to give a comprehensive health history.
   B. Opposed to having a staff member as an interpreter.
   C. More comfortable with a health provider of the same gender.
   D. Mistrustful of clinic staff.

4. From a legal perspective, responsibility for educating agricultural workers about pesticide risks rest with:
   A. Crew leaders
   B. Immigration officers
   C. Migrant health clinic staff
   D. Growers

5. The key to effective outreach efforts to migrant farm workers traveling the stream is:
   A. Availability of educational materials written in a variety of languages.
   B. Scheduling camp visits to coincide with hours when workers are not in the fields.
   C. Developing collaborative relationships with growers and crew leaders.
   D. Targeting female workers and enlisting their help in circulating information.

AACN COMPETENCIES ADDRESSED IN THIS CHAPTER

All AACN end-of-program competencies for baccalaureate nursing education are addressed in this chapter with the exception of Competency 2, which focuses on the use of best evidence in providing culturally competent care. Development of evidence related to the care of migratory populations is slow to emerge and remains in the nascent phase.

1. Apply knowledge of social and cultural factors that affect nursing and health care across multiple contexts.
3. Promote achievement of safe and quality outcomes of care for diverse populations.
4. Advocate for social justice, including commitment to the health of vulnerable populations and the elimination of health disparities.
5. Participate in continuous cultural competence development.

BIBLIOGRAPHY

Aguirre-Molina, M., Molina, C. W., & Zambrana, R. E. (2001). *Health issues in the latino community*. San Francisco, CA: Jossey-Bass.

Anthony, M. A. (2011). Caring for migrant farm workers on medical-surgical units. *MedSurg Nursing, 20*(3), 123–126.

California-Mexico Health Initiative. (2003). *Agricultural workers in California: Health Fact Sheet*. Berkely, CA: University of California, California Policy Research Center. Retrieved October 20, 2003, from www.ucop.edu/cprc/cmhi.htm

California Environmental Protection Agency. (2004). *Pesticide safety rules for farmworkers*. Sacramento, CA: Author.

Centers for Disease Control. *Catch-up immunization schedule for persons aged 4 months through 18 years*. Retrieved January 9, 2012, from www.cdc.gov/vaccines

Cutter, S. L., Boruff, B. J., & Shirley, W. L. (2003). Social vulnerability to environmental hazards. *Social Science Quarterly, 84*(2), 242–261.

De La Torre, A., & Estrada, A. (2001). *Mexican Americans and health*. Tucson, AZ: University of Arizona Press.

Diaz, V. A. (2002). Cultural factors in preventive care: Latinos. *Primary Care: Clinics in Office Practice, 29*(3), 1105–1112.

Kamel, F., Rowland, A. S., Stallone, L., Ramirez-Garnica, G., & Sanders, D. F. (2003). Neurobehavioral performance and work experience in Florida farm workers. *Environmental Health Perspective, 111,* 1765–1772.

McQuiston, C., Larson, K., Parrado, E., & Flaskerud, J. (2002). AIDS knowledge and measurement considerations with unacculturated latinos. *Western Journal of Nursing Research, 24*(4), 354–372.

National Center for Farmworker Health. (2003). Fact sheets about farmworkers. Retrieved October 30, 2003, from www.ncfh.org/factsheets.html

Poss, J. E. (2000). Factors associated with participation by Mexican migrant farmworkers in a tuberculosis screening program. *Nursing Research, 49*(1), 20–28.

Poss, J., Pierce, R., & Prieto, V. (2005). Herbal remedies used by selected migrant farmworkers in El Paso, Texas. *Journal of Rural Health, 21*(2), 187–191.

Snipes, S. A., Thompson, B., O'Connor, K., Shell-Duncan, B., King, D., Herrera, A., & Navarro, B. (2009). Pesticides protect the fruit, but not the people: Using community-based ethnography to understand farmworker pesticide-exposure risks. *American Journal of Public Health, 99*(53) S616–S621.

Patient Education Management. (2011). Trained peers provide education to refugees. Retrieved from http://web.ebscohost.com/ehost/pdfviewer/pdfviewer?sid=5ad91d8c-dba5-4904-abaf-2fd67b950e18%40sessionmgr10&vid=4&hid=9

U. S. Department of Agriculture. (2002). *Migrant and Seasonal Agricultural Worker Protection Act.* Retrieved January 9, 2012, from www.usda.gov/oce/labor-affairs/mspasumm.htm

Villaruel, A., & Rodriguez, D. (2003). Beyond stereotypes: Promoting safer sex behaviors among latino adolescents. *JOGNN, 32*(2), 258–263.

Weyr, T. (1989). *Hispanic U.S.A.: Breaking the melting pot.* New York, NY: Harper and Row.

IMPORTANT WEBSITES

California Department of Pesticide Regulation
1001 I Street
Sacramento, California 95814
Farmworker Justice
www.fwjustice.org/about_farmworker_justice/ourmission/52_who are farm workers.html.
National Center for Farmworker Health
Buda, Texas 78610
800–531–5120
info@ncfh.org
Pesticide Information Office
University of Florida
PO Box 110710, Gainesville, FL 32611–0680
(352) 392–4721, Fax: (352) 846–0206

Cultural Considerations When Working With Patients With a Sexual Orientation That Differs From One's Own

CLAIRE DENTE

LEARNING OBJECTIVES

1. Identify and understand who comprises the lesbian, gay, bisexual, transgender, queer, questioning, intersex, and ally population (**LGBTQQIA**).
2. Articulate the distinction between sexual orientation and gender identity.
3. Gain knowledge of the health care concerns and institutional barriers facing the LGBTQQIA population.
4. Identify personal gaps in knowledge, skills, and comfort in working with members of the LGBTQQIA community.
5. Develop awareness of strategies to increase competence in working with the LGBTQQIA population.

KEY TERMS

Ally
Bisexual
Coming out
Gay
Gender identity
Heterosexism
Heterosexual/straight
Homophobia
Homosexuality
Intersex
Lesbian
LGBTQQIA (also, LGBT, LGBTQA)
Queer

Sexual orientation
Transgender

OVERVIEW

Most of us give little thought to our own sexual orientation, especially if we identify as **heterosexual**, or **straight**, those individuals who are attracted to members of the opposite sex. Straight people don't have to come to terms with their attraction to members of the opposite sex, or explain to friends and family that they are different from the majority. Straight people don't have to **come out** to self, family, friends, work, colleagues, or a faith system. Your initial reactions to this chapter can provide a starting point for assessing your own attitudes and beliefs about working with individuals whose sexual orientation may differ from yours, especially if you are part of the majority group that identifies as heterosexual. If you are someone who identifies as a member of the lesbian, gay, bisexual, or transgender population, you may also find your own self-understanding expanded and your skills refined in working with others in this context as you continue to integrate your own personal identity with your emerging professional nursing identity.

This chapter presents an overview of some of the key issues facing gay, lesbian, bisexual, and transgender patients. It includes a glossary of terms and a case scenario where sexual orientation is an important element in the treatment considerations for patients and in professional nursing relationships. In accordance with the Staircase Model presented earlier in this text, the chapter utilizes self-reflection questions as they relate to the issue of sexual orientation. Finally, we include references and resources that may assist you in expanding your knowledge and clinical skills when working with gay, lesbian, bisexual, and transgender individuals.

LGBTQQIA: DEFINING THE UMBRELLA

Note that the population included under gender and sexual orientation encompasses individuals who identify as lesbian, gay, bisexual, transgender, "queer" and "questioning," often abbreviated as LGBTQQ. Sometimes individuals who identify as "intersex" (I) and "allies" (A) also gather under the sexual orientation and gender identity umbrella. Before proceeding, it is helpful to review about whom we are speaking. Individuals who "are sexually and emotionally attracted to persons of the same sex" are considered **gay** if men and **lesbians** if women (Ritter & Terndrup, 2002, pp. 11–12). Gay is also sometimes used as a catchall phrase for a man or woman who identifies as gay, lesbian, or bisexual. Individuals who identify as **bisexual** may have attraction, behaviors, and self-identification to either males or females, though definitions of bisexual identity continue to emerge (Ritter & Terndrup, 2002, pp. 40–41). **Transgender** refers to those individuals "whose self-image as male or female differs from the norms traditionally associated with their anatomical sex at birth" (Lambda Legal, 2006). It is important for nurses to know that while some transgender people find having a diagnosis of gender identity disorder helpful for obtaining medical care and challenging discrimination, others find it less helpful to have gender classified as an illness and would prefer to see it removed as a diagnosis, akin to the removal of homosexuality from the *Diagnostic and Statistical Manual of Mental Disorders* (*DSM*) in the early 1970s (Lambda Legal, 2006). **Intersex** is defined as "a person born with an anatomy or a physiology that differs from cultural ideals of male and female," which can involve differences in genitalia or hormones (Lambda Legal & National Youth Advocacy Coalition, 2007). As the *DSM* evolves in later editions with *DSM-5* publication anticipated for 2013, it will be important for nurses to be attentive and sensitive not only to the medical and scientific understanding of gender, but to the political repercussions and impact of these transformations and definitions on the legal standards and access to care for the transgender community.

Nurses should be sensitive to the use of the word *queer*. **Queer** is a term that some people in this diverse community are using to reclaim this word in an effort to lessen the intensity of its power, as some people of color have done in attempting to reclaim "the N word." There is disagreement among members of the community about the effectiveness of such a strategy, so some gay people are comfortable using the term, while others are not. Some see the use of this term as liberating, while others feel that it reaffirms a negative connotation to individuals who already have negative feelings to lesbian, gay, bisexual, and transgender individuals. *Questioning* refers to those individuals who are uncertain about their sexual identity and are exploring what their feelings and urgings might mean for them and their sexual identity. Finally, the LGBTQQI acronym sometimes also includes an "A" (**LGBTQQIA**), signifying a person who may not identify as LGBTQQI, but stands as a supportive **ally** to such individuals. This person usually identifies as heterosexual. Although the term heterosexuality is used frequently by most people to define individuals with opposite-sex attraction, the term **homosexuality** historically has been used to identify individuals with same-sex attraction. Nurses should recognize that many individuals in the LGBTQQIA community do not use or like this term because of its previous clinical use to define same-sex attraction as pathological and deviant.

Our purpose here is to address the issue of sensitivity around sexual orientation and gender identity, with a specific focus on issues surrounding sexual orientation. This is not to negate the importance of sensitivity to the unique physical needs of people who identify as transgender or intersex. As the literature has noted, research with transgender individuals is sparse and such individuals have "social and psychological dimensions unique to their identity" that may impact their experiences (Palma & Stanley, 2002, p. 74). It is important for nursing students to understand the difference between **sexual orientation**—to whom one is attracted—and **gender identity**—how one identifies as female or male (Yarhouse, 2001), though there is also a growing awareness to avoid polarizing gender and to include transgender individuals along this continuum. The primary focus of this chapter includes the provision of sensitive and culturally competent nursing care to individuals who identify as lesbian, gay, and bisexual (sexual orientation). Although much of the discussion on the following pages also applies to transgender and intersex individuals, the focus here is primarily on sexual orientation rather than gender identity, though many concerns related to sensitivity in providing care can certainly carry over to both areas. Further reading related to transgender and intersex concerns can be found in the literature (Bieschke, Perez, & DeBord, 2007; Carroll, Gilroy, & Ryan, 2002; Koder, 2006; Messinger & Morrow, 2005, 2006; O'Shaughnessy & Carroll, 2007; Proulx, 2006). Individuals who identify as transgender and those who have listened to their voices have provided tremendous insights in recent years. Readers are referred to these experts for greater clarity and voice of transgender concerns related to identity development and adolescent needs (Morgan & Stevens, 2008; Welle, Fuller, Mauk, & Clatts, 2006), health care and service delivery (Bauer et al., 2009; Cobos & Jones, 2009; Gorton, 2007; Green, 2010; Kenagy, 2005; Melendez, Bonem, & Sember, 2006; Williams & Freeman, 2005), and specific needs related to transgender aging (Persson, 2009; Witten, 2009). There are growing numbers of facilities that provide specialized health and mental health services to transgender individuals. The unique constellation of physical and emotional transitions for transgender individuals requires health care providers who are specially trained to provide care during transition periods; many transgender individuals choose to continue to receive services from these health care providers.

HEALTH CARE AND SEXUAL ORIENTATION: A REVIEW OF THE LITERATURE

Sexual orientation has been identified as an issue of cultural diversity for nursing from the early 1990s to the present (Eliason, 1993b; Giddings, 2005; Misener, Sowell, Phillips, & Harris, 1997; Raso, 2006; Vickers, 2008). Analysis of the nursing and health care literature reveals a history of invisibility to the needs of gays and lesbians in health care and their subsequent marginalization in the receipt of services resulting from this lack of awareness (Albarran & Salmon, 2000; Brogan, 1997; Fredriksen-Goldsen & Hooyman, 2005; Ott & Eilers, 1997). The literature suggests signs of growing acceptance of diverse sexual orientation internationally among nurses and other health care providers (Röndahl, Innala, & Carlsson, 2004), and increased awareness of the need for a diverse workplace (Harrison, 2008; Maxwell, 2005). Yet, there is still room for improvement in knowledge and service. There is a call for nursing education to address issues around the provision of care to gay and lesbian patients (Bretas, Ohara, & Querino, 2008; Kendall-Raynor, 2007; Payne, 2006; Peate, 2006a; Peate, 2006b; Platzer & James, 2000; Röndahl, Innala, & Carlsson, 2004; Snow, 2006; Veldon, 2001).

Studies have examined the experiences and service utilization of gay, lesbian, bisexual, and transgender individuals in the health care system (Makadon, 2006; Meads, Buckley, & Sanderson, 2007; Röndahl, 2009). Some found a need for greater sensitivity and acceptance and others reported perceived discrimination or prejudice from health care providers (Bakker, Sandfort, Vanswesenbeeck, van Lindert, & Westert, 2006; Bjorkman & Malterud, 2009; Cant & Taket, 2006; Facione & Facione, 2007; Fish & Anthony, 2005). Many patients struggle with the issue of disclosure to their health care provider (Lee et al., 2008; Polek, Hardie, & Crowley, 2008). These patients often make conscious attempts to find educated, sensitive, and informed primary care providers (Labig & Peterson, 2006; Neville & Henrickson, 2006). Scholars have examined health care preferences and utilization of services for these patients (Seaver, Freund, Wright, Tjia, & Frayne, 2008) and have offered recommendations for care (Starr, Greco, & Glusman, 1998; Steele, Tinmouth, & Lu, 2006; Wimberly, Hogben, Moore-Ruffin, Moore, & Fry-Johnson, 2006).

Nurses, pre-nursing students, and other health care providers are often unaware of or have difficulty accepting the sexual orientation of patients who identify as gay, lesbian, or bisexual. These patients may suffer health consequences if they are not comfortable identifying themselves to their health care providers (Bjorkman & Malterud, 2007; Burgess, Lee, Tran, & van Ryn, 2007; Eliason & Raheim, 2000; Greco & Glusman, 1998; Khan, Plummer, Hussain, & Minichiello, 2008; Wamala, Merlo, Boström, & Hogstedt, 2007). Studies have indicated that women in this group may be particularly disadvantaged and experience higher rates of disparity in health care (Hollander, 2006; Hutchinson, Thompson, & Cederbaum, 2006). Consequences include delays in seeking health care, decreased participation in routine prevention and wellness care, poorer quality of care provided, and the failure to establish positive nurse–patient relationships (Brogan, 1997; Eliason, 1993b; Wagner, 1997).

Nurses who work with older adults especially note the invisibility of gay, lesbian, bisexual, and transgender patients and their needs (Peate, 2008; Price, 2005). There is a growing awareness of the need for attention specific to older gay adults and their issues, including grief (Bent & Magilvy, 2006), long-term and residential care (Edwards, 2001; Johnson, Jackson, Arnette, & Koffman, 2005; Meneses & Monrow, 2007; Springfield, 2002), caregiving (Grossman, D'Augelli, & Dragowski, 2005), and other aging needs (Goldberg, Sickler, & Dibble, 2005; Hughes, 2007; Kean, 2006). Midlife health and coming out later in life have also been identified as issues of focus (Dibble, Sato, & Haller, 2007; Politi, Clark, Armstrong, McGarry, & Sciamanna, 2009; Rickards & Wuest, 2006).

Nurses involved in the provision of care to families and adolescents find a growing need to learn more about gay adoptions, identity development, school safety, and culturally competent care ("A School Nurse Perspective," 2002; Bakker & Cavender, 2003; Benton, 2003; Berlan, Corliss, Rield, Goodman, & Austin, 2010; Dootson, 2000; Lobaugh, Clements, Averill, & Olguin, 2006; Saewyc, Bearinger, McMahon & Evans, 2006; Sawyer, Porter, Lehman,

Anderson, & Anderson, 2006; Stevens & Morgan, 1999; Weber, 2009). The literature also includes increasing attention to the health of lesbian, gay, bisexual, and transgender adolescents (Coker, Austin, & Schuster, 2009; Coker, Austin, & Schuster, 2010; Ridner, Frost, & LaJoie, 2006). Adolescent mental health and substance abuse issues have also been identified as specific areas of great concern (Ciro et al., 2005; Eisenberg & Resnick, 2006; Riley, 2010; Rostosky, Danner, & Riggle, 2007; Weber, 2010; Weber & Poster, 2010).

Researchers have examined lesbian pregnancy and parenting experiences, often finding that while lesbians have similar health care needs to heterosexual women, other issues arise in the provision of services, such as presumed heterosexuality and the role of their partners in the birth process (Larsson & Dykes, 2009; McManus, Hunter, & Renn, 2006; McNair et al., 2008; Mercier & Harold, 2006; Röndahl, Bruhner, & Lindhe, 2009; Stewart, 1999; Wojnar, 2007). Studies have also broadened to address the unique needs of lesbian, gay, bisexual, and transgender individuals facing mental health issues (Koh & Ross, 2006; Owens & Khalil, 2007; Owens, Riggle, & Rostosky, 2007; Razzano, Cook, Hamilton, Hughes, & Matthews, 2006; Willging, Salvador, & Kano, 2006) and substance abuse (Cochran & Cauce, 2006; Cochran, Peavy, & Cauce, 2007; Hughes, Johnson, Wilsnack, & Szalacha, 2007; Parks & Hughes, 2005; Pettinato, 2008). Research has also focused on women's health concerns (Brandenburg, Matthews, Johnson, & Hughes, 2007; DeHart, 2008; Mravcak, 2006), men's health concerns (Gee, 2006; McAndrew & Warne, 2010; Wang, Häusermann, Vounatsou, Aggleton, & Weiss, 2007), bisexual concerns (Champion, Wilford, Shain, & Piper, 2005; Saewyc et al., 2009), orthopedic and spinal cord injury (Burch, 2008; Dykes & White, 2009), unique dimensions of service delivery to members of the military, particularly during the era of "Don't Ask, Don't Tell" (Johnson & Buhrke, 2006; Nusbaum, Frasier, Rojas, Trotter, & Tudor, 2008), and special concerns regarding weight and body image (Kelly, 2007; Polimeni, Austin, & Kavanagh, 2009). Recent editions of professional journals have published special editions addressing gay, lesbian, bisexual, and transgender health, health psychology, and other needs (Kerr & Mathey, 2007; Peel & Thomson, 2009; Shattell, 2008). Thus, it is imperative that nurses and other health care providers become educated about the needs and concerns of gay, lesbian, bisexual, and transgender patients, and work toward helping these individuals to feel accepted and welcome in the health care setting.

HETEROSEXISM AND HOMOPHOBIA

Think back to your initial thoughts and feelings on reading the title of this chapter, "Cultural Considerations When Working With Patients With a Sexual Orientation That Differs From One's Own." Most likely you thought the chapter was written for straight people who would care for gay people, and you probably thought that it was written by a person who was not gay. If this is true for you, you may have just engaged in what is termed **heterosexism**. Did you presume the readers of the chapter would be straight and therefore the chapter would address how straight nurses can work with gay people? How did you come to the decision that the majority of the readers would be straight and not gay, lesbian, or bisexual? You might argue that the number of gay, lesbian, and bisexual individuals is much smaller in comparison to the number of people who are not gay, and thus the chapter would more likely be read from the perspective of a nongay person. That may be statistically true, but this assumption that the chapter would be written "by heterosexuals for heterosexuals" is an example of heterosexism.

In heterosexism, an individual presumes a basic stance of understanding stemming from the dominant heterosexual perspective. Thus, heterosexism involves "the automatic assumption that everyone is heterosexual unless proved otherwise, and that heterosexuality is, therefore, superior to and dominant over all other sexual orientations" (Evans, 2001, p. 22). Herek (1995), a pioneer in research on gay and lesbian concerns, proposed that psychological heterosexism concerns negative beliefs and attitudes about gays and lesbians that can even be expressed through violent behaviors. Through cultural conditioning, society reinforces heterosexism as the only normal manner of relating, and this heterosexist belief system is intricately entwined with the oppression of people who do not fit this mold (Gray et al., 1996).

Within nursing education heterosexism exists through gender stereotypes that presume that male nurses are more likely to be gay, through the adherence to traditional developmental theories that do not take gay identity formation into consideration, and through the reinforcement of the invisibility of the sexual orientation of historically relevant nurses who were gay or lesbian (Gray et al., 1996). Irwin (2007) argued that patients experienced discrimination because of heterosexism and homophobia in nursing practice, and further noted that heterosexism interferes not only with patient experiences, but also for gay, lesbian, bisexual, and transgender nurses in the workplace, who face unique challenges such as whether to be "out" at work. Chinn (2008) expounded on the challenges of identifying as a lesbian in the nursing profession, and Warriner (2008) emphasized the need for nurses to feel confident to be out in the workplace. For many nurses, choosing to be out or not requires reflection and careful measure of the costs and benefits of this decision (Röndahl, Innala & Carlsson, 2007). Heterosexism and homophobia are cited as reasons not to disclose one's sexual orientation in these studies.

In addition to assuming that the focus of discussion will be on heterosexuals and from the heterosexual perspective, heterosexism can also include an element of ranking. In such ranking, one deems that heterosexuality is better than homosexuality, or, that being gay is somewhat inferior or less than normal to being heterosexual (Evans, 2001; Gray et al., 1996). This classification of gays and lesbians as inferior may result from **homophobia**. In addition to viewing heterosexuality as the only acceptable orientation, homophobia can move beyond the mere presumption of heterosexuality to the fear and hatred of gays and lesbians (Blumenfield, 1992; Wells, 1997). In the extreme, heterosexism and homophobia can lead to hate crimes against gay men (Willis, 2004).

Homophobia refers to a discomfort, fear, or distaste for gay persons. Richmond and McKenna (1998) provided an excellent overview of the intricacies of defining homophobia. The authors argued that homophobia is "inappropriately labeled a 'phobia'" and rather refers to distaste and aversion, thus arguing that homophobia is a complex concept involving "the psychology of negative attitudes" (Richmond & McKenna, 1998, p. 364). According to the work of Richmond and McKenna (1998), homophobia involves references (the breadth and depth of situations in which homophobia occurs), antecedents (patterns, values, or experiences that preclude or contribute to the experience of homophobia, such as a conservative religious upbringing), and consequences (the results of homophobia, including the avoidance of a person who is gay or dreading exposure to gay people) (p. 365). It can exist with different focuses that include from heterosexual men to gays or lesbians, from heterosexual women to gays or lesbians, and through internalized homophobia, the self-hatred and fear that gay, lesbian, and bisexual individuals feel about themselves as gays or lesbians (Pellegrini, 1992). Internalized homophobia is recognized as having negative effects on gay, lesbian, and bisexual people (Shidlo, 1994). Other research identified five "themes" that form the basis of cultural expressions of homophobia toward lesbians that included "anxiety about sexual difference, fear of female sexuality, the sexualisation of lesbianism, the characterisation of lesbianism as 'sick' or 'unnatural'; and the inability to identify lesbians with any certainty" (Wilton, 1999, p. 154). The fear of gays and lesbians can result in extremely negative reactions, including "hatred, harassment and acts of violence" (Gray et al., 1996, p. 207; Herek, 1995).

Heterosexism and homophobia present barriers to gay and lesbian access to health care. Too often in the provision of health care gays and lesbians go unnoticed because of heterosexist assumptions by doctors and nurses that all patients are straight (Ungvarski, 2001). Neville and Henrickson (2006) suggest that women reported that "their healthcare provider usually or always presumed that they were heterosexual" (p. 407). For both men and women, their "healthcare professional's attitude toward sexual identity was important to them when they chose a provider" (Neville & Henrickson, 2006, p. 412).

Gay, lesbian, and bisexual patients fear "discrimination or recrimination" and thus withhold the important information of sexual orientation from health care providers at the cost of their own well-being (Ungvarski, 2001, p. 7). It is well noted in the literature that lesbians are often hesitant to come out (reveal their sexual orientation) to their health care providers because of heterosexism and homophobia on the part of health care providers (Ott & Eilers, 1997; Wagner, 1997). Health care providers have been rated poorly in the past in the provision of services to gay, lesbian, and bisexual patients (Stevens, 1992), and on their negative reactions and attitudes to homosexuality both broadly defined and specifically to individual gay, lesbian, and bisexual patients who disclose their sexual orientation (Morrissey, 1996; Smith, Johnson, & Guenther, 1985). Gay and lesbian people who must endure these biases against them may feel marginalized as they receive health care services (Platzer, 1993). For many gay, lesbian, and bisexual individuals, the mere process of coming out to one's health care provider requires a high level of self-esteem to take this risk. The gay, lesbian, and bisexual community is a population that has had to struggle with self-acceptance and low self-esteem in a culture that historically valued heterosexuality (Hardin, 1999). The literature contains in-depth study from the 1990s into the 2000s of the identity development, coming out process, relationships, and mental health needs of gay, lesbian, and bisexual individuals (D'Augelli & Patterson, 1995; Dworkin & Gutierrez, 1992; Gonsiorek, 1985; Greene & Herek, 1994; Perez, DeBord, & Bieschke, 2000; Ritter & Terndrup, 2002; Taylor, 1999). To provide effective care, nurses must understand the identity and development of gay and lesbian patients, the impact of heterosexism on health care, and the implications for clinical practice (Walpin, 1997). Recent challenges to nurses call for understanding heterosexism and homophobia in health care (Fish, 2007), how these constructs contribute to the oppression faced by gay, lesbian, bisexual, and transgender people, and how they impact health care practice and research for these populations (Foster, 2008; Payne, 2007; Sinding, Barnoff, & Grassau, 2004; Tate & Longo, 2004; Ussher, 2009).

RELIGION AND SEXUAL ORIENTATION: IS IT A SIN?

Before proceeding further, it is important to caution readers that this chapter focuses on the clinical sensitivity required for the professional nurse to address the needs and issues of gay, lesbian, bisexual, and transgender patients. It is not intended to serve as a chapter on morality or religious belief. Nurses should know that some faiths provide support and nurturance to their gay, lesbian, bisexual, and transgender members. Nonetheless, institutional religion traditionally has been unsupportive of gay, lesbian, bisexual, and transgender people, and at times has served to promote outright oppression and intolerance (Davidson, 2000; Hardin, 1999; Ritter & Terndrup, 2002). For this reason, many LGBTQQIA individuals are cautious when approaching formal religious institutions.

Many conservative religious traditions that do not espouse inclusive definitions of sexuality beyond heterosexuality may promote "reparative" and "conversion" therapies and interventions that claim to be able to cure an individual's sexual orientation from a homosexual to a heterosexual orientation (National Committee on Lesbian and Gay Issues, National Association of Social Workers, 1992). In viewing sexual orientation as something that can be "fixed," this stance views homosexuality as disordered. Research does not support the effectiveness of these therapies (Davison, 1991; Haldeman, 1994), and there has been much debate on this topic (Drescher & Zucker, 2006, provided a series of articles on this topic; Carter, edited a special focus on this in the September 2004 edition of the *Counseling Psychologist*; see also Johnston & Jenkins, 2006). The idea of homosexuality as a disorder is also in direct contrast to the major health and mental health organizations that have issued public statements opposing reparative and conversion therapies and transformational ministries, including the American Academy of Pediatrics, the American Counseling Association, the American Psychiatric Association, the American Psychological Association, the National Association of School Psychologists, and the National Association of Social Workers (Just the Facts About Sexual Orientation & Youth, 1999). In 2009, the American Psychological Association (APA) issued a statement that clearly rejected therapies that purport to change an individual's sexual orientation from gay to straight (Associated Press, 2009, p. A16). The APA indicated that such strategies might actually incur depression and suicidality in gay and lesbian people. Nursing research has also addressed the dangers of conversion and reparative therapies (Blackwell, 2008; Hein & Matthews, 2010). In exploring nurses' views of sexual orientation, Blackwell (2007) found that nurses who view homosexuality as a "choice" tended to have higher levels of homophobia.

Although many religious gay, lesbian, bisexual, and transgender people have experienced alienation from various mainstream denominations, the role of spirituality and faith often remains important in their lives (McNeill, 1988; Ritter & Terndrup, 2002). For some, a personal relationship with a deity helps them to overcome the rejection experienced by family, society, and religious institutions. The literature demonstrates a growing interest in understanding the development of spirituality and the coming out process for gay, lesbian, and bisexual people (Helminiak, 2006; O'Neill & Ritter, 1992). Even those from more conservative denominations have explored ministry to gay people by assuming a "listening" stance (Liuzzi, 2001; Nugent & Gramick, 1995) and through traditional religious practices such as spiritual direction (Empereur, 1998). In any case, although some mainstream denominations are taking steps toward the inclusion of gay, lesbian, bisexual, and transgender people into full participation, many congregations are split in their openness to accept the full participation of gay people. In 2003, the Episcopal Church ordained its first openly gay bishop, resulting in news headlines and talk of a schism by some members who opposed the ordination (Goodstein, 2003). Thus, nurses need to accept that each patient brings his or her own experience of the interplay of liberation and oppression from organized religion. Other gay, lesbian, and bisexual patients may not participate in traditional religious institutions at all because of the oppression and alienation they have suffered (Ritter & Terndrup; 2002). It is important for nurses to consider these issues carefully, especially if planning to refer a patient to the hospital's pastoral care team or for a chaplain to visit the patient.

Likewise, each nurse brings an experience and view of gay people as formed by each one's own unique religious tradition and the experience of living in a culture built on a Judeo-Christian tradition (Ritter & Terndrup, 2002). Some nurses may find it difficult to reconcile their own religious beliefs that view homosexuality as sinful with providing sensitive care to gay, lesbian, bisexual, and transgender patients. It is important for nurses to be aware of their own beliefs with how they will act when caring for a patient who is gay. A first step is to validate the discomfort and to recognize that working with this patient will require extra attentiveness to the possible impact that nurses' discomfort could have on the patient. The patient's well-being—physical, psychosocial, and spiritual—should not be at risk. Additional training, professional workshops, and reading nursing journals can inform and educate professional nurses about any misconceptions they may have. Although nurses are not required to abandon their own value system, it may be helpful to refer the patient to other resources if the discomfort is too high (Ungvarski, 2001). The literature offers a discussion of the challenge between personal rights and professional responsibilities (Martino Maze, 2005; Shaw & Degazon, 2008). Some countries have posited legislation requiring equal care and nondiscrimination (Cayton, 2010; Fish, 2007; Peel, 2008), while other discussions have centered on the impact of public recognition of same-sex relationships (de Vries, Mason, Quam, & Aquaviva, 2009), the need for enhanced public policies to support greater equality of care (Coleman, 2007), and policies to reduce discrimination against gay and lesbian employees (Kendall-Raynor, 2009). Some nurses may even view advocacy for lesbian, gay, bisexual, and transgender patients and coworkers as the next step in the provision of competent care (MacDonnell, 2009). Others recognize the complicated interplay of funding and attitudes that might limit research on health issues for these populations (Chesla, 2005). What is most essential is that professional nurses provide competent, sensitive care to all patients, including those who are gay, lesbian, bisexual, and transgender.

CASE ANALYSIS

The case that follows does not represent an actual medical case, though the characters Maria and Beth are based on a real lesbian couple. Rather, the situation below reflects a composite of issues that affect gay, lesbian, bisexual, and transgender individuals who seek health care services. As the reader, you may also be wondering if this chapter will discuss the issue of HIV and AIDS, particularly as it is related to homophobia and heterosexism. The literature contains extensive references to working with patients with HIV and AIDS and the issues of homophobia and heterosexism (Bond et al., 1990; Breault

& Polifroni, 1992; Clauvieul, 1983; D'Augelli, 1989; Eliason, 1993a; Melby, Boore, & Murray, 1992; Powell-Cope, 1998; Royse & Birge, 1987; van Wissen & Siebers, 1993; Young, Knock, & Preston, 1989). The reader is directed to these sources to explore this intersection further.

The case presented here is not intended to focus on the identification and treatment of specific medical diagnoses associated with gay, lesbian, bisexual, and transgender people. Nonetheless, these medical facts are important and nurses should be aware of trends in health care service delivery and the needs of gay, lesbian, bisexual, and transgender individuals. Numerous concerns, such as barriers to health care (e.g., provider bias and psychotherapeutic issues), chemical dependency and its relationship to internalized homophobia, as well as lesbian health concerns related to breast cancer, gynecological problems, HIV, physical and sexual abuse, and mental health, must be addressed (Dibble & Roberts, 2003; Kauth, Hartwig, & Kalichman, 2000; Peate, 2006c; Ritter & Terndrup, 2002). Similarly, an understanding of the concerns of gay men related to high-risk sexual behaviors, substance abuse, HIV infection, and coping with compassion fatigue and multiple losses from HIV and AIDS is also essential (Kauth, Hartwig, & Kalichman, 2000; Ritter & Terndrup, 2002).

Although it is important to be aware of areas of the increased health risk for specific populations, nursing professionals must also be careful to avoid making assumptions about patients, which ultimately can be a form of discrimination. For example, a gay man might present to a hospital emergency room for complications related to cancer or another illness. It would be extremely important to approach that patient according to his specific diagnosis and unique needs rather than to assume that because he is gay, he must be in the hospital for HIV or an AIDS-related illness. This does not negate the importance of awareness by nurses of the increased health risks for certain diseases and disorders more prevalent among gays and lesbians. A key component of good nursing is educating patients about good health practices and risk factors specific to them. The focus in the following case, however, is mainly on the clinical sensitivity required of nurses in a professional health care setting when working with or delivering health services to individuals who are gay, lesbian, bisexual, or transgender. It should be noted that although the case is not true in its entirety, some elements are based on an actual couple's experiences.

IMPORTANT POINTS

1. The LGBTQQIA population consists of many different individuals. They range in socioeconomic status, education level, race, ethnicity, age, religion, gender, and veteran status.

(continued)

IMPORTANT POINTS

(continued)

2. Gender identity (how a person identifies as male, female, transgender, etc.) differs from gender role or expression (how one chooses to present oneself in dress, style, mannerisms, etc.). An individual's gender identity and gender expression may or may not match one's biological sex (one's anatomical configuration). Sexual orientation (to whom one is attracted) and sexual behavior (with whom one chooses to be sexual) may or may not match how one views the self in terms of sexuality and attraction (sexual identity).

3. Historically, individuals who have identified as LGBTQQIA have experienced oppression and discrimination from health and mental health providers, and from religious institutions. This experience has resulted in reluctance to seek health care, wariness of service providers, and lack of disclosure ("coming out") to one's health care providers. For this reason, many LGBTQQIA individuals consciously seek providers who appear knowledgeable and educated on their needs and concerns. They are also sensitized to those providers who dismiss their concerns or where they feel invisible.

4. Cultural identities such as race, ethnicity, age, and religion may impact an individual's decision to disclose to a health care provider. Health care concerns change at different developmental points across the lifespan for LGBTQQIA individuals. The social and political climate toward LGBTQQIA people may negatively or positively impact their access to care, available resources, and stressors to well-being.

5. Heterosexism and homophobia may impact service delivery of care to LGBTQQIA individuals. Nurses need to understand these concepts and reduce discrimination or prejudice against all patients, including those identified as LGBTQQIA.

6. Most health and mental health organizations do not view sexual orientation as a "choice." They reject conversion and reparative therapies as forms of treatment to "change" one's sexual orientation from same-sex attraction to opposite-sex attraction. These organizations view sexual orientation as a variation of "normal," in the same way one might view left-handedness in a right-hand-dominated world.

7. Knowledge of the interaction between gender identity, gender role/expression, biological sex, sexual orientation, sexual behavior, and sexual identity continues to unfold. Thus, culturally sensitive practice with LGBTQQIA individuals is an ongoing process informed by research in health and mental health, advocacy, and the social science professions.

CASE SCENARIO

Maria is a 45-year-old lesbian who has been in a long-term relationship for the past 16 years with her partner, Beth. Maria teaches fourth grade in a public school and Beth works as a social worker in a local Roman Catholic nursing home. Maria is extremely respected by the parents, teachers, and students in her school. Her principal frequently selects her to represent their school on district-wide committees. Maria's reputation among students is one of being fair and approachable. Because of her patience, Maria has had great success in helping students in class who are also receiving special services for learning and emotional disabilities. She works hard to teach her students to respect each other and participates as a mentor in the school district's mediation and conflict-resolution training program for students.

Maria and Beth have chosen not to be "out" in the workplace. Both fear they could lose their jobs. Working with children, Maria fears negative and inaccurate stereotypes of gay people as interested in "recruiting" young people. Beth's employment in an institution with a religious affiliation that condemns homosexuality precludes her sharing that part of her life with her coworkers. Each will occasionally bring the other to a work event as "my best friend who happens to be free" the night of that particular event. Although there are some individuals at each one's workplace who suspect that the two are a couple, most other staff members have not yet figured this out. Maria fears that although many of the teachers in her school respect her enough that finding out she is a lesbian may not tarnish her reputation with them, she fears that parents, students, and perhaps the district administration would not accept this revelation. The suburban community in which she works consists of many families who openly espouse traditional and conservative religious beliefs, and the school district superintendent belongs to an Evangelical Christian Church. Maria once relayed a conversation to Beth where a parent pulled her aside to say that the reason she stopped sending her son to his much-needed counseling sessions was because she suspected the therapist was "one of those homosexuals...I don't want one of *those* people near my son," the parent confided. Maria noted her own discomfort and fear as she grasped the true meaning of the parent's words.

About 6 months ago, Maria was in a serious car accident on her way home from work. She severely fractured her left femur and required immediate surgery. Maria was in the ICU for a few days due to complications following the surgery. The reader should note that it was only as recently as 2010 that President Obama's administration mandated that hospitals receiving Medicare or Medicaid funds must permit patients to determine who can visit them in the hospital and make decisions on their behalf (Shear, 2010). Previous to this, hospitals could prevent anyone but immediate family from visiting, a situation that often became complicated when a biological family member who did not accept the patient's sexual orientation prevented the patient's partner from visiting the patient. Maria was able to inform her doctor about the nature of her relationship with Beth, and requested that she be considered "family." This would afford Beth permission to visit Maria in line with ICU visitation policies. Beth also brought a copy of Maria's living will and medical power of attorney papers to the hospital, which the couple had drawn up with their attorney in case of just such an emergency situation. Although the additional attorney fees had been an extra cost that heterosexual couples did not have to face, Beth was relieved now that they had taken this step (for a discussion of legal documentation and gay individuals, see Riggle, Rostosky, Prather, & Hamrin, 2005). The hospital and Maria's doctor permitted Beth to visit Maria, just as close family members were permitted to do so for other patients. (Although hospitals are now recognizing gay and lesbian relationships and the legal paperwork couples bring, DeHope [2006] presents an excellent example of a case where parents of a lesbian with a traumatic brain injury challenged her partner in court and won legal rights to guardianship despite the couple having obtained a medical power of attorney before the injury had even occurred. This case occurred prior to the Obama administration order.) Although most of the staff was supportive and helpful during this difficult time, Beth felt uncomfortable around one nurse, Kelly, who reminded Beth of a nurse she had once worked with in her nursing home and rehabilitation center employment. Although Kelly said nothing overt, Beth couldn't help remembering her former colleague's reactions to a lesbian couple one time, after the visiting partner had passed the nursing station. Her colleague had rolled her eyes and looked away, not realizing that Beth had seen her reaction. Beth knew that her colleague was very religious and thought of gays and lesbians as living an "alternative lifestyle" and that her church was opposed to it. Beth feared that Kelly may have had similar feelings to her colleague, because she also was overtly religious in the jewelry she wore and the words she spoke. Kelly spent as little time as possible in Maria's room and usually managed to be assigned to other patients, although she made sure to stop in the room to advise Beth when visiting hours were over. She interacted with Beth as little as possible and shrugged off her questions about Maria's care, indicating that "the doctor will explain all of that to the patient."

Beth stayed with Maria in the hospital as often as her schedule would allow, wanting to use her personal and vacation days to assist Maria after her discharge home. She helped to coordinate Maria's care with her visiting nurse on the first few days after discharge. Maria wondered if the visiting nurse could tell that she shared the bedroom with Beth or if she even cared. Usually the visiting therapists and nurses were extremely supportive and took their relationship in stride. Sometimes, there was awkwardness where Beth could tell they had never been around gay people and didn't know what to do or say. In these cases, the visiting nurse might become quiet and task-focused, or somewhat giddy trying hard to appear comfortable in the situation.

Beth also accompanied Maria to many follow-up visits to her doctor appointments and physical therapy sessions. At each new medical office, Maria was required to answer questions verbally or to fill out forms providing her personal information. Frequently the paperwork required her to indicate her marital status: single, married, widowed, divorced. She also needed to indicate an emergency contact (sometimes listed as "next of kin") and that person's relationship to her. Although it was not a new question, each time she was asked, Maria automatically hesitated in her response. She did not fit any of the categories listed, which required her to identify as "single," or to make the clarification that she was "partnered," and thus "out" herself in the process. In each situation, Maria tried to assess the nurse, doctor, or therapist in the room as to his or her acceptance level and understanding of her relationship with Beth. If she said nothing, some thought that Beth was Maria's supportive sister who accompanied her to her medical appointments. Others seemed confused when Maria looked to Beth when decisions about care were made.

The hospital where Maria was treated and the other health care services she obtained were in the same county as the school in which Maria taught, and she recognized a few nurses and aides who were parents from the school where she was employed. She worried at times that the staff who knew who she was would recognize the nature of her and Beth's relationship, and was concerned about their level of professionalism. Maria knew that laws such as HIPPA protected her health care information, but she also knew that the presence of her constant visitor could raise eyebrows and be too tempting for some staff not to relay back to other parents in her school community.

WHAT NURSES NEED TO KNOW ABOUT THEMSELVES

APPLICATION OF THE STAIRCASE MODEL: SELF-REFLECTION QUESTIONS

1. Where am I on the Cultural Competency Staircase? What do I need to do to progress to the next level?
2. How many interactions have I had with people who identify as gay, lesbian, bisexual, or transgender? Would I have known at the time that my patient was LGBTQ? How might these experiences have prepared me for interactions with patients such as Maria and Beth?
3. What assumptions, stereotypes, or generalizations shape my beliefs about Maria and Beth or other members of the LGBTQ community? Do I hold any bias against them?
4. How much have I communicated with Maria and Beth? How much do I understand the need for privacy because of workplace concerns? Do I minimize their concerns about their experiences?
5. How do I present myself to patients who are LGBTQ? Do I seem comfortable and accepting, or nervous and unsure?
6. What steps can I take to improve my ability to be genuine, sincere, and interested in the concerns of my LGBTQ patients?
7. Do heterosexism and homophobia really exist? In what ways do I participate in heterosexism, and what does it mean for me personally to be homophobic?
8. Do I make insensitive statements to or about gay, lesbian, bisexual, and transgender people, or laugh at jokes others tell that involve these individuals?

9. What is the most sensitive way to elicit information about health practices that allows the gay/lesbian/bisexual/transgender patient to answer questions honestly and enables the nurse to complete an effective assessment? Do I believe I currently have the skills needed to do this?
10. Do I have knowledge of the LGBTQ patient's experiences and attitudes toward health care? What do I know about the health risks and behaviors of gay, lesbian, bisexual, and transgender patients?

Responses to Self-Reflection Questions

Response to Where am I on the Cultural Competency Staircase? What do I need to do to progress to the next level?

Review the Staircase Model presented in Chapter 1. Identify where you are in this model on the issue of sexual orientation and gender identity. What specific steps can you take to progress to the next step?

Response to How many interactions have I had with people who identify as gay, lesbian, bisexual, or transgender? Would I have known at the time that my patient was LGBTQ? How might these experiences have prepared me for interactions with patients such as Maria and Beth?

Take a moment to recall any gay, lesbian, or bisexual patients for whom you have cared in your training or work experiences. Now think about the number of gay, lesbian, or bisexual people you know on a personal level. You may think that you have a short list if you cannot quickly think of any specific individual. How did you know that you were working with an individual who was gay, lesbian, or bisexual? Although there are some stereotypical behaviors that people identify with gay and lesbian people based on movies and television shows, most gay, lesbian, or bisexual people look like everyone else. It is most probable that you have worked with many more gay people than you know about, but perhaps you were unaware of their sexual orientation because they did not come out to you. Perhaps your own heterosexism presumes that everyone you know, care for, and work with is heterosexual. As you continue to grow professionally and expand your work experiences, you will encounter more gay and lesbian people. It is important to be sensitive in your encounters with them and to learn from these contacts.

Response to What assumptions, stereotypes, or generalizations shape my beliefs about Maria and Beth or other members of the LGBTQ community? Do I hold any bias against them?

Our belief system is informed by our community, parents and family, religious traditions, and societal values. Each person is a product of the society in which we exist. Take a moment now to make a list of everything that comes to mind when you think of the words "gay," "lesbian," "bisexual," and "transgender." What enters your consciousness as you jot down your ideas? Did you think of clinical terms like "homosexuality"? Was your focus on excessive sexual activity and promiscuity, or sexually transmitted diseases such as HIV and AIDS? Did you think of social oppression or political issues such as gay marriage and hate crimes legislation? How many derogatory terms such as "fag," "homo," or "queer" came into your mind? Do you believe that a gay person is acting out behaviorally, "going through a stage," or psychologically ill? Perhaps like the nurse, Kelly, you might have strong religious beliefs that shape your understanding of gay, lesbian, bisexual, and transgender people.

It is important to consider your own starting point in your understanding of gays and lesbians. Try to identify what your beliefs are about the origins of being gay. Do you believe that gay people choose to be gay or that they are gay because of some genetic predisposition or other scientific reason? Let's presume in Case 1 that Nurse Kelly had made statements suggesting that gay people choose to be gay. By doing so, she indicated by her words that she believes it is not natural to be gay. She views the issue of same-sex attraction as a moral issue where an individual chooses such behaviors. Identifying your own beliefs will help you to be aware of the perspective you take. Your beliefs can influence your attitudes and treatment of other individuals, especially the patients to whom you provide clinical care. It is important that your beliefs be founded on accurate knowledge of the facts about sexual orientation. In addition to nursing associations, professional organizations such as the American Psychological Association, National Association of Social Workers, American Academy of Pediatrics, and the American Counseling Association can serve as resources for current research on issues pertaining to the understanding of sexual orientation and the needs of such individuals.

Response to How much have I communicated with Maria and Beth? How much do I understand the need for privacy because of workplace concerns? Do I minimize the concerns of LGBTQ people's experiences?

When we are uncomfortable with something or someone, we may tend to avoid that topic or person. Avoidance can impact communication styles. It is important to use good communication skills to engage patients, including both verbal and nonverbal communication strategies.

It is also important to recognize that even if a nurse is following HIPPA by upholding confidentiality, there are still subtle ways that may call for prudence. If a patient is in a small community where everyone knows everyone, it is important to ask patients how they want you to address them and their partner. If they are closeted because of work or other issues, the most well-intentioned nurse could ask if a patient's partner is visiting tonight just as someone else passes by the room. This isn't intentional or malicious; however, clients who are in the closet may be extra vigilant about their relationship. On the other hand, another LGBTQ couple that is out might hope that the nurse speaks to them in the same way as is done with a heterosexual couple. It is important to understand that privacy may be more of an issue for an LGBTQ couple or not, but one only will know through assessing the situation with sensitivity.

Response to How do I present myself to patients who are LGBTQ? Do I seem comfortable and accepting, or nervous and unsure?

It cannot be stated enough how important it is to present oneself as a professional. Although this most importantly includes knowledge of one's nursing tasks and duties, it also involves speaking with confidence and respect. Patients will perceive the confidence and dignity of professionals. Confident professionals are not threatened or intimidated by what they do not know, but rather are curious to understand so that they can provide more effective services. Patients who identify as LGBTQ often have experienced negative and rejecting messages about their identity at some point in their past. Many will be particularly adept at picking up signals a nurse may send that being LGBTQ is not okay. Thus, it is important that nurses present a positive demeanor to LGBTQ patients.

Response to What steps can I take to improve my ability to be genuine, sincere, and interested in the concerns of my LGBTQ patients?

This question taps into your fundamental awareness of your feelings about gay people and your core desires about your role as a nursing professional. Most nurses feel drawn to the nursing profession because of a concern for and desire to help others. How much do I care about the needs of people who are marginalized and discriminated against both socially and legally? What attitudes might I need to change to be more accepting of gay people who are patients on my unit? How can I genuinely provide competent, sensitive care to this particular group of individuals? A genuine desire to learn more about the specific needs and health care issues facing the gay, lesbian, and bisexual population will help nurses to provide more competent, sensitive care.

Response to Do heterosexism and homophobia really exist? In what ways do I participate in heterosexism, and what does it mean for me personally to be homophobic?

Perhaps the concept of heterosexism is new for you. Do you believe that it really exists or do you scoff at the idea? Think back to the last patient you met. Many health care workers don't even consider that a patient might be gay. If the patient was wearing a ring, perhaps a band on his or her fourth finger, did you presume the individual was married (Walpin, 1997)? How did you know the person was not in a relationship with another individual of the same gender? It is essential to identify the way you speak to your patients and the presumptions you might be making about them. Patients need to feel accepted and comfortable so that they can entrust you with their care. If a nurse believes that heterosexuals are somehow superior or "more normal" than gay people, she or he may alienate gay or lesbian patients and discourage them from seeking health care information or reporting new symptoms.

In considering your awareness about your presumptions and biases around sexual orientation, it is important to assess your own comfort level with gay, lesbian, and bisexual people. Research indicates that individuals who know someone personally who is gay, such as a family member or close friend, have lower levels of homophobia (Misener et al., 1997). Such individuals are more likely to be accepting of that person, to feel comfortable around him or her, and are less likely to feel threatened by that person's identity as gay or lesbian. Think of your friends, family members, and coworkers and see if you can identify any who are gay or lesbian. If you suspect that someone might be gay but that person has not come out to you formally, why might she or he have avoided coming out to you? Certainly it is challenging for gay people to know to whom they can come out, but in focusing on your own self-awareness, it is important to note if you are giving off subtle messages that you are uncomfortable with such information. Your own homophobia may be sending messages loud and clear that you are uncomfortable with or disgusted by the idea of same-sex relationships. Kelly spent as little time as possible with Maria and avoided Beth at the nursing station. She was clearly giving off a "you are not welcome here" message, a signal that she did not desire to grow in her level of competence in understanding the needs of gay, lesbian, and bisexual patients. Her own misinformation, belief system, and lack of comfort about individuals who are gay heightened her fears, disgust, and avoidance of gay and lesbian patients. She did not desire to learn more or to challenge her current knowledge of what it means to be gay, lesbian, bisexual, or transgender.

Response to *Do I make insensitive statements to or about gay, lesbian, bisexual, and transgender people, or laugh at jokes others tell that involve these individuals?*

Certainly the statements by Beth's colleague and possibly also the nurse, Kelly, may have evoked a level of discomfort in some of the other nurses on her unit who felt that it was not their role to pass judgment but to provide medical care to Maria. It would not be surprising for an individual like Kelly to refer to gays and lesbians in a derogatory manner, or to tell jokes about gays and lesbians on the unit. These insensitive statements reflect biases and beliefs that gay people are somehow bad or flawed.

Although many professionals are not likely to be as overt as Beth's colleague or Kelly, even the most sensitive people can still unintentionally create dissonance between themselves and gay, lesbian, bisexual, and transgender patients. Gray et al. (1996) noted the subtler ways that heterosexism and homophobia emerge even among nursing professionals. If such attitudes exist in professional-to-professional relationships, it is not a huge leap to consider that the subtleness also can exist in the nurse–patient relationship.

Perhaps Maria wears a wedding band on her left hand. Nurse Smith works the 3-to-11 shift on A-wing, but this week she was asked to cover B-wing where Maria's room is located. Shortly before evening visiting hours she stops in Maria's room, and, unconsciously noticing the ring on Maria's hand, asks if her husband will be visiting this evening. Although her intentions are good, Nurse Smith has put Maria in the awkward position of correcting the inaccurate information, ignoring her inquiry, or even lying because she may be too tired to explain. Thus, it is essential to be aware of and sensitive to even the most mundane presumptions, as in the case of Maria's ring. Perhaps Nurse Smith could have rephrased her question to say, "Are you expecting any visitors this evening?"

The more interaction with gay, lesbian, bisexual, and transgender patients nurses have, the more aware they can be to increasing sensitivity to the unique needs of this population. The desire to understand the oppression and discrimination faced by gay, lesbian, bisexual, and transgender people can help nurses to see that insensitive comments and jokes can be harmful to the well-being of the gay, lesbian, or bisexual individual.

Response to What is the most sensitive way to elicit information about health practices that allows the gay/lesbian/bisexual/transgender patient to answer questions honestly and enables the nurse to complete an effective assessment? Do I believe I currently have the skills needed to do this?

Imagine that you are the nurse completing the admission for Maria at the hospital or in the doctor's office. What is the most sensitive manner in which to obtain needed information? Some nurses feel uncomfortable requesting personal information from any patient, but especially in areas related to sexual relationships and activity. If you are such a person, you may find that rehearsing your interviewing skills with a clinical supervisor or a trusted colleague will help you to reduce your discomfort. Strategies for effective clinical interviewing that do not presume heterosexuality can be found in the literature as well (Walpin, 1997). Practice asking questions that make you feel uncomfortable until you are able to ask them smoothly and without judgment or hesitation.

There are specific strategies that a nurse can use to identify a patient's support system without putting those questions in a heterosexual context. For example, rather than asking if the patient is married, the nurse can ask if the individual is in a significant relationship or romantic relationship and with whom. Certainly some gay and lesbian patients have been married in the past even though they may now be in a same-sex relationship. It is clinically appropriate for a gynecologist's office to know a woman's sexual history, as certain activities may put the woman at risk for different forms of cancer or other diseases. Asking a woman if she is straight or gay may not elicit this information; rather, the nurse can inquire about the patient's prior behaviors, for example, "Have you had sexual contact with men, women, both or neither?" Effective communication with gay, lesbian, bisexual, and transgender patients requires skillful interviewing, knowledge about the health care needs relevant to this population, and experience through relationships with individuals as nurses increase their comfort level in providing care to individuals who do not fit traditional family constellations and relationships.

Response to Do I have knowledge of the LGBTQ patient's experiences and attitudes toward health care? What do I know about the health risks and behaviors of gay, lesbian, bisexual, and transgender patients?

It is important for the nurse to know some of the history of gays and lesbians and the health care system. It was not until 1973 that the American Psychiatric Association transitioned from its view of homosexuality as a mental disorder in the *Diagnostic and Statistical Manual* and began to classify homosexuality as an orientation or expression (American Academy of Pediatrics, 1993). Prior to this, gay and lesbian patients were subjected to numerous interventions ranging from institutionalization to electroconvulsive shock therapy (Bullough, 1976; Kauth, Hartwig, & Kalichman, 2000; Murphy, 1992). Given this historical background and the negative attitudes of health practitioners reported earlier, it is not difficult to understand why many gay, lesbian, bisexual, and transgender individuals might approach the health care system with caution and hesitation.

The case of Maria demonstrates the ambivalence and concern of gay, lesbian, bisexual, or transgender patients in how to complete admission forms and paperwork that ask for marital status: single, married, widowed, divorced. Think back to Maria's case. The emergency room nurse asks Maria about her marital status. As Maria is admitted to the floor, the admitting nurse also inquires about the patient's social support. Each time, Maria must assess the safety of "coming out." Is this person safe? Will I be discriminated against? The patient expends a lot of energy assessing each health care worker's attitude and acceptance level, while other patients spend their energy on getting well. There is a cost to telling the truth and a cost to holding back this information. If the patient is not in a relationship, it may not matter, but if the patient is in a committed relationship, she may be worried about the visitation rights of her partner. Are certain units off limits to anyone but spouse and direct family? Will the institution respect the mandate for visitation privileges? What does it mean to be family? What is the policy of the health care setting regarding same-sex relationships where you currently work or intern?

If the patient is unconscious or confused, how is the partner of the same gender treated? Because of warnings against just such discrimination, many same-sex couples have drawn up medical powers of attorney and living wills for such situations, but not all same-sex couples can afford this expense, which married couples do not face. Even when same-sex couples take this extra step, other family members can challenge guardianship in court, and have won such cases, as described earlier in this chapter. As a nurse, one must consider the added burden same-sex couples may encounter in an emergency situation. Not only must the well partner (Beth) worry about her loved one's well-being, she must also worry about being able to prove her right to be present in the room, a right not generally guaranteed unless one is legally married. When a loved one is rushed to the hospital or facing medical treatment, most of us would want to leave our location immediately to be at our loved one's side, not frantically rush around trying to remember to bring legal papers with us to the hospital. Do we ask each married person to prove the legitimacy of his or her relationship by presenting a marriage certificate or other legal document in order to visit the patient in an ICU unit? Of course not. Yet, gay couples may face this type of challenge any time there is a medical concern.

As mentioned earlier, there are specific health care concerns that appear to have a higher incidence among gay or lesbian people. HIV/AIDS and other sexually transmitted diseases are well known, and recent research has explored lesbian health risks for breast cancer as well as other health issues for gay men (Kauth, Hartwig, & Kalichman, 2000; O'Hanlan, 2000). It is essential for nurses to know the risk factors unique to any patients they treat so that the most effective care and education can be provided. It is important for the nurse to keep her knowledge current by reading professional journals and attending professional conferences to continue to learn about the health care concerns of gay, lesbian, and bisexual patients.

A FINAL WORD TO GAY, LESBIAN, BISEXUAL, AND TRANSGENDER NURSES

At the opening of this chapter, the reader was invited to consider for whom and by whom this chapter was written. Although most readers probably approached the chapter as geared to heterosexual readers, it is quite likely that gay, lesbian, bisexual, and transgender nurses might be reading this chapter as well. What are the unique challenges that these nurses face in the health care workplace? Despite the important issues presented earlier, it is both hopeful and reassuring that there are many caring straight and gay people working in various roles in the health care system who are sensitive to the issues faced by gay, lesbian, bisexual, and transgender patients.

For gay, lesbian, bisexual, and transgender nurses, coming out and one's identity as a gay person can also be a primary concern in the workplace. This concern extends in the direction of working with patients as well as working with coworkers. Will the patient not want me to provide care if my sexual orientation is known? Stereotypes of gay people as highly sexualized, focused only on sex and wanting to "hit" on everyone and anyone still abound, despite the absurdity of such beliefs. How will the patient react to me as a nurse if the patient learns of my sexual orientation? Will the patient not want me to assist with toileting, bathing, and other activities of daily living or medical treatments?

Workplace discrimination against gay people may also be a concern for the gay, lesbian, or bisexual nurse. Will my coworkers treat me differently if they know that I am gay or lesbian? Will administration withhold promotions or compensations? If I make an error, will it be attributed to characteristics of my sexual identity? If I receive extra challenging work assignments, how will I know whether this is just my turn to receive a challenging assignment or whether someone has some hidden feelings against homosexuality or my expression of my sexual orientation or gender identity? These uncertainties challenge gay, lesbian, and bisexual people in any workplace. As a microcosm of a larger society, the health care world reflects many of the same concerns found in other workplaces.

On a positive note, gay, lesbian, bisexual, and transgender nurses can offer the health care workplace a wealth of knowledge and skill. As gay people, gay nurses are sensitized to issues of concern to gay, lesbian, bisexual, and transgender patients, such as forms and paperwork that are noninclusive of their relationships. Gay nurses can be a visible sign of safety to gay, lesbian, bisexual, and transgender patients who can view such staff members as sensitive allies, helpers, and advocates to the unique circumstances of their care. In some cases, gay, lesbian, bisexual, and transgender nurses can serve as cultural translators to other health care providers unfamiliar with the challenges and fears faced by gay, lesbian, and bisexual patients. They can provide education to staff, patients, and families of patients, and they can work on committees to improve sensitivity to issues of concern for gay, lesbian, bisexual, and transgender patients and staff.

CONCLUSION

The case analysis of Maria's experience with the health care system highlights some of the key issues relevant to working with an individual with a minority sexual orientation. Heterosexism and homophobia can creep into the practice of even the most well-intentioned health care provider. It is important to promote a health care environment that accepts all people, regardless of sexual orientation. As noted, the Staircase Model can provide a structure for assessing the key areas of cultural competency as they pertain to sexual orientation. Staff education can provide a valuable avenue for raising nurses' awareness, knowledge, skill level, and encounters with gay, lesbian, bisexual, and transgender individuals (Walpin, 1997). Gay, lesbian, bisexual, and transgender people can be found across all ages, disability status, religion, race, ethnicity, and socioeconomic status. Thus, nurses can expect to care for gay, lesbian, bisexual, and transgender patients at some time in their career. School nurses can work to promote safety in the schools, reduce harassment of gay students and the resulting physical and emotional injuries that occur because of it, and help young people just coming out to feel supported and safe. Homecare nurses can be sure that patients are receiving sensitive care in their homes, and in-patient hospital unit nurses can help to raise awareness of gay, lesbian, bisexual, and transgender patients' needs, both clinical and psychosocial.

NCLEX-TYPE QUESTIONS

1. The culturally competent nurse leads a staff development workshop for nurses on the care of patients who are LGBTQQIA. What statement by the nurse conveys the most accurate information about the acronym LGBTQQIA?
   A. It is a term that describes an organization in support of gay people.
   B. It is an umbrella term for individuals who are anti-gay.
   C. It is an umbrella term that reflects both gender and sexual orientation identities.
   D. It is a term that refers only to males who are gay.

2. A nurse is assigned to care for a newly admitted patient who sustained multiple injuries in a car crash and requires complete care. The patient self-identifies as a lesbian and is accompanied by her partner of 10 years. What action by the nurse suggests a need for further staff development in the care of patients who are LGBTQQA?
   A. The nurse asks the patient's partner if she has any questions and allows her to assist the nurses by feeding the patient.
   B. The nurse reminds the patient's partner that visiting hours are not until 2 p.m., but only close members of the family will be permitted in to see the patient at that time.
   C. The nurse includes the patient's partner in the discussion during the interview when collecting information about the patient's medical history.
   D. The nurse documents the patient's partner's contact information on the chart.

3. A nurse is working on a pediatric unit where a 15-year-old male patient has confided to the nurse that he is uncomfortable sharing with his parents that he believes he is probably gay. On reflecting on this situation the nurse considers that the young man has expressed a concern about his (select all that apply):
   A. Gender identity
   B. Sexual orientation
   C. Attraction to members of the same sex
   D. View of himself as a female

4. What statement is true about the impact of attitudinal barriers on individuals who are LGBTQQ?
   A. The impact of stereotyping and discrimination is evident throughout the lifespan of persons who are LGBTQQ.
   B. Only teenagers and young adults who are LGBTQQ and sexually active are affected by discrimination.
   C. The impact of discrimination against LGBTQQ is most notable in mid-life.
   D. Senior citizens who are LGBTQQ are no longer impacted by discrimination toward persons who are LGBTQQ.

5. When giving the change of shift report to the other nurses on her unit, a young female nurse explains that a middle-aged male patient on the unit "appears to be gay." She further states that as a result she is uncomfortable caring for the patient until she is certain about his HIV status. The culturally competent nurse receiving

the report appreciates that the nurse's comments probably reflect the younger nurse's:

A. Ageism
B. Heterosexism
C. Homophobia
D. Germ phobia

6. A nurse states to one of her colleagues that she believes that any patient who self-identifies as being a member of the LGBTQQ population is experiencing some type of psychological problem. What statement by the nurse colleague offers the most appropriate response?

A. "Psychological problems are found among members of every cultural group."
B. "Some gay and lesbian patients have psychological problems, some do not."
C. "Everyone has attitudes based on their own beliefs; however, the APA removed homosexuality from the *Diagnostic and Statistical Manual of Mental Disorders* in the early 1970s."
D. "This is probably true, but nurses should not judge anyone."

7. The nurse who expresses the belief that being gay is a choice made by individuals who are deviating from the normal or appropriate sexual behavior pattern is exemplifying what characteristic?

A. Heterosexism
B. Ethnocentrism
C. Homophobia
D. Centrism

8. The first action by nurses who are seeking to provide culturally sensitive care to patients who are LGBTQQIA is to:

A. Gain an understanding of their own beliefs and attitudes about members of this group.
B. Seek information about the health risks in this population.
C. Attempt to learn about what it means to be LGBTQQIA.
D. Involve themselves in advocacy groups to assist members of the group.

9. What statement best describes the role of the culturally competent nurse in providing care to patients who are LGBTQQIA. Culturally competent nurses:

A. Abandon their own values and beliefs and adopt those of the patients for whom they are caring.
B. Recognize their personal discomfort level and refer patients to other resources when they are personally unable to assist them.
C. Seek training, professional workshops, and journals to explore information about topics related to patients who are LGBTQQIA.
D. Advocate for patients and coworkers as the first step on the staircase of cultural competency.

10. The ER nurse interviews a 32-year-old patient who has come to the ER alone complaining of severe headache. Her blood pressure is 160/110 and she is being admitted until her hypertension is stabilized. During the interview, the nurse asks if the patient is married or single. The patient hesitates and then responds,

"No, I'm unmarried." What statement by the nurse reflects an effort to be culturally sensitive in this situation?

A. "Well, are you single, divorced, or widowed?
B. "Is there a significant person or family member you would like me to contact?"
C. "Who is your next of kin; are there children I might get in touch with?"
D. "Have you always been single"?

AACN COMPETENCIES ADDRESSED IN THIS CHAPTER

1. Apply knowledge of social and cultural factors that affect nursing and health care across multiple contexts.
2. Use relevant data sources and best evidence in providing culturally competent care.
3. Promote achievement of safe and quality outcomes of care for diverse populations.
4. Advocate for social justice, including commitment to the health of vulnerable populations and the elimination of health care disparities.
5. Participate in continuous cultural competence development.

REFERENCES

A school nurse perspective on lesbian and gay adolescents: Identity development. (1993, May). *School Nurse News 19*(3), 22.

Albarran, J. W., & Salmon, D. (2000). Lesbian, gay and bisexual experiences within critical care nursing, 1988–1998: A survey of the literature. *International Journal of Nursing Studies, 37*(5), 445–455.

American Academy of Pediatrics. (1993). Policy statement on homosexuality and adolescence (RE9332) [Electronic Version]. *Pediatrics, 92*(4), 631–634.

Associated Press. (2009, August 6). Psychologist reject gay "therapy." *New York Times*, p. A16.

Bakker, L. & Cavender, A. (2003). Promoting culturally competent care for gay youth. *Journal of School Nursing, 19*(2), 65–72.

Bakker, F., Sandfort, T., Vanwesenbeeck, I., van Lindert, H., & Westert, G. (2006). Do homosexual persons use health care services more frequently than heterosexual persons: Findings from a Dutch population survey. *Social Science & Medicine, 63*(8), 2022–2030. doi:10.1016/j.socscimed.2006.05.024

Bauer, G., Hammond, R., Travers, R., Kaay, M., Hohenadel, K., & Boyce, M. (2009). 'I don't think this is theoretical; This is our lives': How erasure impacts health care for transgender people. *JANAC: Journal of the Association of Nurses in AIDS Care, 20*(5), 348–361. doi:10.1016/j.jana.2009.07.004.

Bent, K., & Magilvy, J. (2006). When a partner dies: Lesbian widows. *Issues in Mental Health Nursing, 27*(5), 447–459. doi:10.1080/01612840600599960

Benton, J. (2003). Making schools safer and healthier for lesbian, gay, bisexual, and questioning students. *Journal of School Nursing, 19*(5), 251–259.

Berlan, E., Corliss, H., Field, A., Goodman, E., & Austin, S. (2010). Sexual orientation and bullying among adolescents in the growing up today study. *Journal of Adolescent Health, 46*(4), 366–371. doi:10.1016/j.jadohealth.2009.10.015

Bieschke, K. J., Perez, R. M., & DeBord, K. A. (2007). *Handbook of counseling and psychotherapy with lesbian, gay, bisexual, and transgender clients* (2nd ed.). Washington, DC: American Psychological Association.

Bjorkman, M., & Malterud, K. (2009). Lesbian women's experiences with health care: A qualitative study. *Scandinavian Journal of Primary Health Care, 27*(4), 238–243. doi:10.3109/02813430903226548

Bjorkman, M., & Malterud, K. (2007). Being lesbian—does the doctor need to know? *Scandinavian Journal of Primary Health Care, 25*(1), 58–62. doi:10.1080/02813430601086178

Blackwell, C. (2008). Nursing implications in the application of conversion therapies on gay, lesbian, bisexual, and transgender clients. *Issues in Mental Health Nursing, 29*(6), 651–665. doi:10.1080/01612840802048915.

Blackwell, C. (2007). Belief in the "free choice" model of homosexuality: A correlate of homophobia in registered nurses. *Journal of LGBT Health Research, 3*(3), 31–40. doi:10.1080/15574090802093117

Blumenfield, W. J. (1992). *Homophobia: How we all pay the price.* Boston, MA: Beacon Press.

Bond, S., Rhodes, T., Philips, P., Setters, J., Foy, C., & Bond, J. (1990). HIV infection and AIDS in England: The experience, knowledge and intentions of community nursing staff. *Journal of Advanced Nursing, 15*, 249–255.

Brandenburg, D., Matthews, A., Johnson, T., & Hughes, T. (2007). Breast cancer risk and screening: A comparison of lesbian and heterosexual women. *Women & Health, 45*(4), 109–130. doi:10.1300/J013v45n04-06

Breault, A. J. & Polifroni, E. O. (1992). Caring for people with AIDS: Nurses' attitudes and feelings. *Journal of Advanced Nursing, 17,*21–27.

Bretas, J., Ohara, C., & Querino, I. (2008). Orientation about sexuality for nursing students. *Acta Paulista de Enfermagem, 21*(4), 568–574.

Brogan, M. (1997). Healthcare for lesbians: Attitudes and experiences. *Nursing Standard, 11*(45), 39–42.

Bullough, V. L. (1976). *Sex, society & history.* New York, NY: Science History Publications.

Burch, A. (2008). Health care providers' knowledge, attitudes, and self-efficacy for working with patients with spinal cord injury who have diverse sexual orientations. *Physical Therapy, 88*(2), 191–198.

Burgess, D., Lee, R., Tran, A., & van Ryn, M. (2007). Effects of perceived discrimination on mental health and mental health services utilization among gay, lesbian, bisexual and transgender persons. *Journal of LGBT Health Research, 3*(4), 1–14. doi:10.1080/15574090802226626

Cant, B., & Taket, A. (2006). Lesbian and gay experiences of primary care in one borough in North London, UK. *Diversity in Health & Social Care, 3*(4), 271–279.

Carroll, L., Gilroy, P. J., & Ryan, J. (2002). Counseling transgendered, transsexual, and gendervariant clients. *Journal of Counseling & Development, 80*, 131–139.

Carter, R. T. (Ed.). (2004, September). Religious beliefs and sexual orientation [Special issue]. *The Counseling Psychologist, 32*(5).

Cayton, E. (2010). Equal access to health care: Sexual orientation and state public accommodation antidiscrimination statutes. *Law & Sexuality: A Review of Lesbian, Gay, Bisexual & Transgender Legal Issues, 19*, 193–214.

Champion, J., Wilford, K., Shain, R., & Piper, J. (2005). Risk and protective behaviours of bisexual minority women: A qualitative analysis. *International Nursing Review, 52*(2), 115–122. doi:10.1111/j.1466–2435.2005.00246.x

Chesla, C. (2005). Family nursing: Challenges and opportunities: The hand that feeds us: Strings and restrictions on funding for family nursing research. *Journal of Family Nursing, 11*(4), 340–343. doi:10.1177/1074840705280819

Chinn, P. (2008). Lesbian nurses: What's the big deal? *Issues in Mental Health Nursing,* 29(6), 551–554. doi:10.1080/01612840802046604

Ciro, D., Surko, M., Bhandarkar, K., Helfgott, N., Peake, K., & Epstein, I. (2005). Lesbian, gay, bisexual, sexual-orientation questioning adolescents seeking mental health services: Risk factors, worries, and desire to talk about them. *Social Work in Mental Health,* 3(3), 213–234. doi:10.1300/J200v03n03_05

Clauvieul, G. (1983). *Evaluation of AIDS: Apprehension among nursing personnel and its observed effects on levels of patient care.* Bethesda, MD: National Institute of Health.

Cobos, D., & Jones, J. (2009). Moving forward: Transgender persons as change agents in health care access and human rights. *Journal of the Association of Nurses in AIDS Care,* 20(5), 341–347. doi:10.1016/j.jana.2009.06.004

Cochran, B., & Cauce, A. (2006). Characteristics of lesbian, gay, bisexual, and transgender individuals entering substance abuse treatment. *Journal of Substance Abuse Treatment,* 30(2), 135–146. doi:10.1016/j.jsat.2005.11.009

Cochran, B., Peavy, K., & Cauce, A. (2007). Substance abuse treatment providers' explicit and implicit attitudes regarding sexual minorities. *Journal of Homosexuality,* 53(3), 181–207. doi:10.1300/J082v53n03_10

Coker, T., Austin, S., & Schuster, M. (2010). The health and health care of lesbian, gay, and bisexual adolescents. *Annual Review of Public Health,* 31(1), 457–477. doi:10.1146/annurev.publhealth.012809.103636.

Coker, T., Austin, S., & Schuster, M. (2009). Health and healthcare for lesbian, bisexual, and transgender youth: Reducing disparities through research, education, and practice. *Journal of Adolescent Health,* 45(3), 213–215. doi:10.1016/j.jadohealth.2009.06.020

Coleman, E. (2007). Creating a sexually healthier world through effective public policy. *International Journal of Sexual Health,* 19(3), 5–24. doi:10.1300/J514v19n03_02

D'Augelli, A.R. (1989). AIDS fears and homophobia among rural nursing personnel. *AIDS Education and Preventions,* 1(14), 277–284.

D'Augelli, A. R. & Patterson, C. J. (Eds.). (1995). *Lesbian, gay and bisexual identities over the lifespan: Psychological perspectives.* New York, NY: Oxford University Press.

Davidson, M.G. (2002). Religion and spirituality. In R. M Perez, K. A. DeBord and K. J. Bieschke (Eds.), *Handbook of counseling and psychotherapy with lesbian, gay and bisexual clients* (pp. 435–456). Washington, DC: American Psychological Association.

Davison, G. C. (1991). Construction and morality in therapy for homosexuality. In J.C. Gonsiorek & J.D. Weinrich (Eds.), *With compassion toward some: Homosexuality and social work in America* (pp. 115–136). New York, NY: Harrington Press.

DeHart, D. (2008). Breast health behavior among lesbians: The role of health beliefs, heterosexism, and homophobia. *Women & Health,* 48(4), 409–427. doi:10.1080/03630240802575146

DeHope, E. (2006). The case of Joan and Terri: Implications of society's treatment of sexual orientation for lesbians and gays with disabilities. In L. Messinger & D. F. Morrow (Eds.), *Case studies on sexual orientation and gender expression in social work practice* (pp. 44–46). New York, NY: Columbia University Press.

de Vries, B., Mason, A., Quam, J., & Acquaviva, K. (2009). State recognition of same-sex relationships and preparations for end of life among lesbian and gay boomers. *Sexuality Research & Social Policy: A Journal of the NSRC,* 6(1), 90–101. doi:10.1525/srsp.2009.6.1.90

Dibble, S. L., & Roberts, S. A. (2003). Improving cancer screening among lesbians over 50: Results of a pilot study. *Oncology Nursing Forum, 30*(4), E71–E79.

Dibble, S., Sato, N., & Haller, E. (2007). Asians and native Hawaiian or other Pacific Islanders midlife lesbians' health: A pilot study. *Women & Therapy, 30*(3–4), 129–143.

Dootson, L. (2000). Adolescent homosexuality and culturally competent nursing. *Nursing Forum, 35*(3), 13–20.

Drescher, J., & Zucker, K. J. (Eds.). (2006). *Ex-Gay research: Analyzing the Spitzer study and its relation to science, religion, politics, and culture.* Binghamton, NY: Harrington Park Press/The Haworth Press.

Dworkin, S. H., & Gutierrez, F. J. (Eds.). (1992). *Counseling gay men & lesbians: Journey to the end of the rainbow.* Alexandria, VA: American Counseling Association.

Dykes, D., & White, A. (2009). Getting to equal: Strategies to understand and eliminate general and orthopaedic healthcare disparities. *Clinical Orthopaedics & Related Research, 467*(10), 2598–2605.

Edwards, D. (2001). Outing the issue: Gay and lesbian residents are seeing the development of long-term care communities marketed for the them—and opportunities for existing ones to make them feel more welcome. *Nursing Homes: Long Term Care Management, 50*(8), 40.

Eisenberg, M., & Resnick, M. (2006). Suicidality among gay, lesbian and bisexual youth: The role of protective factors. *Journal of Adolescent Health, 39*(5), 662–668. doi:10.1016/j.jadohealth.2006.04.024

Eliason, M. J. (1993a). AIDS-related stigma and homophobia: Implications for nursing education. *Nurse Educator, 18*(6), 27–30.

Eliason, M.J. (1993b). Cultural diversity in nursing care: The lesbian, gay or bisexual client. *Journal of Transcultural Nursing, 5*(1), 14–20.

Eliason, M. J., & Raheim, S. (2000). Experiences and comfort with culturally diverse groups in undergraduate pre-nursing students. *Journal of Nursing Education, 39*(4), 161–165.

Empereur, J. L. (1998). *Spiritual direction and the gay person.* New York, NY: Continuum.

Evans, D. (2001). Out in the open. *Nursing Standard, 15*(41), 22.

Facione, N., & Facione, P. (2007). Perceived prejudice in healthcare and women's health protective behavior. *Nursing Research, 56*(3), 175–184.

Fish, J. (2007). Getting equal: The implications of new regulations to prohibit sexual orientation discrimination for health and social care. *Diversity in Health & Social Care, 4*(3), 221–228.

Fish, J. (2007). *Heterosexism in health and social care.* New York, NY: Palgrave Macmillan.

Fish, J., & Anthony, D. (2005). UK national lesbians and health care survey. *Women & Health, 41*(3), 27–45. doi:10.1300/J013v41n03_02

Foster, E. (2008). Commitment, communication, and contending with heteronormativity: An invitation to greater reflexivity in interpersonal research. *Southern Communication Journal, 73*(1), 84–101. doi:10.1080/10417940701815683

Fredriksen-Goldsen, K., & Hooyman, N. (2005). Caregiving research, services, and policies in historically marginalized communities: Where do we go from here? *Journal of Gay & Lesbian Social Services: Issues in Practice, Policy & Research, 18*(3–4), 129–145. doi:10.1300/J041v18n03_08

Gee, R. (2006). Primary care health issues among men who have sex with men. *Journal of the American Academy of Nurse Practitioners, 18*(4), 144–153. doi:10.1111/j.1745-7599.2006.00117.x

Giddings, L. (2005). Health disparities, social injustice, and the culture of nursing. *Nursing Research, 54*(5), 304–312.

Goldberg, S., Sickler, J., & Dibble, S. (2005). Lesbians over sixty: The consistency of findings from twenty years of survey data. *Journal of Lesbian Studies, 9*(1–2), 195–213. doi:10.1300/J155v09n01_18

Gonsiorek, J. C. (Ed.). (1985). *A guide to psychotherapy with gay and lesbian clients.* New York, NY: Harrington Park Press.

Goodstein, L. (2003, October 17). Anglicans warn of a split if gay man is consecrated. *New York Times.* Retrieved October 17, 2003, from www.nytimes.com

Gorton, R. (2007). Transgender health benefits: Collateral damage in the resolution of the national health care financing dilemma. *Sexuality Research & Social Policy: A Journal of the NSRC, 4*(4), 81–91. doi:10.1525/srsp.2007.4.4.81

Gray, D. P., Kramer, M., Minick, P., McGehee, L., Thomas, D., & Greiner, D. (1996). Heterosexism in nursing education. *Journal of Nursing Education, 35*(5), 204–210.

Greco, J. A. & Glusman, J. B. (1998). Providing effective care for gay and lesbian patients. *Patient Care, 32*(12), 159–162.

Green, R. (2010). Transsexual legal rights in the United States and United Kingdom: Employment, medical treatment, and civil status. *Archives of Sexual Behavior, 39*(1), 153–160. doi:10.1007/s10508–008-9447–5

Greene, B., & Herek, G. M. (Eds.). (1994). *Lesbian and gay psychology: Theory, research, and clinical applications: Vol. 1. Psychological perspectives on lesbian and gay issues.* Thousand Oaks, CA: Sage Publications.

Grossman, A., D'Augelli, A., & Dragowski, E. (2005). Caregiving and care receiving among older lesbian, gay, and bisexual adults. *Journal of Gay & Lesbian Social Services, 18*(3/4), 15–38. doi:10.1300/J041v18n03–02

Haldeman, D.C. (1994). The practice and ethics of sexual orientation conversion therapy. *Journal of Consulting and Clinical Psychology, 62,* 211–221.

Hardin, K. N. (1999). *The gay and lesbian self-esteem book: A guide to loving ourselves.* Oakland, CA: New Harbinger Publications, Inc.

Harrison, S. (2008). Equality for gay staff can only be good for the workforce as a whole. *Nursing Standard, 22*(22), 12–13.

Hein, L., & Matthews, A. (2010). Reparative therapy: The adolescent, the psych nurse, and the issues. *Journal of Child & Adolescent Psychiatric Nursing, 23*(1), 29–35. doi:10.1111/j.1744–6171.2009.00214.x

Helminiak, D. A. (2006). *Sex and the sacred: Gay identity and spiritual growth.* New York, NY: The Haworth Press.

Herek, G. M. (1995). Psychological heterosexism in the United States. In A. R. D'Augelli and C. J. Patterson (Eds.), *Lesbian, gay, and bisexual identities over the lifespan: Psychological perspectives* (pp. 321–346). New York, NY: Oxford University Press.

Hollander, D. (2006). Women, but not men, living with a same-sex partner are disadvantaged with regard to health care access. *Perspectives on Sexual & Reproductive Health, 38*(3), 169–170.

Hughes, M. (2007). Older lesbians and gays accessing health and aged-care services. *Australian Social Work, 60*(2), 197–209. doi:10.1080/03124070701323824

Hughes, T., Johnson, T., Wilsnack, S., & Szalacha, L. (2007). Childhood risk factors for alcohol abuse and psychological distress among adult lesbians. *Child Abuse & Neglect, 31*(7), 769–789. doi:10.1016/j.chiabu.2006.12.014

Hutchinson, M., Thompson, A., & Cederbaum, J. (2006). Multisystem factors contributing to disparities in preventive health care among lesbian women. *Journal of Obstetric, Gynecologic & Neonatal Nursing, 35*(3), 393–402.

Irwin, L. (2007). Homophobia and heterosexism: Implications for nursing and nursing practice. *Australian Journal of Advanced Nursing, 25*(1), 70–76.

Johnson, W., & Buhrke, R. (2006). Service delivery in a "don't ask, don't tell" world: Ethical care of gay, lesbian, and bisexual military personnel. *Professional Psychology: Research and Practice, 37*(1), 91–98. doi:10.1037/0735–7028.37.1.91

Johnson, M., Jackson, N., Arnette, J., & Koffman, S. (2005). Gay and lesbian perceptions of discrimination in retirement care facilities. *Journal of Homosexuality, 49*(2), 83–102. doi:10.1300/J082v49n02_05

Johnston, L. B., & Jenkins, D. (2006). Lesbians and gay men embrace their sexual orientation after conversion therapy and ex-gay ministries: A qualitative study. *Social Work in Mental Health, 4*(3), 61–82.

Just the Facts About Sexual Orientation & Youth. (1999). [Electronic version]. Retrieved March 4, 2004, from www.glsen.org/binary-data/GLSEN_ATTACHMENTS/file/123–1.pdf

Kauth, M. R., Hartwig, M. J. & Kalichman, S. C. (2002). Health behavior relevant to psychotherapy with lesbian, gay and bisexual clients. In R. M Perez, K. A. DeBord, & K. J. Bieschke (Eds.), *Handbook of counseling and psychotherapy with lesbian, gay and bisexual clients* (pp. 435–456). Washington, DC: American Psychological Association.

Kean, R. (2006). Understanding the lives of older gay people. *Nursing Older People, 18*(8), 31–36.

Kelly, L. (2007). Lesbian body image perceptions: The context of body silence. *Qualitative Health Research, 17*(7), 873–883. doi:10.1177/1049732307306172

Kenagy, G. (2005). Transgender health: Findings from two needs assessment studies in Philadelphia. *Health & Social Work, 30*(1), 19–26. Retrieved from PsycINFO database.

Kendall-Raynor, P. (2009). DH guidance aims to end unfair treatment of gay and lesbian staff. *Nursing Standard, 23*(27), 8.

Kendall-Raynor, P. (2007). Step forward in fight against healthcare discrimination. *Nursing Standard, 21*(22), 14–15.

Kerr, S., & Mathey, R. (2007). Preface. *Women & Health, 44*(2), xxiii–xxx. doi:10.1300/J013v44n02_a

Khan, A., Plummer, D., Hussain, R., & Minichiello, V. (2008). Does physician bias affect the quality of care they deliver? Evidence in the care of sexually transmitted infections. *Sexually Transmitted Infections, 84*(2), 150–151. doi:10.1136/sti.2007.028050

Knowledge and attitudes of nurses in Northern Ireland. *Journal of Advanced Nursing, 17*, 1068–1077.

Koder, S. (2006). Transgender emergence: Therapeutic guidelines for working with gender-variant people and their families. *Journal of the American Academy of Child & Adolescent Psychiatry, 45*(5), 630–631.

Koh, A., & Ross, L. (2006). Mental health issues: A comparison of lesbian, bisexual and heterosexual women. *Journal of Homosexuality, 51*(1), 33–57.

Labig, C., & Peterson, T. (2006). Sexual minorities and selection of a primary care physician in a midwestern U.S. city. *Journal of Homosexuality, 51*(3), 1–5. doi:10.1300/J082v51n03_01

Lambda Legal. (2006). *Basic facts about being LGBTQ: Getting down to basics toolkit.* [Electronic version]. Retrieved May 8, 2007, from http://www.lambdalegal.org/take-action/tool-kits/getting-down-to-basics/basic-facts.html

Lambda Legal & National Youth Advocacy Coalition. (2007). *Bending the Mold: An Action Kit for Transgender Youth.* [Electronic version]. Retrieved May 7, 2007, from http://data.lambdalegal.org/pdf/305.pdf

Larsson, A., & Dykes, A. (2009). Care during pregnancy and childbirth in Sweden: perspectives of lesbian women. *Midwifery, 25*(6), 682–690. doi:10.1016/j.midw.2007.10.004

Lee, R., Melhado, T., Chacko, K., White, K., Huebschmann, A., & Crane, L. (2008). The dilemma of disclosure: Patient perspectives on gay and lesbian providers. *Journal of General Internal Medicine, 23*(2), 142–147. doi:10.1007/s11606–007-0461–4

Liuzzi, P. J. (2001). *With listening hearts: Understanding the voices of lesbian and gay Catholics.* New York, NY: Paulist Press.

Lobaugh, E., Clements, P., Averill, J., & Olguin, D. (2006). Gay-male couples who adopt: Challenging historical and contemporary social trends toward becoming a family. *Perspectives in Psychiatric Care, 42*(3), 184–195.

MacDonnell, J. (2009). Fostering nurses' political knowledges and practices: Education and political activation in relation to lesbian health. *Advances in Nursing Science, 32*(2), 158–172.

Makadon, H. (2006). Improving health care for the lesbian and gay communities. *The New England Journal of Medicine, 354*(9), 895–897. doi:10.1056/NEJMp058259.

Martino Maze, C. (2005). Registered nurses' personal rights vs. professional responsibility in caring for members of underserved and disenfranchised populations. *Journal of Clinical Nursing, 14*(5), 546–554. doi:10.1111/j.1365–2702.2004.01107.x

Maxwell, M. (2005). Human resource solution. It's not just black and white: How diverse is your workforce?. *Nursing Economics, 23*(3), 139–140.

McAndrew, S., & Warne, T. (2010). Coming out to talk about suicide: Gay men and suicidality. *International Journal of Mental Health Nursing, 19*(2), 92–101. doi:10.1111/j.1447–0349.2009.00644.x

McManus, A., Hunter, L., & Renn, H. (2006). Lesbian experiences and needs during childbirth: Guidance for health care providers. *Journal of Obstetric, Gynecologic & Neonatal Nursing, 35*(1), 13–23.

McNair, R., Brown, R., Perlesz, A., Lindsay, J., de Vaus, D., & Pitts, M. (2008). Lesbian parents negotiating the health care system in Australia. *Health Care for Women International, 29*(2), 91–114. doi:10.1080/07399330701827094

McNeill, J. J. (1988). *Taking a chance on God: Liberating theology for gays, lesbians, and their lovers, families and friends.* Boston, MA: Beacon Press.

Meads, C., Buckley, E., & Sanderson, P. (2007). Ten years of lesbian health survey research in the UK West Midlands. *BMC Public Health, 7251–7259.* doi:10.1186/1471–2458-7–251

Melby, V., Boore, J. R. P. & Murray, M. (1992). Acquired immune deficiency syndrome:

Melendez, R., Bonem, L., & Sember, R. (2006). On bodies and research: Transgender issues in health and HIV research articles. *Sexuality Research & Social Policy: A Journal of the NSRC, 3*(4), 21–38. doi:10.1525/srsp.2006.3.4.21

Meneses, C., & Monroe, J. (2007). Health inequities in long-term care: Through the eyes of the consumer. *American Journal of Recreation Therapy, 6*(3), 20–26.

Mercier, L., & Harold, R. (2006). Preface: We are family: Lesbian parenting. *Journal of Gay & Lesbian Social Services: Issues in Practice, Policy & Research, 19*(2), S1–S5.

Messinger, L., & Morrow, D. F. (Eds.). (2005). *Sexual orientation and gender expression in social work practice: Working with gay, lesbian, bisexual and transgender people.* New York, NY: Columbia University Press.

Messinger, L., & Morrow, D. F. (Eds.). (2006). *Case studies on sexual orientation & gender expression in social work practice.* New York, NY: Columbia University Press.

Misener, T. R., Sowell, R., Phillips, K. D., & Harris, C. (1997). Sexual orientation: A cultural diversity issue for nursing. *Nursing Outlook, 45*(4), 178–181.

Morgan, S., & Stevens, P. (2008). Transgender identity development as represented by a group of female-to-male transgendered adults. *Issues in Mental Health Nursing, 29*(6), 585–599. doi:10.1080/01612840802048782

Morrissey, M. (1996). Clinical: Attitudes of practitioners to lesbian, gay and bisexual clients. *British Journal of Nursing, 5*(16), 980–982.

Mravcak, S. (2006). Primary care for lesbians and bisexual women. *American Family Physician, 74*(2), 279.

Murphy, T.F. (1992). Redirecting sexual orientation: Techniques and justifications. *The Journal of Sex Research, 2,* 501–523.

National Committee on Lesbian, Gay and Bisexual Issues, National Association of Social Workers. (2000). *Position statement: "Reparative" and "conversion" therapies for lesbians and gay men* [Electronic Version]. Washington, DC: National Association of Social Workers.

Neville, S., & Henrickson, M. (2006). Perceptions of lesbian, gay and bisexual people of primary healthcare services. *Journal of Advanced Nursing, 55*(4), 407–415. doi:10.1111/j.1365–2648.2006.03944.x

Nugent, R., & Gramick, J. (1995). *Building Bridges: Gay & lesbian reality and the Catholic church.* Mystic, CT: Twenty-Third Publications.

Nusbaum, M., Frasier, P., Rojas, F., Trotter, K., & Tudor, G. (2008). Sexual orientation and sexual health care needs: A comparison of women beneficiaries in outpatient military health care settings. *Journal of Homosexuality, 54*(3), 259–276.

O'Hanlan, K. (2000). Health concerns of lesbians. In R. M. Eisler & H. Hersen (Eds.), *Handbook of gender, culture, and health* (pp. 377–404). Mahwah, NJ: Erlbaum.

O'Neill, C. & Ritter, K. (1992). *Coming out within: Stages of spiritual awakening for lesbians and gay men.* San Francisco, CA: Harper.

O'Shaughnessy, T., & Carroll, L. (2007). Coming to terms with gender identity: Counseling transgender students. In J. A. Lippincott & R. B. Lippincott (Eds.), *Special populations in college counseling: A handbook for mental health professionals* (pp. 49–60). Alexandria, VA: American Counseling Association.

Ott, C., & Eilers, J. (1997). Breast cancer and women partnering with women. *Nebraska Nurse, 30*(2), 29, 41–42.

Owens, G., Riggle, E., & Rostosky, S. (2007). Mental health services access for sexual minority individuals. *Sexuality Research & Social Policy: A Journal of the NSRC, 4*(3), 92–99. doi: 10.1525/srsp.2007.4.3.92

Owen, S., & Khalil, E. (2007). Addressing diversity in mental health care: A review of guidance documents. *International Journal of Nursing Studies, 44*(3), 467–478. doi:10.1016/j.ijnurstu.2006.08.024

Palma, T. V., & Stanley, J. L. (2002). Effective counseling with lesbian, gay and bisexual clients. *Journal of College Counseling, 5*(1), 74–89.

Parks, C., & Hughes, T. (2005). Alcohol use and alcohol-related problems in self-identified lesbians: An historical cohort analysis. *Journal of Lesbian Studies, 9*(3), 31–44. doi:10.1300/J155v09n03_04

Payne, D. (2006). Attitude change leaves a skills gap. *Nursing Standard, 20*(21), 72.

Payne, D. (2007). Heterosexism in health and social care. *Nursing Standard, 21*(22), 30.

Peate, I. (2008). The older gay, lesbian and bisexual population. *Nursing & Residential Care, 10*(4), 192–194.

Peate, I. (2006a). Caring for gay men 1: Specific health needs. *Practice Nursing, 17*(2), 64–68.

Peate, I. (2006b). Caring for gay men 2: A welcoming practice. *Practice Nursing, 17*(3), 139–143.

Peate, I. (2006c). Men's health: The provision of nursing care for gay men with GI issues. *British Journal of Nursing, 15*(4), 220–225.

Peel, E. (2008). De-heterosexualising health: Exploring lesbian, gay, bisexual and trans health issues and policy in Britain. *Sex Roles, 59*(7–8), 609–610. doi:10.1007/s11199–008-9434–2

Peel, E., & Thomson, M. (2009). Editorial introduction: Lesbian, gay, bisexual, trans and queer health psychology: Historical development and future possibilities. *Feminism & Psychology, 19*(4), 427–436. doi:10.1177/0959353509342691

Pellegrini, A. (1992). S(h)ifting the terms of hetero/sexism: Gender, power, homophobias. In W. Blumenfield, *Homophobia: How we all pay the price* (pp. 39–56). Boston, MA: Beacon Press.

Perez, R. M., DeBord, K. A. & Bieschke, K. J. (Eds.). (2000). *Handbook of counseling and psychotherapy with lesbian, gay and bisexual clients.* Washington, DC: American Psychological Association.

Persson, D. (2009). Unique challenges of transgender aging: Implications from the literature. *Journal of Gerontological Social Work, 52*(6), 633–646. doi:10.1080/01634370802609056

Pettinato, M. (2008). Nobody was out back then: A grounded theory study of midlife and older lesbians with alcohol problems. *Issues in Mental Health Nursing, 29*(6), 619–638. doi:10.1080/01612840802048865

Platzer, H. (1993). Nursing care of gay and lesbian patients. *Nursing Standard, 7*(17), 34–37.

Platzer, H., & James, T. (2000). Lesbians' experiences of healthcare. Including commentary by Maggs C. *NT Research, 5*(3), 194–203.

Polek, C., Hardie, T., & Crowley, E. (2008). Lesbians' disclosure of sexual orientation and satisfaction with care. *Journal of Transcultural Nursing, 19*(3), 243–249. Retrieved from CINAHL with Full Text database.

Polimeni, A., Austin, S., & Kavanagh, A. (2009). Sexual orientation and weight, body image, and weight control practices among young Australian women. *Journal of Women's Health, 18*(3), 355–362. doi:10.1089/jwh.2007.0765

Politi, M., Clark, M., Armstrong, G., McGarry, K., & Sciamanna, C. (2009). Patient–provider communication about sexual health among unmarried middle-aged and older women. *JGIM: Journal of General Internal Medicine, 24*(4), 511–516. doi:10.1007/s11606–009-0930-z

Powell-Cope, G. M. (1998). Heterosexism and gay couples with HIV infection. *Western Journal of Nursing Research, 20*(4), 478–496.

Price, E. (2005). All but invisible: Older gay men and lesbians. *Nursing Older People, 17*(4), 16–18.

Proulx, A. M. (2006). Transgender care resources for family physicians. *American Family Physician, 74*(6): 924, 926

Raso, R. (2006). Cultural competence: Integral in diverse populations. *Nursing Management, 37*(7), 56.

Razzano, L., Cook, J., Hamilton, M., Hughes, T., & Matthews, A. (2006). Predictors of mental health services use among lesbian and heterosexual women. *Psychiatric Rehabilitation Journal, 29*(4), 289–298. doi:10.2975/29.2006.289.298

Richmond, J. P. & McKenna, H. (1998). Homophobia: An evolutionary analysis of the concept as applied to nursing. *Journal of Advanced Nursing, 28*(2), 362–369.

Rickards, T., & Wuest, J. (2006). The process of losing and regaining credibility when coming-out at midlife. *Health Care for Women International, 27*(6), 530–547. doi:10.1080/07399330600770254

Ridner, S., Frost, K., & LaJoie, A. (2006). Health information and risk behaviors among lesbian, gay, and bisexual college students. *Journal of the American Academy of Nurse Practitioners, 18*(8), 374–378. doi:10.1111/j.1745–7599.2006.00142.x

Riggle, E., Rostosky, S., Prather, R., & Hamrin, R. (2005). The execution of legal documents by sexual minority individuals. *Psychology, Public Policy, and Law, 11*(1), 138–163. doi:10.1037/1076–8971.11.1.138

Riley, B. (2010). GLB Adolescent's "Coming out". *Journal of Child & Adolescent Psychiatric Nursing, 23*(1), 3–10. doi:10.1111/j.1744–6171.2009.00210.x

Ritter, K. Y. & Tendrup, A. I. (2002). *Handbook of affirmative psychotherapy with lesbians and gay men.* New York, NY: The Guilford Press.

Röndahl, G. (2009). Lesbians' and gay men's narratives about attitudes in nursing. *Scandinavian Journal of Caring Sciences, 23*(1), 146–152. doi:10.1111/j.1471–6712.2008.00603.x

Röndahl, G., Bruhner, E., & Lindhe, J. (2009). Heteronormative communication with lesbian families in antenatal care, childbirth and postnatal care. *Journal of Advanced Nursing, 65*(11), 2337–2344. doi:10.1111/j.1365–2648.2009.05092.x

Röndahl, G., Innala, S., & Carlsson, M. (2007). To hide or not to hide, that is the question? Lesbians and gay men describe experiences from nursing work environment. *Journal of Homosexuality, 52*(3/4), 211–233.

Röndahl, G., Innala, S., & Carlsson, M. (2004). Nurses' attitudes towards lesbians and gay men. *Journal of Advanced Nursing, 47*(4), 386–392.

Rostosky, S., Danner, F., & Riggle, E. (2007). Is religiosity a protective factor against substance use in young adulthood? Only if you're straight! *Journal of Adolescent Health, 40*(5), 440–447. doi:10.1016/j.jadohealth.2006.11.144

Royse, D., & Birge, B. (1987). Homophobia and attitudes towards AIDS patients among medical, nursing and paramedical students. *Psychological Reports, 61*, 867–870.

Saewyc, E., Bearinger, L., McMahon, G., & Evans, T. (2006). A national needs assessment of nurses providing health care to adolescents. *Journal of Professional Nursing, 22*(5), 304–313.

Saewyc, E., Homma, Y., Skay, C., Bearinger, L., Resnick, M., & Reis, E. (2009). Protective factors in the lives of bisexual adolescents in North America. *American Journal of Public Health, 99*(1), 110–117. doi:10.2105/AJPH.2007.123109

Sawyer, R., Porter, J., Lehman, T, Anderson, C., & Anderson, K. (2006). Education and training needs of school staff relevant to preventing risk behaviors and promoting health behaviors among gay, lesbian, bisexual and questioning youth. *Journal of HIV/AIDS Prevention in Children & Youth, 7*(1), 37–53.

Seaver, M., Freund, K., Wright, L., Tjia, J., & Frayne, S. (2008). Healthcare preferences among lesbians: A focus group analysis. *Journal of Women's Health, 17*(2), 215–225. doi:10.1089/jwh.2007.0083

Shattell, M. (2008). From the guest editor—Issues affecting gay, lesbian, bisexual, and transgender persons. *Issues in Mental Health Nursing, 29*(6), 549–550. doi:10.1080/01612840802046562

Shaw, H., & Degazon, C. (2008). Integrating the core professional values of nursing: A profession, not just a career. *Journal of Cultural Diversity, 15*(1), 44–50.

Shear, M. D. (2010, April 16). Obama extends hospital visitation rights to same-sex partners of gays. *The Washington Post*, p. A1. Retrieved November 17, 2011, from www. washingtonpost.com/wp-dyn/content/article/2010/04/15/AR2010041505502. html?sid=ST2010052403690

Shidlo, A. (1994). Internalized homophobia: Conceptual and empirical issues in measurement. In B. Greene & G. M. Herek (Eds.), *Lesbian and gay psychology: Theory, research and clinical applications: Vol. 1. Psychological perspectives on lesbian and gay issues* (pp. 176–205). Thousand Oaks, CA: Sage Publications.

Sinding, C., Barnoff, L., & Grassau, P. (2004). Homophobia and heterosexism in cancer care: The experiences of lesbians. *Canadian Journal of Nursing Research, 36*(4), 170–188.

Smith, E., Johnson, S., Guenther, S. (1985). Health care attitudes and experiences during gynecologic care among lesbians and bisexuals. *American Journal of Public Health, 75*(9), 1085–1087.

Snow, T. (2006). Diversity agenda must widen to cover sexual orientation. *Nursing Standard, 20*(38), 9.

Springfield, F. (2002). Lesbians, gays and transsexuals in care homes. *Nursing & Residential Care, 4*(12), 586–588.

Starr, C., Greco, J., & Glusman, J. (1998). Providing effective care for gay and lesbian patients. *Patient Care, 32*(12), 159.

Steele, L., Tinmouth, J., & Lu, A. (2006). Regular health care use by lesbians: A path analysis of predictive factors. *Family Practice, 23*(6), 631–636. doi:10.1093/fam pra/cml030

Stevens, P. (1992). Lesbian health care research: A review of the literature from 1970 to 1990. *Health Care for Women International, 13*(2), 91–120.

Stevens, P.E., & Morgan, S. (1999). Health of lesbian, gay, bisexual and transgender youth. *Journal of Child and Family Nursing, 2*(4), 237–251.

Stewart, M. (1999). Women's health. Lesbian parents talk about their birth experiences. *British Journal of Midwifery, 7*(2), 96–101.

Tate, F. & Longo, D. (2004). Homophobia: A challenge for psychosocial nursing. *Journal of Psychosocial Nursing & Mental Health Services, 42*(8), 26–33.

Taylor, B. (1999). 'Coming out' as a life transition: homosexual identity formation and its implications for health care practice. *Journal of Advanced Nursing, 30*(2), 520–525.

Ungvarski, P. J. (2001). HIV: Still a problem of sex: Still a problem of bigotry. *American Journal of Nursing, 101*(6), 7.

Ussher, J. (2009). Heterocentric practices in health research and health care: Implications for mental health and subjectivity of LGBTQ individuals. *Feminism & Psychology, 19*(4), 561–567. doi:10.1177/0959353509342933

van Wissen, K. A., & Siebers, R. W. L. (1993). Nurses' attitudes and concerns pertaining to HIV and AIDS. *Journal of Advanced Nursing, 18*, 912–917.

Vickers, D. (2008). Social justice: A concept for undergraduate nursing curricula? *Southern Online Journal of Nursing Research, 8*(1), 1–18.

Wagner, L. (1997). Lesbian health and homophobia. *Tennessee Nurse, 60*(4), 15–16.

Walpin, L. (1997). Combating heterosexism: Implications for nursing. *Clinical Nurse Specialist, 11*(3), 126–132.

Wamala, S., Merlo, J., Boström, G., & Hogstedt, C. (2007). Perceived discrimination, socioeconomic disadvantage and refraining from seeking medical treatment in Sweden. *Journal of Epidemiology and Community Health, 61*(5), 409–415. doi: 10.1136/jech.2006.049999

Wang, J., Häusermann, M., Vounatsou, P., Aggleton, P., & Weiss, M. (2007). Health status, behavior, and care utilization in the Geneva Gay Men's Health Survey. *Preventive Medicine, 44*(1), 70–75. doi: 10.1016/j.ypmed.2006.08.013

Warriner, J. (2008, February 6). Confident to come out. *Nursing Standard, 22*(22), 64.

Weber, S. (2010). Guest editorial: Special issue on mental health nursing care of LGBT adolescents and young adults. *Journal of Child and Adolescent Psychiatric Nursing, 23*(1), 1–2. doi: 10.1111/j.1744–6171.2009.00209.x

Weber, S. (2009). Policy aspects and nursing care of families with parents who are sexual minorities. *Journal of Family Nursing, 15*(3), 384–399. Retrieved from Academic Search Complete database.

Weber, S., & Poster, E. (2010, February). Guest editorial: Special issue on mental health nursing care of lgbt adolescents and young adults. *Journal of Child & Adolescent Psychiatric Nursing, 23*(1), 1–2. doi:10.1111/j.1744–6171.2009.00209.x

Welle, D., Fuller, S., Mauk, D., & Clatts, M. (2006). The invisible body of queer youth: Identity and health in the margins of lesbian and trans communities. *Journal of Lesbian Studies, 10*(1–2), 43–71. doi:10.1300/J155v10n01_03

Wells, A. (1997). Homophobia and nursing care. *Nursing Standard, 12*(6), 41–42.

Williams, M., & Freeman, P. (2005). Transgender health: Implications for aging and caregiving. *Journal of Gay & Lesbian Social Services: Issues in Practice, Policy & Research, 18*(3–4), 93–108. doi:10.1300/J041v18n03_06

Willging, C., Salvador, M., & Kano, M. (2006). Unequal treatment: Mental health care for sexual and gender minority groups in a rural state. *Psychiatric Services, 57*(6), 867–870. doi:10.1176/appi.ps.57.6.867

Willis, D. (2004). Hate crimes against gay males: An overview. *Issues in Mental Health Nursing, 25*(2), 115–132.

Wilton, T. (1999). Towards an understanding of the cultural roots of homophobia in order to provide a better midwifery service for lesbian clients. *Midwifery, 15*(3), 154–164.

Wimberly, Y., Hogben, M., Moore-Ruffin, J., Moore, S., & Fry-Johnson, Y. (2006). Sexual history-taking among primary care physicians. *Journal of the National Medical Association, 98*(12), 1924–1929.

Witten, T. (2009). Graceful exits: Intersection of aging, transgender identities, and the family/community. *Journal of GLBT Family Studies, 5*(1–2), 35–61. doi:10.1080/15504280802595378

Wojnar, D. (2007). Miscarriage experiences of lesbian couples. *Journal of Midwifery & Women's Health, 52*(5), 479–485. doi:10.1016/j.jmwh.2007.03.015

Veldon, J. (2001). Time to out the lack of gay research. *Nursing Times, 97*(35), 16.

Yarhouse, M. A. (2001). Sexual identity development: The influence of valuative frameworks on identity synthesis. *Psychotherapy: Theory, Research, Practice, Training, 38*(3), 331–341.

Young, E. W., Knock, P. B., & Preston, D. B. (1989). AIDS and homosexuality: A longitudinal study of knowledge and attitude change among rural nurses. *Public Health Nursing, 6*(4), 189–196.

RESOURCES

There are numerous resources available to nurses who wish to become more informed about the issues of concern for gay, lesbian, bisexual, and transgender individuals. An extensive collection of resources can be found in the *Handbook of Affirmative Psychotherapy with Lesbians and Gay Men* (Ritter & Terndrup, 2002). Many major cities have a gay and lesbian community center that can provide referrals and information. Other cities also have gay and lesbian health centers that focus primarily on addressing the health concerns of gay, lesbian, and bisexual individuals. Some important resources that provide a starting point for obtaining information are also listed below.

American Academy of Pediatrics (AAP)
www.aap.org
The AAP consists of physicians who address the needs of youth on a regular basis. The Committee on Adolescence has developed a statement on sexual orientation.
American Nurses Association (ANA)
www.nursingworld.org
The ANA is the association for professional nurses. It provides information on nursing standards, ethics, policy statements, and other important information related to the practice of nursing. Visitors to the site can search for information related to nursing care and diverse patients.
American Psychological Association (APA)
www.apa.org
The APA website contains information about sexual orientation and mental health, youth who are gay and lesbian (www.apa.org/ed/hlgb/schclimate.html), and family issues. Division 44 is the Society for the Psychological Study of Lesbian, Gay, and Bisexual Issues and hosts its own webpage (www.apa.org/about/division/div44.html).
Gay, Lesbian, Straight Educators' Network (GLSEN)
www.glsen.org
GLSEN works to educate teachers about the needs of gay youth. It contains information about developing support groups for gay and straight allies and provides resources to students, educators and others interested in learning more.
Gay and Lesbian Medical Association (GLMA)
www.glma.org
The GLMA provides updated information on health concerns of LGBTQ individuals, clinical trials regarding health issues of concern to LGBTQ individuals (HIV, breast cancer, etc.), and provides an opportunity to obtain referrals to LGBTQ-friendly physicians, and advocates on behalf of LGBTQ individuals and their health concerns.
Human Rights Campaign (HRC)
www.hrc.org
HRC addresses legal and political issues of concern for LGBTQ individuals. The website also contains resources on coming out, gay-friendly workplaces, and family issues.
Just the Facts About Sexual Orientation and Youth: A Primer for Principals, Educators, and School Personnel
www.apa.org/pi/lgbc/publications/justthefacts.html
This booklet was developed for educators and contains useful information about sexual orientation for those who are beginning to learn about the issue, and addresses the issue of reparative and conversion therapies. It is sponsored by numerous

health and mental health organizations to inform educators and others about sexual orientation. It is available through the websites of many of the sponsoring organizations.

Lambda Legal

www.lambdalegal.org/cgi-bin/iowa/index.html

Lambda works for civil rights for LGBTQ individuals by addressing legal, education, and public policy issues.

National Association of School Nurses

www.nasn.org/positions/orientation.htm

This site contains the official statement of the organization adopted by the Board of Directors in 1994, recognizing the unique needs of gay, lesbian, bisexual, and transgender youth.

National Association of Social Workers (NASW)

www.naswdc.org

The NASW website contains links to policy statements on issues such as reparative and conversion therapies, gay and lesbian families, and student issues. NASW addresses both mental health and social policy concerns.

Parents, Families, and Friends of Lesbians and Gays (PFLAG)

www.pflag.org

PFLAG is a grassroots organization of the families and friends who care about someone who is gay, lesbian, bisexual, or transgender. A national organization, PFLAG also has local chapters. It provides support, advocacy, and education, and often serves as a starting point for support for parents who learn that their child is gay, lesbian, bisexual, or transgender.

Philadelphia Trans-Health Conference (PTHC)

www.trans-health.org

www.mazzonicenter.org

The PTHC is a conference for the transgender community and their friends and families as well as providers of services to transgender people and the general public. It focuses on transgender health issues broadly defined, encompassing not only physical, but mental and spiritual health. The conference was founded in 2002 and is a program of the Mazzoni Center, the LGBT Health Center located in Philadelphia, Pennsylvania.

Cultural Considerations When Caring for the New Immigrant or Refugee

GLORIA KERSEY-MATUSIAK

The interests we share as human beings are far more powerful than the forces that drive us apart.

—U.S. PRESIDENT BARACK OBAMA, 2009

LEARNING OBJECTIVES

1. Define concepts and terms that are used to differentiate types of immigrants and nonimmigrants who reside permanently or temporarily in the United States.
2. State the geographical origins of the vast majority of immigrants that currently come to America.
3. Discuss the cultural diversity that exists between and among immigrant populations and the implications for nurses.
4. Explain the role of the nurse when caring for members of immigrant populations.
5. Identify resources to assist the nurse and other health care providers when providing care for new immigrants.
6. Describe issues surrounding the debate for and against immigration in the United States and its impact on nursing.

KEY TERMS

Acculturation
Alien (Legalized Alien)
Asylee
Deportation
Detainee

Green card
Illegal or undocumented immigrant or alien
Immigrant
Naturalization
Nonimmigrant
Permanent resident alien or legal permanent resident
Refugee

THE NATURE OF IMMIGRATION

Since the time of Columbus, America has been a nation of **immigrants**. Immigrants come to America to escape poverty or search for personal freedoms not found in their native lands. Others, more desperate, come to escape persecution, or death because of their membership in a particular religious, ethnic, or political group. Many immigrants come with the hope of becoming an American. According to a United States Census Bureau report, in 2009, 12.4% or more than 36 million people in the United States were foreign-born. Included among this number is an estimated 12.6 million **legal permanent residents (LPR)**. Members of this group of immigrants are **green card** recipients who have been granted lawful permanent resident status in the United States. A large percentage of this group, 8.1 million, is eligible for **naturalization**. An immigrant may apply for naturalization or citizenship after a 5-year residency in America (United States Bureau of the Census, 2010).

It is projected that by "2050, nearly 1 in 5 or 19% of Americans, as compared to 1 in 8 or 12% in 2005" (Pew Research Center, 2008) will have been born outside of the United States. Despite these numbers, there is growing evidence that the rapid increases of new immigrants that occurred during the last decade is leveling off (Myers, 2008).

Each year, the President, in collaboration with Congress, determines the annual number of **refugees** permitted to enter the United States within a fiscal year. The United States grants permission to a limited number of refugees seeking asylum in America to enter the country and apply for citizenship. Some of these individuals are given green cards that indicate their status as permanent residents who are free to live and work in the United States. The United States Citizenship and Immigration Services (USCIS) processes "between six and eight million" applications and petitions each year. This process involves "roughly 90,000 *asylum* applications, about 70,000 interviews of refugee applicants, and naturalization of another half million new citizens" (USCIS, 2007). Of those individuals who entered the United States between the years 1990 and 2000, 13.4% or 1,759,386 of them later became United States citizens. "The population of naturalized citizens reached 12.8 million in 2005" (USCIS, 2007). However, not everyone who comes to America has the intention of making it his or her permanent home. For this reason, the USCIS issues both permanent and temporary visas to individuals coming from five regions around the world including: Asia, Africa, Europe, Latin America, and Oceania, a group of Pacific Islands. Currently, the largest groups of immigrants come to the United States from Latin America and Asia. In 2010 Mexico was the leading country with 3.3 million immigrants or 26% of the LPRs who come to America. Table 10.1 illustrates the birth places from which the United States receives immigrants. These include Mexico, the Philippines, the People's Republic of China, India, El Salvador, Vietnam, Cuba, the Dominican Republic, South Korea, and Guatemala.

It is also noteworthy that some states more than others lead the country in receiving immigrants, thereby becoming geographically more multicultural than some others. California, New York, Florida, Texas, and New Jersey are the leading states for immigration as illustrated in Table 10.2.

IMMIGRATION STATUS

Nonimmigrants who enter the country with the intention of returning to their native lands are considered. *Foreign nationals* are granted temporary entry into the United States for business or pleasure, study, temporary employment, or to act as a foreign governmental or organizational representative.

TABLE 10.1   Place of Birth for the Foreign-Born Population in the United States

TOP TEN COUNTRIES	2010	2000	1990
Mexico	11,711,103	9,177,487	4,298,014
China	2,166,526	1,518,652	921,070
India	1,780,322	1,022,552	450,406
Philippines	1,777,588	1,369,070	912,674
Vietnam	1,240,542	988,174	543,262
EL Salvador	1,214,049	817,336	465,433
Cuba	1,104,679	872,716	736,971
South Korea	1,100,422	864,125	568,397
Dominican Republic	879,187	687,677	347,858
Guatemala	830,824	480,665	225,739
All of Latin America	21,224,087	16,086,974	8,407,837
All Immigrants	39,955,854	31,107,889	19,767,316

Source: 1990 and 2000 decennial Census and 2010 American Community Survey.

TABLE 10.2   Immigration by State 2007

STATE	NUMBERS OF IMMIGRANTS	PERCENT OF IMMIGRANTS (%)
California	9,980	36
New York	4,105	21
Florida	3,453	19
Texas	3,438	19.1
New Jersey	1,869	21.6
Illinois	1,702	13.5
Georgia	953	10.2
Massachusetts	897	14.2
Arizona	891	14.2
Virginia	856	11.4
Maryland	731	13
Washington	722	11.4
North Carolina	633	7
Pennsylvania	581	4.7
Michigan	493	4.9

Source: Center for Immigration Statistics.

According to the Office of Immigration Statistics, during 2008 there were 175 million nonimmigrant admissions to the United States.

Detainees

"Each year more than 300,000 non-citizens are held in immigration detention" (Constitution Project, 2010). The Department of Homeland Security is authorized to detain non–U.S. citizens who are alleged to have violated immigration law to await legal proceedings or removal from the country, if their case has already been decided. **Detainees** may include those who have (1) entered the country without proper documentation, (2) received a final removal order, (3) or have been convicted of certain crimes. Although immigration crimes are civil ones, detainees are often incarcerated in local jails and prison facilities for extended periods of time. The average time for detention may be as long as 18 months. Several advocacy groups report that individuals in these facilities often receive inadequate physical and mental health care. Several deaths that have been reported as a result of inadequate or inappropriate health care while immigrants were awaiting their disposition.

Illegal Immigrants

Several agencies, including the Department of Homeland Security, the Urban Institute, the Pew Hispanic Center, and the Census Bureau, gather data to estimate the size of the alien population (Camarata, 2007). Based on the Census Bureau's

Population Survey of 2007, the Center for Immigration Studies estimated that there were 11.3 million or nearly one in three aliens who were illegally staying in the United States. This figure indicated an increase in the **alien** population by 4 million between 2000 and 2007. Data collected by the United States Census Bureau in March 2008 revealed that while unauthorized immigrants accounted for 4% of the nation's population, illegal immigrants represented 5.4% of its workforce. Estimates indicate that there were 8.3 million undocumented immigrants in the United States labor force in March 2008. Despite these numbers, the Center for Immigration Studies reports trends that suggest a decline in the illegal immigrant population due, in part, to "stepped up" immigration enforcement efforts, failed legislation to legalize aliens, and a rise in unemployment among low-level jobs throughout the nation (Camarota & Jensenius, 2008). Further evidence of this decline was provided by the Pew Hispanic Center, which concluded that, "the rapid growth of undocumented immigrant workers has halted" (Pew Hispanic Center, 2008). Among the nation's unauthorized immigrants, "76 percent is Hispanic and 59 percent of this population is believed to come from Mexico, 11 percent, from Asia, 11 percent, from Central America, 7 percent, from South America, 4 percent, from the Caribbean, and less than 2 percent, from the Middle East" (Camarata, 2007).

Some Americans believe that aliens contribute much to the nation's workforce and economy by taking jobs that are less attractive to American citizens (Passel 2009; Suro & Escobar, 2006). However, there are others who view the undocumented immigrant as a drain on the economy, because they are frequently poor, uneducated, and require many social services (Center for Immigration Studies, 2009). In any case, for the immigrant who enters the country illegally, the cost is high. Many desperate Mexicans travel across difficult dessert terrain, placing themselves at risk for **hazard vulnerability**, for which they are unprepared. In addition, when they arrive, unemployment or receiving low-paying jobs and being unqualified for certain social and medical benefits to which they would be entitled as legal aliens or as citizens. Illegal entrance to the United States also means living an underground existence in fear of discovery and **deportation**. Yet, for some immigrants the cost of living in America is priceless when compared with the obstacles faced in their country of origin.

THE PROS AND CONS OF IMMIGRATION

Unfortunately, since September 11, 2001, and the increased rise in terrorism, people throughout the world are experiencing a heightened sense of fear and anxiety. This fear has resulted in a significant reduction in the numbers of refugees and other immigrants that America and other nations are willing to accept. In addition, Americans hold diverse opinions about whether the United States should continue to permit immigration from certain countries at all (Myers, 2008). Some argue that immigration makes America more vulnerable to foreigners who maintain loyalties to their native land while living in America

(Glazov, 2008; Tancredo, 2004). In an effort to cope with the social isolation one experiences arriving in a foreign country, new immigrants often cling to their native language, social customs, and patterns of behavior (Myers, 2008). In addition, today's modern communication and transportation technology affords immigrants easy contact with relatives and friends in their countries of origin. These assets make assimilation less appealing to aliens who choose to reside in America (Glaszov, 2008). In some communities, this lack of assimilation sets immigrants apart from their neighbors, fosters resentment between them and the community, and makes **acculturation** more difficult, especially during poor economic times. Consequently, some citizens fear the potential exhaustion of resources, social services, and jobs for which they must compete with new immigrants. Trends indicate that the longer immigrants stay in a community, the more likely they are to become acculturated to it. Still, there remains skepticism about immigration in some communities that experienced surges in the immigrant population during 1995 to 2006.

This phenomenon was especially true in cities like Atlanta, Georgia; Des Moines, Iowa; and Charlotte, North Carolina, where the sudden influx of new immigrants was most noticeable by natives in the community (Myers, 2008).

Therefore, despite the predicted decline in the numbers of immigrants coming to America there is an ongoing debate among Americans about the future of immigration based on current statistics. Myers (2008) discussed two perspectives on immigration representing both proponents' and dissenters' point of view. Members of these two groups disagree on the current rate of immigration, assimilation, and America's need for immigration. As Myers observed, the state of California may be viewed as a model of long-standing diversity (36% of its population is foreign-born). Members of the immigrant population there demonstrate greater assimilation with the passage of time lived in the state. "Old timers" show a greater tendency toward English proficiency, employment and income, and home ownership than do new immigrants. Thus, it would seem beneficial to all to allow time needed for new immigrants to gain longevity in their newfound communities as one means of boosting the economy.

Perhaps the most compelling argument in support of immigration is the aging of the U.S. population. The aging baby boomers, those born 1946 to 1964, create a need in the near future for younger workers to replace Americans who will retire. The "ratio of seniors (age 65 and older) to working age adults will soar by 67% between 2010 and 2030" (Myers, 2008, p.1). According to Myers's (2008, p. 8) research there will be a ratio of 411 seniors to every 1,000 working-age adults. This difference in ratio will create a myriad of economic problems related to the workforce deficit that will impact retirement supports, health care benefits, housing costs, and entitlements for older Americans. Immigrants can fill the employment gap and strengthen the economy, provided they have had time to acculturate to U.S. society.

Many Americans believe that all persons living in America are entitled to certain rights, privileges, and services; others believe that these services should be limited to those who are classified as citizens or legal immigrants.

At this writing, the debate is mounting among politicians and the general public about the rights and services that should be provided to foreign-born persons. In 1996, the Responsibility and Work Opportunity Reconciliation Act (PRWORA), was passed by President Clinton, which greatly restricted the health care benefits received by undocumented immigrants. However, some states have disregarded this federal law in an attempt to address the needs of individuals who reside within their borders (Kultgren, 2003). More recently, 700 immigrants advocating for immigration reform staged a protest on President Barack Obama's first day in office (Persaud, 2009). In August 2009, the Obama administration announced plans to change policies regarding how the nation detains immigration violators.

Because of the events of September 11, 2001 and the fear of terrorism, as well as the general public's confusion about who is and who is not a citizen, some Americans express negative attitudes toward legal and illegal immigrants and the laws intended to protect them. Consequently, some illegal immigrants avoid seeking medical intervention for fear of being discovered and being deported back to their home country. When immigrants who are ill remain underground and delay treatment for communicable illnesses or diseases, the health and well-being of the population is put at risk. For this reason, the problem of providing health care for immigrants, legal or undocumented, is one that ultimately affects all members of American society.

The experience of living in America is different for each immigrant group and the quality of that experience is influenced in part by the group members' support systems, and their ability to acculturate or assimilate into the American culture. Immigrants' success in the United States may also be affected by the attitudes held toward them by other members of the communities in which they live and work. Specifically, the attainment of health information, health care access, and health care treatment are byproducts of an immigrants' successful navigation of unfamiliar territory, often with a language barrier complicating the process. Although the debates around the pros and cons of immigration continue, there is still the need for nurses to appreciate the diversity that exists among the various groups that immigrate to America and to realize that a vast number of immigrants enter the country legally.

Nurses must help address the challenges posed by immigration that impact on the health and well-being of both citizens and immigrants who already live in the United States. Irrespective of an individual's immigration status, persons entering the country who have or acquire an infectious or contagious illness or disease can potentially infect others with whom they interact. Therefore, the health and well-being of new immigrants is an important consideration for all health care providers in the prevention of disease and the maintenance of health in the general community. Another serious consideration is that of providing adequate and culturally appropriate health care for the large numbers of culturally diverse people who arrive in America with various and complex health care needs (Cain, Mackenzie, Castro, & Lobue 2008; Passell & Cohn, 2009; Porco et al., 2006). Because of the conditions under which some immigrants travel to get to the United States, and the preexisting chronic and acute health problems many already have, some immigrants require health care as soon as they arrive (Rasmussen & Keller, 2009; Venters, Dasch-Goldberg, Rassmussen, & Keller, 2009).

Regardless of immigrants' states of health, or their country of origin, they share many common goals. Most immigrants come to America seeking a welcoming community where they can become active members and overcome the socioeconomic barriers that brought them here. More specifically, newcomers to America seek affordable housing, gainful employment, appropriate health care, and education for their children. They come seeking, as one author puts it, "the American dream" (Takougang, 2003). Yet, although immigrants share these issues and concerns, the various groups differ in cultural and ethnic values, traditions, and beliefs, especially attitudes about health (Giger & Davidhizer, 2008; Purnell & Paulanka, 2008; Spector, 2004). Moreover, both legal and undocumented immigrants, like others living in America, have a desire to receive social and health care benefits and services that address their specific health care needs.

HEALTH AMONG IMMIGRANTS

A 2006 report by the Centers for Disease Control found that while immigrants reported significantly better physical and mental health than their U.S.-born counterparts, despite limited access to health care, they became less healthy the longer they lived in the United States (American Pubic Health Association, 2006; USDHHS, 2009). For example, "[O]verall, U.S.-born adults were more likely to be obese than were their immigrant counterparts. Another study reported weight increases with residency in the United States. Moreover, the prevalence of smoking, hypertension, and cardiovascular disease was also higher among U.S.-born adult" (CDC, 2010). On the other hand, many immigrants have left countries such as Africa and Haiti where they have few health resources and diseases such as tuberculosis and HIV are prevalent (CMAJ, 2011). A study involving 1,283 women from 10 European countries revealed that foreign-born women were three times more likely to receive inadequate prenatal care and 19 times more likely when they did not have health insurance. Foreign-born women in the United States are also less likely to have health insurance and consequently receive much less prenatal care than do American natives. (Commissioner's Prenatal Care Task Force, 2008; Kaiser Commission, 2008; Loue & Cooper, 2005). Another study found a high incidence of diabetes among Arab immigrants living in America (Fakhouri, Dallo, Templin, Khoury, & Fakhouri, 2008).

THE ROLE OF THE NURSE

Nurses, as providers and consumers of health care, are in a unique position to provide health care services to immigrants and nonimmigrants at all levels of illness prevention. With an increased awareness and understanding of the immigrant's need for preventive care and health promotion, nurses can help ensure that the potential spread of disease due to lack of treatment is minimized. Unfortunately most nurses and doctors admit to knowing little about new groups coming to America. Thus the rapid rate at which some groups are arriving poses a challenge for most health care providers. A good place for nurses to start in addressing this matter is by gaining knowledge about the groups for whom they are most likely to be providing care, always keeping in mind the diversity that exists among members of immigrant groups.

An important caveat for nurses as they care for members of various immigrant groups is to first consider each individual patient unique, despite what knowledge the nurse may have about the group as a whole. Another important consideration is to determine whether the immigrant is newly arrived to America or has been here for several years. Research tells us that many immigrants who have been in America a long time begin to assimilate or acculturate to the American lifestyle. When the immigrant is newly arrived, the nurse should determine if the patient has to make any difficult transitions to the new geographical environment. Patients previously accustomed to a different climate or terrain may find it difficult to make the physical and psychological adjustment to a new location. New immigrants may also fail to recognize any previously untreated health issues that may have accompanied them. Having an understanding of the patient's history of immigration, the circumstances under which immigration occurred, and the patient's present living conditions in the United States is also essential for the nurse to understand. For example, immigrants seeking to escape political persecution may have traveled alone and had limited resources when they arrived. Some may even have endured being detained by government officials for a long time. Others who have come at the request and with the support of families already living in America are much more likely to be able to negotiate the health care system and gain access to medical care.

Most importantly, the culturally competent nurse recognizes that even aliens deserve quality care and to be treated with dignity and respect. With each of these things in mind, the nurse attempts to overcome any language barriers by using medical interpreters when needed to ensure effective communication with new immigrants. The nurse also remembers that health education is critical and identifies appropriate resources to assist the new immigrant in promoting health at all levels of illness prevention. A listing of some important websites to assist nurses in this role is included at the end of this chapter.

Selected Immigrant Groups

Because of the large numbers of immigrant groups that come to America each year, it is impossible to include each in this chapter. The section that follows will describe some of the health-related issues of selected Asian, Arab, Black, and Latino immigrants who currently reside either temporarily or permanently in America.

IMPORTANT POINTS

- In the United States in 2009, 36 million people or 12.4% of the population was foreign-born.
- It is projected that by 2050, 19% of the population will have been born outside of the country.
- The large majority of legal permanent residents are eligible for naturalization.
- The five regions from which immigrants currently come to America include Asia, Africa, Europe, Latin America, and Oceania, a group of Pacific Islands.
- The four leading countries from which the majority of new immigrants come include Mexico, Philippines, China, and India.
- The leading states with the most new immigrants include California, New York, Florida, Texas, and New Jersey.
- The CDC reports that immigrants generally enjoy better health on arrival than their U.S. counterparts, yet become increasingly less healthy the longer they stayed in America.
- Smoking, hypertension, and heart disease are greatest among U.S.-born adults.
- Immigrant countries like Haiti and Africa have limited health resources and a high prevalence of diseases like tuberculosis and HIV.
- Since September 11, 2001, Americans have mixed attitudes and some confusion about immigration.
- The various groups of immigrants that come to America are diverse in their cultural attitudes and health care beliefs.
- Language barriers are one of the biggest problems influencing immigrants' ability to access quality health care; there may be a need for a medically trained interpreter.
- Nurses enjoy a critical position from which they can prevent illness and promote health in immigrant populations through patient education.
- Nurses can begin to address barriers to health care by gaining knowledge about the immigrant groups for whom they provide care.
- Regardless of immigration status, all patients deserve dignity and respect.

Asian Immigrants

According to the U.S. Census Bureau, one-quarter of foreign-born individuals living in America comes to the United States from Asia. The large collective of people, Americans refer to as Asian/Pacific Islanders represents 47 different countries and includes more than 20 specific ethnic groups. The largest number of Asian immigrants comes to America from China, India, Korea, the Philippines, and Vietnam. Asian populations are concentrated in metropolitan areas such as Los Angeles, New York, and San Francisco. Asians enjoy the highest citizenship rates among the foreign-born living in America and have a high school education or higher at similar rates to natives (U.S. Census Bureau, 2010). Asians also enjoy the highest income and are more likely to be employed in managerial or professional positions than either native or all other foreign-born workers. Fifty-two percent have health insurance coverage at a similar rate to natives. As a reflection of the wide variety of Asian ethnic groups coming from the various Asian countries, religious practices among Asians also vary. The American Religious Identification Survey (ARIS, 2008) and the U.S. Religious Landscape Survey, conducted by the Pew Forum on Religious Life, offer insight into some of these variations. With the exception of China and Vietnam, for which data about religious affiliations are not readily available, one can assume that the religions "within an Asian country are similar to that within its community in the U.S." (Asian Nation, 2004). Thus, Asian immigrants from India are more likely to be Hindu, Muslim, Buddhist, or Sikh as compared to Asians from the Philippines who are more likely to be Roman Catholic or Protestant. According to the ARIS 2008 Report, among Asians, religious practices may be subdivided into three major groups (ARIS Report, 2008). These groups include agnostics or no religion (27%), Eastern religions (21%), and Catholics (17%), a decline from 27% in 1990. Among Eastern faiths, Hinduism is the most popular followed by Buddhism. In 2008, the category of "Christian Generic" was identified as the fourth largest group (10%), which included Protestants, Evangelical, Born Again Christian, Fundamentalist, and Nondenominational Christian. Muslims represented 8% of the Asian population. Other groups including Scientologists, Pagans, Druids, Rastafarian, and others comprised 2% of the Asian population. Members of these groups, although sharing some common health beliefs, differ in their tendency to practice cultural traditions. For example, among Chinese and Vietnamese, practices like coining, cupping, and the belief in the relevance of maintaining the internal balance of hot and cold forces in the body are a part of their health belief system. Even within the same ethnic group, some members may place more value on using folk healers, herbal remedies, or practices than others. Differences in language and communication styles between the patient and the nurse can interfere with the nurse's ability to identify patients' unique needs and to provide culturally appropriate care.

As one writer noted, "the fact that Americans often categorize Asians and Pacific Islanders into one large demographic, makes it hard to identify each of these group's unique health care needs" (Temple University, 2009). In a study that sought to determine the impact of differing Asian cultures and attitudes on cancer-screening rates, researchers found differences among Cambodian, Chinese, Vietnamese, and Korean Americans on their tendencies to get screenings for various types of cancer. However, another important finding in the study was the high number of participants across all four groups who reported never being screened for prostate, colorectal, or HBV. The researchers believed that this study provided evidence of the need for preventive health services in the Asian communities and gave some direction to health care providers as to where to focus their efforts. To address early detection in Asian communities, the researcher suggested a range of cultural and language-sensitive interventions to stress the need for education and access to preventive care.

In a study of Chinese and Vietnamese patients, conducted by Ngo-Metzger et al. (2003), the frequent health care concerns of immigrants were described, including the need for ready access to care, information and education, respect by providers for patients' preferences, the demonstration of emotional support, and facilitation of continuity and transition in care provision. In addition, three dimensions of quality care not identified in prior research included a desire for providers to have a greater knowledge of non-Western cultural traditions and health practices. Respondents in the study also expressed a preference for trained interpreters over family members, and to have assistance from health care professionals in navigating the health care system.

Kim (2002) outlined a model for providing proactive, preventive health care and health promotion to a community of Korean immigrants. This effort involved collaboration between the University of Illinois, School of Nursing, the Chicago Department of Public Health, and a bilingual interdisciplinary team that included a physician and a certified advanced nurse practitioner. Among the clinical problems treated most often in the Korean community under study were: hypertension, hepatitis B, gastric problems, high cholesterol, and diabetes mellitus. In this study, focus groups revealed that Korean patients felt differently from Americans regarding the need for assistance with emotional or mental health problems. Generally, Koreans' cultural need for privacy, self-sufficiency, family solidarity in problem solving, and "saving face," made it difficult for the researchers to identify and to address the mental health issues of this group. Despite their experiences of high stress related to isolation and lack of ability to utilize health care services, Korean participants were unaccustomed to discussing their emotional needs. Another concern of Koreans in this study was the need for changes in the male's familial role as breadwinner due to high unemployment. In addition, Korean and American children differed in their attitudes toward their parents. Traditionally, Korean children were more respectful of older adults, but were being influenced by their American peers. This difference in parental expectations between American and Asian parents created additional stress for some Asian families. Based on their findings, the collaborative health team adopted a psycho-educative approach and developed three booklets in the Korean language to address family issues and explain the concept of mental illness to the Korean patients. Medical health care needs of this group were also addressed. A major accomplishment of this collaboration was to ensure the availability of culturally competent health care services to members of this Korean immigrant community.

Chinese, Cambodian, Vietnamese, and Koreans represent only a small sample of Asian patients. This point underscores the need for nurses to identify the specific health care problems of the Asian groups for whom they provide care. Most importantly the nurse needs to learn about whether the patient and family are new or long-term immigrants, from what geographical region and under what circumstances are they presently living in the United States. Equally important is the determination of the patients' values and beliefs about health care, especially their attitudes toward Western medicine and/or traditional folk practices.

IMPORTANT POINTS

- In 2010 Asians grew by 43% reaching 14.7 million people.
- The largest groups of Asians immigrate from China, India, Korea, the Philippines, and Vietnam.
- Asians tend to live in large metropolitan areas like Los Angeles, New York, and San Francisco.
- Asians have the highest level of citizenship.
- High school completion and higher is similar to natives.
- Asians are more likely to be employed in management or professional positions more than other foreign born.
- Religious diversity among Asians includes Buddhists, Hindu, Muslim, Sikh, and Roman Catholics.
- Asians vary in language and communication styles, and their use of folk practices such as coining, cupping, and the use of healers even among the same ethnic group.
- Family solidarity and the concept of "saving face" ranked high among cultural values.

Black Immigrants

The largest majority (94%) of individuals who self-identify as Black were born in the United States. However, the Black immigrant populations come to the United States from around the world. The many places from which America receives Black immigrants include Africa, Europe, South America, the Caribbean, and West Indies Islands. The largest group of Black immigrants comes to America from Haiti. Although one-third of Black immigrants speak a foreign language, the majority (94%) speaks English fluently. Thus, most Black immigrants are bilingual.

According to the Agency for Healthcare Research and Quality, African- and Caribbean-born Blacks generally experience better cardiovascular, mental health, and cancer outcomes than their American-born counterparts with the exception of prostate cancer, which is more prevalent among Caribbean males. In several earlier studies on Black immigration, the authors noted many differences between Black immigrants and African American natives that are important to include here (Logan & Deane, 2003; Lukas, Barr-Anderson, Daheia, & Kington, 2003; Takougang, 2003; Wilkinson, 2003).

Logan and Deane (2003) distinguished the Afro-Caribbean and sub-Saharan African populations from native-born African Americans and found the "social and economic profile of Afro-Caribbean and Africans is far above that of African Americans." America's African population is much more dispersed with the largest numbers coming from Ghana and Nigeria in the west of Africa and Ethiopia and Somalia in the east. The majority of these immigrants then settle in Washington and New York. "Like African Americans,

Afro-Caribbean's and Africans are segregated from Whites" (Logan & Deane, 2003, p. 2). Segregation among Black ethnic groups reflects important social differences between them. Africans tend to live in neighborhoods with higher median incomes and educational levels. Afro-Caribbeans tend to live in neighborhoods with a higher percent of homeowners than either African Americans or Africans.

On Black immigrant health, Lukas, Barr-Anderson, Daheia, and Kington (2003) described the health status, health insurance, and health care utilization patterns of the growing population of immigrant Black men. These researchers found that foreign-born Blacks resided in large central cities of metropolitan areas in the Northeast much like African Americans and more than 55% of them have lived in the United States for more than 15 years. They are bilingual, speaking their native language and fluent English. These authors further noted, "foreign born Black men were less likely than either U.S.-born Black or White men to report being heavy smokers or drinkers or other adverse health behaviors; however, although foreign-born Black men were in better overall health than their U.S.-born Black and White counterparts, they were more likely then either to be uninsured" (p. 1740). Thus, these writers concluded that Black immigrants who are in poor health, especially new immigrants, may find it difficult to access appropriate health care because they lack private and federally subsidized medical insurance. As Takougang (2003) and Migration Information Source (2007) reported, despite the fact that "African born immigrants are often highly educated professionals when they arrive in America they must seek employment where less skills and education are required. This happens because, in America Black immigrants are forced to confront some of the same stereotypes, and prejudices often associated with their African American counterparts" (Takougang, 2003). Wilkinson (2003) described the struggle of thousands of Somali Bandu of eastern Africa to reach American soil during this period of increased apprehension toward foreigners. Despite efforts by some to assist those seeking asylum from war-torn countries in Africa and elsewhere, tighter security needed to thwart acts of terrorism is making it much harder for refugees to settle in the United States. One man who was seeking asylum took 10 years before he arrived on American soil.

Afro-Caribbean Immigrants From Haiti

Haiti is said to be "the poorest country in the Western Hemisphere, which has been plagued by political violence for most of its history" (CIA, World Factbook, 2009). In 2004 there were 419,317 foreign-born Black immigrants from Haiti living in the United States. At that time, the political unrest and armed revolts, as well as the devastation caused by a major tropical storm, left many Haitians fleeing by boat from their homeland seeking refuge on American shores. During that period, food supplies and basic services were disrupted and 80% of all crops were destroyed. About 300 people died during the revolt and 300,000 became homeless. The U.S. ambassador declared the area a disaster area (Grieco, 2004). Haiti remains a place from which many documented and undocumented immigrants seek refuge in the United States. The native languages of Haiti are French and Creole. Because of poor health conditions, the people of Haiti are exposed to major infectious diseases including HIV, food- and waterborne diseases, such as hepatitis A and E, typhoid fever, and vector-borne diseases like malaria. The ongoing political turmoil in Haiti has correlated with an increase in new LPR in the United States from Haiti (Grieco, 2004). Immigrants from Haiti qualify for a family-sponsored or employment-based immigrant visa or through temporary or **asylee** visas. However, there is ongoing controversy about Haitians who come by boat to the United States without legal documentation. Some consider these immigrants refugees and asylum seekers, while others view the undocumented Haitian a serious threat to homeland security. Presently, the U.S. policy toward undocumented Haitians is to prohibit their entry and to enforce mandatory detention. Human rights advocates have expressed "concern that Haitians are not afforded the same treatment as other asylum seekers" (Wasem, 2005). The five states with the largest number of foreign-born Haitians include Florida, New York, Massachusetts, New Jersey, and Connecticut. In 2004, the largest (43.5%) contingent of Haitian immigrants lives in Florida. Some African Caribbean groups, while sharing physical traits like skin color and facial features with African Americans, do not identify culturally with them. For example, many Haitians, in contrast to some African immigrant groups, come from more impoverished backgrounds, are often less educated, and speak Creole or French as their primary language. However, many do speak fluent English. Haitian immigrants are predominately Roman Catholic (80%), but many Protestant religions are also represented among them (16%). Protestant groups include Baptist (10%), Pentecostal (4%), Adventist (1%), and other (1%). Only 1% of Haitians claim to practice no religion, while approximately half of the population practices voodoo (CIA World Factbook, 2009). Like many African Americans, Haitians are at high risk for a number of health problems and diseases. For example, one study indicated 26% of Haitians smoked, and 67% were overweight (although Haitians consider obesity a sign of good health). In Haiti some common diseases include malnutrition, sexually transmitted diseases (due partially to a belief in polygamous practices), tuberculosis, malaria, typhoid, and hypertension. The life expectancy in Haiti is reported to be 49.5 years.

On January 12, 2009, the Haitian people experienced one of the worst earthquakes ever to hit the island. The earthquake registered 7 on the Richter scale and, as of this writing, has left 170,000 Haitians dead and 1.5 million people homeless. Others who had been buried under rubble for several days awaited decisions about whether the doctors would be able to save their crushed limbs. The U.S. government and France have sent military aides to assist in the mass distribution of food and supplies. The Haitian government plans to move 40,000 individuals out of the capital city of Port-au-Prince, which was devastated by the earthquake, to nearby villages.

Black Immigrants From Africa

According to figures from the former Immigration and Naturalization Service (INS), the number of African immigrants has quadrupled over the past two decades (Takougang, 2003). Among Africans who reside in America, 53% are U.S. citizens (born in the United States, or of at least one American parent), while 46.3% are foreign-born. In 2004, there were more than 1.2 million African immigrants in the United States (Takougang & Tidjani, 2009). In the past, immigrants coming to the United States from Africa typically came to the United States from the west and east coasts of sub-Saharan Africa. As a result, immigrants from Ghana and Nigeria on the west and Ethiopia and Somalia on the east and South Africa represent the largest number of sub-Saharan African immigrants living in the United States. Today, due to civil wars and limited economic opportunities throughout the continent, corrupt and oppressive regimes, and a more relaxed U.S. diversity policy toward African immigrants, a more diverse population of Africans, are attracted to America. Africans from former Portugese, French, and Spanish colonies are now choosing to come to America rather than to go to Europe, their former destination. According to Takougang and Tidjani (2009), "the U.S. has also allowed some illegal immigrants to have working permits under conditions of human resource shortages" (p. 31).

Over the past two decades, the African-born population has grown to nearly 1.5 million people from only 200,000 in 1980. Like other groups, Africans enter the country under various classes of admission. The Immigration Act of 1990 established the U.S. Diversity Program that offers certain countries with low immigration rates an opportunity to enter a "green card lottery."

As a result, 24% of African immigrants were admitted via this program. In 2010, of all LPR (46,763), 48% (or 23,903) were African-born. An additional 22% of refugees and asylum seekers were born in Africa. Another 5% of individuals who were born in Africa entered through their employment. According to the 2010 Census Report, among Africans 74.5% self-identified as Black as compared to 33% of all foreign-born. African immigrants reported higher levels of English proficiency and educational attainment than other immigrants and American-born citizens. Nearly 75% of African immigrants were also more likely to be employed in service, construction, or transportation jobs. African immigrants are among the most highly educated and many highly skilled and trained professionals have been forced to leave their country. As one writer observes, Nigeria's health care system was adversely affected by the absence of 21,000 practicing Nigerian physicians in the United States (Takougang, 2003). These new immigrants come with the intention of staying in America, unlike previous Africans, who sought to educate themselves and return home. Both the unskilled and professionals take jobs in a variety of fields, for which some are often overeducated. There are conflicting reports about the economic status of African immigrants in America. Logan (2003) noted, "among Blacks, immigrants have a surprising edge over those born in the U. S., higher education and income, and a substantially lower percentage unemployed or below the poverty line." However, by 2009 the U.S. Census Bureau reported that despite being more highly educated and being fluent in English, the African-born were more likely to live below the poverty line.

As in the past, African immigrants still prefer major cities like New York, Chicago, Los Angeles, Dallas, Atlanta, Boston, and Washington, D.C. However, new African immigrants can also be found in smaller numbers in Idaho, Iowa, Maine, and North and South Dakota. Often these immigrants join friends and relatives who are already established in the community. Their goal is to improve their economic situation, become an active part of the community, and send money back home to love ones. However, because African immigrants come from countries across the continent, they are culturally diverse from one another, speak different languages, and have different religious affiliations. Table 10.3 lists common places for African settlement in the United States.

African immigrants who come to America are often viewed by natives as simply African. However, immigrants from Africa come from different cultures and geographical regions, many from agricultural areas, while others have left more urban settings. For example, people coming from Ghana in western Africa come from a variety of distinct ethnic groups speaking one or more of 11 different languages, although English is the official language taught in school. There is also religious diversity among Ghanaians with Christian 68.8% (Pentecostal/Charismatic 24.1%, Protestant 18.6%, Catholic 15.1%, other 11%), Muslim 15.9%, traditional 8.5%, other 0.7%, and none 6.1% (CIA World Factbook, 2009). Among Ethiopian immigrants, who come from eastern Africa, there are eight ethnic groups who speak one or more of eight languages between them. Christians, Muslims, and other religious groups can also be found among Ethiopian immigrants. On the other hand, Somalis, immigrants coming from Somalia, share the same language, religion, and culture and tend to follow Islamic practices and law (Koshen, 2007). Because of the diversity within African groups, it is important for nurses to keep these differences in mind when attempting to identify African patients' cultural or spiritual needs.

TABLE 10.3 Top 7 U.S. States of African Immigration (2009)

STATE	NUMBERS OF AFRICAN IMMIGRANTS	PERCENT OF AFRICAN IMMIGRANTS (%)
New York	151,697	10.7
California	14,335	10.2
Texas	119,116	8.4
Maryland	111,698	7.9
Virginia	79,661	5.6
New Jersey	74,031	5.2
Massachusetts	7,231	4.9

Source: Migration Policy Institute: Migration Information Source: February, 2009 www.migrationinformation. org/usfocus/display.cfm?1d=719.

In most of the countries in Africa food- and waterborne diseases like typhoid, hepatitis A bacterial diarrhea, and meningitis are among some of the health risks most Africans encounter. Across the continent, too, severe poverty and the HIV virus have taken a devastating toll on the lives of children and adults. In 2007, 260,000 people in Ghana were living with HIV and in Ethiopia, 890,000. Considering the poverty, waterborne diseases, and high prevalence of HIV, it is not surprising that the life expectancy in these countries is 57 years for a female and 52 for a male in Ethiopia and age 60 for both genders in Ghana (CIA World Factbook, 2009).

As is the case for all other immigrants, the United States conducts pre- and posthealth screening to assess Black immigrants for tuberculosis, venereal, and other infectious diseases. Since 2010, screening for HIV is no longer done prior to admission, but is done on arrival to the United States, particularly for those immigrants coming from sub-Sahara African countries and Haiti where the prevalence of HIV is high (CDC, 2011).

It is also not surprising that many who are able would seek refuge elsewhere. Although it is probably true that the best and brightest and healthiest among Africans are those most likely to reach American shores, African immigrants do not have it easy once they arrive in America. Irrespective of their place of origin, educational background, or ability to speak fluent English, African immigrants, in their search for the "American dream," often encounter a less than receptive environment. Many authors have described the factors that influence African immigrants' experiences in America (Abdullah, 2009; Camarota, 2008; Logan, 2003; Takougang, 2004; Takougang & Tidjani, 2009). As Abdullah (2009) explains, new immigrants today "are integrated into one of three segments of society, rather than a linear path to middle-class society" (p. 39). Immigrants find themselves assimilated into one of three groups, the White middle class, the Hispanic or Black lower class, or their own cohesive ethnic group in the community. Abdullah discussed the recent influx of 100,000 West African immigrants to what is now called "Little Africa in Harlem." The majority of these ethnic group members is Muslim. This particular group is attempting to bridge the cultural gap that exists between themselves and native-born Blacks in the community. At the same time, some African American natives in the community expressed displeasure at having the African cultural influence in the neighborhood and spoke disparagingly of the new immigrants. Ngugi (2009) explains this phenomenon and states, "while there is a strong tradition of African and African American solidarity, at the top, there is also contempt between them at the bottom where, Africans and African Americans see one another with contempt...through racist eyes." Africans, because they have an accent, are seen as foreigners, students in good standing, professors, and professionals that have a "foreigner privilege." Comparing Africans to native African Americans engenders the "you are not like them" mentality that minimizes their encounters with racism. According to Ngugi, "some Africans in the U.S. view African Americans as some whites view them, as ingrates of the great American democracy"

(p. 521). Thus it is clear that at times the nature of Black immigrants and African American relationships is one of ambivalence. Camarota (2008) in describing the impact of Black immigration on Black Americans identified three factors including the strain of illegal immigration on public services; the increasing demand for low-income rental housing; and job competition at the bottom end of the labor market, particularly in categories such as building, cleaning, maintenance, food service and preparation, and construction. Black men are disproportionately employed at the bottom end of the labor market, so they are more likely to compete with new immigrants for these jobs. Moreover, employment rates, wages, and benefits like health insurance have declined. Because of the differences in the cost of labor, employers "often prefer immigrants, particularly Hispanic and Asian over native born Black Americans." Despite these facts, there remains a debate over the real impact of Black immigration on native Black Americans (Camarota, 2008).

IMPORTANT POINTS

- There is much cultural and language diversity among Black immigrants.
- The majority of Africans and Caribbean-born Blacks are bilingual and speak fluent English.
- Most immigrant Blacks arrive in America in a better state of health than their African American counterparts.
- African immigrants, despite being highly educated professionals, usually find employment where less skills and education are required.
- Black immigrants experience the same stereotypes and prejudice as African Americans.
- Haitians are among the poorest Black immigrants and many come to America as refugees.
- African Caribbean groups do not identify culturally with African Americans.
- Obesity is high among Haitians and considered a sign of good health.
- U.S.-born Blacks disproportionately experience coronary heart disease (CHD), higher intake of calories from fat, low infant birth weight, and worse cardiovascular (CV) and mental health outcomes then both African- and Caribbean-born immigrants.

CASE SCENARIO 1

Chinaza Okonkwo, a 62-year-old Nigerian woman, came to America after her daughter and her husband were selected by lottery. Cecelia, Chinaza's daughter, was fearful that her mother would die before she could bring her to the States, because they lived in a small rural town in which there was little to eat. Food was obtained through farming and women had to walk several miles before reaching a place where they might harvest something substantial to eat. In this town, there was only one general doctor who took care of everything from childbirth to more serious health problems. As soon as Chinaza's daughter was eligible, she applied for a green card for her mother, a recent widow, to join her in America. All of Chinaza's other children remained in the small village in eastern Nigeria. When Cecelia met Chinaza at the airport, she could not believe her eyes. Chinaza, at 5 feet 8 inches, weighed only 108 pounds. That night Chinaza told her daughter that she was having burning on urination, difficulty passing her urine, and itching around the perineal area. Mrs. Okonkwo told her daughter that her urine had had a foul odor for the past several days. Cecelia took her mother to the medical clinic to visit her gynecologist. During the interview, the doctor attempted to get a health history from Chinaza, but to each question he asked, Chinaza had no answer. This was Chinaza's first visit to any doctor in her entire life. She was terrified when the tall, young, White doctor entered the room with a female nurse accompanying him. Chinaza spoke some English, but needed to rely on Cecelia to translate for her. The doctor became more and more upset as Chinaza answered no to each of his questions. "When was your last Pap smear?" "No," she replied. "Your last breast examination?" "No," said Chianza. "Your last vaginal examination?" the doctor asked. "No," Chianza replied. "No means never," said Cecelia. The doctor was so upset on learning that Chinaza had seven children, but had never once seen a doctor before or after her deliveries, that he left the room and asked the nurse to complete the interview. He did return later to perform the physical. The nurse remained with Chinaza and attempted to comfort her throughout the procedure.

WHAT NURSES NEED TO KNOW ABOUT THEMSELVES

APPLICATION OF THE STAIRCASE MODEL: SELF-REFLECTION QUESTIONS

1. How prepared would you be to care for this patient; how many encounters have you had with patients from this background?
2. Where would you place yourself on the staircase with regard to this patient?
3. What steps could you take to move to the next level? (see Chapter 1)
4. If you were the nurse, what attitudes and feelings would you have about this patient or her situation?
5. How would you have managed this situation if you were the nurse?
6. What skills do you need when caring for this patient?
7. What do you need to know about this patient to deliver culturally relevant care?

Responses to Self-Reflection Questions 5 and 7

Response to How would you have managed this situation if you were the nurse?

Clearly, health care providers in this situation need good cultural assessment skills to determine how the patient who is unable to speak English well is feeling about the visit. Because the patient has an adult daughter with her, the nurse may be able to get some information through her. It would be advisable to use a medical interpreter, if one is available, to explain the doctor's findings and or to ask questions as needed. Because there are a variety of dialects spoken in Nigeria, it might be difficult to find someone to interpret for Chinaza. It would be helpful for the provider to communicate nonverbally in a way that is assuring and comforting when the patient is stressed.

Response to What do you need to know about this patient to deliver culturally relevant care?

Knowledge of this patient's cultural history would be helpful, but as the patient admits, there have been no medical assessments or treatments by a doctor in the past. Knowing Chinaza's attitudes and beliefs and usual methods of caring for her illnesses would also be useful. Are there folk practices that Chinaza has used in the past to manage infections or other illnesses? Is Chinaza likely to follow the doctor's orders to take the medication he prescribes? A cultural assessment is needed to comprehensively determine this patient's needs. The nurse selects an appropriate model and proceeds using the model as guidance.

Hispanic Immigrants

According to the United States Census Bureau in 2003, the Hispanic population became the largest minority group in America, comprising 39.9 million people, or more than 13.7% of the population. Spanish-speaking people from around the world share an ethnic identity and a common language, but may be of any race. The 2010 Census reported that the percentage of the U.S. population that self-identifies as Hispanic has risen to more 16% or 48.4 million people. Although the term *Hispanic* generally refers to persons who can trace their heritage and lineage from Spain (Purnell, 2008), Latino and Latinas are persons living in America who come from Latin American countries where both Spanish and Portugese is spoken. However, the two terms Hispanic and Latino/a are used interchangeably throughout the literature to describe members of either or both groups. The term Hispanic is used in this chapter to refer to members of either group.

Hispanic immigrants come to America from more than 23 different Spanish-speaking nations (Shah & Carasquallo, 2006). The federal government considers race and Hispanic origin to be two separate and distinct concepts and categorizes an individual's ethnicity as Hispanic or non-Hispanic irrespective of his or her race. Many Hispanics prefer to be referred to by their place of origin rather than a more collective term. For example, many Puerto Ricans self-identify as Puerto Ricans, not Latino or Hispanic just as Mexicans living in America might prefer the term Chicano or Mexican (Purnell, 2008). Between the years 2000 and 2010, Hispanics accounted for the largest percentage of America's population growth (Fry, 2008; U.S. Census Bureau, 2010). Shah and Carrasquallo (2006) identified the four largest subgroups of Hispanic immigrants that come to America: Mexicans, Puerto Ricans, Cubans, and Dominicans. Nearly 66.9% of Hispanics continue to come to America from Mexico, 14.3% from Central and South America, 8% from Puerto Rico, and 3.7% from Cuba. The Hispanic population is younger than the national average with 35% being under 18 years of age. The median age for Hispanics is 27.6 years as compared to 35.2, the median age of the U.S. population. The largest percentage of persons of Hispanic ancestry lives in either the West or the South with half of all Hispanics living in California or Texas, two of the states that form the 1,933-mile border between the United States and Mexico. Other states with large populations of Hispanic immigrants include Florida, New York, and Illinois. States that are experiencing a new growth of the Hispanic population include Arkansas, Georgia, South Carolina, Tennessee, and North Carolina (Bureau of the Census, 2010).

As a group, Hispanics are among the poorest and less educated groups living in America. When compared to their American counterparts, only 62% of Hispanic immigrants have a high school diploma or greater as compared to 84% of Americans. Only 11.5% of male Hispanics and 13.1% of females have a bachelor's degree or more (Shah & Carrasquallo, 2006). As a result of this education gap, Hispanic immigrants are employed largely within service, construction and maintenance, production, and transport jobs as compared to others living in America. Consequently, the income for most Hispanics falls below that of the general population, as well as with the median income for males at $27,490 compared to $42,210. For Hispanic females the difference is less dramatic, with the median being $24,738 as compared to $32,649 for American females. In 2009, more than 40 million Hispanics in the United States were without medical insurance.

Chronic illnesses among the older Hispanics include diabetes, obesity, liver disease, pneumonia, influenza, cervical cancer, and HIV. Some Hispanics utilize plant roots or leaves to prevent, heal, or cure illness and delay seeking medical help until other remedies have proven unsuccessful. Magilvy, Congdon, Martinez, Davis, and Averil (2000) examined the results of four studies that explored Hispanic families' experiences with health care and identified three major themes. First, as Hispanics grow older, family members feel an obligation to "care for their own," and they find it difficult to relinquish the responsibility of caring for one's older adults, despite having work and parenting responsibilities. Second, spirituality is essential in Hispanic people's lives and serves as a strong source of support for them, particularly during times of crisis. A study of 4,600 Hispanics revealed that two-thirds (68%) of Hispanics identify as Roman Catholic; however, among Hispanic Catholics, 54% of them have embraced a distinctive form of Catholicism, the Charismatic movement. A small group of Hispanics have converted to an Evangelical Protestant movement and 8% of Hispanics profess no religion at all (Pew Hispanic Center, 2007).

Third, in the same study, some Hispanics reported experiences of prejudice toward them by health care workers. In summarizing the findings of the four studies, the researchers identified several important beliefs of the Hispanic respondents about the care they received. The respondents believed that Hispanics who were poor, lacked health insurance, arrived in the country illegally, or who were unable to speak English fluently were treated poorly and in some cases denied care. The respondents also related concerns about being misunderstood by care providers and expressed a continuing need for health care providers to give culturally congruent care and sensitive care. Bilingual health care providers who could communicate with Hispanics in their own language were better able to allay some of the anxiety and mistrust of some of the older patients. Because Hispanics have become and are predicted to remain the largest minority group in the United States, it is critical for nurses and other health care providers to work toward minimizing the effects of communication problems and language differences if they are to administer culturally sensitive care to these patients. The nurse who is fluent in the patient's language or who is able to gain the support of an appropriate interpreter to assist in providing culturally sensitive care will be better able to gain Hispanic patients' trust and establish a cooperative and therapeutic relationship with them. Although the earlier discussion describes some socioeconomic characteristics of Hispanics in general, like other groups, Hispanics are not a monolithic group. Within-group differences exist among Cubans, Puerto Ricans, and Mexicans and all other Hispanic groups. These differences are a result of many factors that include immigration status, age, education, language fluency, and available family and other support systems in the United States.

Mexican Americans

Mexico is the country from which the majority (32%) of all immigrants and 66% of Hispanic immigrants comes to America. About 10% of all people born in Mexico now live in the United States (Pew, 2009). However, although many Mexicans come with the intention of staying, there is also "circular migration" that tends to be seasonal based on employment opportunities in the spring and summer. Mexico's National Survey of Employment and Occupation estimated that 433,000 Mexican migrants returned home from February 2008 to February 2009. This number indicates a small decline in the numbers returning home during the same periods in 2006 to 2008 (Pew Hispanic Center, 2009). Data further suggest that there are substantial declines in the number of new arrivals from Mexico. Unfortunately, not all Hispanic groups wanting to come to America are received with welcoming arms. For example, the 1996 Immigration Act sought to minimize the illegal entry of Mexicans across the border. Proponents of the Immigration Act believe that Mexican immigrants take low-skilled jobs from Americans; others consider undocumented immigrants a ready source of cheap labor and value the Mexican contribution to the economy. Thus, attitudes toward Mexican immigrants vary among Americans. In January 2004 President George Bush proposed a temporary worker program that would allow foreign workers, including those who are undocumented, to fill positions that are unfilled by American citizens. Although many citizens praised the president for this action, many conservatives expressed their strong opposition.

Mexicans, as the largest subgroup of Hispanics, share commonalities with other Hispanics; however, there is much within group diversity. For example, among Mexicans, besides the Spanish language, there are 54 indigenous languages and 7,500 dialects spoken. Among Hispanics, Mexicans are the least educated, the most likely to be living in poverty (26%), and to be working in farming, mining, oil production, construction, landscaping, domestic jobs, and the restaurant and hotel industries (Purnell, 2008). Unemployment also remains highest among members of this group as compared to other Hispanics.

Variations among Hispanic immigrants reflect subgroup differences and immigration status. Shah and Carrasquallo (2006) found "notable subgroup variations in education, socioeconomic status, geographic localization, and access to health care." In 2002, 30% of Mexicans were without medical insurance as compared to 18% of Puerto Rican Americans. When one considers immigration status, "50 percent of Latino immigrants who are not U.S. citizens lack (insurance) coverage versus 23 percent U.S.-born Latinos" (Shah & Carraquallo, 2006). Like other Hispanic people, Mexicans place a high value on family, friends, and sustaining close personal relationships. *Respeto* (giving and receiving respect in communications with others) is an important consideration among Mexicans as well as other Hispanics.

Health considerations of particular significance to Mexicans living in America today include the high rate of cigarette smoking, which for men is at 20% and for women is at 8.5%; obesity, which is at 29% for men and 41% for women; and hypertension at 17% for men and 20% for women. With all of these risk factors for heart disease, 36% of Mexican immigrants are without health insurance (CDC, 2009).

Puerto Ricans

Puerto Ricans represent the second-largest Hispanic group living in the United States (2.7 million) or 11% of the U.S. Hispanic population. As a result of the Spanish American War, Puerto Rico became a commonwealth of the United States and its citizens are granted full U.S. citizenship (CIA World Factbook, 2009). Most Hispanics who can trace their lineage to Puerto Rico were actually born within the continental United States. According to the Pew Hispanic Center, only about one-third of all Puerto Ricans or 1.4 million were actually born there. Those born outside of either the United States or Puerto Rico and who were not citizens by birth are considered "foreign born" (Pew Hispanic Center, 2007). Ethnicity among Puerto Ricans includes White Spanish 76.2%, Black 6.9%, Asian 0.3%, and Amerindian 0.2%, Puerto

Ricans who self identify as mixed, 4.4%, and other 12% (CIA World Factbook, 2007). Puerto Ricans migrate most often to large urban areas and are dispersed throughout the country but more concentrated in the Northeast. States with the largest population of Puerto Ricans include New York, New Jersey, Pennsylvania, Illinois, Florida, and California. Among Hispanics, Puerto Ricans are the least likely to be married.

Puerto Ricans share many of the cultural values of other Hispanic groups; therefore, they are family-oriented and value interpersonal interactions, respect for adults, especially older people, and hold a relativistic view of time (Purnell, 2008). Like other Hispanics, Puerto Ricans speak Spanish and English, although many report speaking English with greater fluency than do other Hispanics. Twenty percent of Puerto Ricans say they speak English less well as compared to 38% of the total Hispanic population. Puerto Ricans are typically Catholic (85%) with the rest of the population represented in Protestant and other religions (CIA World Factbook, 2012).

Puerto Ricans have lower levels of education and income, are less likely to be in the labor force, and have a higher rate of unemployment when compared to the U.S. population (Pew Hispanic Center, 2007). In 2000, the CDC reported that Puerto Ricans' health outcomes were worse than other Hispanics in the mainland United States. This study revealed that 18% of Puerto Ricans reported being in fair or poor health compared to 14% of Cubans and 12% of other Hispanics. Puerto Ricans also reported more days spent in bed due to illness than other Hispanic groups. In 2006, the CDC reported higher death rates for Puerto Ricans linked to hypertension than Whites, Blacks, or other Hispanic groups. Another study that same year, identified several chronic health problems (Robert Wood Johnson, 2006) encountered by Puerto Ricans in the United States, which included cardiovascular disease including hypertension, diabetes, and asthma. A 2006 CDC report revealed a steady increase in diabetes among Puerto Ricans over 65 years of age over the past five years. Ho, Qian, Kim et al. (2006, p. 336). identified obesity, diabetes, smoking, and physical illness among the indicators of health among Puerto Ricans. These researchers found disparities between mainland Puerto Ricans and those living on the island with mainlanders having a higher prevalence of diabetes mellitus (DM) and physical illness; those with diabetes also showed a higher prevalence of smoking. The researchers stressed the need for health education, greater health access to primary care for mainlanders, and further studies to identify factors accounting for poor health in mainland Puerto Ricans. According to reports by the CDC in 2010 Puerto Ricans continue to suffer disease from asthma, HIV/AIDS, and infant mortality at rates higher than other minority groups. Unfortunately, more than 30% of all Hispanics lack health insurance.

For more information about Hispanic Americans see (2010 Shows Hispanic Population Growth) http://2010.census.gov/news/releases/operations/cb11-cn146.html.

IMPORTANT POINTS

- In 2010 Hispanics accounted for 48.4 million people and represented 16% of U.S. population.
- The terms Hispanic and Latino/a are often used interchangeably.
- Most Hispanics prefer references to their nation of origin.
- Hispanics come to America from more than 23 different Spanish-speaking countries.
- Most Hispanics immigrate to America from Mexico; others from Puerto Rico, Cuba.
- Half of all Hispanics live in California and Texas; also in Florida, New York, and Illinois.
- Chronic illness among Hispanics includes diabetes, hypertension, obesity, cardiovascular disease, liver disease, and HIV.
- The population of Hispanics is younger than the American-born.
- There is religious diversity among Hispanics with the majority being Catholics; however, there are also Protestants and other religions among them.
- Hispanics place a high value on family and close relationships.
- Sixty-two percent have a high school diploma as compared to 84% of natives.
- Unemployment is higher and income and health insurance lower among Hispanics than natives and other minorities.
- Hispanics vary in use of folk practices, and use of herbal remedies.
- Cultural variations may be based on immigration status.

Arab Immigrants

There are variable size estimates of the Arab population in America ranging from 2 million to 8 million (Ghazal Read, 2008). Between 2007 and 2009, the U.S. government reported that more than 1.7 million people of Arab ancestry lived in the United States. (U.S. Census Bureau, American Community Survey, 2009). The numbers are believed to be an underestimate because the question of ancestry is separated from questions of race and ethnicity. The U.S. government defines persons of Arab heritage as those who can trace one or more ancestries to an Arab-speaking country or region such as the Middle East or Northern Africa. Although 54% of Arabs are foreign-born, nearly half of the individuals living in the United States (46%) and claiming Arab ancestry were actually born in America (We the People of Arab Ancestry, 2005). The first of three waves of Arab immigrants were Christians from Lebanon and Syria who immigrated to New York and to Boston between 1887 and 1913 with the intention of improving their life circumstances and one day returning home. Many were unskilled workers, some poets and writers who became permanent residents, and their descendants are now natives. A second wave of Arab immigration included displaced Palestinians and more Muslims after Britain gave Palestine to the Jews in 1948 (Ghazal Reed, 2007). This wave included many more refugees fleeing a war-torn existence. Among this group were many professionals and those seeking educational degrees (Purnell, 2008). A third wave in the mid-1960s brought more professionals and entrepreneurs who fled the ongoing political unrest and wars in the Middle East. Arabs who came during this wave were more educated and affluent and many became U.S. citizens (Nobles & Sciarra, 2000). Thus, Arab people have been a significant part of American life for several generations.

The largest groups of foreign-born Arabs who come to America are Lebanese (25%), Egyptian (14%), Syrian (8.9%), Palestinian (7.3%), Jordanian (4.2%), Moroccan (3.6%), Iraqi, (3.5%), and other Arab groups like Saudi Arabians, Algerians, and Tunisians. Half of the foreign-born Arab population arrived in the United States between 1990 and 2000. Sixty-eight percent of the Lebanese population lived here since 1990. Most recent arrivals have come from Morroco and Iraq (1990–2000). Among Arab populations, there are several ethnic categories and 17 religious sects. Muslims (59.7%), which include Shias, Sunni, Druze, Ismalites, and Nusayr, constitute the largest group. Muslims are themselves a diverse ethnic group in that one-third is Arab, another one-third South Asian, and one-fifth is U.S.- born Black Muslim. There is also an increasing population of U.S.-born Anglo and Hispanic Muslims who are converting to Islam (Ghazal Read, 2008). Thus, not all Muslims are Arab, nor are all Arabs Muslim. Like other religious groups, there are also variations among Muslims regarding their degree of religiosity (Ghazal Read, 2008). Therefore, one cannot assume the degree to which religion plays a role in a particular Muslim's life. Many Muslims are very devout, although others are less influenced by their religion. A second group of Arabs are Christians, which include Maronita, Catholic, Greek Orthodox, Armenian, Syrian Catholic, Armenian Catholic, Roman Catholic, and Protestant, accounting for 39% (CIA World Factbook, 2000). Muslim groups tend to be more traditional then their non-Muslim peers and are also more likely to be immigrants, have an Arab spouse, and believe in *inerrancy*, the belief that the Qu'ran is completely without error. Among women, the degree of attachment to the Arab community is a significant factor influencing their beliefs about gender roles.

In 2005, U.S. citizenship among Arab peoples varied with only 12% of Lebanese reporting not being citizens, but 45% of Iraqis and Moroccans reporting not being naturalized. There is also variation among Arabs in their fluency of the English language. Eighty-two percent speak English at home. Lebanese are the most fluent (53.5%); Jordanians (11.5%) and Iraqis were the least fluent with 42% speaking non-English languages at home. Iraqis also reported speaking English less than very well (We the People of Arab Ancestry, 2005).

Unfortunately, since September 11, 2001, "Increased racial and ethnic animosity has left Arabs, other Middle Easterners, Muslims, and those that bear physical resemblance to members of these groups, fearful" (Giger & Davidhizar, 2002, p. 79). This is a reciprocal fear as members of this group fear retaliation for the events of September 11th and some individuals outside the group look on the group members with suspicion, and at times misplaced anger and mistrust. "Ignorance and fear breed discrimination" (Abu El-Haj, 2007). Although some of this attitude has dissipated, there remains an undercurrent of tension surrounding relationships between new and old Arab immigrants and others living in America. Ironically, according to the 2000 United States Census, Americans of Arab descent live in all 50 states with 94% living in metropolitan areas including: Los Angeles, Detroit, New York, New Jersey, Chicago, and Washington, D.C. Most of these citizens come from Lebanon, Egypt, Syria, Palestine, and Iraq. The largest Arab immigrant population is found in Metropolitan Detroit (Shah, Ayash, Phararon, & Gany, 2008).

Arab Americans are among the most highly educated and skilled workers in the nation; 84% of all Arabs hold a high school diploma or better. More than 40% of Arabs have a bachelor's degree compared to 24% of other Americans. Nearly twice as many Arabs hold postgraduate degrees, as compared to other Americans. Among Arabs, Egyptians are the most highly educated at 94% with high school diplomas or better and 64% with a bachelor's degree or higher as compared to Iraqis at 73% with a high school education and above and only 36% with bachelor's degrees. As a result, Egyptians are more likely (51%) to work in professional and management positions. Seventy-three percent of working Arabs is employed in managerial, professional, sales, or administrative fields. As a result, Arabs living in the United States generally enjoy a higher income than most other Americans. In 2005, the median Arab family income was $52,000. Fifty-five percent of Arabs own their homes. Nevertheless, a high percent of Arabs (17%) in America live below poverty as compared to 12% of the total U.S. population. Unlike other groups there is a significant labor force and earning gap between Arab men and women, with 73% of men and 46% of women in the labor force. Among Jordanians, that gap is even wider at 42%, with men 78% and females 42% (We the People, 2005). A $10,000 earning gap exists between male and female Arabs with men earning significantly higher pay. Perhaps these differences reflect educational differences between men and women and less emphasis placed by the culture on females working outside the home.

Community-based studies of Arabs in America point to significant health problems among immigrants. However, "Arab immigrants are not uniformly disadvantaged in health outcomes" (University of California, 2005). Yet, as Shah, Ayash, Phararon, and Gary (2008) observed, there is limited health research focused on the Arab population in the United States. Research that does exist suggests a need for health care providers to become knowledgeable about the health beliefs, attitudes, and practices of Arab immigrants as a means of determining ways to provide culturally competent care for this population (Almakhzoomy, 2005; Baron-Epel, 2009; Shah, Ayash, Phararon, & Gary, 2008; Yosef, 2006). Several studies that focused on Arabs in America lend some insight into the problems these immigrants encounter.

In a study of the health care and cancer knowledge, attitudes, and beliefs of Arab Americans, Shah, Ayash, Phararon, and Gary (2008) identified barriers to the utilization of health services in cancer prevention and treatment. Data in this study underscored the importance of providing culturally and linguistically appropriate health interventions in partnership with community leaders for this population. Johnson, Nriagu, Hammad, Savoie, and Jamil (2005) studied asthma prevalence and severity in Arab American households in Detroit. In this study environmental factors and socioeconomic status were found to be predictors of asthma prevention. English fluency and birth in the United States were linked to health care access and utilization behaviors that influence asthma management. These researchers also found a significant relationship between asthma prevalence and degree of acculturation. Asthma prevalence was highest among moderately acculturated immigrants as compared to new immigrants. Abdulrahim (2009) discussed differences in self-rated health by immigrant status and language preference among Arab Americans and found that health status of Arabs improves with acculturation. This researcher also observed that Arab-speaking immigrants were more likely to self-report poorer health than both U.S.-born Arab Americans and English-speaking immigrants. Almakhzoomy (2005) studied the impact of cultural understandings and experiences in managing diabetes among Arab immigrant women. This research revealed that Arabs' understanding of the illness experience does not conform to the biomedical model of illness. Rather, Arab understanding of illness is intricately tied to factors such as culture, family roles, and identities. One important cultural norm that may impact patient care is Arab patients' desire and expectation to be cared for by someone of the same gender, especially during personal care when sensitivity and privacy are needed. Therefore, to develop therapeutic and culturally sensitive interventions to address health care needs in this population, providers must understand these variables and the role they play in determining Arabs' health behaviors. In a study of 20 Arab Muslims in Orange County, California, Yosef (2006) identified several factors that influence health and healthful behaviors. These researchers concluded that to bridge the gap between minority and majority populations, "an in-depth understanding of health perceptions and health promotion beliefs and practices among immigrant populations in the United States should be used to provide culturally sensitive health care and health promotion services." Baron-Epel (2009) found that Arab women reported more fatalistic beliefs compared to other women. Arab women believed that external forces were the cause of cancer among Arab immigrants, which may inhibit them from having mammograms. These researchers advocate nursing interventions to help decrease fatalism in Arab women. Regardless of the nature of the health risk or problem, nurses and other health care providers—through their routine encounters with Arab patients—must gain insights into what the illness experience actually means to the patient who is experiencing it. In understanding the sociocultural context in which the individual experiences illness, the nurse is more likely to be able to identify appropriate strategies for providing Arab patients with culturally competent health care.

Each immigrant population comes to America under a particular set of circumstances, bringing with them their own unique value systems, goals, and aspirations for living in America. As we have discussed throughout this chapter, many factors influence immigrants' ability to live healthy and productive lives in a foreign land. These factors include immigration status, a family support system, ability to speak the English language, economic resources, and receptiveness of the host community. As nurses, we are most concerned about the factors that influence immigrants' health and access to health care irrespective of their country of origin, or immigration status. Providing culturally competent care requires that we maximize the time we spend with patients during each encounter with them. Learning as much as we can about the cultural needs of the individuals we serve ensures that we will be able make informed decisions about how best to care for them. For more information about Arab Americans see http://aai.3cdn.net/7b78d6b07baf301c26_zrm6b9qoj.pdf.

IMPORTANT POINTS

- As many as 2 to 8 million individuals of Arab ancestry are estimated to be living in the United States; these numbers are considered an underestimation.
- Among Arabs, although 54% are foreign-born, 46% are American-born.
- The earliest Arabs came to the United States from Lebanon.
- The majority of Arabs come to the United States from Lebanon, Egypt, Syria, Palestine, Jordan, Morocco, and Iraq.
- There are several ethnic categories represented among Arabs, including Shias, Sunni, Druze, Ismalites, and Nusayr.
- Among Muslims there are Arabs, South Asians, Blacks, and increasing numbers of Hispanics.
- Arabs are among the most highly educated with more than 40% having bachelor degrees compared to 24% of other Americans.
- Not all Arabs are Muslim; there are Catholics and Protestants among them as well.
- Many Muslims are deeply devout in their religiosity.
- Gender roles are influenced by the attachment to the Arab community.
- Since September 11, 2001, there is ambivalence and some anger and hostility toward Arabs.
- There is limited health research about the Arab population.

CASE SCENARIO 2

Hasim Amad is a merchant who was born and raised in the Middle East in an urban area near Lebanon. Mr. Amad struggled all his life to acquire a modest income to support his family. He always wanted his son Youseff to become a physician and enjoy a better life in America. Mr. Amad made sure that each of his six children learned English, as well as both the classical Arabic and the Arabic dialect spoken in his region. Youseff honored his father's wishes, studied English as well as classical Arabic, and received excellent grades in school. He applied to many universities in America. After being accepted to medical school, Youseff came to America with the intention of ultimately returning home. Following his residency, Youseff returned home and married Raja, age 16, the daughter of a family friend, and brought her to America. Today, Youseff Amad and his wife Raja have three children, Nour, Naseem, and Nizir. Raja is expecting her fourth child and is 38 weeks pregnant. They have lived in America for 5 years. Raja has learned to speak English, but has trouble reading it. Youseff and Raja are practicing Muslims and live a quiet life in Dearborn, Michigan, within a large Arab community. Youseff practices as a physician at a local clinic, while Raja cares for their children and their modest home near the clinic where Youseff works. She sometimes socializes with the women of her community, but spends most of her time at home. One morning as Raja is returning home from taking the children to school, she is involved in a car accident. Although Raja experiences no critical injuries, the accident causes her to go into premature labor and she is rushed to a nearby hospital. On Raja's arrival in the labor room, Sarah, the nurse, determines that Raja is very upset, but is limited in her ability to provide information in English. After performing a brief assessment, she notifies the physician on call that Raja is in labor and needs to be examined immediately. She also contacts Dr. Hassan, an Arab doctor on staff, who she knows is on duty today. She explains that she needs an interpreter to assist in communicating with Raja. Dr. Hassan says that he will be happy to assist, but warns that not all people of Arab heritage speak the same dialect. Dr. Hassan tells Sarah that they will need to have a female physician and nurses, if possible, if the patient is Muslim. Raja is taken to the labor room and her husband Dr. Amad is notified. The nurse shares her conversation with the other staff members. Raja's contractions are occurring every 15 minutes. Although Raja is pain-free, Cindy, the nurse in the labor room, decides to learn more about Raja and utilizes Purnell's cultural assessment (Purnell, 2008). This model includes considerations of patients' country of origin, communication, family roles and organization, workforce issues, biocultural ecology, high-risk behaviors, nutrition, pregnancy and child-bearing practices, death rituals, spirituality, health care practices, and health care practitioners (Purnell, 2008). By considering these areas, Cindy is able to learn much about Raja and to determine the best approach for her care. Despite the fact that Raja appears to be about Cindy's age, the nurse begins by asking the patient what she prefers the nurses to call her. Raja states that she prefers being called by her first name, rather than Mrs. Amad. Cindy is also unsure about whether it is appropriate to touch Raja. When assisting her patients in labor, Cindy likes to hold their hand or rub their backs, but she has never cared for an Arab patient before. She learns from Raja that touching is permitted between members of the same gender. She is relieved to know that she can comfort Raja in her usual way throughout her labor. Between labor contractions, Raja is offered but refuses ice chips to her lips. Many Arabs believe that receiving cold or icy beverages during the morning or during illness is inappropriate. Despite being offered comfort measures, Raja moans and screams out as contractions occur. Some staff members are annoyed by Raja's screaming. "All that screaming is not necessary," one nurse comments. Cindy recognizes that this behavior is an acceptable cultural norm for many Arab women and other ethnic groups. When Raja's contractions are 3 minutes apart, Dr. Amad, Raja's husband, arrives in the delivery room. His sister accompanies him. Dr. Amad asks Raja's uncles and two brothers to wait in the reception room. On entering the room, Dr. Amad asks to speak with the physician in charge and is pleased when Dr. Joy Kim approaches him. The doctor introduces herself to Dr. Amad and tells him, "Your baby is coming early, but baby and mom are doing well." Dr. Amad asks the nurses to give Raja something for pain. He also tells his sister to put something cool over Raja's head. The nurses explain that Raja received an epidural anesthetic before he arrived. Cindy realizes that it is the role of Arab family members to speak to the health care professionals on behalf of the patient and to actively participate in their care. She provides Raja's sister-in-law with a cool cloth to place on Raja's head. Typically, the male is not supposed to participate in the actual birth; however, because Dr. Amad is a physician, albeit not an obstetrician, he chooses to remain with Raja. Raja's contractions occur closer and closer together and are now 2 minutes apart. Dr. Amad frowns each time a male nurse or doctor stands at the door to speak with one of the individuals in the room. "That is our way," he says. "There should be no males in the room except me." As the staff prepares to take Raja into the delivery room, Cindy reassures Dr. Amad that the nurses will do their best to adhere to the Amads' traditional practices. She further explains that there will be a need to have a pediatrician in the room once the baby is born and there is no female pediatrician on call today. Dr. Amad states that he understands and together with the staff anxiously awaits the birth of his child.

WHAT NURSES NEED TO KNOW ABOUT THEMSELVES

APPLICATION OF THE STAIRCASE MODEL: SELF-REFLECTION QUESTIONS

1. What feelings and attitudes would you have toward the Amads?
2. Where are you on the Cultural Competency Staircase when caring for Arab patients?

3. How will you progress to the next step?
4. What skills are needed when caring for the Amads?
5. If you were the nurse, what would you and the other staff members need to know to provide culturally competent care to the Amads?

Responses to Self-Reflection Questions

Response to What feelings and attitudes would you have toward the Amads?

Your personal attitudes and feelings will depend on the number of clinical or personal encounters you've had with Arab patients and the nature of those experiences. As you gain more knowledge about this cultural group and understand their values, norms, and health needs, you will feel more comfortable caring for Arab patients. Both of the nurses assigned to care for Raja in this case example demonstrate an awareness of the possible influences cultural differences may have on this patient's hospital experience. As examples, the first nurse seeks an interpreter and raises the awareness of others, that is, by informing the labor room nurses that the patient is Muslim so that the some of the patient's known cultural needs may be anticipated. The second nurse demonstrates an understanding of her own preference for calling the patient by her first name because she is about the same age. The nurse also recognizes her tendency to hold patients' hands as a way of showing support. However, in both these instances, the nurse understands that in some cultures these behaviors may be offensive and decides to speak with the patient first, before acting on assumptions or misperceptions. Both nurses remain nonjudgmental and responsive to the patient's cultural needs. It is mentioned that some nurses resent Raja's screaming during labor. They consider this behavior inappropriate, because it is culturally incongruent with their own values and attitudes. These nurses lack cultural understanding and respect for cultural differences.

Response to Where are you on the Cultural Competency Staircase? and How will you progress to the next step?

From the moment the nurse first meets the patient and throughout each subsequent meeting, the nurse must utilize skills in cultural assessment to identify and prioritize the patient's cultural needs. Each encounter between the patient and the nurse is also an opportunity to identify the nursing behaviors that are most likely to positively affect patient care outcomes. Since a patient–nurse encounter may take many forms, these opportunities can occur even before the nurse actually meets the patient. For example, when receiving documentation or a verbal report about the patient of Arab heritage, the nurse may begin to collect data about potential cultural issues that can impact care. Culturally competent nurses proactively explore potential areas of cultural conflicts between the medical staff and the patient. By so doing, they are able to anticipate potential problems and address them before they occur. Despite cultural differences that might exist, the nurse consistently strives to demonstrate respect and caring to the patient and family, even when the patient's views are incongruent with the nurse's own values and beliefs. By exploring cultural differences, the nurse is able to build on previous cultural knowledge. When caring for Arab patients, nurses should explore gender roles and determine to what extent a female patient might wish to defer to her husband in health care decision making. Because family relationships are important to Arab patients, family members should be considered when planning care. Speaking with the family's designated spokesperson, asking appropriate questions, and explaining technical information will enable the nurse to establish a positive working relationship with the patient and the family. When time permits, speaking with other members of the Arab community through formal (continuing education, staff development) or informal means to gain insight about the health issues and concerns of this cultural group helps prepare the nurse for future encounters with Arab patients. All of these nurse behaviors enable the nurse to build skill and confidence to progress to the next step in cultural competency.

Response to What skills are needed when caring for the Amads?

The nurses in this case, and nurses during any encounter with patients, need to have skills in cultural assessment. Being skilled involves having several cultural assessment models in one's repertoire from which to choose the one that best fits the clinical situation and time frame (see earlier in this chapter). One model that might be useful is Purnell's *Twelve Domains of Culture*, which includes considerations of patients' country of origin, communication, family roles and organization, workforce issues, biocultural ecology, high-risk behaviors, nutrition, pregnancy and child-bearing practices, death rituals, spirituality, health care practices, and health care practitioners (Purnell, 2008). When conducting the cultural assessment, the nurse must have the ability to listen actively to determine the most effective approach for care. Communication skills that incorporate the use of an interpreter are also needed should the patient or the nurse have difficulty exchanging information. Fortunately, in this case there is a doctor on staff who may be able to assist. However, in some cases, the nurse will need to be skilled at recognizing and utilizing nonverbal cues, body language, or other strategies to communicate effectively with the patient who speaks English as a second language.

Response to What do you and other staff members need to know to provide culturally competent care to the Amads?

When caring for the Amads, or any other Arab patients, the nurses need an *understanding* of Arab culture. This knowledge includes the recognition that Arab cultures are diverse and that even the language may vary between Arab groups, although most Arabs are fluent in English. Differences between groups are influenced by the geographical origins of a particular group, length of time in the United States, and other variables such as age, socioeconomic status, education, and language ability. Because many Arabs practice Islam, nurses need some knowledge of what that means in terms of patients' dietary restrictions, religious practices or spirituality needs, health beliefs, and lifestyle. However, not all Arabs are Muslim, so the nurse must acquire knowledge of the patient's specific religion and determine what relevance it has in the patient's life. In this case, knowledge of cultural attitudes about labor and delivery is helpful; however, in other situations, cultural beliefs and attitudes around death and dying may be more relevant. Having knowledge of these things enables the nurse to work with the patient in establishing meaningful health care goals and implementing culturally appropriate interventions. Knowledge of other resources such as interpreters, language banks, or reference texts that offer detailed information about the culture is also useful for nurses who are attempting to communicate with people from culturally diverse groups. As in this case, the patient's and family's acknowledgment of the nurse's respect for their cultural values and beliefs is demonstrated by their expressions of satisfaction with the care they receive.

SUMMARY

Despite current policies and attitudes toward immigration, America remains a refuge for thousands of immigrants each year. Each new group of immigrants comes with the hope of experiencing a welcoming social environment, decent housing, employment, and social and health care services. Generally, immigrants come with the expectation of receiving health care that is viewed superior to that received in many other countries. Health care professionals who desire to provide superior health care for their patients recognize the need to become culturally competent. Culturally competent nurses appreciate the need to partner with their patients in determining culturally relevant health care goals and interventions. The health and well-being of immigrants, whether legal or illegal, impacts the health of the communities in which they live. The more nurses and other health care workers can do to ensure culturally competent, preventive, and supportive care, the more they are able to minimize disease and illness and promote health in their communities.

NCLEX-TYPE QUESTIONS

1. The staff development nurse conducts a workshop on the care of new immigrants. The nurse states that according to the U. S. Census, 36 million people or 12.4% of the population is:
   A. A citizen
   B. Residing in the country illegally
   C. A permanent resident
   D. Foreign-born

2. The newly admitted patient explains to the nurse that he recently immigrated to the United States and holds a green card. The nurse understands that this means:
    A. The patient must at some point return to his native land.
    B. The patient has citizenship.
    C. The patient has a legal right to reside permanently in the United States.
    D. The patient is a foreign national.

3. A Mexican migrant farm worker is seen in the emergency room for a work-related injury. During the intake interview, the patient reveals that she is worried about being treated because she has no health insurance. The nurse's best response is:
    A. Only citizens are eligible to receive hospital care.
    B. All persons who live and work in America are entitled to emergency care.
    C. Green-card holders only may receive hospital care.
    D. There is a fee that must be paid by those without health care insurance.

4. The nurses on a busy hospital unit in an urban metropolitan area observed a sudden influx of Hispanic patients from Puerto Rico and Mexico over the past several months. Which statement by the staff is accurate about current demographics and Hispanic populations? (select all that apply)
    A. Hispanics currently represent more than 16% of the population with a projection of 19% by 2050.
    B. Current trends suggest a decrease in the number of Hispanics coming to America.
    C. The largest group of Hispanic immigrants come from Mexico.
    D. Hispanics are typically younger than their U.S. counterparts.

5. A new graduate nurse relocates to California in search of employment and is to begin working in a busy medical-surgical unit in San Diego. What statement by the nurse indicates a good understanding of the diversity of patient populations in California?
    A. According to the 2010 Census, California had the largest immigrant population in the United States.
    B. California is second only to Texas in having the largest numbers of immigrants in the state.
    C. Largely Asian immigrants migrate to California.
    D. There is limited cultural and ethnic diversity in California.

6. The nurse reads the chart of a newly admitted recent immigrant to the United States. The patient's chart reads that the patient was admitted to the country due to a fear of returning to her country of origin because of the danger of political persecution. Based on this information, the patient is best described as:
    A. An alien
    B. An asylee
    C. An LPR
    D. An illegal

7. The culturally competent nurse recognizes that the majority of new immigrants come to the United States from what regions around the world?
    A. Oceania and Europe
    B. Africa and Asia

    C. Asia and Oceania
    D. Latin America and Asia

8. The greatest barrier to health care access for new and older immigrants is:
    A. Problems in communication due to language issues
    B. Religious and value differences
    C. Gender and family roles variations
    D. Gaining access to hospitals due to transportation problems

9. When nurses are caring for new immigrants one of the most important roles of the nurses is that of:
    A. Learning a foreign language
    B. Teaching foreign patients to speak English
    C. Learning illness prevention and health promotion
    D. Providing acute care for those who arrive in an illness state

10. What statement(s) are true about the health care needs of immigrants in the United States? (select all that apply)
    A. Some immigrants require health care as soon as they arrive in the country.
    B. Immigrant's health on arrival to the United States is usually better than their U.S. counterparts.
    C. Obesity and other illnesses among immigrants increase with time spent in the United States.
    D. Hypertension and heart disease are experienced more by U.S.-born adults than foreign-born.

11. According to research, what factors best explain why there are some negative attitudes among citizens toward immigrants?
    A. New immigrants' failure to assimilate and natives' fear of losing jobs and resources.
    B. Language diversity and differences in religious beliefs.
    C. Political misunderstandings and value differences.
    D. Socioeconomic differences.

12. When initiating care for new immigrants nurses should be guided by what important principle?
    A. The patient's culture determines values, attitudes, and beliefs.
    B. The patient is a unique individual with cultural attitudes, values, and beliefs.
    C. The patient's religion will determine values and behavior.
    D. Members of the same cultural group share similar attitudes and ideals.

13. The nurse performs a cultural assessment for a Puerto Rican patient using the Giger and Davidhizar model. When considering biologic variations of members of this group, the nurse realizes that among Puerto Ricans:
    A. There is a high incidence of asthma, hypertension, and diabetes.
    B. There is a high susceptibility to gastrointestinal disorders.
    C. Arthritis and lupus are prevalent.
    D. Neurological and hematological illnesses are common.

14. The ER nurse gives a report to the receiving nurse on a medical-surgical unit. She explains that the unit will receive Mr. G., a 45-year-old Arab patient. The receiving nurse expresses concern about what important consideration impacting this admission?
    A. There is an all-female staff on the unit.
    B. The nursing staff is uncertain about the correct pronunciation of the patient's name.
    C. The nurse assumes the patient will not like the food.
    D. The nurse is confused about the patient's attitudes toward American nurses and doctors.

AACN COMPETENCIES ADDRESSED IN THIS CHAPTER

1. Apply knowledge of social and cultural factors that affect nursing and health care across multiple contexts.
2. Use relevant data sources and best evidence in providing culturally competent care.
3. Promote achievement of safe and quality outcomes of care for diverse populations.
4. Advocate for social justice, including commitment to the health of vulnerable populations and the elimination of health care disparities.
5. Participate in continuous cultural competence development.

REFERENCES

Abdullah, Z. (2009). African Soul brothers in the hood: Immigration, Islam, and the Black encounter. *Anthropological Quarterly, 82*(1), 37–62.

Abdulrahim, S., & Baker, W. (2009). Differences in self-rated health by immigrant status and language preference among Arab Americans in the Detroit Metropolitan Area. *Social Science & Medicine, 68*(12), 2097–2103. doi: 10.1016/j.socscimed.2009.04.017

Abu El-Haj. (2007). I was born here, but my home it's not here: Educating for democratic citizenship in an era of transnational migration and global conflict. *Harvard Educational Review, 77*(3), 300.

Almakzoomy, I. K. (2005). *Cultural understandings and experiences in managing diabetes of women from an Arab immigrant community in Iowa: A focused ethnographic study.* [Doctoral dissertation]. Retrieved from http://webscohost.com/ehost/delivery?vid=22&hid

American Public Health Association. (2006). Immigrant health decline coincides with U.S. residency. *Nation's Health, 36*(4), 6.

American Religious Identity Survey (ARIS). (2008, July). *Summary Report.* Retrieved from http://commons.trincoll.edu/aris/

Asian Nation. (2008). Asian American history, demographics, and issues. Retrieved from www.asian-nation.org/index.shtml

Baron-Epel, O. (2009). Fatalism and mammography in a multicultural population. *Onclogy Nurse Forum, 36*(3), 353–361.Retrieved from http://web.ebscohost.com/ehost/delivery?vid=14&hid

Camarota, S. A., & Jensenius, K. (2008, July). Homeward bound: Recent Immigration enforcement and the decline in the illegal alien population. *Backgrounder,* pp. 1–11

Camarota, S. A., & Jensenius, K. (2008). *Immigration and Black Americans: Assessing the impact. Testimony before the U.S. commission on civil rights.* Retrieved from www. cis.org/articles/2008/sactestimony040508.

Camarota, S. A. (2007). Immigrants in the United States, 2007: A profile of America's foreign-born population. Retrieved from http://www.cis.org/immigrants_profile_2007

Centers for Disease Control. (2010). *Central Intelligence Agency, World Fact Book 2010.* Retrieved from www.cia.gov/library/publications/the-world-factbook/index. html

CMAJ. (2011). *Guidelines. Evidence-based guidelines for immigrants and refugees.* Retrieved from www.cmaj.ca/content/early/2011/07/27/cmaj.090313.full.pdf

Constitution Project. (2010). *Immigration.* Retrieved from www.constitutionproject. org/rolp/immigration.php

Fakhouri, M., Dallo, F., Templin, T., Khoury, R., & Fakhouri. (2008). Disparities in self-reported diabetes mellitus among Arab, Chaldean, and black Americans in Southeast Michigan. *Journal of Immigrant and Minority Health, 10*(5), 397–405. Retrieved from http://web.ebscohost.com/ehost/delivery?vid=17&hid

Ghazal Reed, J. (2007). More of a bridge than a gap: Gender differences in Arab-American political engagement. *Social Science Quarterly, 88*(5), 1072–1089. Retrieved from http://web.ebscohost.com/ehost/delivery?vid=20&hid

Ho, G. Y. F., Quian, H., Kim, M. Y., Melnik, T. A., Tucker, K. L., Jimenez-Velazquez, I. Z., … Rohan, T. E. (2006). Health disparities between island and mainland Puerto Ricans. *Revista Panamericana de Salud Pública, 19*(5), 331–339.

Johnson, M., Nriagu, J., Hammad, A., Savoie, K., & Jamil, H. (2005). Asthma prevalence and severity in Arab American communities in Detroit area, Michigan. *Journal of Immigrant and Minority Health, 7*(3), 165–178.

Loue, S., Cooper, M., & Lloyd, L. (2005). Welfare and immigration reform and use of prenatal care among women of Mexican ethnicity in San Diego, California. *Journal of Immigrant Health, 7*(1), 37–44.

Myers, D. (2008). Thinking ahead about our Immigrant future: New trends and mutual benefits in our aging society. *Immigration Policy Infocus, 6*(1), 1–11.

Ngo-Metzger, Q. (2003). Patient centered quality measures for Americans: Research in progress. *American Journal of Medical Quality, 15*(4), 167–173.

Nobles, A.Y., & Sciarra, D. T. (2000). Cultural determination in the treatment of Arab Americans: A primer for mainstream therapists. *American Journal of Orthopsychiatry, 70*(2), 182–191.

Office of Imigration Statistics. (2008). *Refugees and asylees.* Retrieved from http:// wwdhs.gov/ximgtn/statistics/pulication/yearbook.shtm

Office of Immigration Statistics. (2008). Nonimmigrant admissions to the United States:2008

Persaud, F. (2009). Immigrant advocates turn Obama's famed one-liner into call for reform. *New York Amsterdam News, 100*(4),14.

Pew Research Center, Pew Hispanic Center, Passell, J., & Cohn, D. (2009). *A portrait of unauthorized immigrants in the United States.* Retrieved at www.pewhispanic. org/2009/04/14/a-portrait-of-unauthorized-immigrants-in-the-united-states

Pew Research Center, & Robert Wood Johnson Foundation. (2007). *Hispanics and health care in the United States: Access information and knowledge.* Retrieved from http:// pewhispanic.org/files/reports/91.pdf

Purnell, L. D., & Paulanka, B. J. (2008). *Transcultural health care: A culturally approach* (3rd ed.). Philadelphia, PA. F.A. Davis.

Shah, S. M., Ayash, C., Pharaon, N. A., & Gany, F. M. (2008). Arab American immigrants in New York: Health care and cancer knowledge, attitudes and beliefs. *Journal of Immigrant and Minority Health, 10*(5), 425–436. Retrieved from www.cinahl.com/cgi-bin/refsvc?jid

Takougang, J. (2003). *Contemporary African immigrants to the United States.* Retrieved from www. africamigration.com/archive_02/j_takougang.htm

Takougang, J., & Tidjani, B. (2009). Settlement patterns and organizations among African immigrants in the United States. *Journal of Third World Studies, 26*(1), 31–40.

Tancredo, T. (2004). Immigration, citizenship, and national security: the silent invasion. *Mediterranean Quarterly, 15*(4), 4–15. Retrieved from http://webscohost.com/ehost/delivery?vid=34&hid

U.S. *Bureau of the Census: Newly Arrived Foreign Born.* (2010). Retrieved from http://www.census.gov/prod/2011pubs/acsbr10–16.pdf

U.S. Department of Health and Human Services. Agency for Healthcare Research and Quality. (2009). *Preventive care: Immigrants use fewer preventive services than U.S natives.* Retrieved from www.ahrq.gov/research/apr09/0409RA34.htm

Venters, H. Dasch-Goldberg, D., Ramussen, A., & Keller, A. S. (2009). Into the abyss: Mortality and morbidity among detained immigrants. *Human Rights Quarterly, 31,* 475–495.

Wasem, R. E. (2005). U.S. Immigration Policy on Haitian Migrants. *CRS Report For Congress Congressional Research Service, The Library of Congress. We the People of Arab Ancestry in the United States. Census Special Report (2005).* Retrieved from www.census.gov/prod/2005pubs/censr-21.pdf

Yosef, A. O. (2006). Male Arab-Muslims health and health promotion perceptions and practices. Retrieved from http://webscohost.com/ehost/delivery?vid=2-&hid

IMPORTANT WEBSITES

Commissioner's Prenatal Care Task Force. Retrieved from www.state.nj.us/health/fhs/documents/task_force_report.pdf

Depatment of Homeland Security. Immigration Status 2010. Retrieved from www.dhs.gov/files/statistics/immigration.shtm

Healthcare Guidelines for Refugees. Retrieved from www.cdc.gov/immigrantrefugeehealth/guidelines/refugee-guidelines.html

Hispanic Americans by the numbers. Retrieved from www.infoplease.com/spot/hhmcensus1.html

Kaiser Commission on Medicaid and the Uninsured. (2008). Retrieved from http://www.kff.org/medicaid/upload/7761.pdf

Pew Research Center: Pew Social and Demographic Trends. U.S. Population Projections 2005–2050. Retrieved from www.pewsocialtrends.org/2008/02/11/us-population-projections-2005–2050/

Rytina, N. Estimates of the legal permanent residents in 2010. Retrieved from www.dhs.gov/xlibrary/assets/statistics/publications/ois_lpr_pe_2010.pdf

Cultural Considerations When Caring for the Poor and Uninsured

GLORIA KERSEY-MATUSIAK

If the world seems cold to you, kindle fires to warm it.

—LUCY LAROM

LEARNING OBJECTIVES

1. Examine socioeconomic factors that impact health care decision making and outcomes.
2. Discuss poverty in the United States and its relationship to health care disparities.
3. Describe health-related problems encountered by the poor and uninsured.
4. Examine homelessness and its impact on health.
5. Discuss the intersection of cultural differences, language barriers, and poverty and its impact on health care access.

KEY TERMS

Barriers
Gender bias
Health care disparities
Indigent
Infantilization
Limited English proficiency
Objectification
Poverty
Poverty thresholds

Socioeconomic status
Tuskegee experiments

OVERVIEW

Throughout this text, the authors have focused on clinical situations in which nurses experience various differences between themselves and their patients. These differences may be based on race, ethnicity, religion, culture, or other attributes that reflect the wide range of human diversity. This chapter focuses on yet another area of human diversity—socioeconomic class—more specifically it examines poverty and its impact on health. This topic is included here because **socioeconomic status** has been identified as one of the major determinants of health (WHO, 2011). Therefore, nurses and other health care providers must attempt to find ways to minimize the impact of low income on health care access to reduce health care disparities in the United States. Despite nurses' desire to give optimum care to all patients, the socioeconomic status of the patient can sometimes interfere with nurses' and other health care workers' best efforts to positively influence the quality of health care the patient receives.

SOCIOECONOMIC CLASS AND HEALTH CARE

Indicators of socioeconomic class include income, completed education, net worth, and private health insurance (Armstrong, Ravenell, & McMurphy; Muchier & Burr, 2009; Putt, 2007). Research indicates that there is a positive relationship between these indicators of socioeconomic status and health (Coddington & Sands, 2008; Keller, 2008; McGibbon, Etowa, & McPherson, 2008; Wiltshire, Person, & Kiefe, 2009). In the United States variations exist between racial and ethnic groups on each of these indicators. For example, in a study that examined the effect of socioeconomic status on health, Mulchier and Burr (2009) observed, "Life experiences of Blacks and Whites in the United States have been characterized by different patterns of education, economic success, and employment, as well as different access to the goods, resources, and privileges available within the larger society" (p. 1). In this study, the researchers concluded that one explanation for the health disparities that exist between Blacks and Whites is that Blacks are "less advantaged in terms of income, wealth, and access to care." Often race has been thought of as a factor influencing one's health; however, when socioeconomic factors were controlled for, the influence of race became less significant.

Results of this study and others indicate that persons who are poor, irrespective of their race or ethnicity, experience health and health care differently from their wealthier counterparts in society (Mclanahan, 2009; Rose & Hatzenbuehler, 2009). Poverty, then, acts as a **barrier** to quality health care. For this reason, patients who are poor are in need of care that focuses on identifying ways to help the patient overcome its impact on their health care outcomes.

Poverty in the United States

In 2008, 13.2% of all persons living in America lived in poverty. By 2010 an additional 2.6 million people for a total of 46.2 million people or one in six fell below the poverty line (McLaughlin, 2011).

The United States Census Bureau defines **poverty** based on predetermined **thresholds** for cash income relative to family size. An individual or family is considered poor if their pretax income falls below the poverty threshold (U.S. Census Bureau, 2008). For example, in 2008 the threshold for a single parent family with two children was $17,346. A single mother whose total cash income was $15,000 or less would be considered poor. Among those who are poor, there is much variation between racial and ethnic groups. The greatest differences can be seen between Blacks and Whites; however, members of other ethnic groups also experience poverty at rates above the national average. In 2008, 24.7% of Blacks and 23.2% of Hispanics were poor, compared to 8.6% of non-Hispanic Whites and 11.8% of Asians (National Poverty Center, 2008). The highest poverty rates are found among families headed by single women (28.7%), especially among those who are Black or Hispanic. In contrast, only 5.5% of married couples lived in poverty. There are also disparities in poverty rates between the native born and foreign-born living in the United States. Foreign-born noncitizens had the highest incidence of poverty at 23% as compared to 12.6 % of residents born in the United States. For patients who are poor and who speak English as a second language, their problems are compounded. Without a clear understanding of the medical terms and jargon used by health care personnel it becomes even more difficult for them to negotiate the health care system or to utilize available resources.

Children living in America experience the most disproportionate share of poverty in that they represent 25% of the total population, but 35% of the poor population (National Poverty Center, 2008). As a consequence, children who experienced chronic poverty were those who were more likely to develop persistent asthma, and moving out of poverty had a protective effect on the children (Cutuli, Herbers, Rinaldi, Masten, & Oberg, 2010; Kozyrskyj, Kendall, Jacob, Sly, & Zubrick, 2010).

For very young children the impact of asthma can have a detrimental effect on their school achievement throughout their lives (Davis, Gordon, & Burns, 2011). Being poor in America often means less access to quality care, higher morbidity, and mortality rates despite living in one of the wealthiest nations in the world. Among those who live in poverty, many also find themselves homeless.

Homelessness

The literature on homelessness is expansive (Coker, Elliot, & Kanouse et al., 2009; Hickler, 2009; Hoffman, 2008; Kamuldeep, Shanahanh, & Harding, 2006; Nunez, 2001; Otoole, Polinni, Ford, & Bigelow, 2008). This researcher found that homeless children have "poor health that is exacerbated by hunger and poor nutrition after becoming homeless, are four times more likely to have asthma and receive sporadic care" (p. 367). Homeless children are also more likely than nonhomeless children to encounter domestic and community violence and to be educationally and socially deprived (Walker, Lewis-land, Kub, Touklans, & Butz, 2008). Because of the social conditions associated with homelessness, homeless children are more likely to develop a negative self-image, drop out of school, and get in trouble with the law. The Department of Homeless Services of New York reported in May 2010, 35,882 individuals lived in shelters; this number includes 8,363 families with children. Many others still await placement and are therefore among the homeless currently living in New York. Coker, Elliot, and Kanouse et al. (2009) found the prevalence of homelessness among fifth-grade students as high as 11% in some populations. According to these results, "for a classroom of 28, 2 students will have spent some part of their lives being homeless." The researchers also found a positive association between being homeless and emotional, developmental, and behavioral problems among this population. The authors suggest developing state health care policies that ensure necessary funds to provide emergency housing needs for poor families.

Hickler (2009) examined paths to homelessness, self-perception, and survival strategies on health behaviors and health outcomes of African American and White homeless youth in San Francisco. The researchers found that although the group members had the problem of having a dysfunctional family background in common, they differed in their access to housing, street survival strategies, and utilization of health services. Although White youth perceived themselves as homeless, African American youth associated homelessness with stigma. Therefore, in this study, African Americans were less likely to use available services. In a study of 600 people's experiences of homelessness, Hoffman (2008) identified two major perceptions of service users, **infantilization**, and **objectification**. The term *infantilization* was used to describe the themes that summarized service users' beliefs that they were treated like children by the staff or service providers. Objectification was a summary term for service users' belief that often they were treated by providers with "rudeness, lack of compassion, and unethical behavior," which was "dehumanizing." Kamuldeep, Shanahanh, and Harding (2006) studied homelessness rates and mental illness in East London and found decreased rates of health services uptake, unmet needs, and a significant decrease in life expectancy among people who "slept rough" (slept on the streets). The national life expectancy was 74 years for men and 79 for women, as compared to 42 years for homeless persons on the streets. The researchers also found a high prevalence of alcoholism, drug misuse, depression, and personality disorders when compared to the general population. Many respondents in this study also believed that the stigma of being homeless was compounded when a homeless person also had a mental illness. Some perceived stereotyping and prejudice by providers. Generally, homeless persons in this study placed a higher priority on meeting physical and social needs above mental health issues. They were also dissatisfied with services and believed the supports they received were inadequate.

Another study examined health care–seeking behavior in homeless persons who were also substance abusers (Otoole, Pollini, For, & Bigelow, 2008). In this study the researchers found that this population was likely to be younger, uninsured, have hepatitis B/C, and have a 12th-grade education. Being homeless resulted in a delay in seeking treatment.

Problems of the Uninsured

Not surprisingly, those who live in poverty are also those who are most likely to be uninsured, although nearly 39% of the uninsured have a family income above $50,000 and 20% have family incomes above $75,000 (DHHS, 2008). Higher rates of insurance were found among those who were employed, because the largest numbers of those who were insured obtained coverage through their employers. The Department of Health and Human Services reported that in 2007, 45.7 million people or 15.3% of the population was uninsured. Although this figure represents a decline in the percent of uninsured, from 15.8% in the previous year, there was an increase in the numbers of those who were insured through public insurance programs such as Medicare and Medicaid. The largest age category of uninsured was 18- to 24-year-olds who live in households with incomes below $25,000. Based on ethnicity, 32.1% of Hispanics and 19.5% of Blacks lacked health insurance in 2007. Gresenz, Rokowski, and Escarce (2009) found that "among U.S. born Mexican Americans who are uninsured, living in areas more heavily populated with Spanish-speaking immigrants is negatively associated with access to care" (p. 1542). These staggering statistics underscore the need for care that is sensitive to the needs of the poor to ameliorate the influence that poverty has on health.

THE ROLE OF THE NURSE

Nurses, like physicians, have an opportunity and a responsibility to ensure quality care, especially by strengthening their interpersonal skills and by helping to facilitate access to care for patients who are poor (Maze, 2005; Montgomery & Schubart, 2010). By developing skills at the interpersonal level, nurses can enhance communication between themselves and other health care providers and with patients to have a positive influence on their health care outcomes. Moreover, advocating for the poor can take many forms, but nurses start by establishing relationships with those who are empowered to make a difference in the life of the poor such as hospital administrators, community activists, local, and federal politicians, and social networks and organizations.

Although nurses may be generally aware of patients' **socioeconomic status**, they seldom focus their attention on it. Thus, it is unlikely that they set out to provide a different kind of care to those who are poor. Yet, the literature attests to differences in the quality of care that patients who are **indigent** receive (Hernandez, Fornos, Milkas, Urbansky, & Villarreal, 2009; McGibbon,

Etowa, & McPherson, 2008). Often these differences can be attributed to institutional or patient–physician dynamics that inadvertently create barriers to the provision of comprehensive or culturally competent care. For example, Armstrong, Ravenell, and McMurphy (2007) examined racial/ethnic differences in levels of mistrust in physicians in the United States and found higher levels of mistrust toward physicians among Blacks and Hispanics than among Whites. These dynamics are often beyond the control of the nurse. However, as the largest group of health care providers, nurses can do much to provide the missing link that exists between the poor patient and the health care system. By addressing some of the problems that the poor or uninsured patient encounters during health care experiences, nurses can enhance the care provided to them. These problems include variations in access, emergency room overuse, cultural differences, communication barriers, inadequate time for sharing information with the physician, limited trust in health care providers, and decreased patient satisfaction (Wood, Corey, Freeman, & Shapiro, 1992).

ACCESS TO CARE

Research shows that certain groups have limited access to health services because of discrimination, based on their social class, race, ethnicity, or sexual orientation (McGibbon, Etowa, & McPherson, 2008). However, access to care is often directly related to one's ability to pay for medical services and the poor are often those most in need of care. For example, throughout the United States, many who live in areas of extreme poverty such as those found in some parts of the south, the Mexican border states, Appalachia, Native American territories, and impoverished urban areas experience neglected chronic and debilitating parasitic, congenital, and other infections at greater rates than others in the nation (Hotez, Stillwagon, McDonald, Todman, & DiGrazia, 2010). Such untreated infections have a long-lasting negative effect on children, expectant mothers, and workers in impoverished communities that increase their morbidity and mortality.

In other situations, many patients who may have obtained a prescription from a physician in the ER or clinic may never get them filled because of a lack of funds or insurance to pay for such medications. Middle-class young adults, who are no longer young enough to be covered under their parents' health insurance, may be in low-paying jobs and lack health benefits. Consequently, these individuals find health care unaffordable. This age group, especially males, is still within the high-risk population for trauma injury. These injuries often necessitate extensive, prolonged, and costly hospital care. Patients who believe they will be asked to pay amounts for care they cannot afford will delay or avoid seeking health care until they are seriously ill. Those who are underinsured often face similar problems, as their health care needs increase. These behaviors increase the need for more extensive use of health care services in the future.

Patients who are either uninsured or underinsured are least likely to seek preventive care, such as annual physicals, dental check-ups, regular vision screenings, and mammograms. Consequently, they are more likely to be diagnosed with later-stage cancers and to die when hospitalized with serious conditions like heart attacks and strokes (IOM, 2009).

Emergency Room Overuse

Coddington and Sands (2008) discussed the uninsured person's utilization of the emergency department for care. These authors attribute this continuing pattern to recent reductions in Medicaid enrollments to pay for services by primary care providers. By using the emergency room services without follow-up care, the patient is likely to return to the ER when the condition worsens or recurs.

The Emergency Medical Treatment Active Labor Act is a federal statute that was passed into law in 1986 to ensure emergency services to the indigent (Keller, 2008). This law enables care to persons irrespective of their citizenship status, insurance, or employment status. However, uninsured patients often do not realize that hospitals receiving Medicare funding have an obligation to treat all patients' emergent needs when they cannot afford to pay. As a result, many patients who are indigent, delay seeking treatment until they are seriously ill for fear of being turned away. As a result, patients who are poor often wait so long to be treated that by the time they are seen in the ER by a physician, they are seriously ill.

Brink (2004) discussed ER doctors' frustration in trying to accommodate the growing population of uninsured patients' health care needs, while struggling to contain hospital costs. Approximately 18% of trauma patients are uninsured and cost hospitals several thousands of dollars each year (Coddington, 2008). As a result, many trauma centers have had to close their doors leaving some poor communities who may be most in need of trauma or acute care services without them. Emergency room overuse creates a serious problem that ultimately impacts the entire community (Coustasse, Lorden, Nemarugommula, & Singh, 2009).

Additionally, some patients lack knowledge of special programs or other supportive services. For example, some pharmaceutical companies offer assistance through programs that provide prescription medications to medically needy patients (Drug Formulary Review, 2010; Hernandez, Fornos, Milka, Urbansky, & Villarreal, 2009). To address the increasing need of patients who live in poverty, there are more than 1,100 free clinics in the United States. The working poor and uninsured patients who utilize them receive primary care and pharmacy services that would otherwise be unavailable to them and thereby avoid emergency room overuse. Generally, patients report satisfaction with these services (Gertz, Frank, & Blixen, 2011). In Orange County, a medical services initiative assigned uninsured and low-income residents to a patient-centered medical home where they received comprehensive care using a team-based approach. These services greatly reduced the need for ER use (Roby et al., 2010). Additionally, parish nurses and other community health nurses offer health care information through church bulletins and flyers that describe free services or those offered at nominal cost that are available to eligible members of the community to support the growing needs of the poor.

POVERTY, CULTURAL DIFFERENCES, AND LANGUAGE BARRIERS

The combination of poverty, cultural differences, and language barriers makes achieving health care services even more difficult for patients who are poor. A study of 14,317 food pantry users in Los Angeles (Algert, Reibel, & Renvall, 2006) found that among the users of the food pantry, those who are homeless and who have limited English language skills are less likely to receive food stamps. Without a permanent address, these individuals are unable to apply for and receive stamps. New immigrants, especially those who are undocumented, would most likely fall into this category; however, their children, if they are born in the United States, are eligible to receive food stamps. Being unable to speak the English language further inhibits individuals who are poor from negotiating social networks offering this kind of support. Results of a study exploring barriers to treatment among women in poverty revealed that women and racial and ethnic minorities who were living on low incomes were more likely to experience depression than the rest of the U.S. population (Grote, Zuckoff, Swartz, Bledsoe, & Geibel, 2007). For example, postpartum depression was found to be more prevalent among low-income mothers (Abrams & Curran, 2009). Another study of low-income women and women of color found disparities in medical care and **barriers** to service (Francis, Berger, Giardini, Steinman, & Kim, 2009). They concluded that suburban poverty is often overlooked, while it contributes to **health care disparities** in infant mortality. In a report on health and health care needs of minority women living in small towns and rural areas in the United States, the author identified common characteristics found among them that included, "geographic and informational isolation, fragmentation of services, limitations regarding transportation, **gender biases**, and inequalities, educational limitations, and disproportionate poverty" (Hargraves, 2002). Following Hurricane Katrina, one study found Vietnamese and other minority groups were disproportionately more vulnerable to health problems, but cited social support as a protective factor for them (Chen, 2007). Cultural differences attributed to women of color included health beliefs; racism; and political, economic, and access inequalities in addition to those problems above that are encountered by other women living in rural areas. Women in these settings are more likely to have "enforced gender roles, work for lower salaries, and have inadequate health insurance."

Graham, Ivey, and Neuhauser (2009) assessed the needs of patients and caregivers during the transition from hospital to home and identified unmet needs of ethnic minorities, especially those with **limited English proficiency (LEP)** and recent immigrants. These unmet needs included limited social supports, lack of linguistically appropriate information and services, and cultural and financial barriers to using long-term care services. The study results suggest a need to design services that include bilingual information and services, partnerships with community agencies, and culturally competent care to near-poor seniors. In a study that examined the utilization of hospice care, Randall and Csikai (2003) discussed the need to educate the Hispanic community and promote cultural awareness among hospice staff. Although the respondents expressed a willingness to accept hospice in their homes, they did not really understand it. The researchers identified the language barrier as the greatest obstacle to utilization of hospice care.

Patients from culturally diverse backgrounds who live in poverty are more likely than dominant group members to use folk practices as a remedy for certain illnesses and diseases. Because of limited economic resources, these cultural practices, which may include herbal medicine, teas, or the use of folk healers, are sought before the patient would consider going to a physician. Sometimes herbal medicines or folk remedies used by the patient, while being treated for an illness with Western medicine, are incompatible with those that are later administered by health care providers. When there is a trusting relationship between the patient and the nurse, the patient feels free to discuss any home remedies or treatments without fear of being judged by the nurse. Nurses who demonstrate caring and respect for their patients' beliefs and values are able to establish trust and maintain an open and honest working relationship. In such relationships, nurses avoid receiving misinformation or limited information that may compromise care. Sharing critical information is particularly difficult when a language barrier exists between the patient and the nurse.

Moreover, the language of the health care system is particularly difficult for someone who speaks a second language. However, conducting a cultural assessment that identifies the patient's language abilities and communication style or pattern enables the nurse to select the appropriate resources to strengthen communication between them. It is helpful for the nurse to communicate in clear, simple language, avoiding the use of medical jargon. Ideally, information about procedures and treatments should be provided in the patient's own language. If an interpreter is needed, the nurse makes sure that when possible, the interpreter is age- and gender-appropriate and is knowledgeable of medical terminology. See Chapter 6 for guidelines on using an interpreter. In all situations, when speaking with the patient, the nurse places attention on the patient, not the interpreter.

INADEQUATE TIME WITH PRIMARY CARE PROVIDERS

In clinical situations where physicians are forced to see large numbers of patients at a time, they are naturally compelled to limit the time of each visit. Consequently, time needed to provide adequate explanations about the patient's illness, tests results, or treatment is limited. Moreover, patients may sense the physician's hurried demeanor and be reluctant to ask relevant questions pertaining to their care. Although this situation is not unique to minority or disadvantaged patients, patients who are poor are more likely to be less educated and less able to understand medical terminology used by physicians (Patterson & Gong, 2009). Immigrants, for example, are more likely to follow traditional health care practices that deviate from those of Western medicine, have more difficulty understanding medical jargon, have language barriers, and have fewer opportunities to meet with primary care physicians, due to having limited health insurance. Additionally, social and cultural differences between White middle-class physicians and poor minority patients may result in some communication problems due to differences in language usage and styles of communication.

In settings where there are advance practice nurses, they can be used as resources for all staff personnel to provide medical information to patients, and to support the staff in using the nursing process to overcome barriers to access care for patients who are poor. When nurses sense that patients are confused, or lack knowledge or understanding of their illness or treatment, they are in a prime position to offer support. The culturally competent nurse is sensitive to an indigent patient's feelings of inadequacy, particularly in disadvantaged groups when there is a language barrier. Information is provided in simple language and the nurse makes the time to encourage questions about issues of concern to the patient. The nurse also remains nonjudgmental in listening to the patient's own beliefs and ideas about the causes and impact of illness as well as the patient's preferred methods of treatment.

LACK OF CONFIDENCE IN THE HEALTH CARE SYSTEM

Several groups have been described in the literature as having little confidence in Western medicine and the U.S. health care system (Cook, 2009; Jaiyeola & Stabler, 2009; Patterson & Gong, Williams, & Peal, 2009). Some of this lack of confidence comes from past historical events that impacted culturally diverse groups in health care. One of the most notable is the **Tuskegee experiments**. During this research in 1932 to 1972 the U.S. Public Health Service investigated untreated syphilis using poor, illiterate, Black men in rural Alabama. The men in this study were not told of their diagnosis or the availability of treatment. Consequently, these experiments have negatively influenced African Americans views of the health care system. Hospitals and other health care settings can be oppressive, especially to those who already feel oppressed by majority group attitudes and practices. Because hospitals and other health care facilities are microcosms of the society in which we live, disadvantaged groups may fear experiencing in these settings the same oppression, prejudice, and discrimination they encounter elsewhere (McGibbon, Etowa, & McPherson, 2008).

Moreover, it is often the values and health care beliefs of the health care provider that are emphasized when care is being provided. Sometimes these values conflict with those of some patients who present from different cultures. For example, being given intimate care by a member of the opposite gender may be considered an indignity by some cultural group members. Having a lack of privacy for prayers, and for getting washed and dressed, is among some of patients' concerns about avoidable breaches of privacy in hospital care. Because of the mistrust of health care providers by some cultural groups, some patients who are poor may feel they are just being used as guinea pigs. Patients who are poor may also believe that they will be turned away because of an inability to pay, even when they are seriously ill.

Keller (2008) discussed the need for nurses to build trust and confidence in the care they provide to patients. In this study, the researcher found patients were reluctant to ask questions when the nurse appeared hurried or inattentive. Participants described positive experiences as those in which nurses were attentive, unrushed, and "took the time to explain procedures" (p. 37). When culture, race, and poverty intersect, these problems can become even more challenging for the patient. For this reason many persons of color are distrustful of the health care system because their perception is (whether it is accurate or not) that they will be discriminated against either because of their race or because of their lack of ability to pay.

Nurses can assist in minimizing these long-held feelings of mistrust by patients who feel oppressed by the health care system. Placing more emphasis on the patient's own attitudes and beliefs enables the nurse to plan care that is more culturally appropriate and effective in meeting the patient's health care goals. By working collaboratively with social service organizations, the hospital social worker, and other agents of support within the community, the nurse can apprise the patient of ways to obtain needed resources or services that may be available, but unknown to them.

Williams and Peal (2009) suggest overcoming mistrust through partnerships with minority organizations to "allay fears, dispel myths, and to educate the community on the importance of research." Nurses can gain knowledge about available resources and share this information with their respective communities through civic and religious channels.

DECREASED PATIENT SATISFACTION

Wood et al. (1992) found that poor families were twice as likely not to be satisfied with their medical encounters and parents of poor children were less satisfied with their care. Issues of concern for poor families centered on the physicians' inadequate provision of information about the illness, discussion of laboratory findings, medical care, and limited time provided to ask questions that were important from the family or patient's perspective (p. 66). The authors noted that, "consistent with previous research, these findings were independent of race, and health insurance status" (p. 68).

Because nurses often have more frequent encounters with the patient and are knowledgeable of significant clinical information, they are able to share that information with patients and families in a manner that incorporates ethical standards of practice. The knowledgeable, skilled, and culturally competent nurse intervenes on the patient's behalf by providing requested information clearly and honestly. This approach helps allay the fears of patients and families, and enables them to make appropriate health care decisions and fosters greater patient satisfaction regarding the health care experience.

WHAT NURSES CAN DO

Nurses who are knowledgeable about Patients' Bill of Rights and their hospital's policies regarding the care of the poor can help explain these policies to patients who lack this information. By exploring the local city or county websites on the Internet, local newspapers, the hospital and church bulletins, nurses can determine services that are available to persons who are indigent or lack health insurance in their communities. This information enables nurses to educate the community about free or nominal cost services offered by local organizations, hospitals, nurse managed clinics, and health centers. Opportunities for sharing health information exist at community health fairs, church functions, and civic gatherings, as well as during encounters with patients in tertiary care facilities. Individual nurses and nursing organizations, such as the American Nurses Association (ANA) and the National League for Nursing (NLN), can affect health care policy by encouraging legislators to respond to the health needs of the poor both nationally and locally. All of these efforts enable nurses to influence access to care for those who are indigent.

Culturally competent nurses can be effective advocates for patients who are poor. In order to address uninsured patients' health goals, nurses must be knowledgeable about available health services and resources so they can direct needy patients to them. Although individual nurses can do much within their communities, nurses are even stronger as a united body.

Nurse educators play a role in assisting the poor when they expose students to learning situations that enable them to observe and experience the health related issues of the poor and witness the effectiveness of strategies used to achieve health outcomes (Alvin & Eppley, 2009; Botsworth, Haloburdo, Patchett, Thompson, & Welch, 2006; Simmons, DeJoseph, Diamond, & Weinstein, 2009; Smith-Miller, Leak, Harlan, Dieckmann & Sherwood, 2010). These experiences prepare students for their future roles in promoting health and advocating for patients from vulnerable populations.

Advocacy for the uninsured and disadvantaged can be facilitated through nursing organizations and social service group efforts. Over the past 20 years, the ANA has fought for the adoption of health care reform to provide health insurance for the uninsured and the underinsured. In 2002 during a weeklong campaign, the ANA raised awareness of the public, the media, and Congress about the need for health insurance for the masses that are uninsured. During that campaign, nurses from around the nation spoke on behalf of millions who were uninsured. Local chapters held their own campaigns and the

New York State Nurses' Association held a town meeting during which then–Senator Hillary Clinton was the keynote speaker. Presently on the website www.nursingworld.org nurses can trace the historical efforts of the ANA and the historical passage of Patient Protection and Affordable Care Act, which can be viewed in comparison with ANA's Health System Reform Agenda.

Regardless of the patient's power, status, or wealth, culturally competent nurses, despite external pressures, find ways to establish themselves as powerful and professional patient allies. These nurses strive to maintain their professional integrity by carefully determining and prioritizing the immediate needs of all those under their care.

SUMMARY

In this chapter, nurses are asked to consider some of the obstacles they may encounter when caring for the uninsured or indigent patient. When caring for members of this group, nurses are challenged to find creative ways to overcome the circumstantial barriers that inhibit effective nurse–patient interactions and to develop strategies for ensuring the provision of culturally competent care to both the uninsured and indigent patient.

IMPORTANT POINTS

- Research indicates a relationship between socioeconomic status, private health insurance, and access to care.
- Life experiences of Americans that impact health care differ along racial lines.
- Among members of culturally diverse groups, Blacks, Hispanics, and single mothers have the highest poverty rates.
- Poverty more than race alone impacts health care access.
- Poor patients experience multiple health care problems that include variations in access, emergency room overuse, cultural differences, communication barriers, inadequate time for sharing health information, limited trust in health care providers, and decreased patient satisfaction.
- Those who are poor are most likely to be uninsured.
- Middle-class young adults represent a large percent of the medically uninsured.
- Homelessness is a barrier to health care.
- Health care disparities are differences between groups in morbidity and/ or mortality rates.
- Children living in America experience the most disproportionate share of poverty in that they represent 25% of the total population, but 35% of the poor population.

(continued)

IMPORTANT POINTS

(continued)

- Culturally diverse patients who live in poverty are more likely than dominant group members to use folk practices as a remedy for illnesses and diseases.
- The combination of poverty, cultural differences, and language barriers further impedes health care access for the poor.
- The Emergency Medical Treatment Act of 1986 ensures emergency services to those who are unable to pay.
- Nurses can address the problems of poverty, limited access, and health care disparities by providing health education to those who are poor and by determining institutional and community resources to assist them.
- Nurses can also advocate for the poor individually through their legislators or collectively through their nursing organizations.

CASE SCENARIO

Mabel Tucker is a 56-year-old African American widow. She lives in a small, three-bedroom home in a federally subsidized housing development. Mabel has asthma and has been experiencing more frequent asthma attacks. Mabel works as a cook at a nearby housing facility where she earns $9 an hour. Recently, she had to leave work early on two occasions because of breathing difficulties. Mabel has also been having more difficulty managing her hypertension, but only takes her medication when she feels ill. Despite her medical problems, Mabel finds it difficult to give up cigarette smoking and smokes one to two packs a day. She says smoking helps her relax. Mabel also struggles with her weight. At 5 feet 4 inches tall, she weighs 190 pounds. She has no health care benefits.

Mabel shares her home with her 28-year-old daughter, Cherise, and three grandchildren, Charlie, 8; Carey, 6; and Cala who is 2 years old. Together Mabel and Cherise share household chores and expenses and Mabel cares for the children when Charise, a clerk typist, attends classes in the evening at a community college.

Mabel worries daily about the stressors of her work environment, being able to make ends meet, and the increasing crime in the neighborhood. Her anxiety often exacerbates her symptoms.

Today Mabel awakens with a severe headache, which signals a need to take her blood pressure medicine. Mabel is worried about the cost of an ER visit and does not wish to go to the hospital. She also feels that some of the ER staff members have treated her unkindly in the past. To Mabel, doctors and nurses always seem rushed and annoyed. On her last visit, after examining Mabel, the doctor advised her to lose weight and stop smoking. He wrote a prescription for an antihypertensive treatment and asked her to follow up with her medical doctor. Mabel could not bring herself to admit to the ER doctor that she did not have a private doctor, nor could she afford one. Mabel feels guilty about not attempting to lose weight or give up smoking, or follow up with another doctor as the ER doctor suggested. As Mabel's headache worsens, she reluctantly decides to go to the ER. Upon her arrival to the ER, the triage nurse takes Mabel's blood pressure and finds it to be 192/100. After the physical examination and review of lab studies, the physician admits Mabel to a medical-surgical unit. Mabel is extremely anxious and concerned about leaving her grandchildren and the possibility of missing work and losing her job.

WHAT NURSES NEEDS TO KNOW ABOUT THEMSELVES

APPLYING THE STAIRCASE MODEL: SELF-REFLECTION QUESTIONS

1. How comfortable are you caring for this patient?
2. Where do you see yourself on the Cultural Competency Staircase?
3. How would you progress to the next level? (see Chapter 1)
4. Do you have any biases, prejudices, or have you made any assumptions about patients from this cultural background? Are your preconceived notions or attitudes likely to impact the kind of care you can provide?
5. What information do you and other nurses need about this patient to provide her with quality care?
6. What nurse behaviors and resources do you need to provide culturally competent care for this patient?

Responses to Self-Reflection Questions

Response to How comfortable are you caring for this patient?

Your experience or number of encounters communicating with female African American patients from this socioeconomic background will determine your level of comfort working with members of this cultural group. Although there is probably no language barrier, as English is the shared language, there may be cultural differences between the nurse and the patient in language usage or communication style. This is an important difference. For this reason, during the initial interview, the nurse should make an effort to project courtesy and respect, without becoming too familiar, especially with an older patient like Mabel.

Response to Where do you see yourself on the staircase?

First go to Chapter 1 and review the Cultural Competency Staircase table. Place yourself at the level that best describes you when working with patients from this cultural group.

Response to How will you progress?

Examine the area of the table in Chapter 1 that describes ways to progress from where you are to the next level.

Response to Do you have any biases or prejudices or make any assumptions about members of this group?

In today's society, despite our best efforts, it is difficult for any nurse to escape the impact of racism and ethnocentrism on our psyche. Consider any long-held assumptions you've made about members of this cultural group. Are these assumptions or generalizations evidence-based or are they derived from personal opinions related to experiences with a few representatives from this group? In either case, consider this patient and all others as unique individuals from which you might gain some knowledge or insights about the groups they represent. However, that knowledge cannot ever be used to predict an individual's values, attitudes, and beliefs. Care planning should be specific to the assessed needs of the individual.

WHAT NURSES NEED TO KNOW ABOUT THE PATIENT

Selecting a Cultural Assessment Model

Response to What information about this patient does the nurse need to provide her with culturally competent care?

The nurse must consider patients in light of the entire circumstances surrounding their illness. The patient's social history is important in this case, as many environmental factors may be influencing this patient's health care situation. Having knowledge of the socioeconomic conditions under which this patient lives on a daily basis is essential to planning effective care. Having knowledge of the patient's cultural background, lifestyle, health beliefs, and values is equally important for the nurse to gain insight into the patient's health care needs. The nurse also needs to know appropriate health resources in the institution or the community that will be useful in addressing the patient's health related issues.

Response to What nurse behaviors and resources do you need to provide culturally competent care to this patient?

To gain an understanding of the cultural needs of this patient, the nurse begins by selecting a cultural assessment model. In this chapter, the author recommends using the ETHNIC assessment model, as described in Chapter 2. The mnemonic ETHNIC stands for *explanation, treatment, healers, negotiation, intervention,* and *collaboration.* The ETHNIC model affords a collaboration between the nurse and the client in planning culturally appropriate care. By using the ETHNIC model, the nurse is reminded to place emphasis on determining the patient's health concerns from her perspective. In this case, the nurse aims to establish a relaxed, supportive rapport with the patient, and makes an effort to convey empathy and respect. These nurse's behavior facilitates the patient's sharing of her concerns about her asthma, hypertension, and obesity, and factors such as cigarette smoking and stress, that may be contributing to them.

During the initial meeting with the patient, the nurse uses the time to build trust, gather pertinent information, and assist the patient in planning a new approach to managing her health problems. The nurse also explores the patient's current home situation and looks for clues about stressors that might be impacting the patient's health.

Some examples of questions the nurse might ask when using this approach are:

"Why do you believe you have hypertension and how do you usually treat it?"

"Do you have people other than nurses and doctors to whom you go for medical advice or use herbal medicine, or other folk practices?"

Using this model, the nurse speaks to the patient using clear, simple language the patient is able to understand, avoiding any medical jargon, if possible. The nurse offers to answer any questions or concerns, which enables the patient to identify areas of interest that the nurse may not have considered. During the interaction, the nurse listens reflectively to the patient to determine what the client expects to happen during the illness, based on that person's health care beliefs and attitudes. Having this knowledge enables the nurse to establish mutually acceptable health care goals and appropriate interventions (Campinha-Bacote, 2003).

It is also important for the nurse to determine why Mabel has neglected to take her medications regularly, which is likely to be linked to Mabel's understanding about its significance and her ability to pay for it. While Mabel describes her personal concerns, the nurse listens attentively and identifies any factors that may be causing stress in Mabel's life. The nurse collaborates with social services to discuss any socioeconomic concerns and to ensure Mabel's utilization of any available hospital or community resources for patients who need financial support. At this point, the nurse might describe controllable and uncontrollable factors influencing hypertension, such as diet, exercise, and efforts to manage stress. It is important that the nurse remains attentive and nonjudgmental as Mabel shares her thoughts and feelings about her asthma attacks, hypertension, and practice of taking her medication only when she feels ill. Considering all the factors that may be influencing Mabel's health, the nurse identifies several important issues of concern.

Problems and Concerns

Considering Mabel's ethnic background, stressful lifestyle, poor dietary habits, and cigarette smoking, the nurse recognizes that these factors place her at high risk for cardiovascular and cerebro-vascular complications. In addition, Mabel's lack of understanding about the management of asthma and hypertension, and limited financial resources, interfere with her access to care.

Planning Care

Using lay terms, the nurse explains the relationship among Mabel's dietary habits, exercise, smoking, asthma, and hypertension and the possible complications that may result (see Table 11.1). The nurse also offers Mabel some literature on managing hypertension that is written in simple nonjargon terms. Identifying any available pamphlets or other materials that list both free and inexpensive community services and their contact information will also be useful. To assist the patient in staying on track with prescribed medications, the nurse can explore pharmacy-assistance programs for which the patient can apply. Such programs offered by the pharmaceutical companies provide some medications free of charge to those who are unable to afford them. The individual must be ineligible for Medicare and Medicaid and have no other insurance plan. For medications that are needed immediately, the nurse might ask the physician if samples are available that the patient can use while waiting for prescriptions to be filled. The nurse should explain the danger of using other's medication even when the patients share the diagnosis like hypertension with a near relative.

Another important nursing strategy in the care of this patient is to identify any support groups in the area for patients with asthma, and/or exercise programs at local hospitals or community centers that the patient might attend. The nurse should explain the benefits of exercise and stress reduction in addressing this patient's health problems.

Finally, the nurse explains to Mabel the benefit of seeing one health care provider on a more consistent basis, rather than waiting to go to the emergency room when she becomes ill. However, it is also important for the patient to understand that when there is a real clinical emergency, patients have a right to be seen in the emergency room, irrespective of their ability to pay.

Because of this patient's socioeconomic issues, the nurse will need to find creative ways to ensure that the patient's identified health goals are met. In many cities there are medical clinics and nurse-operated health centers where patients who are indigent can be seen and can pay for services based on a sliding scale fee. Under certain circumstances, some hospitals offer special clinic services where needed tests, laboratory work, or procedures are done at the hospital without charge to the patient. Nurses should explore whether this is an option at their place of employment on behalf of the patients they serve who are unable to afford care.

Caring for patients who are poor or who lack medical insurance is one of the most challenging clinical situations for nurses. Nurses faced with this challenge must have effective cross-cultural skills in communication that allow them to listen attentively so that care can be planned from the patients' perspectives. The culturally competent nurse is also knowledgeable about appropriate cultural assessment tools, and has an arsenal of resources from which to choose to address patients' specific needs. Over time, the culturally competent nurse develops skill in each of these areas and is able to offer each patient quality care while maintaining their dignity and respect. Ultimately,

TABLE 11.1 Plan of Care

GOALS	INTERVENTIONS	EVALUATION
The patient will have an enhanced understanding of her illness, including risk factors, clinical manifestations, treatment, and potential complications. The patient establishes contact with a medical provider on a regular basis. The patient takes medication on a regular basis. The patient will reduce weight and stressors impacting hypertension.	The nurse explains the relationship among diet, exercise, smoking, asthma, and hypertension in lay terms. The nurse provides written information about asthma, hypertension, and obesity and gives Mabel a list of free community workshops and presentations at the local hospitals on these topics. The nurse encourages Mabel to visit a local nurse-run health clinic that charges based on a sliding scale to establish a working relationship with a nurse practitioner and/ or physician on a more regular basis. Mabel is given information about a pharmacy-assistance program for patients who are indigent. The nurse encourages Mabel to participate in a local hospital's exercise program as a means of reducing stress and weight.	Mabel takes all prescribed medications regularly and begins to reduce or seek help in reducing her cigarette smoking. Mabel has ongoing monitoring and management of her multiple chronic illnesses. Mabel takes medications regularly and controls hypertension.

the nurse empowers the patient who is poor to manage his or her own health problems in a more effective way.

SUMMARY

Caring for the patient who is indigent or uninsured poses many challenges for the culturally competent nurse. In caring for these patients, the nurse needs to be knowledgeable about the degree to which socioeconomic factors are impacting the patient's access to care. By using an appropriate cultural assessment tool, the nurse is able to gain insight into the patient's cultural perspective on health care problems. Having an understanding of cultural influences on the patient's health care decision making will enable the nurse to determine areas for patient teaching. Nurses caring for indigent patients will need to develop knowledge regarding useful community agencies and other resources to assist patients on an emergency basis until more permanent supports can be attained. The problems of limited access, emergency room over dependence, cultural differences, communication barriers, inadequate time with physicians, limited trust of the health care system, and decreased patient satisfaction can be addressed by the knowledgeable, skillful, and culturally sensitive nurse. By working collaboratively with patients who are uninsured, and utilizing available hospital and community resources culturally competent nurses can assist in removing some of the barriers patients who are uninsured encounter.

NCLEX-TYPE QUESTIONS

1. Research indicates that _____ is one of the **most significant** factors in determining health care outcomes.
   A. Race and ethnicity
   B. Socioeconomic status
   C. Language skills
   D. Religious beliefs

2. The nurse is planning the discharge of a patient who is unemployed. The nurse realizes that it is important to include what strategies in the patient's discharge planning? (select all that apply)
   A. Teach the patient preventive health measures.
   B. Identify community resources.
   C. Provide any medical information in the patient's own language.
   D. Determine the patient's ability to pay for prescriptions.

3. The nurse who works in a busy urban area has frequent encounters with patients from multicultural populations. When working with members of ethnically diverse groups the nurse understands that the poorest patients are most likely to be found among:
   A. Asian immigrants
   B. Pacific Islanders
   C. Blacks and Hispanics
   D. Ethnic Whites

4. When discussing a patient's eligibility for indigent programs based on U.S. government definitions of poverty, what statement by the nurse demonstrates a good understanding of poverty thresholds?
   A. Thresholds vary based on individual states' determinations.
   B. Thresholds are based on the income of the person designated head of household.
   C. Thresholds are consistent throughout the nation and are based on family size and age of its members.
   D. Thresholds are determined by townships and/or municipalities.

5. A patient explains to the nurse that she delayed coming to the emergency room after experiencing a severe burn because she did not have any money to pay for the visit. What statement by the culturally competent nurse is most appropriate?
   A. Patients who are unable to pay are guaranteed emergency services by the Civil Rights Act of 1963.
   B. Patients are provided services through the Patients' Bill of Rights.
   C. Patients are protected by the Equal Opportunities Amendment.
   D. Patients are guaranteed services by the Emergency Medical Treatment Act.

6. According to research, what problems are most often encountered by patients who live in poverty? (select all that apply)
   A. Bilingualism
   B. Too little time for sharing information with providers
   C. Emergency room overuse
   D. Mistrust of health care providers

7. What statement by the nurse is true regarding the intersection of cultural differences, language barriers, lack of health insurance and poverty?
   A. The combination of these factors compounds the problem of access for the poor.
   B. There are no differences between those with language barriers and those without in their impact on health care access.
   C. Cultural differences have little impact on health care access.
   D. All persons who lack private health care insurance are eligible for Medicare or Medicaid.

8. Research shows a positive relationship among income, completed education, net worth, and
   A. Language abilities
   B. Cultural attitudes
   C. Private health insurance
   D. Religious values

9. The nurse admits a patient who is homeless to the unit. When planning care for this patient, what attitude by the nurse is most realistic?
   A. Homelessness poses a serious barrier to health care access.
   B. There are many available health care services provided by governmental agencies for the homeless.
   C. Quality care is provided to the homeless to the same extent it is provided to others.
   D. Persons who are homeless are aided by government subsidies like Medicaid.

10. The nurse encounters multiple patients from culturally diverse groups who are living in poverty in the hospital's local community. The nurse desires to get involved in attempting to address this problem. The most effective *initial* approach by the nurse is to:
    A. Contact the local council members and other legislators to state some of the problems these patients are experiencing.

B. Study a foreign language to reduce the language barrier that exists between the nurse and at least one ethnic cultural group.
C. Join a nursing organization and advocate for the groups through collective action.
D. Attempt to establish a trusting relationship with each individual patient to identify his or her specific health care needs.

AACN COMPETENCIES ADDRESSED IN THIS CHAPTER

1. Apply knowledge of social and cultural factors that affect nursing and health care across multiple contexts.
2. Use relevant data sources and best evidence in providing culturally competent care.
3. Promote achievement of safe and quality outcomes of care for diverse populations.
4. Advocate for social justice, including commitment to the health of vulnerable populations and the elimination of health care disparities.
5. Participate in continuous cultural competence development.

REFERENCES

Abrams, L., & Curran, L. (2009). "And You're Telling Me Not to Stress?" A grounded theory study of postpartum depression symptoms among low-income mothers. *Psychology of Women Quarterly, 33*(3), 351–362. Retrieved May 4, 2010, from Social Sciences Full Text database.

Algert, S. J., Reibel, M., Renvall, M. S. (2006). Barriers to participation in the food stamp program among food pantry clients in Los Angeles. *American Journal of Public Health, 96*(5), 807–809. Retrieved from http://vnweb.hwwilsonweb.com/hww/results/results_single_ftPES.jhtml

Alvin, C., & Eppley, M. (2009). Clinic broadens students' health care perspective. *Reflections on Nursing Leadership, 35*(4), Retrieved from CINAHL Plus with Full Text database.

Armstrong, K., Ravenell, K., & McMurphy, S. (2007). Racial/ethnic differences in physician distrust in the United States. *American Journal of Public **Health**, 97*(7), 1283–1289. Retrieved May 8, 2010, from Social Sciences Full Text database.

Botsworth, T. L., Haloburdo, E. P., Patchett, K., Thompson,M. A., &Welch, M., (2006). International partnerships to promote quality care: Faculty groundwork, student projects, and outcomes. *The Journal of Continuing Education in Nursing, 37*(1), 32–38.

Chen, A. C., Keith, V. M., Leong, K. J., Airriess, C. C., Li, W. W., Chung, K. Y., & Lee, C. C. (2007). Hurricane Katrina: Prior trauma, poverty and health among Vietnamese-American survivors. *International Nursing Review, 54*(4), 324–331. doi:10.1111/j.1466–7657.2007.00597.x

Coburn, D. (2004). Beyond the income inequality hypothesis: *Class*, neo-liberalism, and *health* inequalities. *Social Science & Medicine, 58*(1), 41–56. Retrieved May 4, 2010, from Social Sciences Full Text database.

Coddington, J. A. & Sands, L. P. (2008). Cost of health care and quality outcomes of patients at nurse-managed clinics. *Nursing Economics, 26*(2), 75–83.

Cook, C. (2009). Minority attitudes and perception of health care: A comparison of comments from a cultural competency questionnaire and focus group discussion. In S. Kosoko-Lasaki, C. T. Kook, & R. L. Obrien (Eds.), *Cultural proficiency in addressing health care disparities* (pp. 281–309). Boston, MA: Jones and Bartlett.

Coustasse, A., Lorden, A., Nemarugommula, V., & Singh, K. (2009). Uncompensated care cost: A pilot study using hospitals in a Texas county. *Hospital Topics, 87*(2), 3–11. Retrieved from CINAHL Plus with Full Text database.

Cutuli, J., Herbers, J., Rinaldi, M., Masten, A., & Oberg, C. (2010). Asthma and behavior in homeless 4- to 7-year-olds. *Pediatrics, 125*(1), 145–151. doi:10.1542/peds.2009–0103

Davis, D., Gordon, M. K., & Burns, B. M. (2011). Educational interventions for childhood asthma: A review and integrative model for preschoolers from low-income families. *Pediatric Nursing, 37*(1), 31–38.

Department of Homeless Services. (2010). *Daily report.* New York, NY: Author. Retrieved from www.nyc.gov/html/dhs/html/home

Francis L. E., Berger, C. S., Giardini, M., Steinman, C., & Kim, K. (2009). Pregnant and poor in the suburb: The experiences of economically disadvantaged women of color with prenatal services in a wealthy suburban county. *Journal of Sociology and Social Welfare, 36*(3), 133–157.

Gertz, A., Frank, S., & Blixen, C. (2011). A survey of patients and providers at free clinics across the United States. *Journal Of Community Health, 36*(1), 83–93. doi:10.1007/s10900–010-9286-x

Graham, C. L., Ivey, S. L., Nehauser, L. (2009). From hospitals to home: Asssessing the transitional care needs of vulnerable seniors. *The Gerontologist, 49*(1), 23–33. Retrieved from http://vnweb.hwwilsonweb.com/hww/results/results

Gresenz, C. R., Rogowski, J., & Escarce, J. J. (2009). Community demographics and access to health care among U.S. Hispanics. *Health Research and Educational Trust,* 44(5p1), 1542–1562. doi: 10.1111/j.1475–6773.2009.00997.x

Grote, N. K., Zukoff, A., Swartz, H., Bledsoe, S. E., & Geibel, S. (2007). Engaging women who are depressed and economically disadvantaged in mental health treatment. *Social Work, 52*(4), 295–308.

Hernández, G., Fornos, L., Mika, V., Urbansky, K., & Villarreal, R. (2009). One regional health system's innovative steps to deal with the uninsured. *Journal of Health Care Finance, 36*(1), 70–84. Retrieved from CINAHL Plus with Full Text database.

Hospitals involve pharmacists in care of indigent patients: pharmacists' involvement helps improve outcomes, costs. (2010). *Drug Formulary Review, 26*(3), 25–27. Retrieved from CINAHL Plus with Full Text database.

Hotez, P., Stillwaggon, E., McDonald, M., Todman, L., DiGrazia, L. (2010) *National summit on neglected infections of poverty in the United States* [conference summary]. Emerging infectious diseases. Retrieved from www.cdc.gov/EID/content/16/5/e1.htm

Institute of Medicine. Committee on Health Insurance Status and Its Consequences. (2009). America's uninsured crisis: Consequences of health and health care. Retrieved from www.nationalacademies.org/opinewsitem.aspx?

Jonson-Reid, M., Drake, B., & Kohl, P. (2009). Is the overrepresentation of the poor in child welfare caseloads due to bias or need? *Children & Youth Services Review, 31*(3), 422–7. Retrieved May 4, 2010, from Social Sciences Full Text database.

Keller, T. (2008). Mexican American parent's perceptions of culturally congruent interpersonal processes of care during childhood immunization episodes—a pilot study. *Online Journal of Rural Nursing & Health Care, 8*(2), 33–41. Retrieved from CINAHL Plus with Full Text database.

Kozyrskyj, A., Kendall, G., Jacoby, P., Sly, P., & Zubrick, S. (2010). Association between socioeconomic status and the development of asthma: Analyses of income trajectories. *American Journal of Public Health, 100*(3), 540–546. doi:10.2105/AJPH.2008.150771

Maze, C. (2005). Registered nurses' personal rights vs. professional responsibility in caring for members of underserved and disenfranchised populations. *Journal of Clinical Nursing, 14*(5), 546–554. Retrieved from CINAHL Plus with Full Text database.

McGibbon, E., Etowa, J., & McPherson, C. (2008). Health-care access as a social determinant of health. *Canadian Nurse, 104*(7), 22–27. Retrieved from CINAHL Plus with Full Text database.

McLanahan, S. (2009). Fragile families and the reproduction of poverty. *The Annals of the American Academy of Political and Social Science, 621*, 111–31. Retrieved 4 May 2010, from Social Sciences Full Text database.

McLaughlin, N. (2011, September 19). Depressing numbers: Poverty, insurance, treatment: Could these be jobs for Watson?. *Modern Healthcare, 41*, 170.

Montgomery, K., & Schubart, K. (2010). Health promotion in culturally diverse and vulnerable populations. *Home Health Care Management & Practice, 22*(2), 131–139. Retrieved from CINAHL Plus with Full Text database.

Mulchier, J.E. & Burr, J.A. (2009). The survey of income and program participation Racial differences in health and healthcare service utilization: the effects of socioeconomic status.

National Poverty Center. (2008). Poverty in the United States: Frequently asked questions. Retrieved from http://www.npc.umich.edu

Okunade, A. A. & Suratdecha, C. (2009).The relevance of economics for public policies in multidisciplinary health disparities research. In S. Kosoko-Lasaki, C. Cook, & R. O'Brien (Eds.), *Cultural proficiency in addressing health disparities.* Boston: Jones and Bartlett.

Randall, H. & Cskai, E. (2003). Issues affecting utilization of hospice services by rural Hispanics. *Journal of Ethnic and Cultural Diversity,12*(2), 79–94.

Roby, D., Pourat, N., Pirritano, M., Vrungos, S., Dajee, H., Castillo, D., & Kominski, G. (2010). Impact of patient-centered medical home assignment on emergency room visits among uninsured patients in a county health system. *Medical Care Research & Review, 67*(4), 412–430. doi:10.1177/1077558710368682

Rose, S., & Hatzenbuehler, S. (2009). Embodying social *class:* The link between *poverty,* income inequality and *health. International Social Work, 52*(4), 459–71. Retrieved 4 May 2010, from Social Sciences Full Text database.

Simmons, B., DeJoseph, D., Diamond, J., & Weinstein, L. (2009). Students who participate in a student-run free health clinic need education about access to care issues. *Journal of Health Care for the Poor & Underserved, 20*(4), 964–968. Retrieved from CINAHL Plus with Full Text database.

Smith-Miller, C., Leak, A., Harlan, C., Dieckmann, J., & Sherwood, G. (2010). "Leaving the comfort of the familiar": Fostering workplace cultural awareness through short-term global experiences. *Nursing Forum, 45*(1), 18–28. Retrieved from CINAHL Plus with Full Text database.

U.S. Department of Health and Human Services. (2008) Overview of the Uninsured in the United States: A Summary of the 2008 Current Population Survey. Retrieved at http://aspe.hhs.gov/healthreports/08/uninsuredoverview/index.shtml

Walker, J., Lewis-Land, C., Kub, J., Tsoukleris, M., & Butz, A. (2008). The effect of violence on asthma: are our children facing a double-edged sword?. *Journal Of Community Health, 33*(6), 384–388.

Williams, E. & Peal, F.T. (2009) Addressing health care in communities. In S. Kosoko-Lasaki, C. T. Cook, & R.L. Obrien (Eds.), *Cultural Proficiency in Addressing Health Disparities* (pp. 357–371). Boston: Jones and Bartlett.

Wiltshire, J., Person, S., & Kiefe, C. (2009). Disentangling the influence of *socioeconomic status* on differences between african american and white women in unmet medical needs. *American Journal of Public Health, 99*(9), 1659–65. Retrieved 8 May 2010, from Social Sciences Full Text database

World Health Organization. Commission on Social Determinants of Health. Social determinants of health. (2011). Retrieved at http://www.who.int/social_determinants/thecommission/en

IMPORTANT WEBSITES

Alliance for Children & Families
www.alliance1.org
Catholic Charities USA
www.catholiccharitiesusa.org
Center for People in Need
http://centerforpeopleinneed.org
Coalition on Human Needs: An alliance of national organizations working together to promote public policies which address the needs of low-income and vulnerable populations
www.chn.org
National Coalition for the Homeless
www.nationalhomeless.org/factsheets/How_Many.html
National Alliance to End Homelessness
www.endhomelessness.org/content/article/detail/4335
Poverty & Race Research Action Council (PRRACH)
www.prrac.org

Appendix

Consistent with *The Essentials of Baccalaureate Education for Professional Nursing Practice*, five competencies have been developed to encompass the key elements considered essential for baccalaureate nursing graduates to provide culturally competent care in partnership with the interprofessional team. These competencies are not exhaustive, but serve as a framework for integrating suggested content and learning experiences into existing curricula.

COMPETENCY 1: APPLY KNOWLEDGE OF SOCIAL AND CULTURAL FACTORS THAT AFFECT NURSING AND HEALTH CARE ACROSS MULTIPLE CONTEXTS

Rationale

This competency is important to baccalaureate nurses because understanding and applying knowledge about patient's value systems, beliefs, and practices relevant to health and illness, affect nursing care and practice. Nurses should have increased awareness of historical, political, and socioeconomic factors that determine health and disease in patient populations. The baccalaureate program prepares the graduate to:

1. Demonstrate an understanding of culture and cultural competence in practice
2. Compare similarities and differences in values, beliefs, and practices among and within diverse populations
3. Explain the relationships among cultural, physiological, ecological, pharmacologic, and genetic factors
4. Integrate social and cultural assessment data (including language and health literacy) in planning, implementing and evaluating care

Content may include:

- Acculturation, assimilation, and enculturation
- Cultural as well as social determinants

- Cultural awareness, cultural sensitivity, and cultural competence
- Cultural self-awareness
- Health disparity as well as healthcare disparity
- Health literacy and linguistic competence
- Population as well as population health
- Population based health disparities
- Patient culture as well as healthcare provider culture as well as organizational culture

Examples of Integrative Learning Strategies

- Critique case studies that include examples of key concepts and terms
- Present selected theories, models, and approaches to cultural assessment
- Compare and contrast dominant cultural characteristics for selected patients, families, and groups
- Create cultural care plans for patients and families from a variety of cultures and across the life span
- Discuss students' cultural self-awareness
- Invite people from the community to tell their cultural stories
- Identify population-based health and health care disparities
- Discuss the document "culturally and linguistically appropriate standards"
- Discuss *Hospitals, Language and Culture: A Snapshot of the Nation*, a report from the Joint Commission on Accreditation of Healthcare Organizations

COMPETENCY 2: USE RELEVANT DATA SOURCES AND BEST EVIDENCE IN PROVIDING CULTURALLY COMPETENT CARE

Rationale

This competency is important to baccalaureate nurses because using relevant data sources and best evidence are vital in providing culturally competent care. While there are critical gaps in the quality and quantity of relevant data, nurses must be cognizant of sources of evidence (e.g., research studies, community, and traditional knowledge) and be able to critically analyze it to design appropriate care. The baccalaureate program prepares the graduate to:

1. Critique existing research and knowledge sources to determine its relevance and applicability to diverse groups
2. Integrate best evidence and patient perspectives in planning care
3. Facilitate access to data resources and services to provide culturally competent care
4. Participate in the collection, documentation, and use of cultural and social data in the planning, delivery, and evaluation of care
5. Advocate for the protection of vulnerable populations in human subjects research

Content may include:

- Practice standards and evidence-based guidelines
- Position statements and research agendas
- Ethical guidelines and standards for the conduct of research (NIH, institutional IRB)
- Guidelines for the critique and conduct of research with racial/ethnic populations
- Research process
- Methods for evaluating related health research as it applies to vulnerable populations
- Ethical conduct of research and scholarship
- Locating and evaluating multiple sources of evidence

Examples of Integrative Learning Strategies

- Conduct cultural assessments
- Conduct community assessments in diverse communities
- Complete human subjects training
- Incorporate research studies from racial and ethnic specific research journals (e.g., *Journal of the National Black Nurses Association, Hispanic Health Care International, Journal of the National Medical Association, Journal of Transcultural Nursing*)
- Discuss systematic reviews of research
- Evaluate sources of knowledge and information
- Identify and evaluate sources of evidence

COMPETENCY 3: PROMOTE ACHIEVEMENT OF SAFE AND QUALITY OUTCOMES OF CARE FOR DIVERSE POPULATIONS

Rationale

This competency is important to baccalaureate nurses because of existing disparities in access provision to quality care and health outcomes across population groups. Graduates should be able to use appropriate standards of care, initiate basic quality and safety investigations, and assist in developing quality improvement plans and monitoring outcomes of care. Positive health outcomes for diverse populations are achieved by care that is grounded in collaborative partnerships between members of the interprofessional team, patients and families. The baccalaureate program prepares the graduate to:

1. Advocate for effective resources to facilitate cross-cultural communication for patients with limited english proficiency (LEP) and health literacy
2. Participate in providing leadership to interprofessional teams to minimize and prevent health disparities and to achieve culturally competent programs and services

3. Recognize quality and patient safety as complex system issues that involve patients and members of the health care team
4. Collaborate with patients and families to identify mutually agreed upon goals and outcomes of care

Content may include:

- Cross-cultural communication
- Cultural conflict management
- Language interpretation and translation
- Teaching and learning principles
- Cultural safety
- Pharmacotherapeutics and cultural diversity
- Alternative and complementary therapy
- Cultural and folk healers
- Participatory decision making
- Cultural brokering, negotiation, accommodation
- Patient navigators
- Workforce diversity
- Leadership and change
- Quality improvement

Examples of Integrative Learning Strategies

- Interview and provide health assessment of culturally diverse patients
- Design a health teaching plan for culturally diverse patients
- Assess organizational and community resources appropriate for patients' needs
- Care for patients with limited english proficiency (LEP) and health literacy
- Work with translators and interpreters in actual patient care situations
- Critique brochures, documents, and videos for cultural competence
- Visit a botanica, bodega, ethnic grocery store, ethnic restaurant
- Observe an espiritista, acupuncturist, herbalist, or other folk practitioner
- Research herb–drug effects, food–drug effects, pharmacological effects of drugs on specific groups of patients
- Assess communication, caring, and leadership styles of diverse staff
- Assist in implementation of quality improvement specific to diverse patient groups

COMPETENCY 4: ADVOCATE FOR SOCIAL JUSTICE, INCLUDING COMMITMENT TO THE HEALTH OF VULNERABLE POPULATIONS AND THE ELIMINATION OF HEALTH DISPARITIES

Rationale

This competency is important to baccalaureate nurses because they work collaboratively with patients, families, and the interprofessional team to eliminate health inequalities and discriminatory healthcare practices and assure an environment supportive of health for all. Cultural competence involves understanding different perspectives of vulnerability and discrimination, and responding to patient-perceived needs for all forms of nursing care. The baccalaureate program prepares the graduate to:

1. Recognize the historic and contemporary implications of public policies and discrimination affecting health, health care systems, and use of health care services by racial, ethnic, and other vulnerable groups
2. Recognize and report individual and institutional discrimination practices, unequal treatment practices, breaches of patients' human and civil rights, or violations of respect for patient autonomy to appropriate authorities
3. Demonstrate leadership in addressing behavior that is insensitive, lacks cultural understanding, or reflects prejudice in order to improve adherence to professional standards of respect and civility
4. Demonstrate cultural competence in ethical decisions about care delivery

Content may include:

- History of discriminatory treatment of population groups in health research and health care
- Contemporary public policy proposals (e.g., Immigration, welfare reform, early childhood education, food distribution to women and children, incarceration, poverty initiatives) and their effects on the health of populations
- Legal and policy requirements for the humane care of patients
- Nurse decision making from among a range of actions that could be undertaken when requirements for the humane care of patients are breached

Examples of Integrative Learning Strategies

- Diagram the appropriate chain of reporting procedures for violation of patients' rights to include reporting to regulators, lawmakers, and enforcement agencies responsible for the full and consistent implementation of policies to protect patients
- Compare and contrast examples of behavior by health care team members that are appropriate, respectful, and inclusive; and behavior that is insensitive, lacks cultural understanding, or reflects prejudice, and discuss how the nurse can intervene in interpersonal and interprofessional situations to improve adherence to professional standards of respect and civility
- Present case studies illustrating an existing practice in clinical care that contains elements of discrimination, unequal treatment practices, breaches of patients' human and civil rights, or violations of respect for patient autonomy and conclude with recommendations for advocacy
- Debate the impact of current health and social policy legislation on the health of populations

- Become involved in the legislative process and public policy formation by reviewing a proposed bill and taking and supporting a position (i.e., through writing an editorial or letter or visiting an elected official)

COMPETENCY 5: PARTICIPATES IN CONTINUOUS CULTURAL COMPETENCE DEVELOPMENT

Rationale

This competency is important to baccalaureate nurses because becoming culturally competent is an active progression of learning and practicing, which evolves over time requiring a lifelong commitment. Changing attitudes and values that support ongoing cultural competence development to provide acceptable cultural care is achieved by acquiring a foundation, which include awareness and knowledge about differences in values in beliefs that can influence practice skills. The baccalaureate program prepares the graduate to:

1. Engage in ongoing self-reflection of own behaviors toward diverse patients and other members of the interprofessional team
2. Articulate the value of pursuing lifelong learning about different cultures to foster professional growth and development and provide culturally competent health care
3. Engage in a variety of activities to develop understanding of cultural differences and similarities about health and health care to improve ability to work with diverse and vulnerable populations

Content may include:

- Development of worldviews
- Stereotypes and biases about racial, ethnic, religious, and other social groups (i.e., disabilities, lower socioeconomic groups, age, gender, sexual orientation, etc.)
- Ethnocentrism, discrimination, and racism in health care settings
- Glossary or cultural definitions of stereotyping, ethnocentrism, discrimination, and racism
- Differences in values and beliefs regarding health and illness
- Cultural differences and similarities in attitudes, values, and expectations (include major groups and other social groups) for health care
- Perceptions by cultural groups about health care providers and health institutions
- Cultural imposition in health care

Examples of Integrative Learning Strategies

- Conduct self-awareness assessments with focus on identifying one's own biases and prejudices

- Review journals to conduct self-reflection exercises about values and prejudices
- Share in pairs or in a group about incidents when of stereotyping, discrimination, and racism were experienced (by the student) and it's effect on one's feelings
- Discuss patient case studies/vignettes that bring to light stereotyping, ethnocentrism, discrimination, and racism
- Conduct presentations of incidences of when cultural groups have been discriminated against
- Participate in role-play situations of stereotyping, racism, discrimination, etc. in health care situations
- Attend lectures/presentations by experts or community members from cultural groups to become aware of values
- Participate in a cultural immersion experience
- Participate in community projects involving community members, such as health fairs, community forums/meetings, and so on, to understand concerns values and beliefs about health care
- Participate or attend cultural celebrations or religious ceremonies to understand foundation of values

SUMMARY

This document provides the framework for the integration of cultural competence in baccalaureate nursing education. The assumptions on education for cultural competence were the foundation for the five essential competencies that are operationalized by teaching content and learning strategies.

RECOMMENDATIONS

In addition to curricular implementation, fostering a learning environment that supports cultural competence development of faculty and students is imperative to successful implementation. The following recommendations are provided:

1. Foster organizational commitment and leadership by:

- Creating structure and processes for implementation
- Allocating resources for faculty and program development
- Articulating the program emphasis to students, faculty, and the broader community
- Developing collaborative relationships to recruit and improve graduation rates of diverse students
- Instituting a foreign language requirement for nursing students
- Establishing an evaluation plan for measuring outcomes of the five program competencies

2. Promote faculty commitment and involvement by

- Participating in ongoing development
- Mentoring colleagues and students
- Providing guided clinical experiences for students
- Recruiting diverse faculty and students

RESOURCES

American Association of Colleges of Nursing (AACN) and Commission on Collegiate Nursing Education. (2003). *Accreditation Standards.* Retrieved April 16, 2008, from http://www.aacn.nche.edu/Accreditation/NewStandards.htm

American Association of Colleges of Nursing (AACN). (2008). *The essentials of Baccalaureate education for professional nursing practice.* Washington, DC: Author.

Anderson, N. L., Calvillo, E. R., & Fongwa, M. (2007). Community-based approaches to strengthen cultural competence learning in nursing education and practice. *Journal of Transcultural Nursing, 18*(1), 49S–59S.

California Endowment. (2003). *Principles and recommended standards for cultural competence education of health care professionals.* Woodland, CA: Author.

Department of Health and Human Services (DHHS). (2005). *Healthy people 2010.* Retrieved April 16, 2008, from http://www.healthypeople.gov/About/hpfact.htm

Institute of Medicine (IOM). (2003). *Health professions education: A bridge to quality.* Washington, DC: National Academies Press.

Institute of Medicine of the National Academies. (2002). *Unequal treatment: Confronting racial and ethnic disparities in health care.* Retrieved April 16, 2008, from http://www.iom.edu

National Center for Minority Health and Health Disparities (NCMHHD). (2003). *Mission and vision.* Retrieved April 16, 2008, from http://ncmhd.nih.gov/about_ncmhd/mission.asp

Paasche-Orlow, M. (2004). The Ethics of cultural competence. *Academic Medicine, 79*(4), 347–350.

Porter, C. P. & Barbee, E. (2004). Race and racism in nursing research: Past, present, and future. *Annual Review of Nursing Research, 22,* 9–37.

Universal Declaration of Human Rights. *United Nations 1948.* Retrieved April 16, 2008, from http://www.un.org/Overview/rights.html

Glossary

Acculturate   To adapt or take on some parts of another culture

Acculturated   Interaction style in which people are willing to abandon their own cultural values and practices and fully embrace another

Acculturation   The adoption of some of the cultural values and beliefs of a host culture without losing one's own

Advance directive   Specific instructions, prepared in advance that direct health care providers regarding the patient's health care preferences. Examples include living wills; a designated power of attorney, a person to make medical decisions for the patient when the patient is unable to do so; organ donation, or verbal instructions (Medline Plus; www.nlm.nih.gov/medlineplus/advancedirectives.html)

Agnosticism   The philosophical and theological view that the existence of God or deities is unknown or unknowable. Persons who are agnostic are unconvinced but are unable to deny the existence of God (McAuliffe & Associates, 2008)

Alien (Legalized Alien)   Any person not a citizen or national of the United States. Certain illegal aliens who were eligible to apply for temporary resident status.

Ally   A heterosexual/straight person who advocates on behalf of LGBTQ people

Americans with Disabilities Act (ADA)   A law that was enacted in 1990 that offers protection against discrimination to Americans with disabilities

Arc   The largest national, community-based organization advocating for people with intellectual and developmental disabilities, including autism and Down syndrome, and their families

Assimilate   Being absorbed into another culture and relinquishing one's own

Asylee   An alien in the United States or a port of entry who is unable or unwilling to return to his or her country of nationality, or to seek the protection of that country because of a fear of persecution. Persecution must be based on the person's race, religion, nationality, particular social group, or political opinion.

Atheism   The belief that there is no God

Barriers   Factors that present an obstacle to care access

Bicultural   Interaction style in which people are able to take pride in their own cultural traditions while interacting comfortably with members of the dominant society

Biocultural ecology   One of Purnell's 12 domains that includes physical, biologic, and physiological variations

Bisexual   Individuals who are attracted either to men or to women

Botanicas   Shops typically found in Latino communities in the Caribbean as well as in Latino communities on the mainland that specialize in articles of folk magic, herbal preparations, blessed candles, elixirs, and similar merchandise

CLAS standards   The National Standards for Culturally and Linguistically Appropriate Services in Health Care; guidelines developed by the Office of Minority Affairs

Coming out   The process of acknowledging one's identity as LGBTQ in widening circles, including first to self, then to family, friends, and work colleagues

Cultural assessment   Systematic review of cultural phenomenon impacting a client/patient in a health care setting using a model or framework designated for that purpose

Cultural competence   Having attitudes, knowledge, and skills needed to provide quality care to culturally diverse groups of patients

Cultural encounter   Campinha-Bacote describes an encounter as nurse–patient interactions that include face-to-face and those that occur through other media

Cultural humility   Efforts by the nurse to eliminate biased, disrespectful, and prejudiced attitudes, beliefs, behaviors, policies, and practices

Cultural sensitivity   The intentional avoidance of words, phrases, and categorizations in appreciation for the diversity of others

Culturally congruent   Care that is based on the values and health beliefs of the patient

Culturally immersed   Interaction style in which people find it difficult to relinquish personal values and beliefs; may be in conflict with staff members representing dominant group

Culture   The totality of socially transmitted behavior patterns, beliefs, values, customs, life ways, and all other products of human work and thought characteristics of a population of people that guides their worldview and decision making (Purnell & Paulanka, 2008)

Culture care   Madeleine Leininger's term for care that is culturally congruent with patients' cultural health beliefs and values

Culture Care Diversity and Universality   Dr. Madeleine Leininger's theory that was the first to direct nurses on providing culture care. It states that nurses must consider the cultural values and health care beliefs of the groups for whom they are caring, in order to provide culturally congruent care. The theory is based on the belief that, while various cultural groups are diverse in their values, attitudes, caring behaviors, and health beliefs, they share many commonalities (Dayer-Berenson, 2011)

Deportation   The formal removal of an alien from the United States for violating immigration laws

Detainee   A person held in custody or confinement

Disability   A person who has a physical or mental impairment that limits one or more life activities (U.S. Equal Employment Opportunity Commission. Retrieved from www.eeoc.gov/facts/fs.ada.html)

Disability disparities   The differences in health indicators and outcomes between persons with disabilities and those who are without disabilities

Diversity   All aspects of difference that may be found among health care populations

Espirituista   Spanish or Portugese folk practitioners who receive their talent from "God." They treat conditions thought to be caused by witchcraft (Purnell & Paulanka, 2008)

Gay   Men who are attracted to men; gay sometimes is used as an all-encompassing term to include men and women who identify as gay, lesbian, or bisexual

Gender bias   Prejudicial attitudes toward someone based solely on gender

Gender identity   How a person identifies as male, female, transgender, or other

Generic or folk systems   Includes traditional health beliefs and practices as well as healers such as shaman's and other folk healers

Green card   Verification of Legal Permanent Residents (LPR) right to reside in the United States

Hazard vulnerability   A set of conditions and processes resulting from physical, social, economic, political, and environmental factors that increase the susceptibility of a community to the impact of hazards

Health care disparities   Differences between groups on access, treatment, and/ or outcomes of care

Heterosexism   An approach that presumes heterosexuality unless otherwise indicated; and, often a ranking of heterosexuality as preferable to same-sex relationships and identity

Heterosexual/straight   Individuals who are attracted to members of the opposite sex

Homophobia   Fear or dislike of LGBTQ people; often, a fear of being perceived as LGBTQ

Homosexuality   Refers to same-sex attraction. Many LGBTQQIA do not use the term because of its previous clinical use associating pathology with same-sex sexual attraction

Hospice   Hospice care provides palliative care to patients at the end of life. Care may be provided in health care facilities, extended care facilities, or in the home. The goal is to maximize patient comfort and provide the highest quality of care at the end of life (Medline 2)

Humanist   One who practices a system of thought based on the interests and ideals of humanity. Humanists believe that nothing should be accepted on faith, people must think for themselves, and values are based in the human person. (McAuliffe & Associates, 2008)

Illegal or undocumented immigrant or alien   People who have overstayed their visa or entered the country illegally

Immigrant   A person who has been granted permanent or conditional residence as recognized by the host nation

Indigent   To be in need, poor, or vulnerable to limited access to resources

Infantilization   To treat someone in a childlike fashion, like an infant

Intersex   Individuals who may be born with anatomy or physiology not clearly identified as male/female

Language barrier   Obstacles to care due to language differences including language style, and nonverbal communication

Learning Disability Association of America (LDA)   The largest nonprofit volunteer organization that advocates for persons with learning disabilities. It has state, local, and national affiliations in 42 states and Puerto Rico (www.ldanatl.org/about/index.asp)

Lesbian   Women who are attracted to women

LGBTQQIA (also, LGBT, LGBTQA)   These letters are often combined to abbreviate inclusion of lesbian (L), gay (G), bisexual (B), transgender (T), queer (Q), questioning (Q), intersex (I), and heterosexual or straight allies (A)

Life support   Emergency life support includes the administration of oxygen and the use of a ventilator to sustain breathing and oxygenation of major organs (Medline 2)

Limited English proficiency   Refers to those whose primary language is not English; speakers of English as a second language

Linguistic style   Preferred method of communicating includes tone, rate of speech, degree of loudness

Literacy   The ability to read and write to a competent level

Migrant worker   An individual who travels significant distances to obtain work, typically contracted work

Monists   One who believe in reality as one integrated whole and the interconnectedness of all creation

Naturalization   The process through which a legal permanent resident becomes a citizen

Nonimmigrant   Foreign nationals granted temporary entry into the United States. Major reasons include business or pleasure, academic or vocational study, temporary employment, or to act as representatives of a foreign government

Nonverbal communication   Body language, including gestures, facial expressions, eye contact, stance, or hand movements

Objectification   Term used in a study to describe some health care consumers' beliefs about being treated with "rudeness, lack of compassion, and unethical behaviors by service providers"

Palliative care Efforts by health care providers to relieve symptoms without curing the disease. The patient may receive palliative care at any stage of disease (Medline 2)

Permanent resident alien or legal permanent resident An alien admitted to the United States as a lawful permanent resident. These individuals are legally accorded the privilege of permanently residing in the United States

Poverty The condition of being poor; U.S. government determines based on money income of all members of a family (U.S. Bureau of Census, 2010)

Poverty thresholds U.S. government assigned dollar amounts based on size of a family and the age of its members; used throughout the United States (U.S. Bureau of Census, 2010)

Promotores de salud Peer health educators

Queer A broad, all-inclusive term reclaimed by many within the LGBTQ community

Reflective listening A process of communication whereby the nurse seeks clarification to ensure accurate interpretation of patients' meaning

Refugee A person unable or unwilling to return to his or her native country due to fear of persecution or because the person's life or freedom would be threatened (Department of Homeland Security, 2010)

Religion A specific system of values and beliefs and a framework for ethical behavior that its members must follow

Santa Ana Test A neurological test of dexterity that focuses on hand–eye coordination

Secularist Nonreligious, nonaffiliated with a church (*Webster's New World Dictionary*, 2002)

Sexual orientation To whom the person is attracted physically, romantically, emotionally, and sexually. Most medical and psychological professional associations believe this is an innate quality (like handedness) that is not a choice by the individual

Socioeconomic status Refers to social and economic factors influencing one's life; includes education, employment status, wealth, and living situation

Spirituality A humanist's definition of spirituality describes it as "an intangible, innate, and mysterious attribute of all humans that provides meaning and a reason for existence"

Stigma A "mark of social disgrace" (*Webster's New World Dictionary*, 2002).

Sunrise Model Madeleine Leininger's model of diversity and universality, which became the first transcultural nursing model

Terminal illness A stage of a disease or illness state for which there is no known cure. Stage during which hospice care may be provided

Theist One who believe in God as an independent creator with humans empowered to make choices as unique individuals

Traditional interaction style   is when people who fail to recognize or acknowledge their own cultural identity

Transgender   Individuals who are born in the body of one gender but believe they are another gender

Tuskegee experiments   Investigational study 1933 to 1972 in which Black men were used to investigate untreated syphilis; subsequently fostered mistrust of health care providers among many Blacks

Vulnerable populations   Refers to social groups with increased relative risk (i.e., exposure to risk factors) or susceptibility to health-related problems. The vulnerability is evidenced in higher comparative mortality rates, lower life expectancy, reduced access to care, and risk for diminished quality of life.

REFERENCES

Dayer-Berenson, L. (2011). *Cultural competencies for nurses: Impact on health and illness.* Boston, MA: Jones and Bartlett.

Department of Homeland Security. (2010). *Immigration status 2010.* Retrieved from www.dhs.gov/files/statistics/immigration.shtm

McAuliffe & Associates (2008). *Culturally alert counseling.* Thousand Oaks, CA: Sage Publications.

Purnell, L., & Paulanka, B. J. (2008). *Transcultural health care: A culturally competent approach.* Philadelphia, PA: F.A. Davis Company.

U.S. Bureau of the Census (2010). *Newly arrived foreign born.* Retrieved from http://www.census.gov/prod/2011pubs/acsbr10-16.pdf

Webster's New World Dictionary and Thesaurus (2nd ed.). (2002). New York, NY: Hungry Minds.

Answers to the NCLEX-Type Questions

CHAPTER 2

1. C
2. A
3. B
4. D

5. C
6. D
7. A & C

8. A
9. B
10. C

CHAPTER 3

1. D
2. C
3. A, B, D
4. A

5. A, C, E
6. B
7. A, B, & D

8. C
9. B
10. A

CHAPTER 4

1. C, D
2. A
3. C
4. A

5. A, B
6. D
7. C
8. B

9. C
10. A, B, C
11. A, B, C, D, E
12. B

CHAPTER 5

1. A
2. C
3. B
4. A
5. B

6. B & D
7. E
8. C
9. A
10. A

11. B
12. C
13. B
14. B

CHAPTER 6

1. A, B, D	5. B	8. B
2. A	6. C	9. A
3. A & D	7. C	10. A
4. B		

CHAPTER 7

1. B	5. D	8. A
2. D	6. A, B, D	9. B
3. A	7. C	10. D
4. B		

CHAPTER 8

1. B	4. D
2. A	5. C
3. C	

CHAPTER 9

1. C	5. C	8. A
2. B	6. C	9. C
3. B & C	7. A	10. B
4. A		

CHAPTER 10

1. D	6. B	11. A
2. C	7. D	12. B
3. B	8. A	13. A
4. A, C, D	9. C	14. A
5. A	10. A, B, C, D	

CHAPTER 11

1. A	5. D	8. C
2. A, B, C, D	6. B, C, D	9. A
3. C	7. A	10. D
4. C		

Index